New York City
2009

A Selection
*of **Restaurants** & **Hotels***

Manufacture française des pneumatiques Michelin
Société en commandite par actions au capital de 304 000 000 EUR
Place des Carmes-Déchaux – 63000 Clermont-Ferrand (France)
R.C.S. Clermont-Fd B 855 200 507

Dépôt légal Octobre 2008

Made in Canada

Published in 2008

Cover photograph : Getty Images / Heath Robbins

Please send your comments to:

Michelin North America, Inc.
Maps & Guides/
One Parkway South
Greenville, SC 29615 USA
www.michelintravel.com
Michelin.guides@us.michelin.com

Dear reader

*W*e are thrilled to present the fourth edition of our Michelin Guide New York City.

Our teams have made every effort to update the selection so that it fully reflects the rich diversity of the restaurant and hotel scene in the Big Apple.

The Michelin Guide provides a comprehensive selection and rating, in all categories of comfort and prices. As part of our meticulous and highly confidential evaluation process, Michelin's American inspectors conducted anonymous visits to restaurants and hotels in New York City. Our inspectors are the eyes and ears of the customers, and thus their anonymity is key to ensure that they receive the same treatment as any other guest. The decision to award a star is a collective one, based on the consensus of all inspectors who have visited a particular establishment.

Our company's two founders, Édouard and André Michelin, published the first Michelin Guide in 1900, to provide motorists with practical information about where they could service and repair their cars, find quality accommodations, and a good meal. The star-rating system for outstanding restaurants was introduced in 1926. The same system is used for our American selections.

We sincerely hope that the Michelin Guide New York City 2009 will become your preferred guide to the city's restaurants and hotels.

The Michelin Guide

"This volume was created at the turn of the century and will last at least as long".

This foreword to the very first edition of the MICHELIN Guide, written in 1900, has become famous over the years and the Guide has lived up to the prediction. It is read across the world and the key to its popularity is the consistency in its commitment to its readers, which is based on the following promises.

The Michelin Guide

→ Anonymous Inspections

Our inspectors make anonymous visits to hotels and restaurants to gauge the quality offered to the ordinary customer. They pay their own bill and make no indication of their presence. These visits are supplemented by comprehensive monitoring of information—our readers' comments are one valuable source, and are always taken into consideration.

→ Independence

Our choice of establishments is a completely independent one, made for the benefit of our readers alone. Decisions are discussed by the inspectors and the editor, with the most important decided at the global level. Inclusion in the guide is always free of charge.

→ The Selection

The Guide offers a selection of the best hotels and restaurants in each category of comfort and price. Inclusion in the guides is a commendable award in itself, and defines the establishment among the "best of the best."

How the MICHELIN Guide Works

→ Annual Updates

All practical information, the classifications, and awards, are revised and updated every year to ensure the most reliable information possible.

→ Consistency & Classifications

The criteria for the classifications are the same in all countries covered by the Michelin Guides. Our system is used worldwide and is easy to apply when choosing a restaurant or hotel.

→ The Classifications

We classify our establishments using XXXXX-X and 🏨🏨🏨-🏚 to indicate the level of comfort. The ❀❀❀-❀ specifically designates an award for cuisine, unique from the classification. For hotels and restaurants, a symbol in red suggests a particularly charming spot with unique décor or ambiance.

→ Our Aim

As part of Michelin's ongoing commitment to improving travel and mobility, we do everything possible to make vacations and eating out a pleasure.

The Michelin Guide

Contents

Contents

Contents

How to use this guide

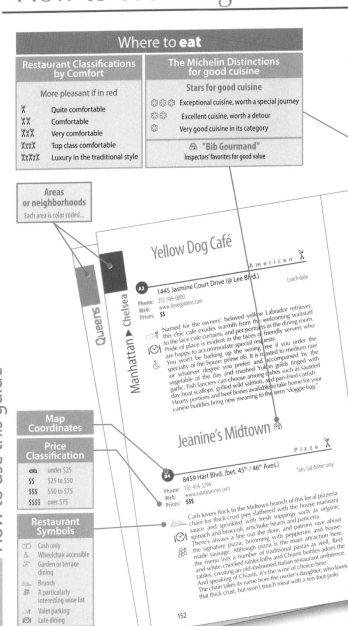

Where to **eat**

Restaurant Classifications by Comfort

More pleasant if in red

X	Quite comfortable
XX	Comfortable
XXX	Very comfortable
XXXX	Top class comfortable
XXXXX	Luxury in the traditional style

The Michelin Distinctions for good cuisine

Stars for good cuisine

✿✿✿	Exceptional cuisine, worth a special journey
✿✿	Excellent cuisine, worth a detour
✿	Very good cuisine in its category

"Bib Gourmand"
Inspectors' favorites for good value

Areas or neighborhoods
Each area is color coded...

Map Coordinates

Price Classification

∞	under $25
$$	$25 to $50
$$$	$50 to $75
$$$$	over $75

Restaurant Symbols

🚭	Cash only
&	Wheelchair accessible
🌿	Garden or terrace dining
	Brunch
🕏	A particularly interesting wine list
	Valet parking
🕐	Late dining

Yellow Dog Café

American X

A2 1445 Jasmine Court Drive (@ Lee Blvd.)   Lunch daily

Phone: 212-599-0000
Web: www.ilovegoldens.com
Prices: $$

Named for the owners' beloved yellow Labrador retriever, this chic cafe exudes warmth from the welcoming waitstaff to the lace cafe curtains, and pet portraits in the dining room. Pride of place is evident in the faces of friendly servers who are happy to accommodate special requests.

You won't be barking up the wrong tree if you order the specialty of the house: prime rib. It is roasted to medium rare (or whatever degree you prefer) and accompanied by the vegetable of the day and mashed Yukon golds tinged with garlic. Fish fanciers can choose among dishes such as sautéed day-boat scallops, grilled wild salmon, and pan-fried catfish. Hearty portions and beef bones available to take home for your canine buddies bring new meaning to the term "doggie bag."

Jeanine's Midtown 🅑

pizza X

B4 8459 Hart Blvd. (bet. 45th / 46th Aves.)   Tues-Sat dinner only

Phone: 310-454-5294
Web: www.eatatjeanines.com
Prices: $$$

Carb lovers flock to the Midtown branch of this local pizzeria chain for thick-crust pies slathered with the house marinara sauce and sprinkled with fresh toppings such as organic spinach and broccoli, artichoke hearts and pancetta. There's always a line out the door, and patrons rave about the signature pizza, brimming with pepperoni and house-made sausage. Although pizza is the main attraction here, the menu lists a number of traditional pastas as well. Red-and-white-checked tablecloths and Chianti bottles adorn the tables, creating an old-fashioned Italian restaurant ambience. And speaking of Chianti, it's the wine of choice here. The chain takes its name from the owner's daughter, who loves that thick crust, but won't touch meat with a ten-foot pole.

152

Where to stay

Average Prices	Hotel Symbols	Hotel Classifications by Comfort

Average Prices

Prices do not include applicable taxes

$	under $200
$$	$200 to $300
$$$	$300 to $400
$$$$	over $400

Map Coordinates

Hotel Symbols

149 rooms No. of rooms and suites
-   Wheelchair access
-   Exercise room
-   Spa
-   Swimming pool
-   Equipped conference room
-   Pet Friendly

Hotel Classifications by Comfort

More pleasant if in red

-   Quite comfortable
-   Comfortable
-   Very comfortable
-   Top class comfortable
-   Luxury in the traditional style

...ya's Palace ✿ ✿ ✿

Italian   XXXX

...Reuther Place (at 30th Street)   Dinner daily
...67-5309
sonyasfabulouspalace.com

Home cooked Italian never tasted so good than at this unpretentious little place. The simple décor claims no big-name designers, and while the Murano glass light fixtures are chic and the velveteen-covered chairs are comfortable, this isn't a restaurant where millions of dollars were spent on the interior.

Instead, food is the focus here. The restaurant's name may not be Italian, but it nonetheless serves some of the best pasta in the city, made fresh in-house. Dishes follow the seasons, thus ravioli may be stuffed with fresh ricotta and herbs in summer, and pumpkin in fall. Most everything is liberally dusted with Parmigiano Reggiano, a favorite ingredient of the chef.

For dessert, you'll have to deliberate between the likes of creamy tiramisu, ricotta cheesecake, and homemade gelato. One thing's for sure: you'll never miss your *nonna's* cooking when you eat at Sonya's.

Appetizers
- Crostini alla Toscana
- Antipasti della Casa
- Funghi con Polenta

Entrées
- Lasagna Bolognese
- Gnocchi alla Sorrentina
- Grilled Lamb Chops "Scotta Dita"

Desserts
- Panna Cotta
- Tiramisú
- Bombolini

153

Manhattan ▶ Chelsea

The Fan Inn

D1

135 Shanghai Road, Oakland

Phone: 650-345-1440 or 888-222-2424
Fax: 650-397-2408
Web: www.superfaninnoakland.com
Prices: $$

45 Rooms
5 Suites

Housed in an Art Deco-era building, the venerable Fan Inn ...ecently underwent a complete facelift. The hotel now fits ... with the new generation of sleekly understated hotels ...fering a Zen-inspired aesthetic, despite its 1930s origins.

...oothing neutral palette runs throughout the property, ...uated with exotic woods, bamboo, and fine fabrics. ... the lobby, the sultry lounge makes a relaxing place for a ...mixed cocktail or a glass of wine.

... linens and down pillows cater to your comfort, while ...een TVs, DVD players with iPod docking stations, ...reless Internet access satisfy the need for modern ...es. For business travelers, nightstands convert to ...tables and credenzas morph into flip-out desks. ...printer, fax or scanner? It's just a phone call away. ...uest, the hotel will even provide office supplies.

...half of the accommodations here are suites, where ...factor ratchets up with marble baths, spacious ... and fully equipped kitchens. Although the inn ... a restaurant, the nearby blocks hold nearly ...ou could want in terms of food, from soup ...haute cuisine.

East of San Francisco

419

A brief History of New York City

INTRODUCTION TO NEW YORK CITY

Cultural magnet, economic powerhouse—so what? New York is first and foremost one great place to eat. With over 17,300 restaurants in 320 square miles, there's practically an eatery on every corner of this consummate food town.

RUM, RICHES, RED SAUCE

From its trade-post beginnings in 1624, New York banked on business. As it expanded, so did the number of boardinghouses, chophouses, oyster bars, cafes, and—of course—taverns that fed workers. Places along Wall Street, especially, were known for drinks, dinner, and deals. Dinner was hearty and plenteous (as was the drink), but even as early as the 1790s, French gastronome Brillat-Savarin commented favorably on the quality and variety of food he enjoyed in the city. Business boomed in the 19th century, and those reaping the profits were eager to eat them up in style. A few grand hotels accommodated, but America's first non-hotel restaurant set the standard for years to come. Coupling European sophistication with American innovation, Delmonico's introduced the *à la carte* menu and dishes that still evoke luxury: baked Alaska, lobster Newburg, and eggs Benedict.

Yet those who powered New York's success with their sweat also did the most to define its cuisine. These new immigrants brought dreams and family recipes to share in the red-sauce joints of Little Italy, Lower East Side Kosher delis, and Chinatown's Cantonese places. As old foodways blended in this new melting pot, ethnic foods became quintessential

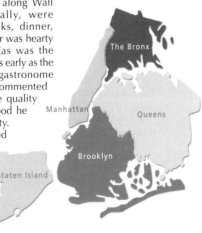

New York fare. A German sausage evolved into the hot dog; a Polish bread became the New York bagel served with lox and a schmear.

WORLD ON A PLATE

Prohibition in the early 20th century brought the demise of elite restaurants as humbler places catering to the average Joe (and Joann, as women entered the work force) flourished. Diners, often run by Greek immigrants, offered American comfort foods like meatloaf, and macaroni and cheese. African Americans from the South brought new riffs on soul food, like fried chicken and waffles, to jazz-age Harlem. Two subsequent international migrations became nothing less than culinary tidal waves, the aftershocks of which still reverberate through the city's kitchens.

A few plucky French chefs stayed on after the raves about their cooking at the 1939 World's Fair. Those chefs and the ones who followed made New York into the New World outpost of haute cuisine, and eventually nouvelle cuisine, not to mention the casual bistro, exalted as it had never been in France. *Cucina Italiana* was revisited, too, going regions beyond red sauce. Immigration restrictions relaxed after 1965, beckoning Southeast Asians, Indians, and many others who continue to bring zesty new flavors to the city. The century's last decades introduced "New American" cuisine and a farm-fresh focus to city dining.

Such are the happy paradoxes that make New York a dynamic, distinctive food town, where Bubbie's heirloom bread recipe might be revived by a Korean artisan baker, some of the most accomplished "French" cooks are Mexican, and macaroni and cheese has gone gourmet. Who knows what's next, but from the oyster bars and chophouses of old to today's sushi temples and steak palaces, diners have always been able to count on the Big Apple for a juicy bite.

History

Where to **eat**

Alphabetical list of Restaurants

A

Abboccato	✗✗	236
Aburiya Kinnosuke	✗✗	192
Adour ✿✿	✗✗✗✗	193
Adrienne's Pizzabar	✗	94
Aesop's Tables	✗	418
Aja	✗✗	192
aki on west 4	✗	130
Alcala	✗✗	194
Al di Là	✗	370
Alexander's Cafe	✗	358
Alfama	✗	130
Allen & Delancey ✿	✗✗	178
Alma	✗	370
Alto ✿	✗✗✗	195
Ama	✗	280
Amalia	✗✗	236
Ammos Estiatorio	✗✗	194
Amy Ruth's ✿	✗	169
Angelo's	✗	196
Annisa ✿	✗✗	131
Anthos ✿	✗✗	237
Antique Garage	✗	280
Ápizz ✿	✗	179
Applewood	✗	371
Aquagrill	✗✗	281
Aquavit	✗✗	196
Arharn Thai	✗	402
Aroma Kitchen & Wine Bar	✗	132
Arqua	✗✗	296
Artisanal	✗✗	197
Asia de Cuba	✗✗	197
Asiate	✗✗✗	338
Atlantic Grill	✗✗	308
August	✗	132
Aureole ✿	✗✗✗	309
A Voce	✗✗	102
Avra Estiatorio	✗✗	198

B

Babbo	✗✗	133
Bacaro	✗	179
Baci & Abbracci ✿	✗	371
Back Forty	✗	74
Balthazar	✗	281
Barbès	✗✗	198
Barbetta	✗✗✗	238
Bar Blanc	✗✗	133
Bar Boulud	✗	338
Barbounia	✗	102
Barbuto	✗✗	134
Bar Masa	✗	238
Bar Milano	✗✗	103
Barney Greengrass	✗	339
Basta Pasta	✗✗	103
Bay Leaf	✗✗	239
Bayou Restaurant	✗	418
Beacon	✗✗	239
Becco	✗✗	240
Beccofino	✗	358
Belcourt	✗	74
Bellavitae	✗	134
Belleville ✿	✗	372
Ben Benson's	✗✗	240
Benoit	✗✗	241
Beppe	✗✗	104
Beso	✗	419
Beyoglu ✿	✗	308
BG	✗✗	241
Bianca ✿	✗	135
Bice	✗✗✗	199
Blaue Gans	✗	296
Blossom	✗	50
BLT Fish	✗✗	104
BLT Market	✗✗	242
BLT Prime	✗✗	105
BLT Steak	✗✗✗	199
Blue Fin	✗✗	242
Blue Hill ✿	✗✗	136
Blue Ribbon	✗	282
Blue Ribbon Bakery ✿	✗	135

Where to **eat** ▶ Alphabetical list of Restaurants

Restaurants by Cuisine type

American

Alexander's Cafe	𝕏	358
Barbuto	𝕏𝕏	134
Beacon	𝕏𝕏	239
BG	𝕏𝕏	241
BLT Market	𝕏𝕏	242
Blue Hill ☼	𝕏𝕏	136
Blue Smoke ☺	𝕏	105
Boathouse Central Park	𝕏𝕏	310
Bridge Cafe	𝕏	94
Café Cluny	𝕏	138
Carol's Cafe	𝕏	419
Community Food & Juice	𝕏	169
Cookshop	𝕏𝕏	51
Craft	𝕏𝕏𝕏	109
Diner	𝕏	375
Dressler ☼	𝕏𝕏	376
DuMont	𝕏	375
Five Points	𝕏𝕏	143
Four Seasons (The)	𝕏𝕏𝕏𝕏	205
Good	𝕏	144
Good Enough to Eat	𝕏	342
Harry's Steak & Cafe	𝕏	95
Henry's End	𝕏	381
Hudson River Cafe	𝕏𝕏	171
J.G. Melon ☺	𝕏	318
Kings' Carriage House	𝕏𝕏	320
Kitchenette	𝕏	300
Maloney & Porcelli	𝕏𝕏𝕏	213
Market Table	𝕏	151
Métrazur	𝕏𝕏	213
New Leaf Café	𝕏	173
Odeon (The)	𝕏𝕏	303
Park Avenue	𝕏𝕏	325
Salt	𝕏	291
Sardi's	𝕏𝕏	267
Savoy	𝕏	292
Taste	𝕏	332
Telepan	𝕏𝕏	350
21 Club	𝕏𝕏	274
Union Square Cafe	𝕏𝕏	123
Vida ☺	𝕏	421
Water's Edge	𝕏𝕏𝕏	412
West Bank Café	𝕏𝕏	275

Argentinian

La Rural	𝕏	343

Asian

Aja	𝕏𝕏	192
Cendrillon	𝕏	283
Chance	𝕏	373
China Grill	𝕏𝕏	245
Garden Court Café ☺	𝕏	316
Kampuchea Noodle Bar	𝕏	181
Kuma Inn	𝕏	182
Momofuku Noodle Bar ☺	𝕏	86
Spice Market	𝕏𝕏	161
Tao	𝕏𝕏	226

Austrian

Blaue Gans	𝕏	296
Café Sabarsky	𝕏	310
Thomas Beisl ☺	𝕏	394
Wallsé ☼	𝕏𝕏	165

Barbecue

Daisy May's BBQ ☺	𝕏	246
Dinosaur Bar-B-Que ☺	𝕏	170
Hill Country	𝕏	111
Smoke Joint (The)	𝕏	393

Basque

Euzkadi	𝕏	77

Belgian

Resto	✗	120

Brazilian

Malagueta	✗	405

Cajun

Bayou Restaurant	✗	418

Caribbean

MoBay Uptown	✗	172

Chinese

Chiam	✗✗	202
Chinatown Brasserie	✗✗	138
Congee Village ⊛	✗	180
Dim Sum Go Go ⊛	✗	60
Fuleen Seafood	✗	61
Golden Unicorn ⊛	✗	62
Great N.Y. Noodletown ⊛	✗	62
Liberty View	✗	96
Lucky Eight	✗	384
Mandarin Court	✗	65
Mr Chow	✗✗	215
New Yeah Shanghai	✗	65
Noodle House	✗	406
Oriental Garden	✗✗	67
Pacificana	✗	387
Peking Duck House	✗✗	68
Philippe	✗✗	327
Phoenix Garden ⊛	✗	218
Shanghai Café	✗	69
Shanghai Pavilion	✗✗	328
Spicy & Tasty	✗	409
Sunrise 27	✗✗	69

Contemporary

Adour ⊛⊛	✗✗✗	193
Aesop's Tables	✗	418
Allen & Delancey ⊛	✗✗	178
Annisa ⊛	✗✗	131
Applewood	✗	371
Aureole ⊛	✗✗✗	309
Back Forty	✗	74
Bar Blanc	✗✗	133
Blue Ribbon	✗	282
Blue Ribbon Bakery ⊛	✗	135
Blue Water Grill	✗✗	106
Bobo	✗✗	137
Brasserie	✗✗	201
Brasserie 8 1/2	✗✗✗	243
Chestnut	✗	374
Commerce	✗	139
Compass	✗✗	340
Craftbar	✗✗	109
Cru ⊛	✗✗✗✗	140
Davidburke & Donatella	✗✗✗	312
DB Bistro Moderne	✗✗	246
Dennis Foy	✗✗✗	298
Django	✗✗✗	203
Dylan Prime	✗✗	299
eighty one ⊛	✗✗✗	341
Eleven Madison Park	✗✗✗	110
Etats-Unis ⊛	✗	315
Five Front	✗	378
44 & X Hell's Kitchen	✗	249
Frederick's Madison	✗✗	316
Garden Café	✗	379
Gilt ⊛⊛	✗✗✗	207
Good Fork (The) ⊛	✗	380
Gordon Ramsay at The London ⊛⊛	✗✗✗✗	251
Gotham Bar and Grill ⊛	✗✗✗	145
Gramercy Tavern ⊛	✗✗✗	113
Grocery (The)	✗	380
Harrison (The)	✗✗✗	300
Irving Mill	✗✗	114
Jean Georges ⊛⊛⊛	✗✗✗✗	344
JoJo ⊛	✗✗	319

Kingswood	✗✗	148
Klee Brasserie	✗	54
Landmark Tavern	✗✗	255
L'Atelier de Joël Robuchon ✿	✗✗	211
Le Cirque	✗✗✗✗	210
Lever House	✗✗✗	212
Little Owl (The)	✗	150
Mas	✗✗✗	152
Mercer Kitchen	✗	288
Michael's	✗✗✗	257
Modern (The) ✿	✗✗✗	259
Momofuku Ko ✿✿	✗	87
Momofuku Ssäm Bar ☺	✗	88
Olana	✗✗	117
Olives	✗✗	117
One if by Land, Two if by Sea	✗✗	153
Orchard (The)	✗✗	183
Ouest	✗✗✗	348
Perilla	✗	155
Perry Street ✿	✗✗✗	156
Per Se ✿✿✿	✗✗✗✗	264
Place (The)	✗✗	157
Prune ☺	✗	88
Red Cat (The)	✗✗	56
River Café (The)	✗✗✗	389
Saul ✿	✗✗	390
Sheridan Square	✗✗	160
Smith's	✗✗	160
South Gate	✗✗✗	269
Stone Park Cafe	✗	393
Tabla	✗✗✗	121
Tocqueville	✗✗	122
Town	✗✗✗	273
Tribeca Grill	✗✗	304
202 ☺	✗	57
Veritas ✿	✗✗	124
wd~50 ✿	✗✗	186

Deli

Barney Greengrass	✗	339
Katz's ☺	✗	182
Sarge's	✗	221
2nd Avenue Deli	✗	222

Ethiopian

Zoma ☺	✗	175

European

August	✗	132
Schiller's Liquor Bar	✗	184

French

Artisanal	✗✗	197
Balthazar	✗	281
Bar Boulud	✗	338
Belleville ☺	✗	372
Benoit	✗✗	241
Brasserie Ruhlmann	✗✗	244
Café Boulud ✿	✗✗✗	311
Capsouto Frères	✗✗	297
Chanterelle	✗✗✗	298
Daniel ✿✿	✗✗✗✗✗	313
Fleur de Sel ✿	✗✗	112
Jarnac	✗✗	147
Jean Claude	✗	286
Jolie	✗✗	381
Jubilee	✗	209
L'Absinthe	✗✗✗	320
La Goulue	✗✗	321
La Grenouille	✗✗✗✗	210
Landmarc	✗✗	301
Le Bilboquet	✗	321
L'Ecole ☺	✗✗	287
Le Gigot	✗	149
Le Périgord	✗✗✗	212
Le Petit Marché	✗	383
Le Refuge Inn	✗	360
Les Halles ☺	✗	115
Marseille	✗✗	257
Orsay	✗	325
Paradou	✗	154
Parigot	✗	67
Park Avenue Bistro ☺	✗✗	118
Pastis	✗	154
Payard	✗✗	326
Petrossian	✗✗✗	263
Quatorze Bis	✗✗	327
Quercy	✗	389
Raoul's	✗	291
718 - Seven One Eight	✗	409

Zest	XX	422

Fusion

Asia de Cuba	XX	197
Asiate	XxX	338
Fushimi	X	420
Koi	XX	254
Morimoto	XxX	55
P*Ong	X	158
Public ✿	X	290
Riingo	XX	220
Stanton Social (The)	XX	185
Vong	XX	228

Gastropub

Marlow & Sons ⊛	X	385
Molly's Pub & Shebeen	X	116
P.J. Clarke's	X	219
Spotted Pig ✿	X	162

German

Nurnberger Bierhaus	X	420

Greek

Ammos Estiatorio	XX	194
Anthos ✿	XX	237
Avra Estiatorio	XX	198
Eliá	X	377
Estiatorio Milos	XxX	248
Molyvos	XX	260
Periyali	XX	118
S'Agapo ⊛	X	407
Snack ⊛	X	292
Stamatis	X	410
Taverna Kyclades	X	411
Trata Estiatorio	XX	333

Indian

Bay Leaf	XX	239
Bombay Talkie	X	50
Brick Lane Curry House	X	75
Copper Chimney	XX	108
Dévi	XX	110
Diwan	XX	203
Jackson Diner ⊛	X	404

Saravanaas ⊛	X	120
Surya ⊛	X	163
Tamarind	XxX	121
Utsav	X	274

International

Mundo	X	405

Italian

Abboccato	XX	236
Al di Là	X	370
Alto ✿	XxX	195
Ama	X	280
Ápizz ⊛	X	179
Aroma Kitchen & Wine Bar	X	132
Arqua	XX	296
A Voce	XX	102
Babbo	XX	133
Bacaro	X	179
Baci & Abbracci ⊛	X	371
Barbetta	XxX	238
Bar Milano	XX	103
Basta Pasta	XX	103
Becco	XX	240
Beccofino	X	358
Bellavitae	X	134
Beppe	XX	104
Bianca ⊛	X	135
Bice	XxX	199
Bocca di Bacco	X	243
Bottega del Vino	XX	200
Bread Tribeca	X	297
Bricco	XX	244
Cacio e Pepe	X	75
Campanile	XX	107
Cellini	XX	202
Centolire	XX	312
Crispo ⊛	XX	139
Da Nico	X	60
da Umberto	XX	52
Del Posto ✿✿	XxxX	53
Enzo's Café	X	359
Etcetera Etcetera	XX	248
Falai	XX	180
Felidia	XX	204
Fiamma ✿	XxX	285

Japanese

Lan	☒	83
Masa ✿✿✿	☒☒	258
Matsuri	☒☒	55
Megu	☒☒☒	301
Momoya	☒☒	346
Nobu	☒☒	302
Nobu Fifty Seven	☒☒☒	261
Omido	☒	261
Osaka	☒	386
Sachiko's On Clinton	☒	184
Sakagura	☒	221
Seo	☒	222
Shaburi	☒☒	223
Sobakoh	☒	90
Soba-Ya ⊕	☒	90
Soto	☒☒	161
Sugiyama	☒	270
SushiAnn	☒☒	225
Sushi Azabu	☒	304
Sushiden	☒☒	225
Sushi Jun	☒	270
Sushi of Gari ✿	☒	330
Sushi of Gari 46	☒☒	271
Sushi Sasabune	☒	329
Sushi Seki	☒	331
Sushi Yasuda	☒☒	226
Sushi Zen	☒☒	271
SUteiShi	☒	98
Tokyo Pop	☒	350
Tomoe Sushi	☒	163
Tori Shin	☒☒	332
Tsushima	☒	227
Ushiwakamaru	☒	164
Yakitori Torys ⊕	☒	230
Yakitori Totto	☒	276
Zenkichi	☒☒	395

Korean

Cho Dang Gol ⊕	☒	245
HanGawi	☒☒	208
KumGangSan	☒	404
Li Hua	☒	64
Mandoo Bar	☒	255
Moim	☒	385
Woo Lae Oak	☒☒	293

Latin American

Rayuela	☒	183

Malaysian

Fatty Crab ⊕	☒	143
Nyonya ⊕	☒	66
Sentosa	☒	408

Mediterranean

Amalia	☒☒	236
Barbès	☒☒	198
Barbounia	☒	102
Belcourt	☒	74
Brick Cafe	☒	402
Extra Virgin	☒	142
Fanny	☒	377
Fig & Olive	☒	314
Hearth	☒☒	78
Isabella's	☒☒	343
Nice Matin	☒	347
Picholine ✿✿	☒☒☒☒	349

Mexican

Alma	☒	370
Café El Portal	☒	283
Café Frida	☒	339
Crema	☒	52
De Mole	☒	403
El Parador ⊕	☒☒	204
El Paso Taqueria	☒	170
Estrellita Poblana III	☒	360
Hell's Kitchen	☒	252
Itzocan ⊕	☒	79
La Esquina	☒	64
Maria's Bistro Mexicano	☒	384
Maya	☒☒	322
Maz Mezcal	☒	323
Mexicana Mama	☒	152
Noche Mexicana	☒	347
Pampano	☒☒	217
Papatzul	☒	289
Rocking Horse Cafe	☒	56
Rosa Mexicano	☒☒	220
Sueños	☒	57
Taco Taco ⊕	☒	331
Toloache	☒☒	272
Zarela	☒	230

Middle Eastern

Mamlouk ⊛	✗	85
Taboon	✗	272
Water Falls Café	✗	395

Moroccan

Café Mogador	✗	76
La Maison du Couscous	✗	382
Park Terrace Bistro	✗	173

New Zealand

Nelson Blue	✗	97

Persian

Persepolis	✗	326

Peruvian

Pio Pio	✗	406

Pizza

Adrienne's Pizzabar	✗	94
Angelo's	✗	196
Luzzo's	✗	85
Nick's	✗	324

Portuguese

Alfama	✗	130

Puerto-Rican

Brisas Del Caribe	✗	359

Russian

Firebird	✗✗✗	249
Russian Samovar	✗	266

Scandinavian

Aquavit	✗✗	196

Seafood

Aquagrill	✗✗	281
Atlantic Grill	✗✗	308
BLT Fish	✗✗	104
Blue Fin	✗✗	242
Brooklyn Fish Camp	✗	373
Ed's Lobster Bar ⊛	✗	284
Esca	✗✗✗	247
Fresh	✗✗	299
Jack's Luxury Oyster Bar	✗	80
Le Bernardin ✿✿✿	✗✗✗✗	256
Lure Fishbar	✗✗	287
Mary's Fish Camp	✗	151
Mermaid Inn (The)	✗	86
Oceana ✿	✗✗✗	216
Pearl Oyster Bar	✗	155
Pearl Room (The)	✗✗	387
Sabry's	✗	407
Sea Grill (The)	✗✗	268
Water Club (The)	✗✗✗	228
Wild Edibles	✗	229

Southern

Amy Ruth's ⊛	✗	169
Madaleine Mae	✗✗	345
Melba's	✗	172
Miss Mamie's Spoonbread Too	✗	346
The River Room	✗	174

Southwestern

Mesa Grill	✗✗	116

Spanish

Alcala	✗✗	194
Beso	✗	419
Boqueria	✗✗	106
Casa Mono	✗	108
Degustation	✗	76
El Cid	✗	141
El Faro	✗	141
La Paella	✗	83
Las Ramblas	✗	149
Picasso	✗✗	219
Sevilla ⊛	✗	159
Suba	✗✗	185

Sri Lankan

Sigiri	✗	89

Steakhouse

Ben Benson's	✗✗	240
BLT Prime	✗✗	105
BLT Steak	✗✗✗	199
Bobby Van's Steakhouse	✗✗	200
Capital Grille (The)	✗✗✗	201
Craftsteak	✗✗✗	51
Del Frisco's	✗✗✗	247
Frankie & Johnnie's	✗✗	250
Gallagher's	✗✗	250
Keens Steakhouse	✗✗	252
MarkJoseph Steakhouse	✗✗	96
Michael Jordan's	✗✗	214
Morton's	✗✗✗	215
Nebraska Beef	✗✗	97
Nick & Stef's	✗✗	260
Peter Luger ✸	✗	388
Porter House	✗✗✗	265
Primehouse New York	✗✗	119
Ricardo Steakhouse	✗	174
Smith & Wollensky	✗✗	224
Sparks Steak House	✗✗	224
Staghorn Steakhouse	✗✗	269
Wolfgang's Steakhouse	✗✗	229

Thai

Arharn Thai	✗	402
Chao Thai	✗	403
Jaiya	✗	115
Kittichai	✗✗	286
Prem-on Thai	✗✗	158
Sea	✗	391
Sripraphai	✗	410
Talay	✗	175
Zabb Queens	✗	412

Turkish

Antique Garage	✗	280
Beyoglu	✗	308
Pera	✗✗	218
Sip Sak	✗	223
Turkish Kitchen	✗✗	122
Zeytin	✗✗	351

Vegan

Blossom	✗	50
Pure Food and Wine	✗	119

Vegetarian

Gobo	✗	144

Vietnamese

Nam	✗	302
Nha Trang Centre	✗	66
Silent H	✗	392
Thai So'n	✗	70

Where to **eat** ▶ Cuisine type

Restaurants by Neighborhood

Where to **eat** ▶ Cuisine type by Neighborhood

28

Where to **eat** ▶ Cuisine type by Neighborhood

31

Where to **eat** ▶ Cuisine type by Neighborhood

SoHo & Nolita

American
Salt	X	291
Savoy	X	292

Asian
Cendrillon	X	283

Contemporary
Blue Ribbon	X	282
Mercer Kitchen	X	288

French
Balthazar	X	281
Jean Claude	X	286
L'Ecole ❀	XX	287
Raoul's	X	291

Fusion
Public ❀	X	290

Greek
Snack ◉	X	292

Italian
Ama	X	280
Fiamma ❀	XxX	285
Giorgione	XX	284
Mezzogiorno	X	288
Peasant	X	289

Japanese
Blue Ribbon Sushi (SoHo)	X	282

Korean
Woo Lae Oak	XX	293

Mexican
Café El Portal	X	283
Papatzul	X	289

Seafood
Aquagrill	XX	281
Ed's Lobster Bar ◉	X	284
Lure Fishbar	XX	287

Thai
Kittichai	XX	286

Turkish
Antique Garage	X	280

TriBeCa

American
Kitchenette	X	300
Odeon (The)	XX	303

Austrian
Blaue Gans	X	296

Contemporary
Dennis Foy	XxX	298
Dylan Prime	XX	299
Harrison (The)	XxX	300
Tribeca Grill	XX	304

French
Capsouto Frères	XX	297
Chanterelle	XxX	298

Landmarc	XX	301

Italian
Arqua	XX	296
Bread Tribeca	X	297
Pepolino	X	303

Japanese
Megu	XxX	301
Nobu	XX	302
Sushi Azabu	X	304

Seafood
Fresh	XX	299

Vietnamese
Nam	X	302

Upper East Side

American
Boathouse Central Park	XX	310
J.G. Melon ◉	X	318
Kings' Carriage House	XX	320
Park Avenue	XX	325
Taste	X	332

Asian
Garden Court Café ◉	X	316

Austrian
Café Sabarsky	X	310

Chinese
Philippe	XX	327
Shanghai Pavilion	XX	328

Contemporary
Aureole ❀	XxX	309
Davidburke & Donatella	XxX	312
Etats-Unis ❀	X	315
Frederick's Madison	XX	316
JoJo ❀	XX	319

French
Café Boulud ❀	XxX	311
Daniel ❀❀	XxXxX	313
L'Absinthe	XxX	320
La Goulue	XX	321
Le Bilboquet	X	321
Orsay	X	325
Payard	XX	326
Quatorze Bis	XX	327

Greek
Trata Estiatorio	XX	333

Italian
Centolire	XX	312
Il Riccio	X	317
Lusardi's	XX	322
Mezzaluna	X	323
Nello	XX	324
Serafina Fabulous Pizza	X	328
Spigolo	XX	329

Starred Restaurants

Within the selection we offer you, some restaurants deserve to be highlighted for their particularly good cuisine. When giving one, two or three Michelin stars, there are a number of things that we judge, including the quality of the ingredients, the technical skill and flair that goes into their preparation, the blend and clarity of flavors, and the balance of the menu. Just as important is the ability to produce excellent cooking time and again. We make as many visits as we need, so that our readers can be sure of quality and consistency.

A two- or three-star restaurant has to offer something very special in its cuisine; a real element of creativity, originality or "personality" that sets it apart from the rest. Three stars – our highest award – are given to the very best restaurants, where the whole dining experience is superb.

Cuisine in any style, modern or traditional, may be eligible for a star. Because we apply the same independent standards everywhere, the awards have become benchmarks of reliability and excellence in more than 20 European countries, particularly in France, where we have awarded stars for almost 80 years, and where the expression "Now that's real three-star quality!" has entered into the language.

The awarding of a star is based solely on the quality of the cuisine.

###

Exceptional cuisine, worth a special journey.

One always eats here extremely well, sometimes superbly. Distinctive dishes are precisely executed, using superlative ingredients.

Jean Georges	XxX	344
Le Bernardin	XxX	256
Masa	XX	258
Per Se	XxXxX	264

✿ ✿

Excellent cuisine, worth a detour.

Skillfully and carefully crafted dishes of outsanding quality.

Adour	XxX	193
Daniel	XxXxX	313
Del Posto	XxX	53
Gilt	XX	207
Gordon Ramsay at The London	XxX	251
Momofuku Ko	X	87
Picholine	XxX	349

###

A very good restaurant in its category.

A place offering cuisine prepared to a consistently high standard.

Allen & Delancey	XX	178	JoJo	XX	319
Alto	XxX	195	Kyo Ya	XX	82
Annisa	XX	131	L'Atelier de		
Anthos	XX	237	Joël Robuchon	XX	211
Aureole	XxX	309	Modern (The)	XxX	259
Blue Hill	XX	136	Oceana	XxX	216
Café Boulud	XxX	311	Perry Street	XxX	156
Cru	XxxX	140	Peter Luger	X	388
Dressler	XX	376	Public	X	290
eighty one	XxX	341	Saul	XX	390
Etats-Unis	X	315	Spotted Pig	X	162
Fiamma	XxX	285	Sushi of Gari	X	330
Fleur de Sel	XX	112	Veritas	XX	124
Gotham Bar and Grill	XxX	145	Wallsé	XX	165
Gramercy Tavern	XxX	113	wd~50	XX	186
Insieme	XX	253			
Jewel Bako	X	81			

37

Bib Gourmand

This symbol indicates our inspector's favorites for good value. For $40 or less, you can enjoy two courses and a glass of wine or a dessert (not including tax or gratuity).

Amy Ruth's	X	169	Les Halles	X	115
Ápizz	X	179	Lil' Frankie's Pizza	X	84
Baci & Abbracci	X	371	Lupa	X	150
Belleville	X	372	Mamlouk	X	85
Beyoglu	X	308	Marlow & Sons	X	385
Bianca	X	135	Momofuku Noodle Bar	X	86
Blue Ribbon Bakery	X	135	Momofuku Ssäm Bar	X	88
Blue Smoke	X	105	Nyonya	X	66
Cho Dang Gol	X	245	Park Avenue Bistro	XX	118
Congee Village	X	180	Phoenix Garden	X	218
Crispo	XX	139	Prune	X	88
Daisy May's BBQ	X	246	S'Agapo	X	407
Dim Sum Go Go	X	60	Saravanaas	X	120
Dinosaur Bar-B-Que	X	170	Sette Enoteca &		
Ed's Lobster Bar	X	284	Cucina	X	392
El Parador	XX	204	Sevilla	X	159
Fatty Crab	X	143	Snack	X	292
Frankies 457 Spuntino	X	378	Soba-Ya	X	90
Garden Court Café	X	316	Sripraphai	X	410
Gennaro	X	342	Surya	X	163
Golden Unicorn	X	62	Taco Taco	X	331
Good Fork (The)	X	380	Thomas Beisl	X	394
Great N.Y. Noodletown	X	62	Turkish Kitchen	XX	122
'inoteca	X	181	202	X	57
Itzocan	X	79	Uva	X	334
Jackson Diner	X	404	Vida	X	421
Jaiya	X	115	Yakitori Torys	X	230
J.G. Melon	X	318	Zabb Queens	X	412
Katz's	X	182	Zoma	X	175
L'Ecole	XX	287			

Where to eat
for less than $25

Adrienne's Pizzabar	✗	94
Amy Ruth's ☺	✗	169
Angelo's	✗	196
Antique Garage	✗	280
Arharn Thai	✗	402
Barney Greengrass	✗	339
Belleville ☺	✗	372
Brisas Del Caribe	✗	359
Café El Portal	✗	283
Café Mogador	✗	76
Chance	✗	373
Chao Thai	✗	403
Cho Dang Gol ☺	✗	245
Congee Village ☺	✗	180
Copper Chimney	✗✗	108
Daisy May's BBQ ☺	✗	246
De Mole	✗	403
Dim Sum Go Go ☺	✗	60
El Paso Taqueria	✗	170
Estrellita Poblana III	✗	360
Frankies 457 Spuntino ☺	✗	378
Fuleen Seafood	✗	61
Gennaro ☺	✗	342
Gobo	✗	144
Great N.Y Noodletown ☺	✗	62
'inoteca ☺	✗	181
Jackson Diner ☺	✗	404
Jaiya ☺	✗	115
J. G. Mellon ☺	✗	318
Katz's ☺	✗	182
Kitchenette	✗	300
Kuma Inn	✗	182
Li Hua	✗	64
Lucky Eight	✗	384
Malagueta	✗	405
Mandarin Court	✗	65
Mandoo Bar	✗	255
Mexicana Mama	✗	152
Miss Mamie's Spoonbread Too	✗	346
Molly's Pub & Shebeen	✗	116
Momofuku Noodle Bar ☺	✗	86
New Yeah Shanghai	✗	65
Nha Trang Centre	✗	66
Nick's	✗	324
Noche Mexicana	✗	347
Noodle House	✗	406
Nyonya ☺	✗	66
Oriental Garden	✗✗	67
Phoenix Garden ☺	✗	218
Pio Pio	✗	406
P.J. Clarke's	✗	219
Saravanaas ☺	✗	120
Sarge's	✗	221
2nd Avenue Deli	✗	222
Sentosa	✗	408
Shanghai Café	✗	69
Shanghai Pavilion	✗✗	328
Sigiri	✗	89
Silent H	✗	392
The Smoke Joint	✗	393
Snack ☺	✗	292
Sobakoh	✗	89
Soba-Ya ☺	✗	90
Spicy & Tasty	✗	409
Sripraphai ☺	✗	410
Sunrise 27	✗✗	69
Taco Taco ☺	✗	331
Taverna Kyclades	✗	411
Thai So'n	✗	70
Tomoe Sushi	✗	163
Turkish Kitchen ☺	✗✗	122
Utsav	✗	274
Water Falls Café	✗	395
Zoma ☺	✗	175

Where to have brunch

Aesop's Tables	✗	418	Bobo	✗✗	137
Alexander's Cafe	✗	358	Boqueria	✗✗	106
Alfama	✗	130	Brasserie	✗✗	201
Alma	✗	370	Brasserie 8 1/2	✗✗✗	243
Antique Garage	✗	280	Brasserie Ruhlmann	✗✗	244
Applewood	✗	371	Bread Tribeca	✗	297
Aquagrill	✗✗	281	Brick Cafe	✗	402
Aquavit	✗✗	196	Bridge Cafe	✗	94
Aroma Kitchen & Wine Bar	✗	132	Café Boulud ✿	✗✗✗	311
Artisanal	✗✗	197	Café Cluny	✗	138
Asiate	✗✗✗	338	Café Frida	✗	339
Atlantic Grill	✗✗	308	Café Mogador	✗	76
August	✗	132	Capsouto Frères	✗✗	297
Avra Estiatorio	✗✗	198	Cendrillon	✗	283
Baci & Abbracci ☺	✗	371	Centolire	✗✗	312
Back Forty	✗	74	Chestnut	✗	374
Balthazar	✗	281	Chiam	✗✗	202
Barbès	✗✗	198	Chinatown Brasserie	✗✗	138
Bar Boulud	✗	338	Community Food & Juice	✗	169
Barbounia	✗	102	Compass	✗✗	340
Bar Milano	✗✗	103	Cookshop	✗✗	51
Barney Greengrass	✗	339	Craftbar	✗✗	109
Beacon	✗✗	239	Crema	✗	52
Belcourt	✗	74	Davidburke & Donatella	✗✗✗	312
Belleville ☺	✗	372	Dim Sum Go Go ☺	✗	60
Beso	✗	419	Diner	✗	375
Beyoglu ☺	✗	308	Dressler ✿	✗✗	376
Blaue Gans	✗	296	DuMont	✗	375
Blossom	✗	50	El Paso Taqueria	✗	170
BLT Market	✗✗	242	Estrellita Poblana III	✗	360
Blue Fin	✗✗	242	Etcetera Etcetera	✗✗	248
Blue Ribbon Bakery ☺	✗	135	Extra Virgin	✗	142
Blue Smoke ☺	✗	105	Fanny	✗	377
Blue Water Grill	✗✗	106	Fatty Crab ☺	✗	143
Boathouse Central Park	✗✗	310	Fig & Olive	✗	314

Where to have a late dinner

Midtown East & Murray Hill

Aja	✗✗	192
Avra Estiatorio	✗✗	198
Barbès	✗✗	198
Bice	✗✗✗	199
Giambelli 50th	✗✗	206
Mr Chow	✗✗	215
P.J. Clarke's	✗	219
Sakagura	✗	221
Sarge's	✗	221
2nd Avenue Deli	✗	222
Smith & Wollensky	✗✗	224
Tao	✗✗	226
Yakitori Torys 🍴	✗	230

Midtown West

Becco	✗✗	240
Blue Fin	✗✗	242
Bocca di Bacco	✗	243
Estiatorio Milos	✗✗✗	248
Gallagher's	✗✗	250
La Masseria	✗✗	254
Marseille	✗✗	257
Omido	✗	261
Russian Samovar	✗	266
West Bank Café	✗✗	275
Yakitori Totto	✗	276

SoHo & Nolita

Balthazar	✗	281
Blue Ribbon	✗	282
Blue Ribbon Sushi (SoHo)	✗	282
Café El Portal	✗	283
Raoul's	✗	291

TriBeCa

Landmarc	✗✗	301
Odeon (The)	✗✗	303

Upper East Side

Atlantic Grill	✗✗	308
J.G. Melon 🍴	✗	318
Mezzaluna	✗	323
Nello	✗✗	324
Philippe	✗✗	327
Serafina Fabulous Pizza	✗	328
Sushi Seki	✗	331
Triangolo	✗	333
Uva 🍴	✗	334

BROOKLYN

Blue Ribbon Sushi (Brooklyn)	✗	372
Diner	✗	375
Lucky Eight	✗	384
Pacificana	✗	387
Sea	✗	391
Zenkichi	✗✗	395

QUEENS

KumGangSan	✗	404
Stamatis	✗	410
Zabb Queens 🍴	✗	412

LOUIS ROEDERER

CHAMPAGNE

Chelsea

Center of New York's art world and former stronghold of the city's gay community, Chelsea is situated west of Avenue of the Americas (Sixth Avenue) between 14th and 30th streets. It's a place of stark contrasts—busy commercial avenues intersect quiet residential side streets, and tiny neighborhood cafes abut gargantuan dance clubs. You'll find restaurants in this eclectic neighborhood cater to a wide range of tastes, from French bistros and Old World Spanish places to sushi bars and authentic Mexican eateries.

Check out **Chelsea Market** (75 Ninth Ave., between 15th & 16th Sts). This 1898 Nabisco factory (where the Oreo cookie was first made in 1912) was reopened in 1997 as an urban food market. Interspersed with stores selling flowers, meats, cheeses, and other gourmet essentials are cafes, bakeries, and several soup-and-sandwich shops.

A PROPER ENGLISH ORIGIN

Chelsea got its name in 1750 when British army captain Thomas Clarke bought a farm here (bound by 21st and 24th streets, Eighth Avenue and the Hudson River) and named it after his London neighborhood. In 1813, the property passed to Clarke's grandson Clement Clarke Moore, a scholar and literary figure best known for writing *A Visit from St. Nicholas* (aka *The Night before Christmas*). In the 1820s Moore helped shape the development of the district by setting aside land for park-like squares, giving the neighborhood a distinctly English feel, even as its population increasingly hailed from Germany, Italy, Scotland, and Ireland. He also specified that residences had to be set back from the street behind spacious front yards.

The Hudson River Railroad opened along 11th Avenue in 1851, spawning slaughterhouses, breweries, and tenements. From about 1905 to 1915, several motion-picture studios operated here. Dock activity along the Hudson River began to decline in the 1960s, opening up warehouses and industrial spaces for new uses. Slowly, artists moved in and town houses began to be refurbished.

CHELSEA'S GALLERY SCENE

More than 100 world-class galleries now occupy garages and lofts on the district's western flank (concentrated between 20th and 30th streets, west of Tenth Avenue), offering museum-quality exhibitions alongside up-and-coming group shows. Be sure to pick up a **Gallery Guide**, which contains a fold-out map locating all the galleries in the area. The guide also lists opening receptions, a fun way to drink in the scene. On 20th, 21st, and 22nd streets, a lovely **historic district** preserves Clement Clarke Moore's vision of elegant city living in some of Chelsea's loveliest brownstones. While you're in the neighborhood, check out the ever-evolving waterfront area, home to the mammoth Chelsea Piers recreation complex and the Hudson River Greenway.

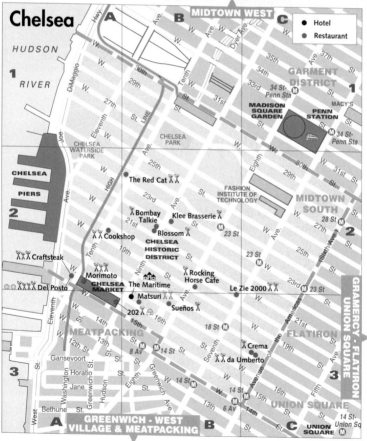

Chelsea

Hotel ●
Restaurant ●

HUDSON RIVER

MIDTOWN WEST

GARMENT DISTRICT

MACY'S

MADISON SQUARE GARDEN

PENN STATION

34 St-Penn Sta

CHELSEA PARK

CHELSEA WATERSIDE PARK

CHELSEA PIERS

The Red Cat

FASHION INSTITUTE OF TECHNOLOGY

MIDTOWN SOUTH

28 St

Bombay Talkie

Klee Brasserie

Cookshop

Blossom

CHELSEA HISTORIC DISTRICT

23 St

Craftsteak

Morimoto

CHELSEA MARKET

Rocking Horse Cafe

Del Posto

The Maritime

Le Zie 2000

23 St

Matsuri

202

Sueños

GRAMERCY · FLATIRON · UNION SQUARE

MEATPACKING

18 St

FLATIRON

Gansevoort

Horatio

Jane

Crema

da Umberto

Bethune

UNION SQUARE

GREENWICH · WEST VILLAGE & MEATPACKING

UNION SQUARE

14 St-Union Sq

Blossom

B2

187 Ninth Ave. (bet. 21st & 22nd Sts.)

Subway: 23 St (Eighth Ave.)
Phone: 212-627-1144
Web: www.blossomnyc.com
Prices: $$

Mon – Thu dinner only
Fri – Sun lunch & dinner

Convivial yet calm, intimate but not claustrophobic, and deliciously satisfying while strictly vegetarian, Blossom is a favorable study in balance. Candles and votives illuminate diners enjoying privacy and pleasant conversations above soft background reggae.

Blossom serves its dynamic cuisine to both vegans and part-time vegetarians. Menu items may include cakes of black-eyed peas and Yukon gold potatoes with fiery pepper sauce; complex and flavorful stuffed portobello caps; or a wonderfully textured tofu cheesecake.

Be sure to reserve, as the small space fills quickly; the restaurant returns calls only if you cannot be accommodated. Upper West Side outpost, Cafe Blossom, offers many of the same dishes.

Bombay Talkie

B2

189 Ninth Ave. (bet. 21st & 22nd Sts.)

Subway: 23 St (Eighth Ave.)
Phone: 212-242-1900
Web: www.bombaytalkie.com
Prices: $$

Dinner daily

As a nod to India's movie craze, owner Sunitha Ramaiah credits her inspiration for Bombay Talkie to a 1970s film of the same name. The Thomas Juul-Hansen designed space followed her lead creating mural paintings of Indian movie stars in the hip room, styled after an Indian tea house. Bollywood films are looped above the downstairs bar, serving a mesmerizing blend of East-meets-West cocktails.

Eat family style at the communal table with friends and enjoy varied "Street Bites," such as Bombay *Bhel*, assorted wheat flour chips, and rice puffs tossed with green mango salsa and mint chutney. "Dinner by the Roadside" and "Curbside" menus include generous servings of more classic regional dishes, permeated with spices and drizzled with cooling sauces.

Cookshop

A2

American ✗✗

156 Tenth Ave. (at 20th St.)

Subway: 23 St (Eighth Ave.)
Phone: 212-924-4440
Web: www.cookshopny.com
Prices: $$

Lunch & dinner daily

Owner Vicki Freeman and husband, Chef Marc Meyer have made an enduring commitment to a philosophy of locally procured ingredients. Whenever possible, they create menus that read as lessons in terroir—with Hudson Valley rabbit and venison, and Vermont lamb. For the herbivores, a large chalkboard highlights the produce—apples, herbs, and squash—that change with the seasons. This is not cookie cutter food simply following the latest green trend. Their food is prepared with pride and their diligence is apparent in every nibble. Be patient because food this thoughtful can only be handcrafted. The room is airy and softly lit during dinner and floods with natural light at lunchtime. Order a cocktail or quartino of wine and relax in the room decked in the season's bounty.

Craftsteak

A2

Steakhouse ✗✗✗

85 Tenth Ave. (at 15th St.)

Subway: 14 St - 8 Av
Phone: 212-400-6699
Web: www.craftrestaurant.com
Prices: $$$$

Dinner daily

Craftsteak is yet another addition to Tom Colicchio's growing restaurant empire. A cavernous space on the edge of the Meatpacking District, this urban-chic steakhouse creates a dramatic ambience, complete with a spacious dining room and separate bar and lounge area. Diners from all over come here, and the banker crowd is certainly an attractive one.

The kitchen turns out flawless fare, high in quality and simplicity. Ingredient-focused, Craftsteak's inventive cuisine attracts celebrities and fashionistas alike. An extensive raw-bar menu rounds out the first-course selections, while Hawaiian grass-fed Angus beef, corn-fed Hereford, and Wagyu from Miyazaki, Japan are main-course standouts. Prices are high, though, so come on an expense account.

Crema

C3

111 W. 17th St. (bet. Sixth & Seventh Aves.)

Subway: 18 St
Phone: 212-691-4477
Web: www.cremarestaurante.com
Prices: $$

Lunch & dinner daily

Mexican regional cuisine is showcased at Monterrey-born chef Julieta Ballesteros's restaurant. Serving equal parts casual and upscale, the bright décor and upbeat Latin music are pure Mexican oasis, while the vibrant presentation of dishes showcase the chef's penchant for dramatic flair. A long, narrow room with colorful walls and a cactus garden are brought to life by the open kitchen. Lovely glass jars filled with a variety of sangrias sit on the bar.

The food at Crema is as artsy as the crowd it draws. For dinner, choose the *flautas en trilogia de salsas* or *cordero en pozole rojo*. A $19 prix-fixe lunch menu features the likes of creamy carrot soup as well as an entrée, side dish, and soft drink.

da Umberto

C3

107 W. 17th St. (bet. Sixth & Seventh Aves.)

Subway: 18 St
Phone: 212-989-0303
Web: N/A
Prices: $$

Mon – Fri lunch & dinner
Sat dinner only

There's something to be said for the tried and true da Umberto. Its inviting bar and natural-light-filled dining room fill nightly with power brokers and others who often rely on expense accounts. There are no surprises here, but consistently good food and attentive service keep a well-heeled crowd of regulars coming back for more.

Start with a selection from the tantalizing array of antipasti displayed on a rustic wooden table. Then choose among house-made pasta, grilled fish, and meat offerings such as the veal chop or *bistecca alla Fiorentina*, a Porterhouse steak for two. Italian dishes, which stay true to their roots while accommodating American tastes, are complemented by a list of daily specials, still recited one by one by the staff.

Del Posto ✿✿

A2

Italian XXXX

85 Tenth Ave. (bet. 15th & 16th Sts.)

Subway: 14 St - 8 Av
Phone: 212-497-8090
Web: www.delposto.com
Prices: $$$$

Wed – Fri lunch & dinner
Sat – Tue dinner only

Maybe it's the shelled-out landscape of warehouses surrounding it, but Del Posto's swirling balconies and dripping chandeliers are guaranteed to elicit gasps from the uninitiated. It's a sexy, over-the-top theatrical setting—but Mario Batali didn't get famous for his interior design skills, now did he? The luxe-rustic Italian menu, conceived by Batali and partners Joe and Lidia Bastianich, reads deceptively simple, but no: soft pockets of *agnolotti*, plump with stewed partridge, send your taste buds on a walk through the forest; and slow-roasted *porchetta* crackles with delicate pork skin. Those with a taste for the grape will find a wine list teeming with regional Italian producers and varietals, not to mention an ample Champagne selection. As to those pesky warehouses? The Highline plans are in full effect—and guess who's seated smack in the middle of Manhattan's next big zip code?

Appetizers

- Horseradish Panna Cotta with Lobster Salad
- Vitello Tonnato with Mustard Seeds & Mâche
- Mixed Salumi Salad with Erbazzone and Stuffed Morels

Entrées

- Agnolotti dal Plin with Golden Butter & Ramps
- Grilled Dover Sole with Spring Vegetable Scafata & Salsa Verde
- Spaghetti with Dungeness Crab, Jalapeño, and Scallions

Desserts

- Apple Strudel, Walnut Praline, Rum-soaked Raisins, Vanilla-Cinnamon-Maple Gelato
- Polenta Crespelle, Ricotta, Rhubarb & Rose Hip Jam
- Chocolate Soufflé

Klee Brasserie

B2

200 Ninth Ave. (bet. 22nd & 23rd Sts.)

Subway: 23 St (Eighth Ave.)
Phone: 212-633-8033
Web: www.kleebrasserie.com
Prices: $$

Thu – Sun lunch & dinner
Mon – Wed dinner only

Opened in 2006 by Chef Daniel Angerer, this ambitious eatery is a favorite among the fashionable, moneyed, and fickle crowds of Chelsea.

The dining room is intriguingly playful and offers glimpses into the semi-open kitchen. One wall's green and black foliage motif adds spice to the room covered in white maple paneling, glowing pink from wine-colored candles on each table.

The fresh and vibrant cuisine explores the culinary map, offering dishes that vary in degree and intensity of flavor. Emphasis is placed on artisanal ingredients prepared with classic technique, as in the Kurobuta pork *tonnato* with plump caper berries in a wonderful mayonnaise-tuna sauce, or the beautifully rendered Austrian classic—Sacher torte—served with sour cream-tinged *schlag*.

Le Zie 2000

B2-3

172 Seventh Ave. (bet. 20th & 21st Sts.)

Subway: 23 St (Seventh Ave.)
Phone: 212-206-8686
Web: www.lezie.com
Prices: $$

Lunch & dinner daily

Italy's Veneto culinary region stars in the pastel dining room, where Le Zie 2000 continues to embody wholesome Italian cuisine. Begin your meal sharing the antipasti sampling—*cicchetti*—which includes several Venetian savory classics and is served with the region's signature starch, grilled polenta. Among several fine *paste* and *secondi piatti* offerings are Venetian-style calf's liver and hearty homemade pastas.

Around the corner on 20th street, Le Zie lounge offers light tasting and cocktail menus. All wines from Le Zie's extensive list, which cites some 200 labels representing all of Italy's viticultural regions, are available in the lounge.

Outside, Le Zie's small patio remains a fine place to while away the sunny days.

Matsuri

B3 Japanese XX

369 W. 16th St. (bet. Eighth & Ninth Aves.)

Subway: 14 St - 8 Av
Phone: 212-243-6400
Web: www.themaritimehotel.com
Prices: $$

Dinner daily

In the heart of the Meatpacking District, the gorgeous, cavernous setting of Matsuri is a knockout space tucked behind the Maritime Hotel. Step downstairs into the wood-spiked dining room that is enormous in height, yet remains an intimate space. The effortless ambiance successfully combines with informally attired servers and delightful food with impressive style.

Only top quality and the freshest ingredients are used to create a rather simple menu geared towards sharing many small and large plates of seasonal Japanese dishes. A menu of two hundred sakes can pair with these as well as classically prepared sushi.

This surprise in the basement is a fantastic destination for dates, groups of friends, a special occasion, or just a drink at the bar.

Morimoto

A2 Fusion XXX

88 Tenth Ave. (at 16th St.)

Subway: 14 St - 8 Av
Phone: 212-989-8883
Web: www.morimotonyc.com
Prices: $$$

Mon – Fri lunch & dinner
Sat – Sun dinner only

Brought to New York by Philadelphia restaurateur Stephen Starr and Executive Chef Masaharu Morimoto, this Chelsea hotspot never seems to stop. A trendy crowd shows up here night after night, while servers pirouette between closely spaced tables. The noise level normally rules out hope of holding a conversation.

This is quite the striking scene. Covering two levels, the arresting interior showcases rice-paper walls and monochromatic dining spaces separated by a wall made from 17,000 glass bottles. Consistent with the flashy décor, dishes emerge from the exhibition kitchen as eye-catching courses. Keeping Japan as a base, entrées like "angry chicken" (a tender roasted half-chicken maddened by fiery green and red chilies) get a modern infusion of European flair.

The Red Cat

Contemporary

B2

227 Tenth Ave. (bet. 23rd & 24th Sts.)

Subway: 23 St (Eighth Ave.)
Phone: 212-242-1122
Web: www.redcatrestaurants.com
Prices: $$

Tue – Sat lunch & dinner
Sun – Mon dinner only

Filled with bold, rich colors as vivid as its cuisine, The Red Cat features a jovial banquette extending the wall opposite a bar that dominates the dining room, lavish with flower arrangements. White-washed pine walls are adorned with fine art worthy of the artists and patrons who frequent this popular Chelsea establishment.

Innovative takes on classic seafood and American dishes include paprika roasted cod and calves liver au poivre. Menus are made according to seasonal availability and are worth return visits. Enjoy the textures and contrasts of goat cheese cheesecake with port wine figs and sweet, heady ribbons of poached fennel for dessert. The waitstaff is affable but inattentive at times, but keep in mind that the bar also offers the full menu.

Rocking Horse Cafe

Mexican

B2

182 Eighth Ave. (bet. 19th & 20th Sts.)

Subway: 14 St - 8 Av
Phone: 212-463-9511
Web: www.rockinghorsecafe.com
Prices: $$

Lunch & dinner daily

Head to Rocking Horse for great Mexican dishes in sophisticated surroundings. The flavors are as vivid as the tangerine and apple-red hues in the hip, contemporary space. Start your meal with handmade tortillas and crispy chips accompanied by a creamy, chunky jalapeño-laced salsa. Soups of the day may include marvelous bowlfuls of warm zucchini thickened with potatoes, and cooled with cilantro and cream. The entrées are myriad and include *budin* Azteca—tortillas layered with tender, free-range chicken breast, Chihuahua cheese, and *salsa verde*. The bar also boasts a serious offering of tequila, mixed in margaritas or served straight up.

Red garage-type doors open to the sidewalk, where a handful of outdoor tables are available for warm-weather dining.

Sueños

B3

Mexican ✗

311 W. 17th St. (bet. Eighth & Ninth Aves.)

Subway: 14 St - 8 Av
Phone: 212-243-1333
Web: www.suenosnyc.com
Prices: $$

Dinner daily

Sueños ("dreams" in Spanish) is a literal dream come true for Chef/owner Sue Torres. This dynamic chef supervises the kitchen and the dining room at this restaurant, which is tucked away down an alley.

There's nothing timid about the place; from the brightly painted magenta and orange brick walls to the bold, chile tasting menu, Sueños celebrates the best of Mexico. Dining spaces center on a glass-enclosed patio, complete with a fountain and flowers. This place has a festive spirit, with flavor-packed signatures like tequila-flamed rock shrimp with avocado and black bean salad.

Sue Torres' latest project is Los Dados *(73 Gansevoort St.)* in the au courant Meatpacking District—where she experiments with fresh ingredients and varied flavors.

202

A3

Contemporary ✗

75 Ninth Ave. (bet. 15th & 16th Sts.)

Subway: 14 St - 8 Av
Phone: 646-638-1173
Web: N/A
Prices: $$

Tue – Sun lunch & dinner
Mon lunch only

Quietly tucked into the Nicole Farhi boutique in Chelsea Market, 202 may be the perfect spot to luxuriate in a handcrafted cocktail while trying to decide which body-hugging dress to try on next. Although high-end shopping opportunities abound, this unique cafe and restaurant remains welcoming, low-key, and very dedicated to presenting high quality, well-prepared cuisine. The silky, tender, juicy, and flavor-packed lamb burger, topped with a melting goat cheese medallion, and served with chick pea fries, is considered one of the best in town. British Chef Annie Wayte's menu also includes crisp seasonal salads and fish tacos. A $35 prix-fixe Sunday brunch menu includes an appetizer, main course, and dessert—a perfect ruse to continue shopping.

Chinatown & Little Italy

As different as chow mein and chicken cacciatore, these two districts are nonetheless neighbors. In recent years, their borders have become blurred, with Chinatown gulping up large parts of Little Italy.

CHINATOWN

Sprawling Chinatown is a veritable city within a city. Markets here stock everything from lychee to lipstick, while storefront restaurants serve up 20 distinct Asian cuisines in more than 200 restaurants. Especially crowded on weekends, the area marked by pagoda-roofed buildings bursts its seams at **Chinese New Year** (the first full moon after January 19th), with dragons dancing down the streets accompanied by costumed revelers and fireworks.

The first Chinese came to New York in the 1870s from the California goldfields or from jobs building the transcontinental railroad. In 1943, following the repeal of the 1882 Chinese Exclusion Act, a new influx of immigrants arrived in New York. They set up garment factories, Chinese laundries, shops, and restaurants in the quarter, which has inexorably spread into Little Italy and the Lower East Side.

Today, Manhattan's Chinatown holds one of the largest Chinese immigrant communities outside Asia. Mulberry and Mott streets teem with shops and exotic food markets. Canal Street, between Broadway and Mulberry Street, is crammed with tiny stalls selling knock-off designer goods. When you get hungry, head for Mott Street and be sure to experience dim sum—a multi-course meal of small buns, pastries, dumplings, and more, served from rolling carts.

LITTLE ITALY

Little Italy, which once ran from Canal Street north to Houston, and from Lafayette Street east to the Bowery, may now be more aptly called Micro Italy. Mulberry Street is the main drag and the tenacious heart of the neighborhood, which is quickly being swallowed up by Chinatown. The onetime stronghold of Manhattan's Italian-American population has dwindled to a mere corridor—Mulberry Street between Canal and Broome streets. A veritable restaurant row, the stretch between Canal and Grand streets booms with white-aproned waiters trying to sweet-talk diners into choosing their linguini over all others. Devotees still frequent Mulberry Street for its authentic delis, gelato shops, and bakeries like Ferrara's (195 Grand St.)—renowned for its Italian pastries and strong espresso.

On weekends from May to mid-October, Mulberry Street is closed to vehicular traffic, making Little Italy one big alfresco party—the **Feast of San Gennaro** in mid-September is particularly raucous. Although these days, you can get better Italian food elsewhere in the city, you still can't beat the Old World ambience on Mulberry Street.

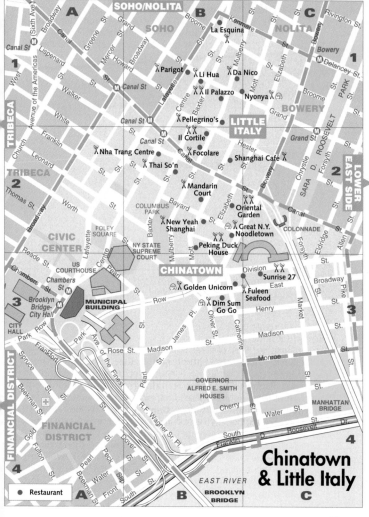

Chinatown & Little Italy

Restaurant ●

59

Da Nico

B1

164 Mulberry St. (bet. Broome & Grand Sts.)

Subway: Canal St (Lafayette St.)   Lunch & dinner daily
Phone: 212-343-1212
Web: www.danicorest.com
Prices: $$

Sister to Il Palazzo and Pellegrino's, Da Nico is another member of the Luizza family's Mulberry Street restaurants. Although the interior was recently refurbished, the place to sit—weather permitting—is on the back patio. This enclosed outdoor terrace (which nearly doubles the restaurant's seating space in summer) provides a quiet, countryside ambience, seemingly far from the commotion of Little Italy's commercial thoroughfare.

From the coal-fired pizza oven come a variety of pizzas, all of which are made using a crust recipe that has been passed down through generations of the Luizza family. Shrimp *fra diavolo*, calamari Luciana, chicken cacciatore, and steak *Fiorentina*—not to mention pasta and risotto—number among the copious choices at dinner.

Dim Sum Go Go

B3

5 East Broadway (at Chatham Sq.)

Subway: Canal St (Lafayette St.)   Lunch & dinner daily
Phone: 212-732-0797
Web: N/A
Prices: ⊜⊜

There are none of those cute little dim sum carts at Dim Sum Go Go; nor, despite the devil-may-care moniker, are there any scantily clad go-go dancers. There is, however, a most excellent selection of dim sum at this bright, funky Chinatown restaurant—loads of it, in fact, with over 24 varieties of the light plates to choose from, even well into the evening (dim sum is traditionally served at lunch). One might gather that owner and French-American food writer, Colette Rossant, has a taste for the stuff, but then there's also the fabulous, often-overlooked, Cantonese cooking to marvel over. Don't miss the sautéed Chinese chives—studded with Chinese celery and crunchy, candied walnuts—the dish offers a divine intermission from the dumpling parade.

Focolare

Italian 🍴

B2

115 Mulberry St. (bet. Canal & Hester Sts.)

Subway: Canal St (Lafayette St.) Lunch & dinner daily
Phone: 212-993-5858
Web: www.focolarenyc.com
Prices: $$

 Unlike most of its neighbors, this Mulberry Street newcomer is free of checkered tablecloths and keeps the red sauce to a minimum. The rustic décor, comprised of parchment-colored walls and dark wood furnishings, is enhanced by a cozy, stone-faced fireplace—a nod to the restaurant's moniker ("hearth" in Italian). A glass of "glowing wine" (warmed cabernet flavored with lemon zest and cinnamon) is a surefire way to ward off any chill. Focolare serves an array of contemporary fare, including rack of lamb with prosciutto-wrapped endive, or marinated chicken breast with fennel and almond couscous. For more traditional tastes, the hearty selection of *piatto del giorno*, like rich and meaty Sunday gravy, is a nostalgic trip back to *nonna's* kitchen.

Fuleen Seafood

Chinese 🍴

B-C3

11 Division St. (bet. Catherine & Market Sts.)

Subway: Canal St (Lafayette St.) Lunch & dinner daily
Phone: 212-941-6888
Web: N/A
Prices:

 This Chinatown mainstay's wall of fully stocked tanks calls out to fans of fish and the like. The attractive dining room is outfitted with large round tables routinely occupied by gregarious groups indulging in revolving platters of well-prepared food. If unsure of what to order, the polite staff will graciously guide you through the menu and make helpful recommendations. Whole fish are presented at the table for approval and then re-emerge steamed with soy, ginger, and scallions. Cantonese-style lobster and harbor-style crabs sautéed with dried shrimp and chilies are but a few of the tasty preparations offered. For those who shy away from the sea, there are plenty of options on the sizeable menu, notably the house rendition of Peking duck.

Golden Unicorn ☺

B3

18 East Broadway (at Catherine St.)

Subway: Canal St (Lafayette St.)　　　　　　　　　Lunch & dinner daily
Phone: 212-941-0911
Web: N/A
Prices: $$

Golden Unicorn has recently hung a new sign on the building housing its multi-story restaurant. Not that it was required as the restaurant is popular enough, especially during weekend brunch when waits are long. The crowds pack in for good reason—delicious dim sum from carts rolling around the lively rooms of families and friends.

It takes a little perseverance and a lot of appetite to truly enjoy Golden Unicorn. Swiftly, you must win the attention of the woman wheeling the cart of goods you're interested in. Post-victory, it takes a prolific appetite to consume the variety of dim sum you've acquired, hopefully including steamed shrimp and snow pea shoot dumplings or barbequed pork buns.

Known by few, fine Cantonese cuisine is served in the evening.

Great N.Y. Noodletown ☺

B2

28 Bowery (at Bayard St.)

Subway: Canal St (Lafayette St.)　　　　　　　　　Lunch & dinner daily
Phone: 212-349-0923
Web: N/A
Prices: ☜☜

At first glance, this unassuming little spot's no-frills décor, menus displayed under glass-topped tables, and lack of alcohol may seem unimpressive. Luckily this is deceiving, for what makes this place special is its reasonably priced, quality food served to a devoted following. Foodies and cognoscenti focus on the house specialties: sweet and salty morsels of barbecued or roasted meats and the selection of salt-baked seafood. When available, the soft-shell crabs are highly recommended. In addition, the menu is augmented with fluffy fried rice and a large variety of noodles. Open from 9 A.M. until 4 A.M., Great Noodletown is available to satisfy your cravings at almost any hour. Credit cards are not accepted so bring cash; gratefully you won't need much.

Il Cortile

B2   Italian ☓☓

125 Mulberry St. (bet. Canal & Hester Sts.)

Subway: Canal St (Lafayette St)   Lunch & dinner daily
Phone: 212-226-6060
Web: www.ilcortile.com
Prices: $$

Several dining rooms at Il Cortile each have their own ambience, but the most pleasant space is the airy garden room (*il cortile* is Italian for "courtyard"), more like an atrium with its glass-paneled ceiling, brick walls, and abundant greenery. Statues may be plentiful here, but this restaurant's décor is among the most restrained in this often over-the-top neighborhood.

Chef Michael DeGeorgio presents a wide array of pastas, meat, and seafood dishes, including his *ragù del Macellaio*, a rich tomato sauce simmered like *nonna* used to make with pork, meatballs, braciola, and sausage—offered only on Sundays. More than 30 years of sharing family recipes have made Il Cortile a favorite of city politicians, neighbors, and tourists.

Il Palazzo

B1   Italian ☓☓

151 Mulberry St. (bet. Grand & Hester Sts.)

Subway: Canal St (Lafayette St.)   Lunch & dinner daily
Phone: 212-343-7000
Web: N/A
Prices: $$

For a good, traditional Italian-American meal, head to this "palace" on Little Italy's celebrated Mulberry Street. A tuxedo-clad host ushers guests into a long room lined with stucco walls and linen-draped tables. Beyond, the sunken dining room recalls a winter garden of lush greenery and natural light.

Repasts begin with a basket of focaccia accompanied by spiced olive oil. Lunchtime frittata specials represent especially good value. Old World dishes reign here, as in *pollo carciofi* (a pan-fried breast of chicken crowned with artichokes and moistened with tomato sauce) or a grilled *bistecca*—a prime aged Porterhouse. For dessert, tiramisu is both innovative and satisfying, as a round of espresso-soaked ladyfingers topped with creamy mascarpone mousse.

La Esquina

Mexican ✗

B1

106 Kenmare St. (bet. Cleveland Pl. & Mulberry St.)

Subway: Spring St (Lafayette St.)　　　　　　　　　Lunch & dinner daily
Phone: 646-613-7100
Web: N/A
Prices: $$

Given all the hype La Esquina has received, it's remarkable that the food is as good as it is. This trendy spot divides its space and parcels its cool clientele into three distinct dining sections, each sharing the same kitchen. The first is a take-out window with sidewalk seating, the second a cozy corner cafe, and the third a lively subterranean dining room (open for dinner only) that requires booking well in advance.

The latter is still perpetually packed, since La Esquina remains a hotspot. Now, though, the buzz has calmed a bit and the food can finally take center stage, where it deserves to be. Flavors from the kitchen are carefully balanced, the cocktails are tasty, and desserts are influenced by the fruits of the season.

Li Hua

Korean ✗

B1

171 Grand St. (at Baxter St.)

Subway: Canal St (Lafayette St.)　　　　　　　　　Lunch & dinner daily
Phone: 212-343-0090
Web: N/A
Prices: ⊗⊗

This appealing establishment graciously serves heartwarming Korean favorites like spicy, bubbling hot stews, and various permutations of the rice casserole, *bibimbab*, served in hot stone bowls. The heat of the bowl continues to cook the rice as it sits, resulting in a layer of golden crusty goodness. The dumplings, known as *mandoo* in Korean, are an especially fine start; this is no surprise, as these owners are also behind Mandoo Bar. Salads, grilled and marinated meats, as well as a list of inexpensive lunch box specials augment the menu. The understated corner location, far away from the sensory overload of midtown's Koreatown, features a simple décor of pale walls and wood furnishings, given pretty touches with panels of graphically scribbled red flowers.

Mandarin Court

B2

Chinese

61 Mott St. (bet. Bayard & Canal Sts.)

Subway: Canal St (Lafayette St.) Lunch & dinner daily
Phone: 212-608-3838
Web: N/A
Prices:

 Dim sum is not just for weekend brunch anymore. At Mandarin Court, dim sum is served every day from 8A.M. to 4P.M. The presentation is Hong Kong-style; the waitresses roll carts full of dumplings, buns, wontons, and other savories past your table so you can take your pick. There's even sweet dim sum for dessert (egg custard; coconut-flavored gelatin; sesame ball).

If you're really hungry, try one of the entrées, which include steaming bowls of broth brimming with noodles, vegetables, meat or seafood. The dining room may not look like much, and it may be a bit noisy with your neighbors a little too close for comfort, but the regulars don't come here for the atmosphere. They're attracted by good Cantonese fare at reasonable prices.

New Yeah Shanghai

Chinese

B2

65 Bayard St. (at Mott St.)

Subway: Canal St (Lafayette St.) Mon – Fri lunch & dinner
Phone: 212-566-4884 Sat – Sun dinner only
Web: N/A
Prices: ☕☕

Just off the bustle of Bayard Street in the heart of Chinatown, New Yeah Shanghai offers a taste of its namesake city. Live plants, arched ceilings, and Asian decorative accents lend a cave-like, Pacific Rim feel to this otherwise casual restaurant.

Decision-making may be difficult here, where an extensive menu features Shanghai favorites, dumplings galore, all sorts of noodles, and many daily specials, as well as seasonal items created specifically for holidays throughout the year. The carefully cooked food is served as promptly as it is prepared by the capable staff, and the large portions are ideal for family-style gatherings (with leftovers to go).

New Yeah Shanghai's loyal crowd of regulars, locals, and tourists feel equally at home here.

Nha Trang Centre

B2

148 Centre St. (bet. Walker & White Sts.)

Subway: Canal St (Lafayette St.)
Phone: 212-941-9292
Web: N/A
Prices: 💰💰

Lunch & dinner daily

Amid a clutch of Vietnamese restaurants in Chinatown, Nha Trang Centre draws a loyal crowd from nearby City Hall. They judge the assortment of *pho*—the beloved Vietnamese noodle soup—the crispy pork spring rolls, and the wealth of seafood, beef, chicken, and pork specialties on the extensive bill of fare to be some of the best around. Preparations are authentic; portions are copious, and prices are low enough to get out for under $15 at lunch. For aficionados of this type of cuisine, a special menu section devotes itself to traditional Vietnamese dishes, including barbecued beef, crispy squid, and frogs' legs.

The jury's still out regarding the ambience, but the staff makes up for any aesthetic weakness with speedy and pleasant service.

Nyonya

B-C1

194 Grand St. (bet. Mott & Mulberry Sts.)

Subway: Canal St (Lafayette St.)
Phone: 212-334-3669
Web: N/A
Prices: 💰💰

Lunch & dinner daily

Beyond the bowlfuls of "arrabbiata," Nyonya's exotic Malaysian cuisine is spicing up Little Italy. Look past the framed accolades adorning the front of the gold-toned dining room and peer into the windowed kitchen, where chefs are preparing *roti canai*—the favorite dish of delicate pancakes served with coconut curry dipping sauce—and allow yourself to be lured inside. Here tumeric, chilies, and shrimp paste are skillfully combined in a warming array of satays, curries, noodles, and clay pot casseroles. More unique house specials include tender slices of pork belly mixing dark, rich flavors with mild sweetness. The restaurant's moniker refers to early Chinese-Malaysian brides, forced to intermarry to strengthen trade ties between the countries.

Oriental Garden

Chinese ✗✗

14 Elizabeth St. (bet. Bayard & Canal Sts.)

Subway: Canal St (Lafayette St.)
Phone: 212-619-0085
Web: N/A
Prices: 🍜

Lunch & dinner daily

Located in the bustling heart of Chinatown, Oriental Garden's mid-block location is easily spotted by the large gold lettering on its stone façade. Inside, the slender windows make the dining room feel decidedly tucked away, amid pale walls simply lined with framed Chinese characters and gold dragons. Towards the front, tanks brimming with fish illustrate the expansive menu's orientation toward seafood in dishes like braised abalone with oyster sauce, drunken live prawns, and sautéed cuttlefish with black bean and green pepper. There is also a hearty selection of dim sum, stir-fried meats as well as a variety of vibrant vegetable and tofu dishes—vegetarians should take caution as some contain pork.

Parigot

French ✗

155 Grand St. (at Lafayette St.)

Subway: Canal St (Lafayette St.)
Phone: 212-274-8859
Web: www.parigotnyc.com
Prices: $$

Tue – Sun lunch & dinner
Mon dinner only

Opened in 2007, this bistro brightens a corner on the boundary between Little Italy and SoHo. The name is slang for a person born and raised in Paris, and the place is owned by Chef Michel Pombet, who can frequently be spotted schmoozing with the regulars.

Two walls of windows line the front of the restaurant, where the bar nestles just inside the entrance. In the dining room, lines of tables stand shoulder-to-shoulder, leaving little room for privacy. No matter. Think of it as a way to make a new friend, or an opportunity to ask your neighbors whether they would recommend the *brandade de morue* over the mussels Parigot as an appetizer from the appealing à la carte selection. Saturday brunch (Parigot is closed Sunday) brings egg dishes and traditional sandwiches (croque monsieur) to the table.

Peking Duck House

Chinese XX

B2

28 Mott St. (bet. Chatham Sq. & Pell St.)

Subway: Canal St (Lafayette St)   Lunch & dinner daily
Phone: 212-227-1810
Web: www.pekingduckhousenyc.com
Prices: $$

Round up a few friends and go for the specialty of the house—you guessed it: Peking duck. The slow-roasted duck comes out juicy inside with pleasingly crispy skin, and it's a surefire crowd pleaser (the dish, which consists of a whole duck or the traditional mulitcourse meal, is better enjoyed by two or more). In ceremonial fashion, the chef slices the bird tableside and serves it with house-made pancakes, scallions, cucumbers, and hoisin sauce.

Don't care for duck? There's a full roster of other selections, from Szechuan-style prawns to "volcano" steak, flamed with Grand Marnier. Those who want a similar dining experience outside Chinatown should visit the restaurant's Midtown sister *(236 E. 53rd St.)*.

Pellegrino's

Italian X

B1

138 Mulberry St. (bet. Grand & Hester Sts.)

Subway: Canal St (Lafayette St)   Lunch & dinner daily
Phone: 212-226-3177
Web: N/A
Prices: $$

On a warm summer day, the view from one of Pellegrino's sidewalk tables takes in the heart of Little Italy. You're likely to find a good number of out-of-towners here, since the long, narrow dining room is attractive, the umbrella-shaded outdoor tables are inviting, and the service is courteous. Children are welcome at Pellegrino's; in fact, the restaurant offers half-portions for smaller appetites.

The food, which stays true to its roots in sunny Italy, includes a balanced selection of pasta, meat, and fish. Linguini alla Sinatra, the signature dish named for the beloved crooner, abounds with lobster, shrimp, clams, mushrooms, and pine nuts in red sauce. Large portions of tasty food make Pellegrino's a good value in this touristy neighborhood.

Shanghai Café

B2

Chinese

100 Mott St. (bet. Canal & Hester Sts.)

Subway: Canal St (Lafayette St.)   Lunch & dinner daily
Phone: 212-966-3988
Web: N/A
Prices:

Head to this Chinatown cafe when you're craving good Shanghai-style cuisine at a fair price in a pleasing, contemporary setting. Dumpling assemblers add these little gems to the enormous steamers in the front window, beckoning diners for an authentic meal.

The enormous menu cites a decision-defying array of dim sum, soups, noodles, and rice dishes. Standouts are the tiny, succulent soup buns. Filled with crabmeat and/or pork, these juicy little jewels explode with flavor in your mouth. A hands-down favorite, "steamed tiny buns," as the menu calls them, appear in steamer baskets on nearly every occupied table. Once you taste them, you'll agree that Shanghai Café ranks a bun above the usual Chinese fare on this stretch of Mott Street.

Sunrise 27

C3

Chinese

27 Division St. (bet. Catherine & Market Sts.)

Subway: Canal St (Lafayette St.)   Lunch & dinner daily
Phone: 212-219-8498
Web: N/A
Prices:

Situated on the edge of Chinatown, this large dining hall is a popular choice to satisfy a midday hankering for dim sum. Warm wood, linen-topped tables, and a rosy glow emanating from the ceiling set a pleasant tone complemented by the well-organized and always accessible waitstaff, who welcome guests with a hot towel. Fully stocked carts laden with an array of freshly prepared dumplings, flavorful buns, or sweets such as black sesame pudding are tirelessly pushed through the lively space and are sure to pique both interest and appetite. When the sun goes down, dinner features pages upon pages of offerings such as chilled jellyfish and snails in black bean sauce as well as steamed, roasted, or crispy chicken available as half or whole portions.

Thai So'n

Vietnamese X

B2

89 Baxter St. (bet. Bayard & Canal Sts.)

Subway: Canal St (Lafayette St.)
Phone: 212-732-2822
Web: N/A
Prices: 🥜🥜

Lunch & dinner daily

Set on busy Baxter Street, Thai So'n is known in the neighborhood for serving high-quality Vietnamese fare at a great value. The place has a dining-hall-like atmosphere and comfort is minimal, but that's not why folks come here. They come for the contrasting flavors and textures that form the basis of the the huge menu of flavorful cuisine, which incorporates fresh vegetables, fiery peppers, and herbs like basil, coriander, mint, and lemongrass. If it's cold out, try a steaming bowl of *pho* (beef or chicken broth full of rice noodles and your choice of other ingredients) to chase away the chill.

The casual atmosphere makes this spot a prime choice for groups or families dining with children; takeout and delivery are also available.

Good food without spending a fortune? Look for the Bib Gourmand ☺.

Sharing the nature of infinity

Route du Fort-de-Brégançon - 83250 La Londe-les-Maures - Tél. 33 (0)4 94 01 53 53
Fax 33 (0)4 94 01 53 54 - domaines-ott.com - ott.particuliers@domaines-ott.com

East Village

Bordered by 14th and Houston streets, the Bowery and the East River, this eclectic neighborhood is the center of New York's alternative culture scene. Bristling with rock concerts, poetry slams, and political Off-Broadway theater productions, the East Village is one of the most artistically diverse areas of the city. Its highly developed cafe culture and throngs of secondhand shops attract an edgy, shabby-chic crowd, as do the bars, eateries, and boutiques. Most patrons of East Village haunts are in their twenties and thirties, many of them artists and performers working in neighboring theaters, or students attending NYU nearby.

FARMERS AND FUR TRADERS

In 1651, **Peter Stuyvesant**, the Dutch-born director-general of the New Netherland colony, purchased the land bound by today's 17th Street, Fifth Street, Fourth Avenue, and the East River from the Indians for use as a farm. After surrendering to the English in 1664, Stuyvesant withdrew from public affairs and moved to his manor house on present-day Stuyvesant Street.

Briefly in the early 1800s, the district west of Second Avenue boasted fashionable town houses, home to a social elite that included **John Jacob Astor**, the fur-trade and real-estate magnate who helped develop the surrounding neighborhood starting in 1825, and railroad tycoon **"Commodore" Cornelius Vanderbilt**. The working-class

neighborhoods farther east were home to Polish, Ukrainian, and German immigrants until the early 20th century. The term "East Village" was coined in the early 1960s to distinguish the neighborhood from the rest of the Lower East Side. The glory days of the East Village were the 1980s, when rock bands like the B-52's, the Talking Heads, and the Ramones made names for themselves at the legendary club CBGB & OMFUG (Country, Bluegrass, Blues and Other Music for Uplifting Gourmandizers).

A TASTE OF EAST VILLAGE

The East Village today contains vestiges of almost all chapters of its history. Laid out in 1834, ten-acre **Tompkins Square Park** sits roughly at the center of the village. Its flowers, fountains, and 150-year-old elms make the park one of downtown Manhattan's most attractive public spaces. Most of the village's side streets are lined by 19th-century brownstones, spiffed-up tenements, and lush trees. **St. Mark's Place** is the most densely commercial street in the East Village, drawing hordes to its sushi bars, jewelry and sunglass stalls, record stores, and head shops. **Second Avenue** is really the district's spine. Here you'll find an astounding variety of ethnic eateries—Italian, Russian, Korean, Thai, Jewish, and Mexican among them. Sixth Street between First and Second Avenues is known as **Little India** for the many super-cheap Indian and Bangladeshi restaurants that line the block.

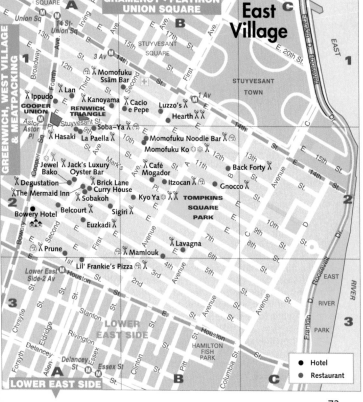

Back Forty

B2

190 Ave. B (at 12th St.)

Subway: 1 Av
Phone: 212-388-1990
Web: www.backfortynyc.com
Prices: $$

Mon – Sat dinner only
Sun lunch & dinner

The folks behind Savoy bring straightforward cooking and simple charm to this East Village newcomer. The mostly unadorned room is spare yet comfortable, with a gently lit mural at the long bar and bare-wood tables topped with brown-paper placemats that double as menus. Start with a perfect Orchard Manhattan, substituting apple brandy for the traditional rye, and dig into the farm-stand inspired fare. Seasonal assortments of locally grown side dishes from "The Garden" menu, such as a chilled green wheat salad of grains dressed with fresh herbs, lemon, and a thick dollop of yogurt; accompany "The Core" selections, including spice-rubbed rotisserie chicken and grass-fed burgers with homemade ketchup.

Belcourt

A2

84 E. 4th St. (at Second Ave.)

Subway: Astor Pl
Phone: 212-979-2034
Web: www.belcourtnyc.com
Prices: $$

Lunch & dinner daily

With antiqued mirror panels, vintage French signs, and mix-and-match tables furnished with simple wooden chairs, this newcomer devises the well worn ambiance of a time-honored neighborhood favorite. An intimate bar mixes innovative cocktails, such as the namesake's blending of champagne and elderflower nectar, which adds to the convivial setting and bistro-inspired fare. With the promise that "everything that can be made in-house, is," the kitchen turns out the likes of slow-roasted pork belly with lavender spaetzle, alluring bowlfuls of well-seasoned Manhattan clam chowder, and a *boudin blanc* "hot dog" with house-made mustard. Brunch cravings need not be reserved for the weekend; Belcourt's daily lunch menu is supplemented with numerous breakfast options.

Brick Lane Curry House

A2

Indian 🍴

306-308 E. 6th St. (bet. First & Second Aves.)

Subway: Astor Pl
Phone: 212-979-2900
Web: www.bricklanecurryhouse.com
Prices: $$

Lunch & dinner daily

Fans of Brick Lane, London's historic Curry Row, will love this East Village curry house, which stands out for its delicious northern Indian food and gracious service. Nods to the Brits are evident in the décor—brick walls lined with charming London metro signs—as well as in the selection of perfectly tapped and poured brews, sure to warm any Anglophile's heart.

The kitchen allows guests to take liberties with Indian dishes, mixing and matching ingredients in classic preparations. For instance, you can request *tikka masala*—traditionally made with chicken—with shrimp, tofu, or vegetables instead. Curries, *saag*, and tandoori entrées can be similarly altered. Excellent yogurt-based *lassi* provides a cooling accompaniment to any of the fiery dishes.

Cacio e Pepe

B1

Italian 🍴

182 Second Ave. (bet. 11th & 12th Sts.)

Subway: 3 Av
Phone: 212-505-5931
Web: www.cacioepepe.com
Prices: $$

Dinner daily

Lower Second Avenue has its share of Italian restaurants, but this one is worth seeking out. Run by a Roman expatriate, Cacio e Pepe focuses on Roman regional specialties, presenting a generous variety of choices on its seasonally changing menu. For example, the signature *tonnarelli cacio e pepe* combines house-made *tonnarelli* tossed in pasta water, olive oil, abundant pecorino cheese, and cracked black pepper; the dish is presented in a hollowed-out pecorino wheel. The wine list is short but carefully selected to highlight less-familiar producers in the most notable Italian regions.

In warm weather, the garden behind the restaurant makes a perfectly lovely setting for dinner. Any time of year, expect service that is warm and attentive.

Café Mogador

Moroccan X

B2

101 St. Mark's Pl. (bet. First Ave. & Ave. A)

Subway: 1 Av
Phone: 212-677-2226
Web: www.cafemogador.com
Prices: ❦❦

Lunch & dinner daily

This family-run, neighborhood favorite serves breakfast, lunch, and dinner daily while exuding an inviting coffee-house vibe. Moorish lanterns, jars of spices, and black-and-white photographs of Morocco impart an air of exoticism. Mediterranean small plates like hummus and tabouli make a fine start leading up to the warm and fluffy house specialty: couscous, offered here with vegetables, lamb, or spicy *merguez* sausage. Traditional *bastilla* fills layers of crispy filo with shredded chicken, eggs, almonds, and cinnamon while the mildly sweet-spicy, simmering tagines are moist, tender, and always popular. Open since 1983, reasonable prices and affable service should ensure Café Mogador's continued longevity. Sidewalk seating is available in warmer weather.

Degustation

Spanish X

A2

239 E. 5th St. (bet. Second & Third Aves.)

Subway: Astor Pl
Phone: 212-979-1012
Web: N/A
Prices: $$

Mon – Sat dinner only

This intimate East Village tapas bar from Jack and Grace Lamb, the proprietors of Jewel Bako located next door, bears the chic vibe New Yorkers would expect from this stylish couple. Dark slate-tiled walls, red leather placemats, and sleek place settings make the dimly lit space feel elegant. Similar to a sushi bar, seating is arranged on a counter facing the open kitchen, where small plates are artfully prepared by this fresh-faced and well-trained team. Offerings may include crunchy and creamy *croquetas*, or caramelized bread pudding served on frozen pink grapefruit segments. The knowledgeable and smartly attired staff ensures care is given to each guest, often guiding them through the menu and making suggestions from the all-Spanish wine list.

Euzkadi

Basque

A2

108 E. 4th St. (bet. First & Second Aves.)

Subway: Lower East Side - 2 Av
Phone: 212-982-9788
Web: www.euzkadirestaurant.com
Prices: $$

Dinner daily

Haven't heard of Euzkadi? Maybe you've been living in a cave. While some restaurants dish out great food but disappoint in the décor department, this one-of-a-kind place delivers both. With textured, exposed walls painted with prehistoric-style cave drawings, thick, velvet curtains shutting out all sunlight, and soft, low lighting, diners can be cave dwellers—even if just for the evening. This cocoon-like restaurant is a great find, despite its cramped quarters.

Of course, no caveman ever ate this well. The menu covers all the bases of traditional Basque cooking, including tapas and the house specialty, *paella mariscos*. Loaded with fish and shellfish, and redolent of saffron, the paella comes sized for two in a traditional cast-iron pan.

Gnocco

Italian

B2

337 E. 10th St. (bet. Aves. A & B)

Subway: 1 Av
Phone: 212-677-1913
Web: www.gnocco.com
Prices: $$

Mon – Fri dinner only
Sat – Sun lunch & dinner

The bohemian vibe of this quaint Alphabet City Italian makes it a favored neighborhood hangout. Large windows look out to the colorful cast of characters that populate Tompkins Square Park; inside, the dining room's rustic charm is accented by rough hewn plank flooring and exposed brick. In summer, the shady back terrace with vine-covered wall and pretty mural, is a great place to enjoy the namesake specialty, *gnocco*: crispy, deep-fried pillows of dough served with thin slices of prosciutto di Parma and salami. Enjoyably straightforward pastas, thin-crusted pizzas, and a well prepared list of meat and fish dishes comprise the tasty offerings here, served by an attentive and gracious staff. The fluffy and creamy white chocolate and coffee semifreddo is a pleasant finish.

Hasaki

A2

210 E. 9th St. (bet. Second & Third Aves.)

Subway: Astor Pl
Phone: 212-473-3327
Web: N/A
Prices: $$$

Wed – Sun lunch & dinner
Mon – Tue dinner only

On weekends, you'll recognize this sushi bar by the line that snakes out the door onto the sidewalk. Hasaki doesn't take reservations, but that doesn't seem to deter the devotees of this little place. The lively sushi bar is where the action is; step up and see what all the fuss is about.

Sashimi (buttery yellowtail, King crab, tuna—not to mention the list of daily specials) is carefully presented and served with soba noodles, a bowl of rice and the requisite wasabi and pickled ginger. Aside from sashimi and sushi, the menu offers tempura, chicken teriyaki, and grilled salmon, among other cooked selections—all at prices that won't break the budget.

Hearth

B1

403 E. 12th St. (at First Ave.)

Subway: 1 Av
Phone: 646-602-1300
Web: www.restauranthearth.com
Prices: $$$

Dinner daily

Guests are warmly greeted and introduced to the comfort and charm of this Mediterranean-inspired restaurant. A candlelit dining room features simple wooden tables and walls lined with copper pots and bookshelves.

Pure, contemporary flavors with a rustic edge are captured by a meticulous kitchen. The menu may feature starters such as a grilled quail, its meat rich and smoky, served with faro, tomato salad, and poached quail egg. Entrées may feature a moist, firm monkfish with caramelized speck, on a bed of heirloom beans, with juniper and sage. A five-course tasting menu, which changes with seasonal availability, can be paired with well-chosen wines. Steps away is Terroir, Marco Canora and Paul Grieco's new wine bar.

Ippudo

✗

A1

65 Fourth Ave. (bet. 9th & 10th Sts.)

Subway: 14 St - Union Sq

Phone: 212-388-0088

Web: www.ippudo.com/ny

Prices: $$

Lunch & dinner daily

A wall covered in soup bowls is your first indication of what to order at this stateside outpost of the popular Japanese chain. Ramen-hungry diners are given a boisterous welcome from the youthful staff upon entering; the same can be said for the farewell. With most seating arranged at communal oak-topped tables and prominently displayed open kitchen, Ippudo feels laid-back and fun. The classic *shiromaru* ramen is a deeply satisfying bowl of rich pork broth and slender, fresh-made noodles garnished with sliced pork and cabbage. In addition, you'll also find *miso* and *shoyu* (soy sauce flavored) ramen. If left with a bowlful of extra broth, simply tell your server "*kae-dama*" and for a small charge you'll receive an additional bowl of noodles.

Itzocan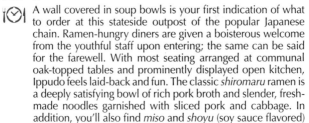

B2

✗

438 E. 9th St. (bet. First Ave. & Ave. A)

Subway: 1 Av

Phone: 212-677-5856

Web: N/A

Prices: $$

Lunch & dinner daily

In the bohemian neighborhood surrounding Tomkins Square Park, aromas of fresh cooking served in copious portions alongside pitchers of sangria lure loyal patrons to one of Manhattan's fusion Mexican restaurants. Beyond the narrow, unpretentious façade, wooden tables seat not more than 15 guests elbow-to elbow in the laid-back dining room, simply adorned with Aztec motifs, colorful statuettes, and Latin music. Lunch focuses on quesadillas and burritos, as well as blackboard specials. A short wine list and more sophisticated offerings of entrées made from carefully selected, quality ingredients include shrimp sautéed with aged tequila, lime juice and *guajillo*. Dessert highlights include the blue corn crepes with goat's milk caramel sauce.

Jack's Luxury Oyster Bar

A2

Seafood ✗

101 Second Ave. (bet. 5th & 6th Sts.)

Subway: Lower East Side - 2 Av

Phone: 212-253-7848

Web: N/A

Prices: $$$

Mon – Sat dinner only

Discreetly tucked away on a busy Second Avenue block, this oyster bar may be tiny in stature but does not fall short of personality thanks to owners Jack and Grace Lamb. You'll find a tempting raw bar menu that includes oysters, peel-and-eat shrimp, and chilled lobster tail as well as confident cooking evident in the substantial listing of small plates. These are not relegated to creatures of the deep and may include tuna paillard, crispy sweetbreads, and braised short rib rounded out by a cheese selection and small dessert menu. The dining counter overlooking the open kitchen is always a popular seating option but upfront, there are cozy wood topped tables. The intimate space has a romantic glow with red and white plaid walls, red painted wainscoting, and red glass votive holders.

Kanoyama

A1

Japanese ✗

175 Second Ave. (at 11th St.)

Subway: 3 Av

Phone: 212-777-5266

Web: www.kanoyama.com

Prices: $$

Dinner daily

The young staff at Kanoyama caters to a clientele that is fanatical about sushi but prefers the mellow East Village vibe to the power-surge of Midtown. Take your place at the sushi bar with the regulars if you want to watch the chefs' amazing knife work and enjoy the warm banter. The energy in the tiny dining room is contagious.

Daily fish specials display incredible variety at top quality, and the daily menu supplements with even more choice . It's not inexpensive, but the quality stands up to the price. After all, it's how much of the buttery toro or creamy uni you consume that determines the final tab.

Kanoyama does not accept reservations on Friday and Saturday nights but there are plenty of fun bars nearby for a drink to pass the time.

Jewel Bako ❀

Japanese ✕

A2

239 E. 5th St. (bet. Second & Third Aves.)

Subway: Astor Pl
Phone: 212-979-1012
Web: N/A
Prices: $$$

Mon – Sat dinner only

One step into the enchanting, gilded interior of Jewel Bako, Jack and Grace Lamb's flagship restaurant, and you'll understand why this husband-and-wife restaurateur team wrote the rules on how the East Village does fine dining. The welcome is warm and understated, but don't be fooled—servers here maintain an eagle's eye for detail. Sushi dominates the menu, where you might find a silky fish tartare, kissed with caviar; or a ten-piece omakase dinner featuring rich, sweet Toro cheek; or delicately butterflied octopus with *yuzu* juice, dusted with green tea salt. A coconut and lychee fruit sorbet, kicked up with key lime, makes for an intense, but refreshing, ending.

Sake lovers should steal a moment to chat up the knowledgeable wait staff, which appears to take a connoisseur's pleasure in parsing the differences bottle-to-bottle.

Appetizers
- Mushrooms "En Papillote" with Sake and Yuzu
- Sashimi of Fluke, with Ponzu, Shiso Flowers
- Sashimi: Hamachi, Konpachi, Hiramasa, and Shima Aji

Entrées
- Tartare Trio: Bluefin Tuna, Salmon, Yellowtail, Lotus Root Chips
- Crispy Scorpion Fish, and Ginko Reduction
- Negitoro with Japanese Pickles

Desserts
- Green Tea Profiteroles with Tofu Cream and Green Tea Powder

Kyo Ya ✿

B2

94 E. 7th St. (at First Ave.)

Subway: Lower East Side - 2 Av

Tue – Sun dinner only

Phone: 212-982-4140
Web: N/A
Prices: **$$$**

It's a sneaky little spot to find, but so very worth the hassle. Duck down an unmarked flight of slate stairs in one of Manhattan's most electric neighborhoods, the East Village—and soon you'll come across a door leading to a quiet little Japanese Narnia. This is Kyo Ya, where the gorgeous, intricate design of this Zen-like lair is matched only by the exquisite *kaiseki*, which is a series of haute cuisine small plates traditionally served with Japanese tea. The menu changes nightly, and presents a fascinating lineup of ingredients: some local, of course, but more of them straight from Japan's waters. An inventive sticky yam and *junsai* tofu is topped with steaming uni; while itty-bitty grilled *ayu* bob in a rich sake broth with soft, green tea somen noodles.

The *kaiseki* has to be ordered a few days in advance, but the restaurant offers an exciting a la carte menu for walk-ins.

Appetizers	*Entrées*	*Desserts*
• Sashimi of the Day	• Seasonal Fish Nitsuke	• Hojicha Ice Cream
• Goma Tofu Cocktail with Cold Dashi Broth served in a Martini Glass	• Grilled Lamb with Hokkaido-style Barbecue Sauce	• Heavenly Custard Pudding
• Ebi Shinjo	• Kamadaki Rice Cooked in a Igayaki Clay Pot	• Black Bean An Mistu

Lan

A1

Japanese

56 Third Ave. (bet. 10th & 11th Sts.)

Subway: 3 Av
Phone: 212-254-1959
Web: www.lan-nyc.com
Prices: $$

Dinner daily

The name translates as orchid, and with its exposed brick walls, white linen-covered tables, and warm candlelight, Lan offers an elegant and refined setting that is a fitting compliment to both its namesake and creative menu. In addition to the rear sushi counter's array of tempting offerings, cooked items are especially well represented here with appetizers like handmade tofu steamed with sea urchin and egg custard *chawan-mushi* with lobster bisque. The kitchen also takes great pride in its meat dishes, serving various cuts of top-quality steak; the shabu shabu (thin slices of beef or pork with an assortment of market vegetables and dipping sauces) is a favorite. The concise wine list is well chosen and bolstered by a large selection of sake and *shochu*.

La Paella

A2

Spanish

214 E. 9th St. (bet. Second & Third Aves.)

Subway: Astor Pl
Phone: 212-598-4321
Web: www.lapaellanyc.com
Prices: $$

Tue – Sun lunch & dinner
Mon dinner only

La Paella recalls the charm of an Old World Iberian inn with its rustic furnishings, wooden ceiling beams draped with bundles of dried flowers, and wrought iron accents. A fresco of a picador on the parchment-colored wall further illustrates the point. Well suited to groups, the aptly prepared menu encourages sharing with its sizable choice of vegetable, seafood, and meat tapas as well as the house specialty: paella. Several variations of this namesake dish include the Catalana with chorizo, chicken, and sausage or the Negra with squid and squid ink. The paella is sized for two and the cozy, dimly lit space makes a tasty date spot... for couples who don't mind the spirited sounds of merrymaking fueled by fruity sangria or a bottle from the Spanish wine list.

Lavagna

B2

545 E. 5th St. (bet. Aves. A & B)

Subway: Lower East Side - 2 Av

Dinner daily

Phone: 212-979-1005

Web: www.lavagnanyc.com

Prices: $$

The steady stream of regulars who frequent this charmingly low-key trattoria is immediately evident at Lavagna. The caring staff often greets guests by name, but this same courteous attention is given to those visiting for the first time. This warm service is enhanced by the cozy dining room, featuring an exposed brick wall hung with framed mirrors, pressed-tin ceiling, and a wood-burning oven in the visible kitchen. The Italian menu may highlight thin, tender ribbons of fresh *pappardelle* tossed in a hearty sauce of shredded, braised rabbit with whole black olives, or individual apple *crostata* topped with an excellent dark caramel sauce and vanilla ice cream. Sunday nights feature a reasonably priced three-course set menu from 5-7 P.M.

Lil' Frankie's Pizza

A3

19 First Ave. (bet. 1st & 2nd Sts.)

Subway: Lower East Side - 2 Av

Lunch & dinner daily

Phone: 212-420-4900

Web: www.lilfrankies.com

Prices: $$

Come with a crowd or expect to wait (reservations are accepted only for parties of six or more), but once you sink your teeth into the pizza at Lil' Frankie's, your grumbling will seem like a distant memory.

As the "it" pizza place in the East Village and an offshoot of the ever-popular Frank Restaurant (*88 Second Ave.*), Lil' Frankie's applies owner Frank Prisinzano's principle of turning quality ingredients into simple and tasty dishes. The menu features salads, pastas and sandwiches, but the real reason to come is the Naples-style pizza. Cooked to crispy perfection in a wood-burning oven with real lava from Vesuvio, pizza is religion here, with ten different varieties. Slake your thirst with a selection from the all-Italian wine list.

Luzzo's

Pizza ✗

B1

211-13 First Ave. (bet. 12th & 13th Sts.)

Subway: 1 Av   Tue – Sun lunch & dinner
Phone: 212-473-7447
Web: www.luzzomania.com
Prices: $$

These days, it seems that New Yorkers can't do anything without breaking some sort of code. There's no smoking or dancing in bars, and the city no longer issues permits for coal-burning ovens. Has all the fun, and taste, left the city? Not at Luzzo's, a former-bakery-turned-Italian-restaurant complete with a coal-burning oven that has been grandfathered. Thank heaven for small miracles and head straight for this rustic, tavern-style spot with its lip-smacking-good pizza.

Choose from 18 varieties, all with a light, chewy crust and a pleasingly charred flavor. Luzzo's also features a large selection of antipasti and pasta. Desserts are as delicious as they are whimsical, as in two menu specials: chocolate "salami" and nutella "pizza."

Mamlouk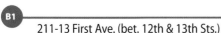

Middle Eastern ✗

B2

211 E. 4th St. (bet. Aves. A & B)

Subway: Lower East Side - 2 Av   Tue – Sun dinner only
Phone: 212-529-3477
Web: N/A
Prices: $$

Want to go out for an authentic Middle Eastern meal, but not up for making decisions? Call a date or a group of friends and shimmy on over to Mamlouk. Inside, you'll be enveloped in an exotic ambience, furnished with octagonal copper-topped tables, and wide cushioned seats. In this cozy den, hosted by the charming owner, you have only to settle back and savor the multicourse, prix-fixe meal (there's no à la carte menu). The feast begins with a tasty assortment of pickles, meze, and fresh-baked pita; then it continues with a couple of appetizers, several entrées, and ends with a sweet. You'll have plenty of good food for the price, and there are two seatings nightly.

As a fitting end to the feast, try a hookah, filled with flavored smokes.

The Mermaid Inn

Seafood ✗

A2

96 Second Ave. (bet. 5th & 6th Sts.)

Subway: Astor Pl   Dinner daily
Phone: 212-674-5870
Web: www.themermaidnyc.com
Prices: $$

When schedules won't permit a sojurn to the sandy shores of Cape Cod, the Mermaid Inn offers a polished take on those familiar sea-sprayed fish shacks. Dark wood furnishings, walls decorated with nautical maps, and a quaint backyard dining area give the setting an undeniable charm. The concise menu begins with a first-rate raw bar and continues with deftly prepared entrées like grilled mahi mahi with orange chervil emulsion or pan-roasted cod with beets and horseradish cream. Their addictive crunchy, golden, Old Bay fries are an essential side dish. A complimentary demitasse of creamy pudding ends things sweetly. West Siders take note—the recently opened uptown location *(568 Amsterdam Ave.)* serves a similarly themed menu as well as weekend brunch.

Momofuku Noodle Bar ☻

Asian ✗

B2

171 First Ave. (bet. 10th & 11th Sts.)

Subway: 1 Av   Lunch & dinner daily
Phone: 212-475-7899
Web: www.momofuku.com
Prices: ☜☜

Chef David Chang's popular destination, and its hoards of hungry fans, recently moved into bigger digs but is still a "lucky peach" of a restaurant (the name's Japanese translation). Momofuku's gutsy menu is fashioned with Asian street food in mind. Iowa Berkshire pork enveloped in steamed buns, topped with thin, cool cucumbers are offered alongside large bowls of chewy Ramen noodles in rich, flavourful broth. Dense and rich soft serve ice cream in flavors like pistachio and cannoli twist may not be Asian but ends meals with a fun and awesome twist. Whether sitting at one of two counters or select a spot at one of the communal tables, join the devotees slurping noodles elbow-to-elbow and watching the chefs' sleight of hand in the open kitchen.

Momofuku Ko ✿✿

Contemporary 🍴

B2	

163 First Ave. (bet. 10th & 11th Sts.)

Subway: 1 Av   Wed – Mon dinner only
Web: www.momofuku.com
Prices: $$$$

Noah Kalina

How much do New Yorkers love Chef David Chang? Let us count the ways. Enough to diligently log on to their computers every morning at 10:00 A.M. sharp, praying for one of 12 backless stools at his newest creation, Momofuku Ko. Enough to fly their visions of formal service in the wind, and gleefully shout: "No menu? No problem!" And what, pray tell, is the return on such unconditional trust?

Those lucky enough to find their way to Momofuku Ko's discrete iron door (look for Chang's token peach symbol), can plunk down $100 to find out. The nightly tasting menu might be the only option, but it's a dazzling one—chili-dusted *chicharones* (think fancy pork rinds) and a crispy English muffin humming with salted pork fat kick things off, and things just heat up from there. Finish with a surreal corn-flake-infused panna cotta, and breathe. It might be a while till you get back.

Appetizers
- Fluke, Spicy Buttermilk, Poppy, White Soy
- Egg & Caviar, Chips, Sweet Potato Vinegar
- Shaved Frozen Torchon of Foie Gras, Pinenut Brittle, Litchi

Entrées
- Galantine of Milk-fed Poulard , Cèpes, Ramps, Kohlrabi Purée
- Roasted Diver Scallops, Radish, Bacon Purée, Almonds
- Deep-fried 48-hour Short Rib

Desserts
- Deep-fried Apple Pie, Toasted Miso, Sour Cream Ice Cream
- Cereal Milk Panna Cotta, Avocado Purée, Gianduja, Caramelized Cornflakes
- Poached Rhubarb-Pea Crunch

Momofuku Ssäm Bar 🐷

Contemporary ✗

B1

207 Second Ave. (at 13th St.)

Subway: 3 Av
Phone: 212-254-3500
Web: www.momofuku.com
Prices: $$

Lunch & dinner daily

Crowds from all walks of life line up at this chicly simple spot for Chef David Chang's free-spirited cooking. Lunch is a focused affair of small dishes, artisanal country hams and *ssäm* (flavorful meats to be wrapped in crisp lettuce leaves). At night, the lights come down, the music goes up and the kitchen turns out ambitious American-fusion fare. Don't miss the order-in-advance *bo ssäm*—lusciously tender pork shoulder served whole with a feast of trimmings. In addition to the porcine-favored items you'll find creative seafood and vegetable creations that bear the chef's distinctive mark. The best way to experience this unique cooking is to order one of the tasting menus. They are served family-style and include menu favorites and daily specials.

Prune 🐷

Contemporary ✗

A2

54 E. 1st St. (bet. First & Second Aves.)

Subway: Lower East Side - 2 Av
Phone: 212-677-6221
Web: www.prunerestaurant.com
Prices: $$

Lunch & dinner daily

This East Village favorite radiates the warm glow of a beloved neighborhood bistro, although it may seem perpetually packed with enthusiasts trekking from afar to enjoy talented Chef/owner Gabrielle Hamilton's straightforward cooking. Prune's mosaic tile floor, paper-topped tables, and swirling ceiling fans create a charming setting in which to converse with a neighboring table, or watch the open kitchen. The diminutive room means scoring a table can be difficult, but dishes like stewed pork shoulder with *salsa verde* or soupy rice with lobster and squid more than compensate for the struggle. Lunch is served daily, and the weekend brunch menu includes a fluffy Dutch-style pancake served warm from the oven as well as a creative Bloody Mary menu.

Sigiri 😊

A2

Sri Lankan 🍴

91 First Ave. (bet. 5th & 6th Sts.)

Subway: 1 Av
Phone: 212-614-9333
Web: www.sigirinyc.com
Prices: 🍴🍴

Lunch & dinner daily

Indian and Bangladeshi cooking reigns on East 6th Street's Curry Row, but for something different in the neighborhood, climb the stairs to the second-floor dining room of Sigiri to discover the unique and flavorful cuisine of Sri Lanka.

Sigiri, with its cinnamon-colored walls, festive table linens, and stylish modern furnishings, is the perfect place to feel worldly on a budget. The well-priced menu features Sri Lankan specialties such as chicken *lamprais* (a baked rice dish studded with chicken, fish, and eggplant, and spiced with whole peppercorns, cinnamon bark, and cardamom). Fruit-based non-alcoholic drinks—mango cordial and apple iced tea—are refreshing, but bring your own if you prefer wine or beer, since Sigiri doesn't serve liquor.

Sobakoh

A2

Japanese 🍴

309 E. 5th St. (bet. First & Second Aves.)

Subway: Lower East Side - 2 Av
Phone: 212-254-2244
Web: N/A
Prices: 🍴🍴

Tue – Fri dinner only
Sat – Sun lunch & dinner

While approaching Sobakoh, stop to see Chef Hiromi Takahashi forming layers of organic, locally grown buckwheat flour dough into impressively uniform noodles—in his diminutive, glass-walled booth. This ritual creation of the mildly nutty, tender noodles is done several times a day; the chef's smiling face is a warming welcome. Steaming pots of richly flavored wild mushroom soba warm wintry evenings just as their chilled, refreshing bowlfuls of noodles and broth topped with sea urchin and salmon roe can thwart a sultry summer night. This is a delightful spot anytime. Many bowls are accompanied with golden, lightly-crisp tempura. Creative variations such as soba risotto and soba gnocchi prove that noodles are not the grain's only guise.

Soba-Ya 😊

A2

Japanese X

229 E. 9th St. (bet. Second & Third Aves.)

Subway: Astor Pl

Phone: 212-533-6966

Web: www.sobaya-nyc.com

Prices: ⊜⊜

Lunch & dinner daily

Students from nearby NYU frequent this place for its Zen-like minimalist ambience and its hearty and inexpensive noodle dishes. Soba (Japanese buckwheat noodles) are made on the premises each morning by the chef, and then presented along with your hot or cold broth and an array of garnishes and ingredients. You can substitute the chewier udon, or wheat noodles (which some say taste more like traditional pasta), if you prefer. Seasonal sashimi or "country-style" soft tofu with edamame sauce are other options.

There's a good selection of Japanese beer and sake to pair with your meal. Made by the owner's wife, ice cream boasts unusual flavors like honey wasabi. Soba-Ya is open seven days a week, but the restaurant doesn't take reservations.

Do not confuse X with ⊛ ! X defines comfort, while ⊛ are awarded for the best cuisine. Stars are awarded across all categories of comfort.

Tierce Majeure

RESERVE DE LA COMTESSE
SECOND VIN DU CHATEAU
PICHON LONGUEVILLE COMTESSE DE LALANDE

CHATEAU PICHON LONGUEVILLE
COMTESSE DE LALANDE
GRAND CRU CLASSE EN 1855 · PAUILLAC

CHATEAU BERNADOTTE
HAUT-MEDOC

33250 Pauillac - France - Tel. 33 (0)5 56 59 19 40 - Fax. 33 (0)5 56 59 29 78

WWW.PICHON-LALANDE.COM

Financial District

Widely considered the financial center of the world, the southern tip of Manhattan isn't as buttoned-up as you might expect. Its ample, U-shaped waterfront, lined with appealing parks, draws hordes of visitors to enjoy views of New York Harbor and catch ferries to The Statue of Liberty and Ellis Island. Cradled within are the narrow, sinuous streets laid out by New York's first Dutch settlers in the 17th century; developers left the curving street plan largely intact when they built their gargantuan office towers. Gaze up and you'll feel as though you're at the bottom of a deep well, with only tiny patches of sky visible among the looming skyscrapers.

BIRTHPLACE OF NEW YORK CITY

The area now known as the Financial District was the birthplace of New York in 1625. Trade flourished here under the Dutch West Indian Company, and the settlement of Nieuw Amsterdam grew quickly. In 1653 colonists built a wall of wooden planks between the Hudson and East Rivers to protect the settlers from Indian attack. Later dismantled by the British (who took over the colony in 1664), the wall is remembered today on **Wall Street**, which traces the original length (less than one mile) of the fortress.

Legend has it that in 1792 a group of 24 brokers met beneath a buttonwood tree at the corner of Wall and Williams streets, and founded the stock exchange. However, the New York Stock Exchange wasn't formally organized until 1817. Inside the classical façade of the Exchange today, you'll find one of the most technically sophisticated financial operations on the globe.

A NEIGHBORHOOD REBORN

As the revitalization of the Financial District continues, construction projects abound: high-rise condominiums compete with upscale shops, not to mention the redevelopment of the World Trade Center site. The National September 11th Memorial is scheduled for completion by 2009, and The Freedom Tower no earlier than 2011.

The publicly owned **Tin Building** and **New Market Building**, home to the former **Fulton Fish Market**, will now house new tenants in the form of **The New Amsterdam Market**. The non-profit organization dedicates itself to the promotion of sustainable agriculture and regionally sourced food, offering space for independent purveyors to sell on behalf of farmers and food producers. Check out their website, www.newamsterdampublic.org. for "market meeting" dates.

Camera-wielding tourists—drawn by attractions such as South Street Seaport, the Museum of Jewish Heritage, and the National Museum of the American Indian—rub shoulders with briefcase-toting bankers on and around Wall Street. Meanwhile, Battery Park, under the watchful eye of Lady Liberty, teems with cyclists, runners, artists, and souvenir-peddlers. Restaurants in the area cater to power-lunchers by day and to business travelers at dinnertime.

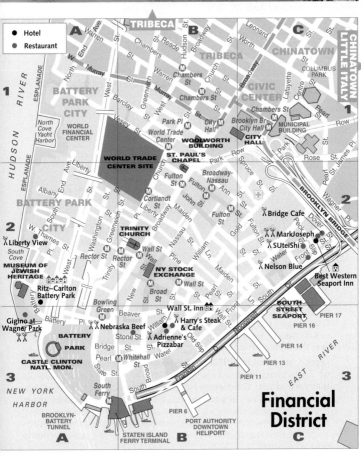

Financial District

Legend:
- Hotel
- Restaurant

Adrienne's Pizzabar

B3

Pizza ✗

54 Stone St. (bet. Coenties Alley & S. William St.)

Subway: Bowling Green
Phone: 212-248-3838
Web: www.adriennespizzabar.com
Prices: 🍽️

Lunch & dinner daily

At midday, Adrienne's is abuzz—its Financial District setting attracts hordes of business types for delectable thin-crust pies. Come evening, the restaurant trades the chaos for calm; this is when diners notice the custom-made oak paneling and upscale touches. This is also when the menu adds a list of baked dishes such as thinly sliced, fried eggplant *rollatini* stuffed with creamy ricotta, as well as 10-inch round pizza to the square pie selection, all presented with toppings at the peak of freshness and flavor. Even the servers are more engaging at dinner, when less rushed by diners needing to get back to work.

Adrienne's owners, the Poulakakos family, reign in the Financial District, where they operate several other establishments.

Bridge Cafe

C2

American ✗

279 Water St. (at Dover St.)

Subway: Fulton St
Phone: 212-227-3344
Web: www.bridgecafenyc.com
Prices: $$

Sun – Fri lunch & dinner
Sat dinner only

Not many establishments in New York City can claim as colorful a history as this one. Billing itself as "New York's oldest drinking establishment," the business opened in 1794 as a grocery in a wooden structure on the bank of the East River. Over the years, the building has housed a restaurant, a brothel, a boardinghouse, and a saloon before it became the Bridge Cafe in 1979. The current 1920s structure stands at the foot of the Brooklyn Bridge.

In a cozy atmosphere, embellished by paintings of the bridge, you'll find upscale American food. Gourmet sandwiches dominate the lunch menu, while dinner is a more formal affair with creative selections like the signature buffalo steak with lingonberry sauce. Go Sunday for the popular Bridge Brunch.

Gigino at Wagner Park

A3

Italian ✖✖

20 Battery Pl. (in Wagner Park)

Subway: Bowling Green
Phone: 212-528-2228
Web: www.gigino-wagnerpark.com
Prices: $$

Lunch & dinner daily

After a long day of downtown sightseeing or a cruise to the Statue of Liberty, this unpretentious Italian restaurant is a welcome, calming oasis. Sister to Gigino Trattoria in TriBeCa, this Gigino is tucked into the ground floor of a wedge-shaped building in Wagner Park.

The best seats are on the raised outdoor terrace where harbor views abound—call ahead to reserve these. Gracious service is assured, no matter where you sit. The dining room has a pleasant air with its palette of creamy whites and large windows.

Select from the well-prepared antipasti before moving to heartier fare, such as the succulent, perfectly grilled veal chop with sweet, smoky red onions. A prix-fixe menu offers good value, and a children's menu keeps picky palates happy.

Harry's Steak & Cafe

B3

American ✖

1 Hanover Sq. (bet. Pearl & Stone Sts.)

Subway: Wall St (William St.)
Phone: 212-785-9200
Web: www.harrysnyc.com
Prices: $$

Mon — Sat lunch & dinner

The ground floor of the historic Hanover Bank building is home to two distinct and equally gratifying experiences from a single kitchen. Both are accessible from entrances on Pearl Street and Hanover Square, though navigating between them may seem mazelike. Those in the mood for a Kobe beef hotdog should make their way to Harry's Cafe. For serious lamb or steak, outstanding pasta specials, and one of New York's better cheesecakes, we suggest the well-ensconced Harry's Steak.

The cafe's large, unencumbered bar area is clearly the place where Wall Street types blow off steam after work. The whitewashed alcoves and private dining at the steakhouse are where politicians come to broker deals. The wine list includes some great vintages and well-priced offerings.

Liberty View

A2

Chinese ✗

21 South End Ave. (below W. Thames St.)

Subway: Rector St (Greenwich St.)
Phone: 212-786-1888
Web: N/A
Prices: $$

Open daily 11am - 11pm

True to its name, Liberty View looks out over the Statue of Liberty from its perch on the ground floor of an upscale condominium at the southern end of Battery Park City. In warm weather, area denizens and Financial District movers and shakers both clamor to claim the restaurant's prime outdoor tables.

Unlike in Chinatown, the clientele here is predominantly Western, and the service orients itself towards these guests. Chopsticks, tea and traditional accompaniments to dishes must be requested, but even so, contented regulars appreciate the pleasant interactions and attentive service. The tremendous menu features a good selection of dim sum—notably the juicy buns—and Liberty View's strength lies in this and in the Shanghai-style specialties.

MarkJoseph

C2

Steakhouse ✗✗

261 Water St. (bet. Peck Slip & Dover St.)

Subway: Fulton St
Phone: 212-277-0020
Web: www.markjosephsteakhouse.com
Prices: $$$

Mon – Fri lunch & dinner
Sat dinner only

Nestled in the shadow of the Brooklyn Bridge in the South Street Seaport Historic District, MarkJoseph's caters to financiers, Wall Street wunderkinds and tourists with deep pockets. The cozy dining room is a notch above the standard steakhouse design, with art-glass vases and pastoral photographs of the wine country adding sleek notes.

At lunch, regulars devour hefty half-pound burgers (there's even a turkey variety). At dinnertime, prime dry-aged Porterhouse takes center stage, accompanied by salads and favorite sides like creamed spinach, caramelized onions and hash browns, along with less guilt-inducing steamed vegetables. And what better to wash your steak down with than one of the selections on the generous list of red wines?

Nebraska Beef

Steakhouse ✗✗

15 Stone St. (bet. Broad & Whitehall Sts.)

Subway: Bowling Green
Phone: 212-952-0620
Web: N/A
Prices: $$$

Mon – Fri lunch & dinner
Sat dinner only

Serious business folk crave serious steak, and they find it at Nebraska Beef. This unpretentious spot, three blocks away from the New York Stock Exchange, is worth seeking out for its grain-fed beef, raised (of course) in Nebraska.

Wall Street traders rushing to get back to the office often sit at the long bar—a lively scene both day and night—and grab a quick steak sandwich, Caesar salad, or house burger. Those with time to kill can settle into the dark, wood-paneled dining room for a heartier repast, which might include a Porterhouse for two, or an appetite-defying 32-ounce prime ribeye that goes by the understated name of The Steak.

This restaurant's discreet façade is easy to miss, so keep an eye out for it while walking down Stone Street.

Manhattan ▶ Financial District

Nelson Blue

C2

New Zealand ✗

233-235 Front St. (at Peck Slip)

Subway: Fulton St
Phone: 212-346-9090
Web: www.nelsonblue.com
Prices: $$

Lunch & dinner daily

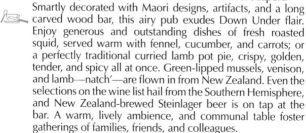

The Kiwi culture comes alive at this casual downtown newcomer, a few short blocks from South Street Seaport.

Smartly decorated with Maori designs, artifacts, and a long carved wood bar, this airy pub exudes Down Under flair. Enjoy generous and outstanding dishes of fresh roasted squid, served warm with fennel, cucumber, and carrots; or a perfectly traditional curried lamb pot pie, crispy, golden, tender, and spicy all at once. Green-lipped mussels, venison, and lamb—natch'—are flown in from New Zealand. Even the selections on the wine list hail from the Southern Hemisphere, and New Zealand-brewed Steinlager beer is on tap at the bar. A warm, lively ambience, and communal table foster gatherings of families, friends, and colleagues.

SUteiShi

Japanese ✗

C2

24 Peck Slip (at Front St.)

Subway: Fulton St
Phone: 212-766-2344
Web: www.suteishi.com
Prices: **$$**

Mon – Sat lunch & dinner
Sun dinner only

Red lacquer, black leather, and backlit bonsai trees behind the bar paint a sleek picture at this corner sushi bar. The clientele of young financial types and tourists seem unfazed by the occasional service flaws; they concentrate instead on the inventive maki. Try the Happy Lobster Roll, with sweet chunks of meat, tucked with mayonaise and delicate greens into warm, perfectly seasoned sushi rice, topped with crunchy, red flying fish roe. Desserts continue this focus on innovation, with offerings such as creamy and nutty black sesame brûlée. At lunch, the Bento box combination lets diners sample a range of fare. In nice weather, the restaurant opens sidewalk seating onto this quiet cobblestone street and surrounding Federal-style buildings.

The sun is out – let's eat alfresco! Look for a terrace 🏠.

Gramercy, Flatiron & Union Square

The retail district that stretches from 14th to 30th Streets between the East River and Avenue of the Americas (Sixth Avenue) contains a concentration of fine restaurants with names you'll no doubt recognize. Large 19th-century and early-20th-century buildings line Broadway, and Fifth and Sixth avenues. Originally built as department stores, many of them now house national chains selling clothing or furniture.

GRAMERCY PARK

New York City's only private park anchors this tranquil, neighborhood known for its lovely brownstones and charming cafes and restaurants. The area was laid out in 1831 by developer Samuel B. Ruggles, who drained an old marsh (Gramercy is a corruption of a Dutch phrase meaning "little crooked swamp") to build an exclusive residential enclave. Enclosed by an eight-foot-high cast-iron fence, to which only local residents have keys, the green rectangle of **Gramercy Park** consists of formal gardens, paths, benches, and trees. In the center stands a statue of Shakespearean actor Edwin Booth, dressed to play Hamlet—his favorite role.

A few blocks northwest of Gramercy Park, lovely six-acre **Madison Square Park** has been transformed recently into one of downtown's most inviting public spaces. From the 1870s to 1925, a succession of entertainment venues stood on the north end of the square, including the first two (of four) arenas called **Madison Square Garden.**

FLATIRON DISTRICT

This moniker refers to the area around the **Flatiron Building** (Daniel Burnham, 1902). Even if you've never been to New York City, you've likely seen this building before—it's a popular backdrop in television shows and movies. Viewed from the north side (the side that faces Madison Square Park), it looks like an iron; the acute angle of its façade is formed by Broadway and Fifth Avenue. Though it's only 6 feet wide on this sharp corner, the building rises 22 stories straight up from the sidewalk.

UNION SQUARE

On the south edge of the district, this pleasant park is crisscrossed with tree-lined paths. The park, so-named because it marked the union of Broadway and the Bowery, was created in 1831; by the mid-19th-century it formed the gated focal point of an elegant residential district. In the early 20th-century, Union Square became a popular place for rallies and demonstrations; today the tiered plaza on the park's southern end still serves as a stage for protesters, who share space with street performers.

Every Monday, Wednesday, Friday, and Saturday year-round, **Union Square Greenmarket** hosts farmers, bakers, flower growers, ranchers, and artisan food makers from all over New York, Pennsylvania, and New Jersey. Neighborhood chefs and residents flock here to forage for the freshest meats, cheeses, and vegetables to incorporate into their menus.

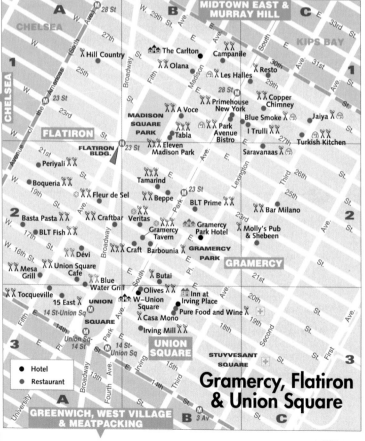

Gramercy, Flatiron & Union Square

MIDTOWN EAST & MURRAY HILL

CHELSEA

KIPS BAY

FLATIRON

MADISON SQUARE PARK

FLATIRON BLDG.

GRAMERCY PARK

GRAMERCY

UNION SQUARE

STUYVESANT SQUARE

GREENWICH, WEST VILLAGE & MEATPACKING

Restaurants and hotels:
- Hill Country
- The Carlton
- Campanile
- Olana
- Les Halles
- Resto
- Primehouse New York
- Copper Chimney
- A Voce
- Blue Smoke
- Jaiya
- Tabla
- Park Avenue Bistro
- I Trulli
- Eleven Madison Park
- Turkish Kitchen
- Periyali
- Saravanaas
- Tamarind
- Boqueria
- Fleur de Sel
- Beppe
- BLT Prime
- Bar Milano
- Basta Pasta
- Craftbar
- Veritas
- Gramercy Park Hotel
- BLT Fish
- Gramercy Tavern
- Molly's Pub & Shebeen
- Dévi
- Craft
- Barbounia
- Mesa Grill
- Union Square Cafe
- Butai
- Tocqueville
- Blue Water Grill
- Olives
- Inn at Irving Place
- 15 East
- W–Union Square
- Pure Food and Wine
- Casa Mono
- Irving Mill

Legend:
- ● Hotel
- ● Restaurant

101

A Voce

B1

Italian ✕✕

41 Madison Ave. (enter on 26th St.)

Subway: 28 St (Park Ave. South)
Phone: 212-545-8555
Web: www.avocerestaurant.com
Prices: $$$

Mon – Fri lunch & dinner
Sat – Sun dinner only

This stylish space packs the requisite slick-and-hip city punch; but the regional Italian food still holds center stage here. Andrew Carmellini and team have departed, but the kitchen is staying the course. A simple ravioli dish showcases soft pillows of pasta, fat with tender, braised beef in a chunky tomato sauce, and exudes rustic grace. An entrée of fennel-glazed duckling breast is succulent and powerful, the delicate skin crisped to golden perfection. Italian regions dominate the wine list, but those in the mood to wander will find some nice French and American offerings, priced for an array of budgets.

A Voce (which translates to "word of mouth") is an energetic spot and still going strong with the "see and be seen."

Barbounia

B2

Mediterranean ✕

250 Park Ave. South (at 20th St.)

Subway: 23 St (Park Ave. South)
Phone: 212-995-0242
Web: www.barbounia.com
Prices: $$

Lunch & dinner daily

A block from Gramercy Park, Barbounia boasts a lovely contemporary look; its sprawling space is broken up by fat columns, arched openings, and pillow-lined banquettes. The bar's long white marble counter is framed by a windowed wall where glass shelves display varied bottles. A rustic wooden communal table adds seating near the bar.

Greece, Turkey, Italy, and France all put their stamp on this cuisine, with dishes ranging from a lamb pita to baked stuffed eggplant or Turkish moussaka. The wood-burning oven, visible in the open kitchen, turns out flatbreads to pair with the mouth-watering mezes including grilled sardines wrapped in grape leaves; pan-fried *kefalotyri* cheese; and zucchini blossoms stuffed with raisins, pine nuts, and yogurt.

Bar Milano

C2

Italian XX

323 Third Ave. (bet. 24th & 25th Sts.)

Subway: 23 St (Park Ave. South)
Phone: 212-683-3035
Web: www.barmilano.com
Prices: $$

Lunch & dinner daily

This newest venture from the brothers Denton (also of 'inoteca) offers an elegant setting in which to feast on tempting Northern Italian fare. Dark grey furnishings, wood-framed cabinetry stocked with wine, and an earth-toned rainbow of hand-selected marble panels adorn the dining room. The corner bar room is furnished with white marble tables and cognac leather seating—a lovely light-filled meeting spot for lunch. The menu offers refined antipasti, pastas like shrimp-filled *agnolotti* with peas and mint, as well as entrées featuring the likes of monkish with foie gras and bittersweet Campari *agrodolce*. This fine cuisine is offset by an extensive all-Italian wine list and friendly, knowledgeable service team that befits this well-run operation.

Basta Pasta

A2

Italian XX

37 W. 17th St. (bet. Fifth & Sixth Aves.)

Subway: 14 St - Union Sq
Phone: 212-366-0888
Web: www.bastapastanyc.com
Prices: $$

Mon – Fri lunch & dinner
Sat – Sun dinner only

New York City has long been considered a cultural melting pot. It seems only fitting that this intriguing combination of first-rate Italian-inspired cuisine prepared and served by a courteous Japanese staff works so well at Basta Pasta. With an interior that draws inspiration from the international television phenomenon *Iron Chef*, diners must walk through the open, working kitchen to reach their tables. Fortunately, the cool, calm, and collected kitchen team saves the drama for the plate. The pastas are excellent and demonstrate, as in the signature spaghetti with *tobiko* and *shiso*, the unique accent of this international union throughout the menu. Basta Pasta also provides a feast for the eyes with a rotating display of bold artwork.

Beppe

Italian ✗✗

B2

45 E. 22nd St. (bet. Broadway & Park Ave. South)

Subway: 23 St (Park Ave. South)
Phone: 212-982-8422
Web: www.beppenyc.com
Prices: $$$

Mon – Fri lunch & dinner
Sat dinner only

Located a half-block from the Flatiron Building, Beppe is a modest place, with an intentionally aged-looking décor made warm and cozy by a working fireplace in winter. Enthusiastic staff members provide knowledgeable, yet informal, service; they are one of the strengths of this welcoming restaurant. From the hospitable waitstaff to the sausage made from pigs raised on the restaurant's own farm, it's the little details that make a big difference here.

Business-lunchers don't seem to mind paying uptown prices for food, like the consistently crowd-pleasing pastas, that reflects the best of each season. The kitchen is committed to offering house-made prosciutto and salami, and locally grown greens from the nearby farmer's market.

BLT Fish

Seafood ✗✗

A2

21 W. 17th St. (bet. Fifth & Sixth Aves.)

Subway: 14 St - Union Sq
Phone: 212-691-8888
Web: www.bltfish.com
Prices: $$$

Mon – Fri lunch & dinner
Sat – Sun dinner only

After establishing BLT Steak in Midtown, Chef Laurent Tourondel turned from turf to surf. His two high-energy seafood restaurants occupy the first and third floors of a Flatiron district town house. Upstairs is the informally elegant dining room; downstairs, New England-style BLT Fish Shack serves weekday lunch and casual dinner, focusing in on favorites like lobster rolls and Maryland crab cakes. Both establishments share the same great raw bar.

Available by the pound, exceptionally fresh fish and shellfish are simply brushed with olive oil and grilled; the popular Cantonese red snapper arrives whole in a colorful display. Seasonally inspired sides (Meyer lemon risotto; baby bok choy) are served à la carte. For meat-lovers, Tourondel always includes one or two "Not Fish" dishes.

BLT Prime

Steakhouse ✗✗

111 E. 22nd St. (bet. Lexington & Park Aves.)

Subway: 23 St (Park Ave. South)   Dinner daily
Phone: 212-995-8500
Web: www.bltprime.com
Prices: $$$

In a city that offers a world of dining options, sometimes there's nothing wrong with meat and potatoes. In fact, there's something very right about BLT Prime, where cuts of USDA prime and certified black Angus are dry-aged in house, served sizzling hot in a cast iron pan, and topped with a slowly melting sheen of herbed butter. To further adorn your steak, choose from an array of homemade sauces and the hearty listing of sides that elevate the humble potato: creamy home fries, blue cheese tater tots, and leek hashbrowns. The Gruyère popovers start meals with a warm and tasty welcome. The handsome room and bar area, popular with local professionals, is done in rich tones of butterscotch and mocha, and furnished with sleek zebrawood tables.

Blue Smoke 😊

C1

American ✗

116 E. 27th St. (bet. Lexington & Park Aves.)

Subway: 28 St (Park Ave. South)   Lunch & dinner daily
Phone: 212-447-7733
Web: www.bluesmoke.com
Prices: $$

Jazz and barbecue make a winning combination, and nowhere more so in the city than at Blue Smoke, where hickory and apple wood are used to flavor the "low and slow" smoked meats. Blue Smoke replaces traditional canned ingredients with fresh versions. Sharing is encouraged, since platters like Rhapsody in 'Cue, a sampler of St. Louis spareribs, pulled pork, smoked chicken, and a hot link are a challenge for one person. With its inclusion of small producers from Europe and North America, the wine list surprises for a barbecue joint. You can enjoy the same food downstairs at Jazz Standard while you listen to live jazz and blues.
Owner Danny Meyer stamps the restaurant with his signature family-friendly service.

Manhattan ▶ Gramercy, Flatiron & Union Square

Blue Water Grill

Contemporary ❧❧

A2-3

31 Union Sq. West (at 16th St.)

Subway: 14 St - Union Sq
Phone: 212-675-9500
Web: www.brguestrestaurants.com
Prices: $$

Lunch & dinner daily

Facing the Union Square greenmarket, Blue Water Grill is housed in a former bank that dates back to the turn of the last century. The dining room bustles with eager guests and a well-trained service team, yet retains a stately air with its soaring molded ceiling, gleaming marble, and large windows overlooking the terraced dining area, ideal for warmer weather.

The crowd-pleasing menu offers a raw bar and selection of sushi or maki. Entrées focus on seafood either simply grilled or accented with international flavors, as in the ginger-soy lacquered Chilean sea bass. Live jazz is served up nightly in the downstairs lounge; and private group dining is available in the Vault Room, a former repository for gold bullion.

Boqueria

Spanish ❧❧

A2

53 W. 19th St. (at Sixth Ave.)

Subway: 18 St (Seventh Ave.)
Phone: 212-255-4160
Web: www.boquerianyc.com
Prices: $$

Lunch & dinner daily

New York's craze for small plates rages on at this sociable Flatiron tapas bar. Boqueria takes its name from the famous Barcelona market. Like the Catalonian *Boqueria*, the restaurant dishes up a dizzying array of offerings, sized from tiny (*pinxto*) and small (*tapas*) to entrée portions (*racion*) and plates for sharing (*compartir*). You can get an idea of the variety—crispy potatoes with roasted garlic aioli; blistered *shisito* peppers; and baby squid with black olive vinaigrette— by eyeing the bar, where examples are set out to tempt you.

To quench your thirst, choose from the all-Spanish wine list, or try a glass of white sangria. You'll find the staff well-versed in all aspects of the menu.

Butai

B2

Japanese 🍴

115 E. 18th St. (bet. Irving Pl. & Park Ave.)

Subway: 14 St - Union Sq
Phone: 212-228-5716
Web: www.butai.us
Prices: $$

Mon – Fri lunch & dinner
Sat – Sun dinner only

Butai is an ideal place to enjoy contemporary Japanese cuisine in a sleek setting. Quietly restrained at lunch, the scene turns hip when the sun sets and young professionals depart the nearby offices. The modern interior is accented with gorgeous marble and dark wood, and lively lounge music adds to the cool ambience.

Attractive presentations of sushi are available throughout the day, but Butai is best known for its robata grill offerings, which are only available in the evening. One of the few Japanese restaurants in the city to offer robata-style cuisine, Butai also impresses with its visually appealing presentations. Japanese classic starters, such as *agedashi* tofu or various *sunomono* are standouts to begin your robata feast.

Campanile

B1

Italian 🍴🍴

30 E. 29th St. (bet. Madison & Park Aves.)

Subway: 28 St (Park Ave.)
Phone: 212-684-4344
Web: www.campanilenyc.com
Prices: $$

Mon – Fri lunch & dinner
Sat dinner only

Pass beyond the discreet windows and through the light wood door for a warm and casual welcome to this authentic Italian-American eatery.

A small bar near the entrance is followed by a long and narrow dining room between pale yellow walls, where small tables are adorned with white linens and flowers in porcelain vases.

The menu focuses more on family style than gastronomic fare, but half-orders of pasta are available. Classic and traditionally prepared offerings may include *penne al'arrabbiata*, served al dente with hot tomato and chili sauce, or a sizeable yellowfin tuna *alla Livornese*, cooked medium and served under homemade tomato sauce with black olives, capers, and olive oil. Montepulciano is served with meals as an honest standby for house red wine.

Casa Mono

B3

Spanish ✗

52 Irving Pl. (at 17th St.)

Subway: 14 St - Union Sq
Phone: 212-253-2773
Web: www.casamononyc.com
Prices: $$

Lunch & dinner daily

Partners Joseph Bastianich and Mario Batali serve a bit of Barcelona on this charming Gramercy corner. Consistently packed with a vivacious crowd, one cannot get enough of Chef/co-owner Andy Nusser's enormous atmosphere with a colorful tiled floor and straw chairs. The dining counter overlooks the working kitchen that perpetually turns out a lengthy lineup of appetizing nibbles like pumpkin and goat cheese *croquetas* or octopus with fennel and grapefruit. The wine list is of note, featuring more than 500 labels, all Spanish. If Casa Mono is overflowing, try baby sister, Bar Jamon (Spanish for "ham bar") next door, to nosh on light snacks like *bocadillos* (Spanish sandwiches) or cheeses paired with interesting condiments, such as quince paste.

Copper Chimney

Indian ✗✗

C1

126 E. 28th St. (bet. Lexington & Park Aves.)

Subway: 28 St (Park Ave. South)
Phone: 212-213-5742
Web: www.copperchimney.com
Prices: 🍸🍸

Lunch & dinner daily

Copper Chimney's impressive Indian fare offers plenty to satisfy, in this attractive room with a hip décor and fun vibe. A meal here begins with a small plate of mini-*pappadums* drizzled with mint and tamarind chutney, surrounding a neat mound of minced tomato, onion, and pepper. The appetizer selection includes tandoori samosas and fried cauliflower florets with honey and garlic. Main courses incorporate a wide range of traditional ingredients while emphasizing refined preparation and elegant presentation. Non-meat eaters will be happy with the ample selection of flavorful vegetarian items. Copper Chimney's youthful ambiance is further accentuated by a second floor lounge area.

Craft

B2

American ✗✗✗

43 E. 19th St. (bet. Broadway & Park Ave. South)

Subway: 14 St - Union Sq   Dinner daily
Phone: 212-780-0880
Web: www.craftrestaurant.com
Prices: $$$$

As host of the popular Bravo reality show, *Top Chef*, Tom Colicchio is a Hollywood natural. But years ago, he shot to fame on his home turf—the New York food scene—by ushering in a new, albeit simple, way of thinking about haute cuisine: let fresh, local, organic ingredients do the work, and let customers design their own plates. At Craft, diners can tailor their meals ingredient by ingredient to suit them perfectly, choosing from a basic lineup of seafood, charcuterie, roasted meats, salad, or vegetables. That they can do it in a beautiful Flatiron space with leather-panelled walls, brick-covered columns, and dramatic filament bulbs dripping from the ceiling, takes the cake. Speaking of, don't miss the to-die-for desserts.

Craftbar

A2

Contemporary ✗✗

900 Broadway (bet. 19th & 20th Sts.)

Subway: 14 St - Union Sq   Lunch & dinner daily
Phone: 212-461-4300
Web: www.craftrestaurant.com
Prices: $$

Craftbar, the seductive and always crowded annex to Tom Colicchio's Craft restaurant, moved to bigger digs around the corner to accommodate its burgeoning guest list. Here, at Craft's casual cousin, you can sample Craft-like, top-quality ingredients at a lower price point.

The cuisine successfully blends modern American style with Mediterranean flair. Many of the small plates that made Craftbar famous may be gone now, but sharing items on the extensive new menu is still welcomed. Although the dishes change frequently so customers can enjoy the fresh flavors of select seasonal products, the famous veal ricotta meatballs remain.

Here, as at Craft, you'll revel in a large wine list, with a host of selections by the glass.

Dévi

A2

8 E. 18th St. (bet. Broadway & Fifth Ave.)

Subway: 14 St - Union Sq
Phone: 212-691-1300
Web: www.devinyc.com
Prices: $$$

Mon – Fri lunch & dinner daily
Sat – Sun dinner only

Cookbook author Suvir Saran and tandoor master Hemant Mathur oversee this sultry spot and lucky for aficionados of regional Indian cooking, the cuisine here honors its roots while receiving a modern spin from these very talented chefs.

The sumptuous setting is indeed fit for the Hindu mother goddess who inspired the restaurant's name. Gauzy jewel-tone fabrics swathe the walls; banquettes covered in patchwork of chocolate, gold, and saffron tones provide cozy seating; and colored-glass lanterns light the transporting room.

A mouthwatering choice of vegetarian dishes appeal to some, while others might prefer Tandoori chicken breast stuffed with shredded lamb or a rich Masala fried quail, redolent with touches of cardamom and coriander.

Eleven Madison Park

B1

11 Madison Ave. (at 24th St.)

Subway: 23 St (Park Ave. South)
Phone: 212-889-0905
Web: www.elevenmadisonpark.com
Prices: $$$

Mon – Fri lunch & dinner
Sat dinner only

Set inside the MetLife Insurance tower across from Madison Square Park, the sculpted wrought-iron gates framing the entrance to Eleven Madison Park hint that something wonderful lies beyond. From its marble floors to the 30-foot-high ceilings, the gorgeous Art Deco-style dining room never fails to impress. Drink in park views through the room's high windows while perusing the menu. Swiss-born Chef Daniel Humm pays strict attention to product sourcing and seasonality in creative offerings such as a poached organic duck egg with sautéed wild mushrooms and parmesan foam. Service is professional and engaging, attentive but not intrusive.

Categorized by varietal and region, the excellent wine list demonstrates the restaurant's dedication to its cellar.

15 East

J a p a n e s e ✗

15 E. 15th St. (bet. Fifth Ave. & Union Sq. West)

Subway: 14 St - Union Sq
Phone: 212-647-0015
Web: www.15eastrestaurant.com
Prices: $$$

Mon – Fri lunch & dinner
Sat dinner only

Its name may be non-descript, but 15 East is no plain Jane. In this attractive sushi bar, ivory tiled walls, a polished-concrete floor and dove-gray furnishings complement the warmly lit monochromatic dining room.

Helmed by chef Masato Shimizu, who apprenticed in Japan for seven years, the team at 15 East slices up tender slivers of pristine-quality fish atop warm rice—characteristic of Edo-style sushi. First-rate touches like freshly grated wasabi root, house-pickled ginger and handmade ceramic serving pieces accentuate the experience.

In addition to sushi, there's a full menu of contemporary Japanese cuisine. Don't miss the house-made soba noodles, and be sure to consider a sake or a *shochu* from the impressive selection.

Hill Country

B a r b e c u e ✗

30 W. 26th St. (bet. Broadway & Sixth Ave.)

Subway: 28 St (Sixth Ave.)
Phone: 212-255-4544
Web: www.hillcountryny.com
Prices: $$

Lunch & dinner daily

Lively, very casual, and a whole lot of fun, owner Marc Glosserman brings this Texas-size roadhouse to space-challenged New York, with two floors of patrons flocking for fantastic barbecue that stands out in the recent boom.

A lower level stage fills the space with loud, live country music (a nod to its Austin roots), making this a festive spot for groups and families alike.

Cords of oak fuel massive smokers to re-recreate a truly Texan Hill Country experience. Flintstone-size ribs are sold by the pound. Kreuz sausages, straight from Lockhart, are sold by the link. Have your meal ticket stamped then head over to the trimmings counter for authentic homestyle sides. Takeout and delivery are good options for those who prefer more traditional service.

Manhattan ▶ Gramercy, Flatiron & Union Square

Fleur de Sel ❀

A2

French 🍴🍴

5 E. 20th St. (bet. Broadway & Fifth Ave.)

Subway: 23 St (Broadway)   Lunch & dinner daily
Phone: 212-460-9100
Web: www.fleurdeselnyc.com
Prices: $$$

Fleur de Sel defines charm in its intimate dining room, which centers on a table topped by a striking seasonal floral arrangement. Elsewhere in the refined yet comfortable room, brick walls, warm colors, and well-selected artwork set a cozy tone for fine dining.

Brittany-born Chef Cyril Renaud triumphantly distills the essence of seasonal ingredients. Premier products and an ideal balance between creative and classic preparations ensure a memorable meal. The chef's technique *magnifique* can turn a simple *poussin* into a *chef-d'oeuvre*, with skin perfectly crisped and flattened meat served atop roasted white asparagus, wilted spinach, and wild mushrooms. A foie gras emulsion brings another dimension to the dish.

With its endearingly sincere and professional service, there are no false notes within this place, named for a prized, pure salt harvested on France's Channel coast.

Appetizers	*Entrées*	*Desserts*
• Escargot and Polenta Gâteaux, Parmesan Crisp, Red Wine Sauce	• Poussin, Wilted Spinach, Mushrooms, Foie Gras Emulsion	• Gaufrette au Chocolat, Black Mint, Chocolate Ice Cream
• Pork Belly, Fingerling Potato Purée, American Paddlefish Caviar	• Halibut, Glazed Endives, Oklahoma Pecans, Bacon, Balsamic Reduction	• Brittany Crêpe, Devonshire Whipped Cream
• Trio of Foie Gras, Rhubarb Gelée	• Venison Loin, Potato and Venison Sausage	• Red-Wine-Glazed Almond Macaroon

Gramercy Tavern ❀

Contemporary 🗡🗡🗡

 B2

42 E. 20th St. (bet. Broadway & Park Ave. South)

Subway: 23 St (Park Ave. South)
Phone: 212-477-0777
Web: www.gramercytavern.com
Prices: $$$

Mon – Fri lunch & dinner
Sat – Sun dinner only

A peek into the enormous front windows of this bustling, beloved institution tells you something about New Yorkers. They may be renowned for their slick, urban spaces; but nothing gets them going like a little country-house-in-Vermont decor. Add top-flight cuisine and the wafting scent of wood-smoke to that lineup, and they might just marry you. And that's exactly why Danny Meyer's Gramercy Tavern will celebrate its 15th birthday this year—which doesn't exactly qualify it as venerable just yet, but hearkens many a foodie back to a rather important era, one where restaurateurs were laying down roots for what would define turn-of-the-century fine dining in America.

Chef Michael Anthony, now three years into his tenure, is ushering in his own delicious era—one where meat ragùs are so rich they glisten; and perfectly caramelized apple tatins melt under warm, golden crusts.

Appetizers
- Thumbelina Carrots with Farro and Swiss Chard
- Smoked Brook Trout, Sunchoke Purée and Pickled Onions Vinaigrette
- Marinated Calamari with Meyer Lemon

Entrées
- Spanish Mackerel, Brussels Sprouts, Kohlrabi
- Flatiron Steak & Short Ribs, Cabbage, Puffed Potatoes
- Smoked Lobster, Celery Root Purée and Ramp Sauce

Desserts
- Warm Chocolate Bread Pudding with Cacao Nib Ice Cream
- Warm Apple Crisp with Cinnamon Ice Cream
- Blueberry and Corn Sundae with Toffee Popcorn

113

Irving Mill

B3

Contemporary ✗✗

116 E. 16th St. (bet. Irving Pl. & Union Sq. East)

Subway: 14 St - Union Sq
Phone: 212-254-1600
Web: www.irvingmill.com
Prices: $$$

Tue – Sun lunch & dinner
Mon dinner only

Serving impressive yet unpretentious cuisine in a rustic yet elegant setting with service that is professional yet warm, this crowd-pleasing newcomer achieves an admiral balancing act. Inspired by its location, this modern day tavern draws from the neighborhood's namesake and "Sleepy Hollow" author, Washington Irving. The words of his classic story decorate the curved booths that furnish the formal back room. The casual front area styles a New England tap room and bar, where a zinc-topped bar dispenses local beers to a lively crowd.

The seasonal menu offers solid fare like richly layered flavors of exceptionally moist braised rabbit or silky, tangy lemon buttermilk pudding cake, creatively accompanied by ruby red grapefruit and crushed pink peppercorns.

I Trulli

C1

Italian ✗✗

122 E. 27th St. (bet. Lexington Ave. & Park Ave. South)

Subway: 28 St (Park Ave. South)
Phone: 212-481-7372
Web: www.itrulli.com
Prices: $$$

Mon – Fri lunch & dinner
Sat dinner only

Located in the heart of Gramercy, the family of establishments that falls under the I Trulli umbrella includes something for almost everyone. Attached to the restaurant is a wine bar called Enoteca I Trulli, and across the street, you'll find Vino, which sells Italian wines and spirits.

I Trulli features the cuisine of Puglia, the owner's native region; the restaurant even has its own label of olive oil, harvested and bottled in Italy. Pastas, including the light-as-a-feather *malloreddus* (dumplings filled with sausage) make a wonderful first or second course.

The dining room's rustic fireplace, open kitchen, and wood-burning oven evoke the Italian countryside. In the warm seasons, the covered terrace will transport you to the European countryside.

Jaiya

C1

Thai 🍴

396 Third Ave. (bet. 28th & 29th Sts.)

Subway: 28 St (Park Ave. South)
Phone: 212-889-1330
Web: www.jaiya.com
Prices: 💷💷

Mon – Fri lunch & dinner
Sat – Sun dinner only

Authentic Thai cuisine brings a mixed crowd of couples, families, and groups of friends back to this simple restaurant. There's a reason that groups are drawn to casual Jaiya: generous family-style portions are big enough for sharing, and a group can eat well here for a reasonable price.

Skip the popular pad Thai and satay. A foray into the large number of curries and chef's specialties is bound to delight your palate with authentic tastes of Thailand. The waitstaff is efficient and tries to be helpful by talking diners down from their spice requests. Since the kitchen here does not Americanize the traditional Thai spice levels, ordering a dish "medium spicy" may well yield a more fiery taste than you bargained for.

Les Halles

C1

French 🍴

411 Park Ave. South (bet. 28th & 29th Sts.)

Subway: 28 St (Park Ave. South)
Phone: 212-679-4111
Web: www.leshalles.net
Prices: $$

Lunch & dinner daily

Everyone's favorite bad boy chef, Anthony Bourdain, may have put this well-worn brasserie on the map (this is his alma mater, though an offshoot now resides in the Financial District), but let's get this straight—it's the simple, unfussy French cooking that continues to pack this joint nightly. Why? Because sometimes a fresh-off-the-boat bundle of mussels served with crackling pommes frites, or soft, delicate crêpe, flambéed tableside, can bring a tear to the eye of even the most jaded foodie; and also because certain French classics are best left untouched—not mucked up or modernized. Add that to a budget-friendly wine list, and you've got a recipe for longevity. After 8:00 P.M., the music jumps up at Les Halles, but the crowd stays delightfully unpretentious.

Mesa Grill

Southwestern XX

 A2

102 Fifth Ave. (bet. 15th & 16th Sts.)

Lunch & dinner daily

Subway: 14 St - Union Sq
Phone: 212-807-7400
Web: www.mesagrill.com
Prices: $$$

As part of the original Food Network rat pack, the French Culinary Institute-trained Bobby Flay was dishing edgy, high-end southwestern fare before Rachael Ray could spell E.V.O.O. The triple-threat star (television, cookbooks, and restaurants) can hardly be expected to man his own grill these days, but the food at Mesa Grill—if a bit wobbly on the master's technique from time to time—still packs Flay's signature spicy punch.

Start with a tender blue corncake, fat with moist, smoky, shredded barbecued duck and surrounded by a vibrant-orange swirl of zesty, habanero chile-star anise sauce. Come for drinks, come for fun—but don't come looking for an intimate hideaway. Like the redhead himself, Mesa Grill is bold, colorful, and boisterous.

Molly's Pub & Shebeen

Gastropub X

C2

287 Third Ave. (bet. 22nd & 23rd Sts.)

Lunch & dinner daily

Subway: 23 St (Park Ave. South)
Phone: 212-889-3361
Web: www.mollysshebeen.com
Prices: 🍲

Molly's is as traditional a pub as you're likely to find in New York. Even the exterior screams "Ireland" with its white stucco façade against dark wood beams, and its carved wooden sign. Inside, low ceilings, dark walls, and sawdust floors are warmed by the wood-burning fireplace—a great place to defrost any winter chills.

The pub draws patrons of all stripes, from twenty-somethings to seasoned regulars, minus the boisterous happy-hour set. An ideal watering hole for a pint and an awesome burger, Molly's also serves corned beef and cabbage, fish and chips, and Shepherd's pie.

You may have to wait for a table here, but if so, the bar staff will take good care of you, and the friendly regulars usually have a few good stories to share.

Olana

B1   Contemporary   ✗✗

72 Madison Ave. (bet. 27th & 28th Sts.)

Subway: 28 St (Park Ave. South)
Phone: 212-725-4900
Web: www.olananyc.com
Prices: $$

Mon – Fri lunch & dinner
Sat dinner only

Named after the Hudson River Valley estate of nineteenth-century landscape painter Frederic Church, this stately establishment near Madison Square Park serves a menu that draws inspiration from the seasons. The dining room is outfitted with striking backlit murals of nature scenes, hefty red-velvet seating, and generous woodwork. The front bar is comfortably spacious, and the organized service staff attends to its patrons in earnest.

Detect an enjoyable Italian accent in a listing of pastas that may include mint *tacconi* with house-made lamb sausage ragù; preparations like slow-roasted halibut display a skilled hand. Desserts are equally impressive with a list of treats that may include rhubarb strudel with *pain d'epices* (gingerbread) ice cream.

Olives

B3   Contemporary   ✗✗

201 Park Ave. South (at 17th St.)

Subway: 14 St - Union Sq
Phone: 212-353-8345
Web: www.toddenglish.com
Prices: $$$

Lunch & dinner daily

Chef Todd English opened this outpost of his popular Boston restaurant on the first floor of the W Hotel. A link in the chain of English's empire of eateries, Olives on Union Square packs 'em in seven nights a week.

The draw? A trendy setting, a lively crowd in the lounge, and English's innovative Mediterranean cuisine. Handmade butternut squash *tortelli*, swordfish *oreganata* with Italian sausage ragù, and lamb Porterhouse with pistachio vinaigrette are seasonal highlights. You might even find the likes of brick-oven-baked flatbread topped with fig and prosciutto, which leaves standard pizza in the dust.

You can purchase a copy of English's cookbook, *The Olives Table,* at the reception desk.

Park Avenue Bistro 😊

French ✕✕

B1

377 Park Ave South (bet. 26th & 27th Sts.)

Subway: 28 St (Park Ave. South)
Phone: 212-689-1360
Web: www.parkavenuebistronyc.com
Prices: $$

Mon – Fri lunch & dinner
Sat dinner only

Park Bistro is finally back and proving worth the wait. A new name, location, and look have transformed this venerable restaurant. Airy and inviting, it now has an elegant European feel, much calmer than the stretch of Park Avenue South on which it lies. Still, a scattering of sidewalk tables is prime real estate in warm weather, for those interested in remaining part of the fray.

Bistro fare remains the heart of this menu, with some contemporary dishes. The signature *petatou* (warm fingerling potatoes with shallots and Niçoise olives, topped with a golden layer of goat cheese) is a wonderful starter. Follow this with any of the main courses—just be sure to order a side of the fantastic pommes frites. The three-course prix-fixe lunch offers terrific value.

Periyali

Greek ✕✕

A2

35 W. 20th St. (bet. Fifth & Sixth Aves.)

Subway: 23 St (Sixth Ave.)
Phone: 212-463-7890
Web: www.periyali.com
Prices: $$$

Mon – Fri lunch & dinner
Sat – Sun dinner only

Periyali has been serving delicious, rustic Greek fare since Nicola Kotsoni and Steve Tzolis opened this captivating place in 1987—long before this cuisine gained such popularity in New York.

Despite its basement location, the restaurant manages to be light and airy, thanks to whitewashed walls, abundant live greenery, and sunlit back rooms. The feel of the Greek countryside washes over the dining space, divided into several sections.

Care is taken in both the preparation and presentation of the unpretentious dishes, whose unadulterated flavors and fresh products burst through in the likes of charcoal-grilled shrimp dressed simply in olive oil and lemon. Remember to save room after starting the meal with outstanding fresh bread and olive oil.

Primehouse New York

Steakhouse ✕✕

381 Park Ave. South (at 27th St.)

Subway: 28 St (Park Ave. South)
Phone: 212-824-2600
Web: www.brguestrestaurants.com
Prices: $$$

Lunch & dinner daily

Primehouse New York fashions a grand ambience that sets it apart from the recognizable herd of traditional steakhouses. Here, glossy multi-room spaces sport walls covered in pale marble and ebony tiles, sleek furnishings, and an impressively stocked smoke-glass-walled wine cellar. However, style does not trump substance. Well prepared cuts of prime Black Angus beef are aged in-house and supported by a tempting selection of "ocean meats" or raw bar combinations like the "Chrysler" and "Empire" seafood towers.

Attentive servers wheel trolleys throughout the room, ladling smooth, flavorful soups and preparing traditional Caesar salads tableside—just remember to order that dessert soufflé in advance. The sexy bar lounge is a chic stop for an after-work cocktail.

Pure Food and Wine

Vegan ✕

54 Irving Pl. (bet. 17th & 18th Sts.)

Subway: 14 St - Union Sq
Phone: 212-477-1010
Web: www.purefoodandwine.com
Prices: $$$

Dinner daily

Carnivores beware: this restaurant's name means what it says. A disciple of the raw-food movement, Pure Food and Wine serves only raw vegan dishes. If you're a first-timer here, the waiters will explain that to preserve vitamins, enzymes, minerals, and flavors in the food, nothing is heated above 118°F.

Mushroom hazelnut crostini with pomegranate reduction and white corn tamales with raw cacao mole don't just taste good, they're good for you—especially if you buy into the purported health benefits of raw cuisine. Either way, the kitchen uses only the freshest organic produce available, and the results are surprisingly flavorful.

The juice bar and take-away counter foster healthy eating on the go.

Manhattan ▶ Gramercy, Flatiron & Union Square

Resto

C1

111 E. 29th St. (bet. Lexington & Park Aves.)

Subway: 28 St (Park Ave. South)
Phone: 212-685-5585
Web: www.restonyc.com
Prices: $$

Lunch & dinner daily

Culinary soulmates, *moules frites* are represented in top form, as steaming pots of plump bivalves and flavorful broth cover wooden tables alongside plates of crisp, golden fries. Resto remains true to its Belgian inspiration by accompanying these with rich mayonnaise, vibrantly enhanced with sweet chilli sauce or tart lime pickle. Starters like alluring double-cooked pork served with quartered endive and desserts of dense Liege-style waffles flecked with crunchy sugar are delicious book-ends to any meal. Peruse their expansive selection of beer to find the perfect accompaniment to this hearty fare, which is no slight to the wine list.

This chicly spare room features a marble-topped bar, tin ceiling, and exposed brick, designed to exude warmth.

Saravanaas 😋

C2

81 Lexington Ave. (at 26th St.)

Subway: 28 St (Park Ave. South)
Phone: 212-679-0204
Web: www.saravanaas.com
Prices: 😋😋

Lunch & dinner daily

Set smack in the midst of Curry Row, Saravanaas stands out with its simple, clean contemporary décor. Pastel-hued walls, colorful votives, and gleaming aluminum serving pieces brighten the dining room.

The menu embraces a contemporary reflection of time-honored Southern Indian dishes. *Thalis*, a selection of different foods served with appropriate condiments, come in small or large sizes for a set price. *Dosas*, made with rice and lentils, are a specialty here. You can order these wonderfully thin pancakes plain or with your choice of vegetarian fillings. The *dosas* are so enormous, it's easy to make a meal of just one—for less than $10. And the veggie fillings are so tasty and satisfying, you'll never miss the meat.

Tabla

Contemporary ✕✕✕

B1

11 Madison Ave. (at 25th St.)

Subway: 23 St (Park Ave. South)
Phone: 212-889-0667
Web: www.tablany.com
Prices: $$$

Mon – Fri lunch & dinner
Sat – Sun dinner only

A stone's throw away from Madison Square Park, Tabla is housed in an Art Deco space done in shades of leafy green and persimmon orange; a vibrant mosaic of tropical fruit lends an exotic air to the grand two-story setting. The boisterous street-level Bread Bar is topped by the more formal upstairs dining room. Polished service displays the trademark of Danny Meyer's Union Square Hospitality Group. Executive Chef, partner, and Mumbai native Floyd Cardoz has been at the helm since the restaurant's beginning 10 years ago, skillfully fusing contemporary American cuisine with flavorful Indian accents. Fresh ingredients combine in refreshing and unexpected ways, as in the pumpkin *rasam* soup, warmed by ginger and other spices providing a pleasant depth of flavor.

Tamarind

Indian ✕✕✕

B2

41-43 E. 22nd St. (bet. Broadway & Park Ave. South)

Subway: 23 St (Park Ave. South)
Phone: 212-674-7400
Web: www.tamarinde22.com
Prices: $$$

Lunch & dinner daily

Unlike the sweet-and-sour tropical fruit for which it's named, Tamarind hits no sour notes. Instead, the restaurant achieves a pleasing harmony between its sophisticated décor (no wild colors here) and its regional Indian cuisine.

A floor-to-ceiling wrought-iron "wall" from a maharajah's palace lends a royal air to the dining room, and the back wall holds mirrored niches for a collection of stylized Indian wooden puppets. Inside the glassed-in kitchen, a serious brigade of cooks prepares piquant dishes from Goa, Punjab, Madras, and Calcutta. The large range of regional cuisine includes masala, curries and tandoori dishes; goat meat here is a tender delight. A broad selection of international wines puts the icing on the cake.

Tocqueville

A3

Contemporary ✗✗

1 E. 15th St. (bet. Fifth Ave. & Union Sq. West)

Subway: 14 St - Union Sq
Phone: 212-647-1515
Web: www.tocquevillerestaurant.com
Prices: $$

Mon – Sat lunch & dinner

Chef/owner Marco Moreira and his wife Jo-Ann Makovitsky named their popular labor of love after the 19th-century French writer Alexis de Tocqueville. Lush fabrics, vintage mirrors, and bold art fashion an elegant décor—a soothing respite in which to enjoy the menu's contemporary French-accented creations. Located just one block from the Union Square Greenmarket, the restaurant displays a creative approach to seasonal cuisine in roasted pear salad with local cheddar, pan-roasted brook trout with rhubarb marmalade, and apple pizza with maple ice cream. During the summer months, three-course lunch and dinner menus showcase the market's bounty.

The 300-label wine list features selections from little-known regions around the world as well as a number of sakes.

Turkish Kitchen ☺

C1

Turkish ✗✗

386 Third Ave. (bet. 27th & 28th Sts.)

Subway: 28 St (Park Ave. South)
Phone: 212-679-6633
Web: www.turkishkitchenny.com
Prices: ☺☺

Sun – Fri lunch & dinner
Sat dinner only

You'll see red when you step inside the Turkish Kitchen's windowed façade—red walls, that is. The inside of the first-floor dining room is painted bright red, with red fabric-covered chairs. Casual enough for jeans, the place feels exotic with copper urns filling shelves and wall alcoves, and colorful martini glasses lining the glowing blue-glass bar. At night, blue-glass votives mounted on the walls cast a romantic light.

Many of the best dishes here are uniquely Turkish, such as the *boregi* (feta-filled phyllo rolls baked to a crisp), or the lamb, grilled and served in a variety of preparations. Try a glass of Turkish wine or beer to round out your experience. For both lunch and dinner, the three-course menu is a terrific deal.

Union Square Cafe

A2

21 E. 16th St. (bet. Fifth Ave. & Union Sq. West)

Subway: 14 St - Union Sq
Phone: 212-243-4020
Web: www.unionsquarecafe.com
Prices: **$$$**

Lunch & dinner daily

Quintessentially New York City, Union Square Cafe is a special place. It was founded by a young entrepreneur named Danny Meyer in 1985, and business has been booming ever since. Given the restaurant's comfortable bistro décor, winning service and excellent modern American cooking, it's easy to see why.

Do as the regulars do, get there early and grab a seat at the bar for a great burger or a three-course meal and a sampling of the cafe's wines by the glass. Chef/partner Michael Romano supplements his entrée selection with daily and weekly specials, and the Union Square Greenmarket next door figures largely in the planning. Worth a special mention is the tremendous wine list, which is diverse, well selected and reasonably priced.

Manhattan ▶ Gramercy, Flatiron & Union Square

Feast for under $25 at all restaurants with ☜.

Veritas ✿

Contemporary ✗✗

B2

43 E. 20th St. (bet. Broadway & Park Ave. South)

Subway: 23 St (Park Ave South)　　　　　　　　　Dinner daily
Phone: 212-353-3700
Web: www.veritas-nyc.com
Prices: $$$$

Veritas/©Emily Cantrell

If you've got a little discretionary dough and wine wets your whistle—look no further. Discreetly located along a tree-lined block near Gramercy Park, Veritas is a frequent haunt of the city's well-heeled grape connoisseurs. They come for the thousands of bottles the restaurant shelves, many of them carrying eye-popping price tags.

The good news is that the food, served as a $90 prix-fixe only, actually deserves its own solo number in this production. Wheel your fork around slender strands of homemade *pappardelle*, tossed with juicy chunks of lamb sausage, and studded with roasted red pepper and celery leaves; or tuck into soft, butter-poached halibut laid over a dollop of turnip puree.

With food and drink this good, it's easy to sink into the soft banquettes and let the clean, cool room—with its pale walls and soft, halogen lighting—envelope you for the evening.

Appetizers
- Lobster Salad, Fava Purée, Peppercorns, Sherry Vinegar
- Mushroom Ravioli, Mascarpone, Hon-Shimeji
- Pork Belly, Balsamic Glaze, Apple Salad

Entrées
- Short Ribs, Parsnip Purée, Glazed Carrots
- Monkfish, Melted Cabbage, Bacon, Red Wine Emulsion
- Scallops, Celery Root Purée, Braised Endive, Vinaigrette

Desserts
- Chocolate Soufflé
- Maple Crème Caramel, Candied Pecans, Sour Cherry Sauce
- Tarte Tatin, Macadamia Nut Brittle, Butter Rum Sauce

Innovation
for the future

www.michelin.com

Greenwich, West Village & Meatpacking District

Among the Big Apple's best neighborhoods for great dining, New York's historic bohemia lies between Houston and 14th streets, and contains within its several distinct areas. From Avenue of the Americas (Sixth Avenue) east to the Bowery, **Greenwich Village** keeps itself young with New York University's student population. The **West Village**, bound on the east by Avenue of the Americas and on the west by the Hudson River, is the prettiest and most historic of these westside neighborhoods. The gritty northwest corner of the West Village has been transformed in recent years into a considerably hip shopping, dining, and clubbing destination known as the **Meatpacking District**.

GREENWICH VILLAGE

Centering on **Washington Square** and lined with trees and Federal and Greek Revival row houses, this beguiling tangle of narrow streets is ideal for wandering. The heart of historic Greenwich Village is anchored by Washington Square and largely defined by the presence of **New York University**, founded in 1831 by Albert Gallatin, secretary of the treasury under Thomas Jefferson. One of the largest private universities in the country, NYU has an undergraduate population of 40,000 and a steadily rising reputation. **Washington Square Park,** a Greenwich Village cultural landmark, is presently undergoing a $16 million renovation. The former theater-in-the-round-fountain (a popular gathering place for students, musicians, performers, tourists, and residents) will experience a serious redesign, a source of contention for locals. Soon to be called the "Tisch Fountain," this beloved fixture simply known as "the fountain" was installed in 1870 and became the focal point of the park. Defining the unique character of the neighborhood, the fountain is also used after NYU graduation ceremonies for a celebratory splash—a tradition among graduates. The renovation is scheduled for completion in Spring of 2009.

The commercial spine of Greenwich Village, Bleecker Street, reveals the full spectrum of this neighborhood's life. The intersection with MacDougal Street forms the epicenter of New York University's student quarter. As it angles north toward the Meatpacking District, Bleecker grows increasingly upscale.

WEST VILLAGE

The West Village is bound by Christopher Street, Seventh Avenue South, St. Luke's Place, and Hudson Street. Within its skewed layout you will find meandering streets lined with charming town houses and a scattering of old trees. A crowd of artists and intellectuals began trickling into the Village in the late 1800s. The trickle turned to a flood in the new century, although these days the struggling-artist crowd has since moved to edgier areas.

After a long day ambling along the cobblestone streets, take a

Peter L. Wrenn / MICHELIN

seat on an antique-style bench inside the recently renovated **Father Demo Square**, a beautiful piazza banked by Sixth Avenue, Bleecker Street, and Carmine Street. Named after Father Antonio Demo, the square lies across from Our Lady of Pompei Church, where the late pastor not only served as emeritus, but also campaigned to have rebuilt and expanded in the early 1900s.

MEATPACKING DISTRICT

Not so long ago, "trendy" was the last word one would use to describe the section of the West Village bound by West 15th,

Hudson and Gansevoort streets, and the Hudson River. The Meatpacking District was a rather perilous place until the 1990s. After meat wholesalers would close for the day, drug dealers and prostitutes prowled its moody, cobblestone streets. The booming economy, along with Mayor Rudy Giuliani's heavy-handed crime policy in the early 1990s, cleaned up the neighborhood. Although some meat companies remain, the neighborhood's grit is, for the most part, a fashion accessory. Big-name chefs have forayed into the district, opening hot and hard-to-get-into restaurants. All these places are packed to the rafters at night, so reserve well in advance.

Greenwich, West Village & Meatpacking District

MEATPACKING DISTRICT

Scarpetta
El Ci
Spice Market
Vento
Pastis
Paradou
Gansevoort
Fatty Crab
El Faro
Barbuto
Jarnac
Café Cluny
The Plac
Spotted Pig
Wallsé
Extra Virgir
Alfama
Mary's Fish Camp
Perry Street
August
Mexicana Mama

HISTORIC GREENWICH VILLAGE

The Little Owl
Commerce

WEST VILLAGE

EN Japanese Brasserie
Market Table
Blue Ribbon Bakery
Mas

SOHO

NEW YORK CITY FIRE MUSEUM

HOLLAND TUNNEL

PIER 40

PIER 34

HUDSON RIVER

CHELSEA MARKET

Christopher Sq
Sheridan Sq

TRIBECA

- Hotels
- Restaurants

128

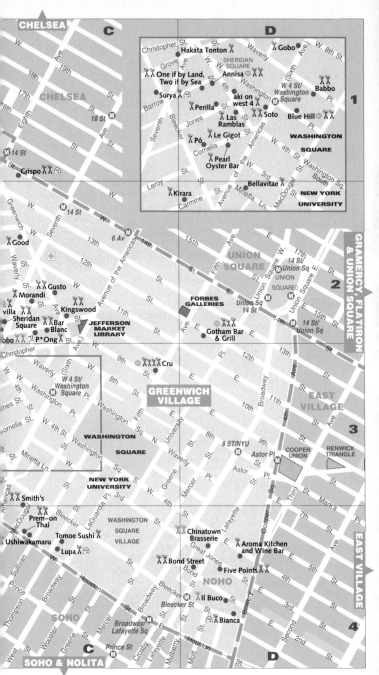

CHELSEA

C

D

Christopher St.   **Hakata Tonton** ✕   St.   Waverly   ✕ **Gobo**

Grove   St.   SHERIDAN   W. 8th. St.
    SQUARE

✕✕ **One if by Land,**   **Annisa** ✕✕
Two if by Sea

Surya ✕   Washington   W 4 St/   ✕✕ **Babbo**
Perilla ✕   **aki on**   Washington
    west 4 ✕   Square

CHELSEA   18 St Ⓜ

Eighth   **Las**   ✕✕✕   **Blue Hill** ✕✕
  Ramblas   **Soto**

Ⓜ 14 St   ✕ **Le Gigot**   WASHINGTON

Crispo ✕✕   ✕ **Pó**   SQUARE
  Cornelia   ✕ **Pearl**   NEW YORK
  Oyster Bar   UNIVERSITY

  Bellavitae ✕

✕ **Kirara**   Carmine

✕ **Good**   14 St Ⓜ   6 Av Ⓜ

GRAMERCY, FLATIRON & UNION SQUARE

UNION
SQUARE

✕✕ **Gusto**   FORBES   Union Sq   UNION
✕ **Morandi**   GALLERIES   SQUARED

villa ✕✕   ✕✕ **Kingswood**   14 St/
Sheridan   ✕✕ **Bar**   JEFFERSON   Union Sq
Square   **Blanc**   MARKET   ✕✕✕ **Gotham Bar**
obo ✕✕   **P*Ong** ✕   LIBRARY   **& Grill**

✕✕✕✕ **Cru**   EAST
  VILLAGE

GREENWICH
VILLAGE

WASHINGTON   8 ST/NYU   COOPER   RENWICK
SQUARE   Astor Pl.   UNION   TRIANGLE

NEW YORK
UNIVERSITY

✕✕ **Smith's**

✕✕   ✕✕ **Chinatown**
Prem-on   **Brasserie**
Thai   ✕ **Aroma Kitchen**
Tomoe Sushi ✕   **and Wine Bar**
Ushiwakamaru   **Lupa** ✕   **Five Points** ✕✕

✕✕ **Bond Street**   NOHO

SOHO   **Il Buco** ✕

  Bianca ✕

C   Prince St Ⓜ   D   4

SOHO & NOLITA

129

aki on west 4

D1

Japanese 🍴

181 W. 4th St. (bet. Sixth & Seventh Aves.)

Subway: W 4 St - Wash Sq
Phone: 212-989-5440
Web: www.members.aol.com/akiw4
Prices: $$

Tue – Sun dinner only

Chef/owner Shigeaki "Siggy" Nakanishi arrived in New York in 1997, bringing with him flavors of the Caribbean from a stint as private chef to the Japanese Ambassador to Jamaica. In this diminuitive restaurant, these two distinct culinary traditions—Jamaican and Japanese—are combined to great effect. Some of the more extraordinary results of this fusion may include the small ramekin of cold, silky *uni mousse* with *junsai*, topped with yuzu-flavored gelée, and a cilantro leaf—perfection in texture, contrast, and creativity. *Satoimo* croquette is a creative fusion of riced taro yam with seafood in a thick dashi soup. A full menu of sushi and sashimi is available to diners seeking more traditional fare. A four-course prix-fixe menu is an economical early dining option, between 6:00-7:00 P.M.

Alfama

B2

Portuguese 🍴

551 Hudson St. (at Perry St.)

Subway: 14 St - 8 Av
Phone: 212-645-2500
Web: www.alfamarestaurant.com
Prices: $$$

Mon – Fri dinner only
Sat – Sun lunch & dinner

Energy surges from every table at Alfama, starting with the vibrant tastes of the Portuguese cuisine and echoed in the cacophony of voices that rise in a room that still packs 'em in (even though it has been open since 1999). The draw? New Chef Mark Twersky prepares classic Portuguese fare (codfish cakes, marinated fresh sardines, and *mariscada Alfama*—a traditional fish stew); theatrical service, from the flaming Portuguese sausages to the *Bife na Pedra*, a filet mignon that's brought to the table on its own sizzling stone grill. Fuel the party further with a bottle from the all-Portuguese wine list or a glass of vintage Port or Madeira.

The decorative handmade tile panel and the Moorish lanterns recall the restaurant's namesake, a historic neighborhood in seaside Lisbon.

Annisa ✿

Contemporary ✗✗

13 Barrow St. (bet. Seventh Ave. South & W. 4th St.)

Subway: Christopher St - Sheridan Sq

Dinner daily

Phone: 212-741-6699

Web: www.annisarestaurant.com

Prices: $$$

From its serene ambiance to its name—which is Arabic for "women"—Annisa celebrates all that is feminine. The interior, designed by co-owner and sommelier Jennifer Scism, employs pastel tones and soft textures to feather its cozy nest. Large windows facing the street add an airy feel to the dining room, which sits on a platform a few steps up from the bar area.

Cuisine by Chef and co-owner Anita Lo pays tribute to the season while integrating global influences. Lo's Chinese-American heritage coupled with the time she spent studying and working in France accounts for clever pairings such as seared foie gras with soup dumplings: half-moon shaped dumplings filled with a rich meaty broth and topped with a thin rectangle of tender foie gras.

Even the wine list continues Annisa's theme; the majority of the 90 labels claim either female vintners and/or vineyards with female owners.

Appetizers
- Seared Foie Gras with Soup Dumplings and Jicama
- Tuna with Three Mints
- Duck and Buckwheat Ochazuke

Entrées
- Skate, Avocado, Radishes and Korean Flavors
- Braised Shortribs, Caperberries, Parmesan
- Pan-roasted Chicken, Sherry, Truffle and Pig's Feet

Desserts
- Poppyseed Bread and Butter Pudding with Meyer Lemon Curd
- Goat Cheese Cheesecake with Candied Beets and Citrus
- White Chocolate and Mint Parfait

Manhattan ▲ Greenwich, West Village & Meatpacking District

Aroma Kitchen & Wine Bar

Italian ✗

36 E. 4th St. (bet. Bowery & Lafayette St.)

Subway: Bleecker St
Phone: 212-375-0100
Web: www.aromanyc.com
Prices: $$

Sun – Fri lunch & dinner
Sat dinner only

Customers return to Aroma for its unique energy and, of course, the food. In warmer weather, the crowd at this Greenwich Village hangout spills onto the sidewalk. Though luckily, its appearance on the Food Network did not leave this tiny space overwhelmed.

Owners Alexandra Degiorgio and Vito Polosa are passionate about the food and wine they serve. This is evident in the house-made pastas, marinated olives, and many fine ingredients—truly a step up from the usual wine bar fare. Pan-regional Italian cooking is balanced with New York's seasons. Enjoy live guitar music Monday nights with the seasonal five-course chef tasting menu and optional wine pairing. The unique and fairly priced wine list contains many varietals rarely found outside Italy.

August

B2

European ✗

359 Bleecker St. (bet. Charles & 10th Sts.)

Subway: Christopher St - Sheridan Sq
Phone: 212-929-8727
Web: www.augustny.com
Prices: $$

Lunch & dinner daily

From the moment you enter this cozy place on a busy Greenwich Village street, your mouth will water at the enticing scents wafting through the room from the wood-burning oven. Billed as "regional European," the honest cuisine here roams the continent from France to Italy to Portugal to Greece. *Garganelli* with seared baby squid, and a braised veal breast served with crayfish, pea shoots, snap peas, and chervil exemplify the changing offerings. Of course, if you want a dish that's closer to home, the August burger—jazzed up with *pimenton* fries and house-made mayonnaise—is available at lunch and brunch.

August radiates warmth from its exposed brick walls and bright glassed-in back patio to its amiable waitstaff, who does whatever is necessary to make a meal here enjoyable.

Babbo

110 Waverly Pl. (bet. MacDougal St. & Sixth Ave.)

Subway: W 4 St - Wash Sq
Phone: 212-777-0303
Web: www.babbonyc.com
Prices: $$$

Dinner daily

Mario Batali's empire of delicious is on cruise control (New York digs include Del Posto, Lupa, Esca, and Casa Mono), but nothing defines the legendary chef like his beloved flagship, Babbo. Packed to the gills every night of the week, this restaurant manages to thrill the critics as much as the tourists. Maybe it's that whole quaint-townhouse thing; or the kitchen's inventive spin on otherwise simple, rustic Italian fare. But we like to imagine it's the soft thrum of rock n' roll wafting through, just loud enough to make you wonder if that famous ponytail is bouncing to the beat back there, cooking your food himself.

The menu changes seasonally, but stays creative: stewed rabbit gets a kick from smoky pancetta; a silky panna cotta is paired with a pink peppercorn and grapefruit sorbet. Batali's trademark Italian wine list is in full effect here, teeming with regions, vintages, and varietals.

Bar Blanc

142 W. 10th St. (bet. Greenwich Ave. & Waverly Pl.)

Subway: 14 St (Seventh Ave.)
Phone: 212-255-2330
Web: www.barblanc.com
Prices: $$$

Dinner daily

The chic interior of this West Village newcomer offers more fine dining than bar, yet remains true to its name with a predominantly white color scheme complemented by espresso-toned accents and marble bar.

The talented team behind this operation met while honing their craft at Bouley and has conceived a concise menu of impressively fine-tuned creations. The crowd, attended to by a warm staff, is as attractive as the candlelit setting, and sups on complex dishes such as slow-roasted chicken sauced with a light jus reduction over potato and brie purée, garnished with dark meat sausages and wild mushroom sauté.

Flavors combine beautifully in the dessert menu, as in the bitter chocolate cake with caramel ice cream and scattered grains of sea salt.

Barbuto

B2

American ⅄⅄

775 Washington St. (at 12th St.)

Subway: 14 St - 8 Av

Lunch & dinner daily

Phone: 212-924-9700

Web: www.barbutonyc.com

Prices: $$

♿

When the weather is warm, the garage-style doors are open, and tables spill out onto the front sidewalk, there's nothing like the ambience at Barbuto. You'll enjoy prime West Village people-watching here on the ground floor of the building that houses Industria Superstudios.

Simple is a good thing here, and Chef Jonathan Waxman's market-based cuisine plays up the best qualities of pristine ingredients. From day to day, spaghetti may be given a delicious lift with pancetta, artichoke *ragù*, and parmesan, while roasted Hudson Valley pears may add a sweet note to a grilled Berkshire pork chop.

The long bar is usually packed, especially later in the evening. From the celebrity-studded crowd to the fresh, flavorful fare, Barbuto still rules as a neighborhood favorite.

Bellavitae

D2

Italian ⅄

24 Minetta Ln. (bet. MacDougal St. & Sixth Ave.)

Subway: W 4 St - Wash Sq

Dinner daily

Phone: 212-473-5121

Web: www.bellavitae.com

Prices: $$

Tucked away in the unique Minetta Lane, this hugely popular charmer is staffed by bustling Italian servers who seem to do everything right. The comprehensive wine list offers a veritable education and includes myriad precious discoveries, with many available by the *quartino* (small carafe) allowing diners to explore the wealth of choices.

Sophisticated comfort food may include a floury fava purée topped with wild dandelion greens over thick toast, or a Bosc pear poached in Sangiovese and mulling spices: simple, delicious, and outstanding. Intoxicating scents from an array of pastas fill the smart, atmospheric room, adorned with beams and dark woods that hint of an old wine vault. Devotees may pick up a bottle of olive oil from Bellavitae's pantry.

Bianca

Italian 🍴

D4

5 Bleecker St. (bet. Bowery & Elizabeth St.)

Subway: Bleecker St   Dinner daily
Phone: 212-260-4666
Web: www.biancarestaurantnyc.com
Prices: $$

From its charming owners (also of Teodora and Celeste) to its intimate seating, Bianca simply radiates warmth. This fetching Italian in the heart of Nolita is perfect for a date or a get-together with friends. Tables are close together, making diners feel like part of the family, and soft lighting adds to the atmosphere.

Bianca's casual personality extends to its cuisine; genuine Italian food with simple, rustic presentations. Rarely found, the *cotechino* (a rustic sausage) is a winner. Generous portions of tasty food and a moderately priced Italian-focused wine list make for a very good value in a city often dominated by overpriced meals.

The restaurant does not take reservations so you may expect a short wait outside when things are busy.

Blue Ribbon Bakery

Contemporary 🍴

B3

35 Downing St. (at Bedford St.)

Subway: Houston St   Lunch & dinner daily
Phone: 212-337-0404
Web: www.blueribbonrestaurants.com
Prices: $$

The story of Blue Ribbon Bakery begins with an oven—an abandoned 140-year-old brick oven that brothers Eric and Bruce Bromberg found in the basement of an old bodega. Their discovery sparked an idea for a bakery, and they hired a master craftsman from Italy to rebuild the oven. That same appliance now forms the centerpiece of Blue Ribbon Bakery, opened in 1998.

Bread, from challah to country white, is baked on-site and stars on sandwiches at lunch and appears in a basket at dinner. On the divine menu you'll find everything from terrine of foie gras to a turkey burger, each dish prepared with outstanding ingredients, rich flavor, and impressive skill. Those in the know frequent the bar when they want a drink and light bite.

Blue Hill ✿

American 🍴🍴

D1

75 Washington Pl. (bet. Sixth Ave. & Washington Sq. Park)
Dinner daily

Subway: W 4 St - Wash Sq
Phone: 212-539-1776
Web: www.bluehillnyc.com
Prices: $$$

Jen Munkvold

Some point to the nine year-old Blue Hill as a pioneer of the organic-farm-to-urban-table movement that's swept the city by storm; but with food this fresh, nobody cares who started it. They're too busy thanking the heavens it's here. It helps to be able to hand-pick ingredients from your personal biodynamic farm up the river—and should you be up that way, the Blue Hill at Stone Barns, located in Pocantico Hills, has its own restaurant.

But for those of us stuck in the city, you can taste a little bit of country in Blue Hill's intimate, storybook townhouse located off Washington Square. Something as simple as a vibrant, hand-selected vegetable salad gets the star treatment from a citrus foam vinaigrette, and a dollop of homemade yogurt; while a slice of perfectly grilled *hamachi* is served over crispy, shredded cabbage, then thumped with a bright green herb and whole-grain mustard sauce.

Appetizers
- Stone Barns Greens Ravioli, Lettuce and Pancetta
- This Morning's Farm Egg, Lettuce and Herb Broth
- Crabmeat, Marinated Fennel, and Garden Gazpacho

Entrées
- Hake with Creamless Corn and Shellfish Chowder, Lardo
- Hudson Valley Duck, Chickpeas, Cranberry Beans, Tomato, Kohlrabi
- Grass-fed Lamb, Summer Beans, Herb, Lettuce Pesto

Desserts
- Cheesecake with Blackberries and Corn Ice Cream
- Chocolate Bread Pudding, Vanilla Ice Cream
- Peaches & Almond-Oatmeal Cobbler,

Bobo

C2

Contemporary 🍴🍴

181 W. 10th St. (at Seventh Ave.)

Subway: 14 St (Seventh Ave.)
Phone: 212-488-2626
Web: www.bobonyc.com
Prices: $$

Mon – Fri dinner only
Sat – Sun lunch & dinner

This turn-of-the-century brownstone, decorated more like a chic home than hip downtown dining destination, proves that cool can be comfortable. Bobo's pale blue and white-washed brick dining salon has an eclectic charm, accented throughout with framed pictures, gilded mirrors, book-filled shelves, and beaded lighting. The equally charming first-floor lounge offers a selection of classic cocktails and board games. To further illustrate the ambience, food is served on a mélange of vintage china. A lovely patio area completes the convivial setting.

The kitchen uses Mediterranean flavors to accent the finely made fare in items like asparagus and morel risotto. The perfectly seared mahi mahi served over crisp, fresh chickpeas, bok choy, and ramps demonstrates how excellent, local ingredients combined with very good preparation highlight the essence of each flavor, without overwhelming.

Bond Street

D4

Japanese 🍴🍴

6 Bond St. (bet. Broadway & Lafayette St.)

Subway: Bleecker St
Phone: 212-777-2500
Web: N/A
Prices: $$$$

Dinner daily

There is no name to mark the three-story brownstone that houses Bond Street—only a brown dot on a banner. And just like that, you just know you're in for a scene. Always stylish, always hopping—the music starts thumping early at Bond Street, where wealthy hedge funders and leggy beauties converge for high-end sushi that looks as beautiful as it tastes. Take a piece of *uni*, served in a purple shell, then laced with a necklace of diced cucumber and crowned with a golden leaf. A plating that is guaranteed to drop some jaws, undoubtedly—but with urchin so fresh it's pudding-sweet, Bond Street can afford to flash some bling. Speaking of, come prepared to flash a little of your own—appetizers start at $16, and prices just go up from there.

Café Cluny

B2

American ✗

284 W. 12th St. (at W. 4th St.)

Subway: 14 St - 8 Av
Phone: 212-255-6900
Web: N/A
Prices: $$

Lunch & dinner daily

Café Cluny just might be the quintessential West Village restaurant. Set amid the cobblestone streets and quaint brick town homes that make the area so well loved, this beguiling place lures patrons with its lineage (its owners are the same winning team responsible for the wildly successful Odeon) and its sweet style. Breezy, with cream-colored chairs, settees and screen doors, the place feels like a beachside bungalow—minus the salty air.

Open every day of the week, from morning morsels until midnight munchies, the cafe features items that progress from a breakfast club sandwich to a grilled duck salad with frisée, spiced walnuts and tangerines for lunch. Dinner fare embraces the likes of house-made ricotta ravioli, and grilled branzino with a baby artichoke salad. No matter what time of day you go, you're likely to leave smiling.

Chinatown Brasserie

D4

Chinese ✗✗

380 Lafayette St. (at Great Jones St.)

Subway: Bleecker St
Phone: 212-533-7000
Web: www.chinatownbrasserie.com
Prices: $$

Lunch & dinner daily

Dim sum all day is a dreamy concept and though it's not traditional, it's been well-received in a city that shuns rules. Chinatown Brasserie follows no code with its all-day menu of dim sum, Cantonese fare, fusion favorites, and creative cocktails in the China-chic cavernous space. Part of the stylish family that includes Lure Fishbar and Lever House, a trendy yet grown-up vibe still pervades here, and it's surely one of the most family-friendly brunches in town.

Modern dim sum prepared artfully include crispy taro root shrimp or lobster cream cheese sticks. A plate of crisp Peking duck is a great way to round out the mix and salads offer a bit of crunch.

Downstairs, the mod lounge—complete with a koi pond—sets the stage for post-dinner canoodling.

Commerce

B3   Contemporary X

50 Commerce St. (near Barrow St.)

Subway: Christopher St - Sheridan Sq
Phone: 212-542-2301
Web: N/A
Prices: $$

Mon – Sat dinner only
Sun lunch & dinner

Nestled into a tiny, curving West Village alleyway so utterly charming, it makes the rest of the city pale in comparison, the bustling new Commerce surely landed one of Manhattan's sweetest locations. If that means that quarters are bit cramped in this former speakeasy (the building dates back to the early 1900's), then so be it. Just relax into your Lilliputian table, let one of the crackerjack servers calm your jangled nerves with a basket of warm, freshly-baked bread, and settle in for Chef Harold Moore's ace cooking. A sanguine beef *tataki*, served rare, gets some zip from a mingling of ginger, scallion, and tiny *shiso* leaves; while a lush, shredded duck *rillettes*, carrying a hint of nutmeg, surrounds a creamy, buttery lobe of foie gras.

Crispo

C1   Italian XX

240 W. 14th St. (bet. Seventh & Eighth Aves.)

Subway: 14 St (Seventh Ave.)
Phone: 212-229-1818
Web: www.crisporestaurant.com
Prices: $$

Dinner daily

Sometimes a restaurant becomes your go-to spot simply because it does everything from the ambience to the food very, very well—without all the unnecessary pomp and fuss. Such is the case with Crispo, a quiet, brick-walled charmer tucked behind a wrought-iron fence along bustling 14th Street. The restaurant is named after Chef Frank Crispo, who honed his skills at La Côte Basque and Zeppole before taking the wheel himself. The result is a menu littered with classically-prepared, rustic Italian staples. But while the menu reads deceptively simple, more than a few items turn out to be flavor powerhouses, such as the house signature of spaghetti carbonara—a simple dish in concept, but a thing of beauty in the deft hands of Mr. Crispo.

Cru

C3

24 Fifth Ave. (at 9th St.)

Subway: 8 St - NYU
Phone: 212-529-1700
Web: www.cru-nyc.com
Prices: $$$$

Mon – Sat dinner only

True to its name, Cru is about wine; their 65,000 bottles encompass a dizzying array of producers, regions, vintages, and prices. This list—one of the best in the city—is so large that it is divided into two leather-bound tomes, one for white and one for red. Selections are drawn from the private collection of owner Roy Welland.

As in the wine list, great precision and ingredients formulate Cru's contemporary cuisine. Chef/partner Shea Gallante's sophisticated dishes sing the praises of each season. Creamy pillows of potato gnocchi make a lovely meal when presented alongside wilted greens, roasted garlic, and bites of fennel-spiked rabbit sausage. A pale-green slice of pistachio cake layered with pistachio mousse and topped with plump blackberries proves an elegant finale.

Prix-fixe options include a three-course menu as well as a set market menu, and a chef's tasting.

Appetizers	*Entrées*	*Desserts*
• Basinga Tomato Gazpacho, Langoustine, Avocado-Wasabi Crème Fraîche	• Sweet Potato Gnocchi, Braised Cinghiale, Thyme Croutons and Raschera Crema	• Cherry "Shortcake", Frog Hollow Cherries, Almond Pound Cake, Amaretto Semifreddo
• Nantucket Bay Scallops, Saffron Squash, Mutsu Apple and Endive-Pumpkin Seed Salad	• Chatham Cod, Cabbage Lasagna with Brandade, Oven-dried Tomato, Roasted Garlic Emulsion	• Valrhona Chocolate Tart, Chai-Caramel Ice Cream, Bourbon-Vanilla Shake

El Cid

B1

Spanish

322 W. 15th St. (bet. Eighth & Ninth Aves.)

Subway: 14 St - 8 Av
Phone: 212-929-9332
Web: N/A
Prices: $$

Tue – Sat dinner only

This unpretentious little neighborhood eatery is located in the vicinity of the hip Meatpacking District, but the truth is, El Cid was here long before the designer boutiques moved in.

Hot and cold tapas provide the food focus in the cramped and anything-but-trendy setting. Count on the proud staff to offer careful, kind service to eager crowds. And count on the tapas, from baby eels to chicken, to be flavorful and redolent with garlic. Tender, smoky *calamari al ajillo, chorizo al vino,* and *croquetas* particularly shine. Sangria makes the perfect accompaniment; it comes in red or white versions with enough fruit to liven up the mix, but not so much to clutter your glass. Save room for the signature *torrejas*, a wine-dipped version of French toast.

El Faro

B2

Spanish

823 Greenwich St. (at Horatio St.)

Subway: 14 St - 8 Av
Phone: 212-929-8210
Web: www.elfaronyc.com
Prices: $$

Tue – Sun lunch & dinner

Located in a part of the West Village once known as "Little Spain," El Faro began as a bar and grill in 1927. Its current owners, the Lugris and Perez families, purchased the restaurant in 1959 and have run it ever since.

Never mind the aging 1960s-era décor, highlighted by a mural of flamenco dancers in the main dining room; it's the food that stands out here. Paella is a favorite, teeming with seafood and sausages and brought to the table in a traditional double-handled dish. If you crave something light, check out the extensive tapas menu; whatever you order, be sure ask for a pitcher of the house sangria to quench your thirst.

Manhattan ▶ Greenwich, West Village & Meatpacking District

141

EN Japanese Brasserie

Japanese XXX

B3

435 Hudson St. (at Leroy St.)

Dinner daily

Subway: Houston St
Phone: 212-647-9196
Web: www.enjb.com
Prices: $$$

How's this for fresh? The silky tofu is made four times an evening at EN Japanese Brasserie. *Yuba* is the name of the game, and those uninitiated to the delicate little sheets (created by heating soy milk) will never dismiss the subject lightly again. Housed in an old furniture shop near the Meatpacking District, the spacious, modern restaurant boasts lofty ceilings, mesmerizingly intricate woodwork, and a vast, open kitchen spinning out great Japanese pub fare a few steps up from the typical *izakaya*. Don't let the word "pub" fool you: expert culinary attention is given to the seasonal omakase dinners (and lo and behold, the service matches), with pristine, high-quality products marking each plate. In particular, the *yuba* sashimi is a milky-sweet revelation.

Extra Virgin

Mediterranean X

B2

259 W. 4th St. (at Perry St.)

Tue – Sun lunch & dinner
Mon dinner only

Subway: Christopher St - Sheridan Sq
Phone: 212-691-9359
Web: www.extravirginrestaurant.com
Prices: $$

Casual yet classy, Extra Virgin is staffed by charming, beautiful people serving fine Mediterranean fare in a pleasant and relaxing environment; every neighborhood should have a restaurant like this.

In the spirit of its name, diners are offered a choice from a parade of top-notch olive oils to sample. The menu features creative yet comforting dishes, such as delicate halibut with tomato carpaccio, anointed with pristine olive oil and deeply flavored herbs, or a goat cheese salad with roasted beets and crisp endive dressed in an apple-based vinaigrette that verges on addictive. Seasonal flower arrangements on the bar set the mood of the cheery and rustic space. Loud rock music pouring from speakers does not detract diners from their food and conversation.

Fatty Crab

B1-2

Malaysian ✗

643 Hudson St. (bet. Gansevoort & Horatio Sts.)

Subway: 14 St - 8 Av   Lunch & dinner daily
Phone: 212-352-3590
Web: www.fattycrab.com
Prices: **$$**

Fatty Crab delivers bold Malaysian cooking just out of earshot of the Meatpacking District. The diminutive dining room is eclectically Asian, with dark wood tables and antique Chinese chairs, red lacquer accents and vases of chopsticks.

Chef Zak Pellacio spent time in Malaysia, and the menu pays tribute to his experience. Go for any of the house specialties, especially the chili crab, a messy bowl of fun with large pieces of Dungeness crab in a spicy-sweet, tomato chili sauce; or the Fatty Duck—brined, steamed, fried, and brushed with a sticky soy-chili glaze. (If you plan to share several dishes, expect an onslaught of food to crowd your tiny table.)

Fatty Crab doesn't accept reservations, but a great selection of beers from Saigon to Singha will take the edge off.

Five Points

D4

American ✗✗

31 Great Jones St. (bet. Bowery & Lafayette St.)

Subway: Bleecker St   Lunch & dinner daily
Phone: 212-253-5700
Web: www.fivepointsrestaurant.com
Prices: **$$**

Still going strong after all these years, Five Points has a universal quality that appeals to almost everyone. Perhaps it's the timeless urban décor, with just the right balance between casual and high design. Perhaps it's the happy-hour specials, the family-friendly attitude, or the reasonably priced American menu that pulls in influences from everywhere. Whatever that special quality is, Five Points has it in spades.

Seasonality drives Chef/owner Marc Meyer to pair pan-seared day-boat halibut with cucumber gazpacho in summer, and to couple house-made ricotta *cavatelli* with pancetta, toasted garlic, caramelized onions, and an organic egg when it's cold outside. The clutch of customers who pack the place on weekends between 11:30 A.M. and 3:00 P.M. will testify to the terrific brunch.

Gobo

Vegetarian 🍴

D1

401 Sixth Ave. (bet. 8th St. & Waverly Pl.)

Subway: W 4 St - Wash Sq
Phone: 212-255-3902
Web: www.goborestaurant.com
Prices: 🍝

Lunch & dinner daily

In keeping with the restaurant's Zen philosophy, the space is dressed in muted tranquil colors, soft lighting, and caters to vegetarian and omnivore diners alike with well-prepared and tasteful "food for the five senses." Start by sipping through the "healthy beverage menu," offering organic fruit and vegetable smoothies, teas, and seltzer tonics. Larger plates may include toothsome green tea noodles with vegan Bolognese, melding Asian ingredients with an Italian classic for rich flavors and silky textures in a truly unique dish.

Light wood shelves contrast with dark plank floors, framing the simple and comfortable furnishings. The energetic staff is stylishly attired in purple polos, jeans, with aprons de rigueur; while sweet, service can be haphazard.

Good

American 🍴

C2

89 Greenwich Ave. (bet. Bank & 12th Sts.)

Subway: 14 St - 8 Av
Phone: 212-691-8080
Web: www.goodrestaurantnyc.com
Prices: $$

Tue – Sun lunch & dinner

Set in the heart of the West Village, this attractive establishment lives up to its name in more ways than one. Slices of Americana (a wooden pig, potted cacti, and a large painting of an ear of corn) spiff up the dining room, while the food finds its roots in rustic dishes and adds a contemporary twist.

Take the signature green-chile macaroni and cheese, for instance. Chef/owner Steven Picker kicks up this American comfort food with spicy chiles and cilantro. Even the hamburger goes uptown as a grilled goodBurger, filled with pulled pork and smoked mozzarella, and served with barbecue sauce.

At just $11.95, the weekday lunch includes your choice of entrée with a beverage and a small salad or a cup of soup—mmm, mmm good.

Gotham Bar and Grill ❀

Contemporary 🍴🍴🍴

12 E. 12th St. (bet. Fifth Ave. & University Pl.)

Subway: 14 St - Union Sq
Phone: 212-620-4020
Web: www.gothambarandgrill.com
Prices: **$$$**

Mon – Fri lunch & dinner
Sat – Sun dinner only

Opened in 1984, yet still hopping most nights of the week—this Village classic wrote the book on New American cuisine. Set along a humming stretch of East 12th Street, Gotham Bar and Grill is one of the last big, bustling restaurants you'll find before the downtown nook-and-cranny spaces take over. Come happy hour, you'll find singles buzzing in from the office, soaking in the jazz and leaning into the long stretch of bar that flanks the front room.

But good vibe or no, it's the ace cuisine—rendered under the careful eye of classically trained Chef Alfred Portale—that keeps the regulars loyal. Try a creamy, Meyer lemon risotto, chock-a-block with tender, snow-white crab, and served with a tangle of young greens; or smoky, golden squab, garnished with a creamy ribbon of potato purée.

If you can swing an afternoon date—the three-course lunch, paired with wine, is a steal.

Appetizers
- Alaskan King Crab Risotto
- Tuna Tartare, Cucumber, Shiso, Sweet Miso, Asian Vinaigrette
- Seafood Salad of Scallops, Squid, Octopus and Lobster

Entrées
- New York Steak: Marrow-Mustard Custard, Vidalia Onion Rings
- Snake River Farms Pork, Parsnip Purée, Wild Barley
- Juniper-spiced Duck, Sour Cherries

Desserts
- Gotham Chocolate Cake with Nutella Ice Cream
- Warm Cinnamon Rolls, Pedro Ximenez Parfait
- Bananas and Cream, Warm Chocolate Sauce, Rum Ice Cream

Manhattan ▲ Greenwich, West Village & Meatpacking District

Gusto

C2

Italian ✗✗

60 Greenwich Ave. (at Perry St.)

Subway: 14 St (Seventh Ave.)
Phone: 212-924-8000
Web: www.gustonyc.com
Prices: $$

Lunch & dinner daily

Sleek and sophisticated, Gusto displays all the drama and charm of a black-and-white movie set. The décor, with its opulent chandelier, white marble bar, and black velvet banquettes, alludes to the elegance of a bygone era.

Gusto's kitchen celebrates traditional Italian cookery. Relying on simple combinations, layers of flavors, and utmost freshness, the appealing menu hones in on regional dishes. The likes of fennel-crusted tuna with Cerignola olives and preserved lemons, or a starter of fresh grilled octopus exemplify the use of pristine ingredients. Food prepared with such passion and knowledge helps diners forget occasional gaffs in service.

For the cocktail set, specialty liquors and libations infused with fresh fruit juices sing with flavor.

Hakata Tonton

CD1

Japanese ✗

61 Grove St. (bet. Bleecker St. & Seventh Ave.)

Subway: Christopher St - Sheridan Sq
Phone: 212-242-3699
Web: www.tontonnyc.com
Prices: $$

Dinner daily

A new cuisine has taken root in New York. Enter this tiny red and yellow dining room to be educated in this other facet of the Japanese culinary repertoire: *tonsoku* (pigs' feet, ears, and the likes).

Varied *tonsoku* dishes may include a luxurious slow roasted pork, or *oreilles du cochon*—French in name only—which are an explosion of crunchy, cool, creamy, sweet, sticky, and vinegary flavors. Truer to its Italian roots, *Tonsoku* carbonara is made with smoky bacon and is a good choice for wary newbies. A "rare cheese cake" of piped cheese and sour cream is a very smart and completely delicious take on the traditional dessert.

Il Buco

D4

Italian ☘

47 Bond St. (bet. Bowery & Lafayette St.)

Subway: Bleecker St
Phone: 212-533-1932
Web: www.ilbuco.com
Prices: $$

Tue – Sat lunch & dinner
Sun – Mon dinner only

It's a classic New York story. Fifteen years ago, an independent filmmaker, Donna Lennard, partnered with an old friend, Alberto Avalle, to take over an artist's studio space in the then-burgeoning NoHo neighborhood. Their original intent was to form a countrified antiques store. But while quirky chandeliers and antiques remain in this adorable farmhouse-style restaurant, the food has long since taken center stage at Il Buco. Though recent years have seen the food become a bit less even, the ever-changing menu continues to push out seasonal, innovative Mediterranean small plates like flaky, baked empanadas, plump with beef tenderloin and caramelized onion; or a succulent pork sausage, accompanied by a fig balsamic *mostarda* and dandelion salad.

Jarnac

B2

French ☘☘

328 W. 12th St. (at Greenwich St.)

Subway: 14 St - 8 Av
Phone: 212-924-3413
Web: www.jarnacny.com
Prices: $$

Tue – Sat dinner only
Sun lunch & dinner

An enchanting light emanates from this dark and elegant corner bistro in one of Manhattan's lovelier areas. Inside, a riot of red, burnt orange, and mirrored walls complement the snug dining room. This pretty setting is matched by the dining experience.

As a departure from these often confusing culinary times, the menu sticks to classic French fare interpreted with American sensibility, as in the rich and silky cassoulet or grilled sea scallops—plump and perfectly sweet. Old world and new complement in well-conceived and balanced selections; dishes are prepared with care and attention is paid to presentation. The helpful staff effortlessly adds another layer to overall enjoyment in this relaxed atmosphere. A nightly pre-fixe menu is offered at $36—a fantastic bargain.

Kingswood

C2

121 W. 10th St. (bet. Greenwich & Sixth Aves.)

Subway: 14 St (Seventh Ave.)   Mon – Fri dinner only
Phone: 212-645-0044   Sat – Sun lunch & dinner
Web: N/A
Prices: $$

Young, hip and fresh on the scene, Kingswood has that of-the-moment cachet that restaurateurs dream about, with more beautiful people clamoring to get in than space allows. What can you do? Plan on catching a little attitude at the door, and then get over yourself—because the woodsy, whimsically-decorated Kingswood is pure fun, with a vibrant bar scene that stays open late, and a meat-and-potatoes menu that turns pub food on its head. Three lovely bone-in lamb chops come sealed in an excellent, charred crust, but stay perfectly baby pink within—and arrive with a rich, creamy tomato orzo finished with a little shaved *fiore sardo*.

A short, focused wine list pays homage to the owner's homeland-down-under, Australia.

Kirara

D2

33 Carmine St. (bet. Bedford & Bleecker Sts.)

Subway: W 4 St - Wash Sq   Mon – Fri lunch & dinner
Phone: 212-741-2123   Sat – Sun dinner only
Web: N/A
Prices: $$

If you're feeling adventurous at this family-run restaurant, ask about the omakase, or tasting menu. In Japanese, omakase means "to put yourself in the chef's hands," so go ahead and trust his judgment regarding your meal. You'll be treated to an assortment of the chef's choice of appetizers, followed by a generous platter of sushi and sashimi; it's a great idea for sharing. Of course, you can always order off the à la carte menu if you prefer. Gentle pricing ensures that Kirara is a local favorite, and takeout is a popular option for those who live nearby.

Whatever you order, you'll be treated to artfully presented dishes, since Chef/owner John Hur is an artist himself. Admire his Japanese-style paintings on the walls of the restaurant.

Las Ramblas

D1

Spanish

170 W. 4th St. (bet. Cornelia & Jones Sts.)

Subway: Christopher St - Sheridan Sq   Dinner daily
Phone: 646-415-7924
Web: www.lasramblasnyc.com
Prices: $$

Serving quality tapas packed with flavor, Las Ramblas' small yet imaginative space complements its cuisine. The restaurant, named for Barcelona's historic commercial thoroughfare, also impresses with its smooth, well-informed, and impeccably timed service.

Pleasantly while away time in this beautifully compact bar, where attention to detail is evident in flower arrangements balancing on a tiny shelf, the water fountain embedded in a brick wall, and a banquette that cozies up against the front windows.

This traditional bar food makes a satisfying meal; go in groups to fully explore the menu. Such small plates as *patatas brava*s (garlicky potatoes with aïoli), and grilled sardines *en escabeche* arrive on an array of colorful crockery and delicate porcelain.

Le Gigot

D1

French

18 Cornelia St. (bet. Bleecker & W. 4th Sts.)

Subway: W 4 St - Wash Sq   Tue – Sun lunch & dinner
Phone: 212-627-3737
Web: N/A
Prices: $$

 Look for a tiny, cheery, apricot-colored façade with a cast iron sign to find this perfectly quaint restaurant nestled into Cornelia Street. Inside, the immaculate and cozy design closely resembles the landmark Left Bank bistro, Polidor, with parquet floors and banquettes lining mirrored walls with wood crisscrossing.

The friendly and professional staff warmly greets regulars by name and are dedicated to creating a lovely dining experience.

Chef Alione Ndiaye serves meticulously prepared cuisine with products of the utmost freshness. Offerings may include a perfectly sweet, briny, and flaky jumbo lump crabcake with baby greens, or daily vegetables bursting with flavor, like blanched sweet peas, leeks, and carrots lightly seasoned with thyme.

The Little Owl

Contemporary ✗

90 Bedford St. (at Grove St.)

Subway: Christopher St - Sheridan Sq
Phone: 212-741-4695
Web: www.thelittleowlnyc.com
Prices: $$

Tue – Sun lunch & dinner
Mon dinner only

Nesting on the corner of Bedford and Grove streets, The Little Owl is a homey roost, one that puts the pleasure back into dining out. Joey Campanaro and Gabriel Stulman, who opened this place in May 2006, work hard at hospitality—a theme that carries through to the staff and even the diners—all of whom seem to leave any attitude at the door.

Inside, natural light floods in through the two large windows that frame the corner of the small room. The menu is limited, but in this case that's a good thing. By focusing on what it does well, the kitchen crew creates earthy and intensely flavorful dishes. The meatball "sliders" appetizer and the utterly satisfying ricotta *cavatelli* both elicit hoots of delight from the regulars.

Lupa

Italian ✗

170 Thompson St. (bet. Bleecker & Houston Sts.)

Subway: W 4 St - Wash Sq
Phone: 212-982-5089
Web: www.luparestaurant.com
Prices: $$

Lunch & dinner daily

Like coming across an old cassette tape from college, the mere mention of tiny, beloved Lupa seems to invoke smiles from even the coldest food critics. Call them sentimental, for this decade-old Roman trattoria, along with its upscale sister, Babbo, ushered in the kind of inventive, rustic cooking that has defined Batali's growing Italian empire—at a fraction of the cost of his more tony places. Relying on fresh, seasonal ingredients and artisanal meats and cheeses as backbone, current executive chef, Steve Connaughton, turns out homemade pastas to die for. Try the fresh *bucatini alla amatriciana*, humming with fresh basil, pecorino cheese, and nutty chunks of *guanciale* (unsmoked pig cheek). Like pasta carbonara, on steroids.

Market Table

B3

American ✗

54 Carmine St. (at Bedford St.)

Subway: W 4 St - Wash Sq
Phone: 212-255-2100
Web: www.markettablenyc.com
Prices: $$

Lunch & dinner daily

Can Joey Campanaro and Gabriel Stulman—the team behind the perpetually-booked downtown darling, The Little Owl—do no wrong? Not when they tap the talents of former Mermaid Inn chef, Mike Price, to create a fresh, unpretentious menu, with a fantastic staff and rustic décor to match. Straddling a sunny corner of the West Village, Market Table has converted its former "General Store" (located in the front room) into a space for additional seating, satisfying critics' wishes for more tables. Now diners can enjoy the fresh lamb ravioli, tumbling with farm-fresh vegetables and soft, crumbled goat cheese; or a luscious, otherworldly cheesecake, oozing with moist chocolate.

Mary's Fish Camp

B2

Seafood ✗

64 Charles St. (at W. 4th St.)

Subway: Christopher St - Sheridan Sq
Phone: 646-486-2185
Web: www.marysfishcamp.com
Prices: $$

Mon — Sat lunch & dinner

Mary Redding opened this tiny Florida-style seafood joint in a West Village brownstone in 2000 and has been enjoying wild success ever since. Her lobster rolls overflow with succulent chunks of meat, slathered in mayonnaise and piled on a buttered hotdog bun—they might be messy, but they sure are good! Other selections such as conch chowder and conch fritters recall Key West cuisine, while lobster potpie and pan-seared diver scallops pay homage to the bounty of New England waters. Old Bay fries, steamed spinach and grilled corn on the cob accompany the delicious, fresh preparations. Bear in mind that Mary's only serves seafood and the restaurant doesn't accept reservations, but the counter couldn't be better for dining on your own.

Mas

B3

39 Downing St. (bet. Bedford & Varick Sts.)

Subway: Houston St   Dinner daily
Phone: 212-255-1790
Web: www.masfarmhouse.com
Prices: $$$

This tasteful jewel box of a restaurant sits on a lovely West Village block, hidden behind an unassuming façade. Behind the worn wood and glass exterior, Mas is reminiscent of a Provençal farmhouse, with weathered wood beams and a bar made of piled sandstones. Then, upscale and modern details—from the warm and well-orchestrated staff, to the Prouvé chairs—are perfect contrasts for the chic clientele.

The seasonal menu changes daily, and plays off the natural sweetness of the organic and seasonal ingredients used. An heirloom tomato tart is "marinated" in its own juices, or tender Flying Pig Farm pork belly is braised to perfection. Dishes are rustic without the drama or pretense.

The bar is an intimate spot for a creative and expertly concocted libation.

Mexicana Mama

B2

525 Hudson St. (bet. Charles & 10th Sts.)

Subway: Christopher St - Sheridan Sq   Tue – Sun lunch & dinner
Phone: 212-924-4119
Web: N/A
Prices:

A tiny restaurant with a big heart, Mexicana Mama stands out for its well-executed and authentic cuisine. A cup of earthy black bean soup warmed with a bit of jalapeño will brighten any chilly day, while a roasted, perfectly skinned poblano chile stuffed with mild Chihuahua cheese, fresh corn, tomato, and accompanied by cilantro-spiked rice proves a satisfying take on the classic chile relleno. For dessert, the dense flan, flavored with almonds and topped with a thick caramel sauce and whole almonds, hazelnuts, and cashews, ranks tiers above the run-of-the-mill custard. The décor is colorful, spare, curious, funky—and completely beside the point. Here the service is unhurried; for less than $25, take your time eating deliciously and well.

Morandi

C2

Italian ✗

211 Waverly Pl. (bet. Charles St. & Seventh Ave. South)

Subway: 14 St (Seventh Ave.)   Lunch & dinner daily
Phone: 212-627-7575
Web: www.morandiny.com
Prices: $$$

This prominent newcomer appears to be both an Italian cantina and farmhouse, with its antique-tiled floor, weather-beaten wood, Italian-speaking waiters, and straw-covered Chianti bottles displayed on shelves, recalling Tuscany with all its glorious clichés. The menu, too, respects its Italian roots, offering dishes such as *polpettini alla siciliana* (meatballs with pine nuts and raisins), *baccalà con ceci* (salt cod with chickpeas, tomatoes, and peppers), and the ever-popular tender, deep-fried artichokes, with outer leaves that crunch like potato chips, served with wedges of lemon on classic butcher paper.

Those who know Gucci better than gnocchi may pack this place, but this Italian comfort food doesn't miss a stiletto-heeled step.

One if by Land, Two if by Sea

D1

Contemporary ✗✗

17 Barrow St. (bet. Seventh Ave. South & W. 4th St.)

Subway: Christopher St - Sheridan Sq   Mon – Sat dinner only
Phone: 212-255-8649   Sun lunch & dinner
Web: www.oneifbyland.com
Prices: $$$

New York City claims more than its fair share of great "date" restaurants, but only a select few can be counted on for bringing so many men to their knees with offers of marriage. One if by Land, Two if by Sea is one of them.

Housed in an 18th-century carriage house infused with old-world sophistication, this lovely brick building fosters romance with four fireplaces, glittering brass chandeliers, tapers, and fresh roses on each table. Live piano music mellows the mood.

A new chef (late of Picholine) has updated the bill of fare with the likes of halibut poached in coconut milk. Despite the modernized menu, long-time fans will be happy that the signature filet of beef Wellington is still available, for an added charge to the three-course prix-fixe menu.

Paradou

B1

8 Little W. 12th St. (bet. Greenwich & Washington Sts.)

Subway: 14 St - 8 Av   Mon – Fri dinner only
Phone: 212-463-8345   Sat – Sun lunch & dinner
Web: www.paradounyc.com
Prices: $$

Paradou is a welcome respite from the spate of gargantuan over-the-top-posh restaurants that have lately opened in the Meatpacking District. Here, a strictly casual crowd shares a carefree French spirit while relaxing over crisp, vivacious glasses of champagne and bowls of plump, tender mussels Provençal, in a tomato broth heady with thyme.

The whimsical covered "magical garden" tent offers winter enchantment with heat lamps warming the space during colder evenings, but comes down in spring and summer. Enjoy unlimited champagne cocktails, truly al fresco, during their weekend brunch. Live music and "Paradou Happenings" are scheduled regularly.

The all-French wine menu offers some reasonably priced selections to compliment the classic and rustic bistro menu.

Pastis

B1

9 Ninth Ave. (at Little W. 12th St.)

Subway: 14 St - 8 Av   Lunch & dinner daily
Phone: 212-929-4844
Web: www.pastisny.com
Prices: $$

With the closing of Florent, the first success story of the then-nascent Meatpacking District, Pastis can now be considered the last holdout of its kind in the neighborhood. Even now it remains a trendy and popular place, which squeezes in a fashionable flock from breakfast through dinner. Expect celebrity sightings in this stylish boîte, where the timeless bistro décor (decorative mirrors, long zinc bar, walls lined with vintage Pastis ads) has that hip, informal charm so difficult to replicate.

The menu is good and satisfying, focusing on neighborhood favorites: *moules* with Pernod; a seared tuna Niçoise salad; and roasted *poussin*. The cocktail list, as expected, leans heavily on the anise-flavored aperitif from which the restaurant takes its name.

Pearl Oyster Bar

Seafood ✗

18 Cornelia St. (bet. Bleecker & W. 4th Sts.)

Subway: W 4 St - Wash Sq
Phone: 212-691-8211
Web: www.pearloysterbar.com
Prices: $$

Mon – Fri lunch & dinner
Sat dinner only

Pearl Oyster Bar is like a sliver of New England in the heart of Manhattan. This beloved eatery has a small dining room and a classic "counter" in order to handle a brisk business of shellfish aficionados. However, its no-reservations policy often means long waits.

Rebecca Charles named her restaurant for her grandmother, in memory of childhood summers she spent in Maine. The food is New England through and through: fried oysters, PEI mussels, and the lobster roll—chunks of fresh lobster moistened with seasoned mayonnaise, tossed with a hint of celery and parsley, and piled on a toasted bun, alongside a mound of shoestring fries. Wash this down with one of their beers on tap or a glass of Rebecca's carefully selected wines. Don't forget the blueberry crumble pie, another Down East staple, for dessert.

Perilla

Contemporary ✗

9 Jones St. (bet. Bleecker & W. 4th Sts.)

Subway: W 4 St - Wash Sq
Phone: 212-929-6868
Web: www.perillanyc.com
Prices: $$$

Mon – Fri dinner daily
Sat – Sun lunch & dinner

Chef Harold Dieterle won a mint of money on the cable-television series, *Top Chef,* so it's only fitting that he named his new restaurant after a member of the mint family (also known as *shiso*). Perilla is simply outfitted with warm woods, swirling ceiling fans, and pale walls. The inviting bar area has windows that open to the tree-lined street, and despite Perilla's unassuming style, the boisterous crowds that fill the narrow space speak of celebrity chefdom.

The eager-to-please staff is forthcoming with suggestions from the concise, seasonally inspired menu that features a world of influences from spicy duck meatballs to pan-roasted langoustines. Created by the chef's managing partner, the wine list matches the menu in its global stature.

 Manhattan ▲ Greenwich, West Village & Meatpacking District

155

Perry Street ❀

Contemporary XXX

B2

176 Perry St. (at West St.)

Subway:	Christopher St - Sheridan Sq	Lunch & dinner daily
Phone:	212-352-1900	
Web:	www.jean-georges.com	
Prices:	$$$	

How the great Jean-Georges Vongerichten does casual: a cutting-edge interior; thoroughly modern fusion food; and a few celebrities in the corner for good measure. Housed in the bottom floor of a Richard Meier glass tower overlooking the Hudson River, Perry Street's look is icy clean—bright and airy, with uncluttered, polished wood tables.

Combing America, Europe, and Asia for culinary inspiration, the menu features a world of fusion. Flaky rolls of peekytoe crab set atop a bundle of spicy, fresh-plucked arugula and tart, green apple might start a dinner that ends with a soft, buttery apple confit—layer upon layer of paper-thin apples.

The young, stylish professionals that frequent Perry Street set the dress code here—casual but sexy, with guests arriving in everything from tailored suits to designer jeans.

Appetizers	*Entrées*	*Desserts*
• King Oyster Mushroom and Avocado Carpaccio, Jalapeño Oil and Lime	• Arctic Char, Maitake, Smoked Sea Salt and Basil	• Chocolate Pudding, Crystallized Violets, Fresh Cream
• Rice Cracker-crusted Tuna, Sriracha-Citrus Emulsion	• Steamed Skate, Juilienne Vegetables, Fennel Purée and Basil Vinaigrette	• Angel Food Cake, Grapefruit, Yogurt
• Poached Eggs, Caviar, Brioche	• Rack of Lamb and Chili Crumbs	• Baked Hazelnut Frangipane, Poached Pear, Amaretto

The Place

B2

310 W. 4th St. (bet. Bank & 12th Sts.)

Subway: 14 St - 8 Av
Phone: 212-924-2711
Web: www.theplaceny.com
Prices: $$

Mon – Fri dinner only
Sat – Sun lunch & dinner

Tucked deep into the West Village, The Place is the kind of cozy, grotto-style dining that makes people want to up and move to the big city. Rendezvous-like, guests duck below street level to find a small bar with lots of flickering votive candles and a few tables with a view of the bustling sidewalk. Wander back a bit, and you'll find low, rustic beams, and white tablecloth seating; behind that, two outdoor terraces beckon in summer.

Even the food seems designed to comfort, like a piping-hot roasted tomato soup, drizzled with chive oil, and pocked with pecorino-baked croutons; or seared duck *moo-shoo* pancakes, drizzled with sweet tamarind. With a kitchen that employs only fresh, organic ingredients, diners are taken on a surprising gastronomic tour.

Pó

D1

31 Cornelia St. (bet. Bleecker & W. 4th Sts.)

Subway: W 4 St - Wash Sq
Phone: 212-645-2189
Web: www.porestaurant.com
Prices: $$

Wed – Sun lunch & dinner
Mon – Tue dinner only

It's no wonder reservations at this longstanding neighborhood gem still fill up a week in advance. A devoted following of regulars are attracted to Pó's cozy and romantic ambiance, well-run front of the house, and its fine, freshly prepared fare. The satisfying menu may include a cured tuna appetizer, beautifully flavored with white beans, raw crunchy baby artichokes, and spicy yet cool chili-mint vinaigrette. As a twist on the typical presentation, the linguini *vongole* is served with crispy pancetta. For a delightful and surprisingly light end to the meal, Vermont maple syrup sauce is poured over a delicate round of flan-like ricotta cheesecake. Brooklyn now has a Pó of its own—located in Carroll Gardens *(276 Smith St.)*.

Manhattan ▲ Greenwich, West Village & Meatpacking District

157

P*Ong

C2

Fusion ✗

150 W. 10th St. (at Waverly Pl.)

Subway: 14 St (Seventh Ave.)   Dinner daily
Phone: 212-929-0898
Web: www.p-ong.com
Prices: $$$

You'll find P*Ong in the West Village, tucked amid apartment buildings and quiet, narrow streets. If you're dining alone, claim a seat at the bar where you can chat with Chef Pichet Ong, who puts the finishing touches on every dish. If you're dining with friends, don't expect privacy; tables in this little space snuggle close together.

A spirited focus pervades the chef's cuisine, which takes the form of small plates. Intriguing tapas-like dishes here don't stick to Spain. They hop from the Mediterranean to Asia, borrowing influences from afar to flavor the likes of woodsy organic mushrooms with mint-infused, black "forbidden rice."

Further illustrating the chef's serious pedigree, located right next to P*Ong is BATCH (*150 B West 10th St.*), a take-out bakery that houses a mélange of everything sweet.

Prem-on Thai

C4

Thai ✗✗

138 Houston St. (bet. MacDougal & Sullivan Sts.)

Subway: Spring St (Sixth Ave.)   Mon – Fri lunch & dinner
Phone: 212-353-2338   Sat – Sun dinner only
Web: www.prem-on.com
Prices: $$

Setting and food at Prem-On Thai converge in an eclectic, appealing mix of modern elements and traditional influences. Large sculptures of Buddha are visual anchors at the back of the long, narrow main area which is brushed in warm, muted tones; the second, a bright, square dining room in black and white. Upbeat, trendy music fashions a lounge-like feel while diners leisurely enjoy a casual dinner.

Thoughtful and creative presentations far exceed typical Thai restaurants, with dishes served on an attractive mix of china, unusual stone pieces, and banana leaves. Decorative cutting of vegetable and garnishes emphasize an appetizing use of color and balance. Flavors are fresh and distinct, with the appropriate level of heat. The two-course lunch is a great deal.

Scarpetta

B1

355 W. 14th St. (bet. Eighth & Ninth Aves.)

Subway: 14 St - 8 Av
Phone: 212-691-0555
Web: www.scarpettanyc.com
Prices: $$$$

Dinner daily

Scarpetta gives New Yorkers reason to rejoice for now there's serious dining to be had in the über-trendy Meatpacking District. The setting features a white marble bar area, strategically located at the front of the room so as not to provide any distractions in the elegant rear dining room done in chocolate brown and warm orange accents with a long skylight overhead. You're sure to leave a clean plate after dining on the likes of braised boneless veal shank with bone marrow gremolata. Pastas like ricotta-filled raviolini with squash blossoms and a warm basket of homemade breads display the skillful cooking that put Chef/owner Scott Conant on the map. Scarpetta's wine menu offers a selection available by the carafe; perfect for sharing and exploring the international listing.

Sevilla

C2

62 Charles St. (at W. 4th St.)

Subway: Christopher St - Sheridan Sq
Phone: 212-929-3189
Web: www.sevillarestaurantandbar.com
Prices: $$

Mon — Sat lunch & dinner
Sun dinner only

There's something to be said for age. Although Sevilla has been around since 1941, it retains a warm patina in its *taberna*-style interior. José Lloves, who hails from northern Spain, acquired the restaurant in 1962 and has been running it ever since. Tradition reigns here, starting with the attentive waiters, and continuing with the menu, which offers a slice of Spain in its delightful paellas, seafood, and meat dishes. Refreshing sangria makes the perfect accompaniment to heaping portions of Spanish favorites, all authentically fragrant and garlicky.

Sevilla doesn't take reservations, but if you go during the week when it's a bit quieter, ask for a table by the windows, which look out on one of the most charming blocks in the West Village.

Manhattan ▲ Greenwich, West Village & Meatpacking District

159

Sheridan Square

C2

Contemporary XX

138 Seventh Ave. South (bet. Charles & 10th Sts.)

Subway: Christopher St - Sheridan Sq   Dinner daily
Phone: 212-352-2237
Web: N/A
Prices: $$$

Named after the well-known area with which it shares the neighborhood, Sheridan Square is a newcomer with a lot of potential. The dining room is elegant yet rustic; earth toned walls blend with silver tin ceilings, linen covered tables commingle with black and white photos, and an electric "wood burning" oven—visible to diners—ties the elements together. An American-style menu offers items such as crisp squash blossom stuffed with succulent jumbo lump crab, avocado, and roasted corn. Service is still a bit shaky, but management is gracious. Don't skip on sweets—sample the blueberry almond tart, a delicious and delicate dessert served with lemon ice cream. Have two if there's room.

Smith's

C3-4

Contemporary XX

79 MacDougal St. (bet. Bleecker & Houston Sts.)

Subway: B'way - Lafayette St   Dinner daily
Phone: 212-260-0100
Web: www.smithsnyc.com
Prices: $$

In a city where new restaurants pop up like mushrooms, it takes chops to slap a forgettable name like Smith's onto your establishment—but partners Danny Abrams and Cindy Smith have enough foodie clout between them to run that gamble. Tucked into a tiny, albeit charming, space in Greenwich Village, Smith's reads like a gothic jewelry box—with gabled ceilings, antique mirrors, and dark wood floors. The menu is delicate as well, with Chef Pablo Romero churning out some serious contemporary American cuisine, like tender, perfectly-peeled stalks of asparagus with béarnaise sauce and sweet, juicy peekytoe crab flakes; or springy buttermilk panna cotta, humming with poached rhubarb, strawberry compote, and delicate toasted almonds.

Soto

D1

357 Sixth Ave. (bet. Washington Pl. & W. 4th St.)

Subway: W 4 St - Wash Sq
Phone: 212-424-3088
Web: N/A
Prices: $$$

Mon – Sat dinner only

Chef/owner Sotohiro Kosugi's luxurious take on Japanese cuisine has New Yorkers happy he left Atlanta for the Big Apple. This third-generation sushi chef crafts a mouth-watering array of pristine seafood into outstanding sushi, as well as inspired appetizers contingent on the season. Attractive offerings may include sweet, velvety shrimp tartare in a pool of chilled ginger and mushroom broth, or a delicate and creamy mousse of monkfish liver and *uni*. Soto's upscale flavor is also evident in the kitchen's cooked offerings, as in the tender, braised black cod. All creations are artfully presented on traditional pottery and sleek white china. Beware that the unmarked dining room entrance is hidden in plain sight, so be careful not to walk past it.

Spice Market

A s i a n   ✗✗

B1

403 W. 13th St. (at Ninth Ave.)

Subway: 14 St - 8 Av
Phone: 212-675-2322
Web: www.jean-georges.com
Prices: $$$

Lunch & dinner daily

Another venture by Jean-Georges Vongerichten, Spice Market is a Meatpacking District hotspot. The cuisine concept is inspired by Southeast Asian food—what you might nosh on while roaming marketplace stalls in Thailand or Malaysia. Subtly seasoned dishes (chicken samosas, red curried duck, pork vindaloo) are placed in the middle of the table, for all to enjoy.

Realized by Jacques Garcia, the design transforms the mood inside this former warehouse from industrial to brooding and sexy, in deep shades of red, violet, and gold. A large teak pagoda takes center stage, while wooden arches divide the seating areas. The crowd is strictly A-list, especially in the evenings. For those who want to party VIP-style, there are private rooms downstairs.

Manhattan ▲ Greenwich, West Village & Meatpacking District

Spotted Pig ✿

B2

Gastropub ✗

314 W. 11th St. (at Greenwich St.)

Subway: Christopher St - Sheridan Sq
Phone: 212-620-0393
Web: www.thespottedpig.com
Prices: $$

Lunch & dinner daily

Other than regular Jay-Z ordering the last plate of gnudi—the naked sheep's milk ricotta dumplings that put April Bloomfield's two-story gastropub on the map—there's not a lot to complain about at the Spotted Pig. It's lively, it's casual, it's sexy, and because of that, yeah, it's insanely busy after 8:00 P.M. No matter—just go on an off-hour (lunch is ideal), or suck it up, throw your name in at the door, grab a cold pint and join the fray.

The butcher-paper covered tables turn over pretty fast; and when you do manage to procure one of those precious stools, you won't be let down. Bloomfield's critically-acclaimed, upscale pub grub is second to none. A rich, rustic chicken liver smeared over toasted country bread is arguably one of the best in town; and crispy *poussin* arrives perfectly cooked, sided with a scoop of savory pommes puree and roasted garlic cloves.

Appetizers
- Crispy Pig's Ear with Bitter Leaves and Lemon-Caper Dressing
- Ricotta Gnudi with Brown Butter, Sage
- Smoked-Haddock Chowder, Homemade Crackers

Entrées
- Char-grilled Burger with Roquefort and Shoestrings
- Pan-fried Calf's Liver with Crispy Pancetta
- Seared Scallops with Basil, Anchovy and Sweet Corn Pudding

Desserts
- Banoffee Pie
- Ginger Cake
- Flourless Chocolate Cake

Surya

C1

302 Bleecker St. (bet. Grove St. & Seventh Ave. South)

Subway: Christopher St - Sheridan Sq
Phone: 212-807-7770
Web: www.suryany.com
Prices: $$

Lunch & dinner daily

The sun truly does shine upon this little West Village restaurant, whose name means "sun" in Tamil. Vibrant colors fashion a sleek, dimly-lit interior, attended by a superb kitchen and service staff. Surya's menu boasts an array of regional Indian fare to please both vegetarians and meat lovers. Start with the hot, crisp aloo *tikkiyas* of spiced, crushed potato in a tamarind sauce that runs the gamut of fresh herbs and tangy flavors, accompanied by blistered, fresh naan, topped with clarified butter. Tandoor dishes, as well as *saag ghost* of lamb cooked in spinach purée, are among the high recommendations.

Budget-conscious diners should be sure to take advantage of the weekday lunch specials, where all items (except dessert) are offered at half price.

Tomoe Sushi

C4

172 Thompson St. (bet. Bleecker & Houston Sts.)

Subway: Spring St (Sixth Ave.)
Phone: 212-777-9346
Web: N/A
Prices:

Tue – Sat lunch & dinner
Sun – Mon dinner only

Patience is clearly the virtue to have if you're planning dinner at Tomoe Sushi, where the wait in the evening can range up to an hour or more. Why all the buzz? Diners don't come for the spartan décor, which consists of a small sushi bar, bare pine tables, and specials scrawled on pieces of paper.

They do come, though, for the high-quality sushi and sashimi, which is cut in large pieces for those who don't relish bite-size morsels. Of course, if you're squeamish about sushi, there's cooked seafood, too. You might want to give a second thought to Japanese desserts here. Tomoe's creamy version of cheesecake is scented with green tea and served with a coulis of red fruits.

The only downside? Long waits followed by rushed service can be a drag.

Manhattan ▶ Greenwich, West Village & Meatpacking District

Ushiwakamaru

Japanese 🍴

C4

136 Houston St. (Bet MacDougal & Sullivan Sts.)

Subway: B'way - Lafayette St — Mon – Sat dinner only
Phone: 212-228-4181
Web: N/A
Prices: $$$$

After a quick-and-slick makeover in late 2007, Ushiwakamaru is back in business and dressed in white linen, fresh panelling, and soothing blond wood tones. No one's happier than Manhattan's sushiphiles, who were perfectly happy to rub elbows in the old, cramped interior for a taste of Chef Hideo Kuribara's outrageously fresh, authentically-prepared Japanese food. Most nights of the week, the place is packed with its loyal Japanese clientele, and the passing plates explain the reason: artfully-arranged *sayori* (needlefish) topped with glistening salmon roe; blow-torched *anago* (salt water eel), delicately licked with sweet sauce; shrimp heads rolled in fluffy tempura batter; and tiny glassy eels, so transparent you might mistake them for gelatin.

Vento

Italian 🍴🍴

B1

675 Hudson St. (at 14th St.)

Subway: 14 St - 8 Av — Lunch & dinner daily
Phone: 212-699-2400
Web: www.brguestrestaurants.com
Prices: $$

If you were trying to show an out-of-towner an example of the clientele shift in the Meatpacking District over the last decade or so, you might start with Vento. Housed in an old S&M club, this once seedy space is now hopping with see-and-be-seen types, sunning themselves at the outdoor tables, soaking in the bustling atmosphere, and enjoying upbeat service. And the grub? Well, it could be tighter, but with all that *spuntini caldi* (small warm plates) migrating around the table, you're likely to find something that sticks. Try the smoky, tender grilled octopus, framed by delicately sweet butternut squash and red onion pickle. If you find yourself lingering late, there's an ultra-sceney downstairs bar, Level V—but good luck getting past the doorman.

Wallsé ✿

Austrian 🍴🍴

B2

344 W. 11th St. (at Washington St.)

Subway: Christopher St - Sheridan Sq
Phone: 212-352-2300
Web: www.wallse.com
Prices: $$$

Mon – Fri dinner only
Sat – Sun lunch & dinner

Maike Paul

Straddling a sunny corner of West 11th and Washington St., this Austrian charmer is the kind of place visitors conjure up when they think "quaint dinner in the West Village," but never actually manage to find. A few key elements make it click—oodles of neighborhood charisma; fresh, innovative cuisine; and a welcoming, understated staff.

The art gracing the walls is by Julian Schnabel and includes portraits of Chef Kurt Gutenbrunner (Wallsé is named for the Austrian town he was born in), whose considerable aesthetic taste doesn't end there. Gutenbrunner's presentations are careful but unfussy—a spot-on spaetzle with tender, braised rabbit brings to mind a creamy risotto; and the seared wild king salmon is served over a pile of lentils studded with root vegetables. Save room for a simple, but divine finale—fresh huckleberries, served under a fluffy pile of sugared egg whites, kissed with lemon and vanilla.

Appetizers

- Spätzle, Braised Rabbit, Peas, Corn, Tarragon
- White Asparagus with Morels in Sherry
- Warm Smoked Salmon, Apples, Celery, and Caviar

Entrées

- Wiener Schnitzel with Parsley, Potato and Cucumber Salad
- Brook Trout, Spinach and Capers
- Canadian Halibut with Cucumbers, Dill and Chanterelle Mushrooms

Desserts

- Salzburger Nockerl with Huckleberries
- Apple-Walnut Strudel with Pistachio Ice Cream
- Chocolate "Lollipops"

Harlem & Washington Heights

The northernmost reaches of Manhattan, Harlem and Washington Heights stand shoulder to shoulder. They are known for their soul food, rich history, and a storied collection of medieval artifacts housed at the Cloisters. This diverse neighborhood has a split personality. East of Fifth Avenue and north of East 97th Street lies East Harlem, with its distinctive Puerto Rican flavor. Northwest of Fifth Avenue, central Harlem ranks as the most famous African-American community in America.

RAILROADS TO RENAISSANCE

Dutch governor Peter Stuyvesant established Nieuw Haarlem in northern Manhattan in 1658. The hamlet remained largely rural until the railroad and the elevated trains linked it to the rest of the city in the first half of the 19th century. By the 1890s, Harlem was an affluent residential area. As a result of a slumping real-estate market early in the 20th century, landlords rented to the increasing numbers of working-class black families who were moving into the area at that time.

Harlem's golden era, the **Harlem Renaissance**, lasted from 1919 to 1929. During this period, writers Langston Hughes and Zora Neale Thurston electrified the world with their originality. Nightclubs—including the original **Cotton Club**—hosted performances by jazz greats Duke Ellington, Count Basie, and Billie Holiday. Everything changed with the Depression. Jobs became scarce and poverty set in. By the 1960s, a climate of violence and crime overran Harlem, forcing many middle-class families to leave.

21ST-CENTURY RENAISSANCE

Today, a renaissance of another sort is taking place. Investors are renovating old brownstones,

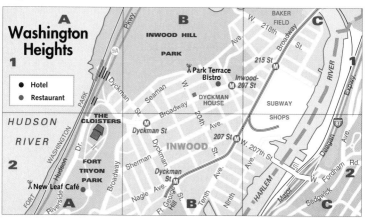

Washington Heights

- ● Hotel
- ● Restaurant

HUDSON RIVER

INWOOD HILL PARK

BAKER FIELD

Park Terrace Bistro

DYCKMAN HOUSE

SUBWAY

SHOPS

THE CLOISTERS

Dyckman St

INWOOD

207 St

FORT TRYON PARK

New Leaf Café

Dyckman St

HARLEM

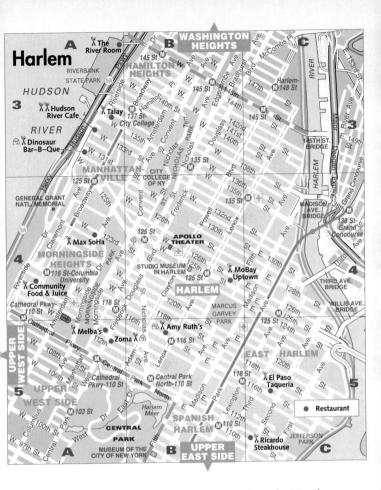

and West 125th Street—the main thoroughfare—is a lively stretch of shopping and restaurants. Tour buses fill with visitors, who come to marvel at the neighborhood's wealth of architectural and cultural treasures, such as the **Sylvan Terrace Mansion,** in Sylvan Terrace—one of Manhattan's most famous historic districts in Harlem.

On your way to Washington Heights stop by **Hamilton Heights** (bounded by West 135th Street to the south, and West 145th Street to the north.) Once owned by Alexander Hamilton, this area houses three historic landmarks: the summer home of Alexander Hamilton, the **Convent Avenue Church,** and **St. Luke's Episcopal Church**. Marvel at the architectural beauty of **Hamilton Heights/Sugar Hill,** a historic district that was once home to the likes of Reverend Adam Clayton Powell and Joe Lewis. **Sugar Hill** was first built in the early 1900s for upper and middle-class white residents. The area was transformed in the 1920s and 1930s, when successful black

167

Brigitte L. House / MICHELIN

professionals moved into the neighborhood, calling it a place where life was prosperous and "sweet."

For a lesson in jazz history, visit the **The National Jazz Museum in Harlem,** where you'll learn about legendary musicians such as Billie Holiday, Charlie Parker, and Duke Ellington. The museum offers educational programs and community events in honor of this great American art form.

Keep going north and you'll enter **Washington Heights**. Ranging from West 145th Street to West 200th Street, this narrow neck of land is rimmed by water: the Hudson River on the west and the Harlem River on the east.

Attracted by the comparatively low rents and spacious apartments, young urban professionals are slowly adding to the ethnic mix in this neighborhood, thanks to a recent real-estate boom. The northwestern section of Washington Heights is dominated by the green spaces of **Fort Tryon Hill** park. **Fort Tryon,** the highest natural point in Manhattan, is home to the **Cloisters**. The main draw for visitors to this area, this re-created

12th-century monastery belongs to the Metropolitan Museum of Art and is fabled for its collection of medieval artifacts, including the 16th-century Unicorn tapestries. While you're visiting, there are several good restaurants to sample in this pleasant quarter.

AN ILLUSTRIOUS PAST

Wealthy New Yorkers sought rural sanctuaries near the water here in the late 18th and 19th centuries. One of these, the 130-acre estate where George Washington planned the battle of Harlem Heights in 1776, welcomes the public as the **Morris-Jumel Mansion**. Lining the mansion's original cobblestone carriage drive, now called **Sylvan Terrace**, are some of the city's few remaining wood-frame houses. African-American luminaries such as jazz great Duke Ellington, Supreme Court Justice Thurgood Marshall, and historian W.E.B. Du Bois—co-founder of the NAACP—all called this neighborhood home at one time.

Amy Ruth's

Southern ✗

B5

113 W. 116th St. (at Lenox Ave.)

Subway: 116 St (Lenox Ave.)
Phone: 212-280-8779
Web: www.amyruthsharlem.com
Prices:

Lunch & dinner daily

When hankerin' for some down-home Southern food, make a beeline for Harlem's famed Amy Ruth's. Established in 1998, this restaurant is named for the owner's grandmother, a fine Southern lady and a good cook to boot.

If you spot a smoker out front, rest assured that it's not a prop; barrels nearby are filled with wood for fueling the fire used to smoke the delectable and meltingly tender barbecue ribs. The place is perpetually packed with locals and out-of-towners who have caught wind of the truly outstanding, soulful cooking here. From freshly prepared corned beef hash for breakfast to sautéed chicken livers or smothered pork chops with a side of collard greens for dinner, one of the best memories New York City can offer is a visit to Amy Ruth's.

Community Food & Juice

American ✗

A4

2893 Broadway (bet. 112th & 113th Sts.)

Subway: Cathedral Pkwy/110 St (Broadway)
Phone: 212-665-2800
Web: www.communityrestaurant.com
Prices: $$

Lunch & dinner daily

A culinary turning point has come to Morningside Heights, with the fantastically popular Community Food & Juice leading the pack of this area's exciting new restaurants. Healthy comfort food, sustainably sourced, complements the warm yet industrial, eco-friendly space.

The menu boasts grass-fed beef, free-roaming chicken, and wild-only fish. Choose from a selection of spreads with breads—baked either on-site or at exclusive, nearby bakeries. The dinner menu includes small plates such as zucchini-scallion pancakes or bowl o' beets, which are perfect for sharing. The large, airy dining room and outdoor seating will not prevent a wait for a table, and reservations are not taken; patience is a must. Moodier, elevated seating offers a calm respite to the main room.

Dinosaur Bar-B-Que

A3

Barbecue ⚕

646 W. 131st St. (at Twelfth Ave.)

Subway: 125 St (Broadway)
Phone: 212-694-1777
Web: www.dinosaurbarbque.com
Prices: $$

Tue – Sun lunch & dinner

The sumptuous smell of smoking meat carries beyond the block, beckoning barbecue lovers for miles. With a roadhouse-style vibe similar to its Syracuse counterpart, this upbeat, unpretentious eatery sports a casual, family-friendly setting with large tables, a lively bar, and fantastic food. Dinosaur Bar-B-Que's monstrous menu demands a colossal appetite—options are as delicious as they are plentiful.

For a starter, try the Jumbo BBQ chicken wings, smoked in-house and doused with your choice of sauce (go for the Wango Tango), complete with bleu cheese dressing. Next, order up the ribs and half chicken combo served with honey hush cornbread and a choice of two sides. After your mammoth meal, buy a bottle of Dino-BBQ sauce to take home.

El Paso Taqueria

C5

Mexican ⚕

237 E. 116th St. (bet. Second & Third Aves.)

Subway: 116 St (Lexington Ave.)
Phone: 212-860-4875
Web: N/A
Prices: ⚅⚅

Lunch & dinner daily

Manhattan may be a hotbed of Latin restaurants these days, but the soul of the city's Mexican population lies along East 116th Street in Harlem. Enter El Paso Taqueria, a promising Harlem newcomer that stands out for its charming, immaculate space, friendly waitstaff, and authentic, affordable Mexican cuisine. Dishes are all worthy of savoring, and include a fluffy corn tamale oozing with fragrant, tender pork, presented with swirls of sour cream and *salsa verde*. Plates of enchiladas rally the tastebuds, from tart and spicy corn tortillas to chipotle-tinged sauces to the *cojita* cheese sprinkled on top. The sweet, fizzy, house-made sangria uses just the right amount of seasonal fruit and proves the perfect complement to a meal.

Hudson River Cafe

A3

697 W. 133rd St. (at Twelfth Ave.)

Subway: 125 St (Broadway)
Phone: 212-491-9111
Web: www.hudsonrivercafe.com
Prices: $$

Mon – Sat dinner daily
Sun lunch & dinner

In an area of Harlem that's prime for development (witness the large marina under construction on the waterfront), this bustling cafe is a welcome addition to the neighborhood.

It's all about fun here, between the strong cocktails, the live music on weekends, and the big flavors in American dishes—such as deep-fried crab cakes served with a tart remoulade sauce and a refreshing salad of greens, fennel, orange segments, and a grapefruit-juice reduction. For dessert, pistachio ice cream plays a cool foil to a warm flourless chocolate cake.

The look inside is sleek and modern, with black molded chairs standing out against stark white walls. Outside, the bi-level patio, surrounded by gated walls and greenery, is a super spot to wash away the day's worries with a mango *mojito* or a Harlem Sidecar.

Max SoHa

A4

1274 Amsterdam Ave. (at 123rd St.)

Subway: 125 St (Broadway)
Phone: 212-531-2221
Web: www.maxsoha.com
Prices: $$

Lunch & dinner daily

Set on a corner in Morningside Heights in the shadow of prestigious Columbia University, Max SoHa rates as a great neighborhood find. Wide sidewalks here make room for outdoor seating, and a good opportunity to observe the avalanche of change that is currently transforming Harlem.

Entrées run from breaded chicken cutlet to grilled flank steak; however, the true reason to dine here is the decadent, well-prepared, satisfying pasta. Tender chunks of lamb in a deeply aromatic sauce drenching the house-made *spaghetti chitarra al ragù d'Agnello* make, quite simply, a great plate of pasta. Gnocchi, fusilli, and lasagna dishes consistently touch all the right rustic notes. To complete your meal, sip a fragrant glass of Italian wine from the well-priced list.

Melba's

S o u t h e r n ✗

300 W. 114th St. (at Frederick Douglass Blvd.)

Subway: 116th (Frederick Douglass Blvd.)
Phone: 212-864-7777
Web: www.melbasrestaurant.com
Prices: $$

Tue – Sat dinner only
Sun lunch and dinner

On a corner of this vibrant and rapidly changing neighborhood is a quaint yet spirited dining room dressed with custom chandeliers, mirror-lined walls, cushioned banquettes, exposed brick, and panel windows. A small bar completes the well-appointed and friendly ambiance.

This young and well-kept secret has been serving reasonably priced Southern "Healthy Comfort" and very satisfying soul food since 2005. Melba's menu features delicious fusions of ingredients despite seemingly uncommon compositions, as in the spring rolls filled with black-eyed peas, yellow rice, and collard greens. The turkey meatloaf topped with smoky, vinegar-laced sauce is a classic (if not haute) American dish. The restaurant features open mike and live music on Tuesdays.

MoBay Uptown

C a r i b b e a n

17 W. 125th St. (bet. Fifth & Lenox Aves.)

Subway: 125 St (Lenox Ave.)
Phone: 212-828-3400
Web: www.mobayrestaurant.com
Prices: $$

Lunch & dinner daily

The upscale and calming ambience, with fresh flowers, deep, sultry colors, and embroidered silk panels, is an oasis in this ever-changing and bustling area of Central Harlem.

Art hangs on the walls paying homage to its African-American roots, with jazzy images evoking Josephine Baker. The small room has gold and brown lacquered tables, and high back leather banquettes. A long communal table is used to maximize seating during live performances Tuesday through Saturday nights, and during the Gospel brunch on Sundays.

Baby back ribs and Maryland crab cakes are served, as well as Caribbean favorites: spicy jerk chicken, fried green plantains, and curry goat with red beans and rice. Rummy rum cake for dessert doubles as a decadent after dinner drink.

New Leaf Café

American 🍴

A2

1 Margaret Corbin Dr. (Fort Tryon Park)

Tue – Sun lunch & dinner

Subway: 190 St
Phone: 212-568-5323
Web: www.nyrp.org/newleaf
Prices: $$

Thanks to the New York Restoration Project and its dedication to reclaim and restore parks, public gardens, and open spaces in forgotten areas of the city, this captivating 1930s stone structure turned over a new leaf in 2001, when it was re-imagined as a cafe.

Despite its location in an urban center, the dining room wears each season's regalia, the bounty of which is mirrored in the changing menu. Locals as well as visitors to The Cloisters (home to the Metropolitan Museum's world-class collection of medieval art) favor the restaurant's outdoor terrace on a sunny day. Proceeds from your meal support the upkeep of Fort Tryon Park, in which it sits.

Dogwalkers rejoice—call ahead and the cafe will reserve a table outside for you and your pup!

Park Terrace Bistro

Moroccan 🍴

B1

4959 Broadway (bet. 207th & Isham Sts.)

Tue – Sun dinner only

Subway: Inwood - 207 St
Phone: 212-567-2828
Web: www.parkterracebistro.com
Prices: $$

A slice of Morocco in Inwood, this sweet bistro sits a couple of blocks east of Inwood Hill Park, just steps from the last stop on the A-train line. Inside they've captured the essence of the Casbah with deep colors, sultry lighting, and soft Moroccan music.

The cuisine of North Africa is celebrated here. Traditional tagines are served with your choice of fish, chicken, or lamb; or opt for a taste of the Moroccan-French connection with the "Fifteenth-Century couscous," a combination of seafood, almonds and stewed fruits in a light saffron cream sauce. French-influenced dishes include filet mignon and grilled pork chops. Casablanca-born owner, Karim Bouskou, and his wife, Natalie Weiss, promote a convivial atmosphere, aided by the delightful waitstaff.

Manhattan ▶ Harlem & Washington Heights

173

Ricardo Steakhouse

Steakhouse ✕

C5

2145 Second Ave. (bet. 110th & 111th Sts.)

Subway: 110 St (Lexington Ave.)   Dinner daily
Phone: 212-289-5895
Web: www.ricardosteakhouse.com
Prices: $$

With a suitcase full of song, if the Mambo Kings were still around, Ricardo Steakhouse would be their haunt. This top-notch steakhouse delivers quality dishes with a Latin beat. Classics such as NY strip steak and filet mignon share space with Angus beef-filled empanadas and other Latin favorites.
In recent years East Harlem has seen substantial gentrification, but Ricardo Steakhouse remains a true destination restaurant. It draws a mix of diners from all over the city lured by the promise of a good, reasonably priced meal. From the brightly colored walls to the distinctive artwork, the mood is decidedly upbeat. An open kitchen and exposed brick add warmth to the dining room, which is serviced by an extremely engaging and professional staff.

The River Room

Southern ✕

A3

750 W. 145th St. (at Riverside Dr.)

Subway: 145 (Broadway)   Wed – Sat dinner only
Phone: 212-491-1500   Sun lunch only
Web: www.theriverroomofharlem.com
Prices: $$

Located in the Riverbank State Park along Riverside Drive, the River Room boasts resplendent views of the Hudson River and the George Washington Bridge, enjoyed through floor-to-ceiling windows—a truly unique dining experience.
A pitched roof creates a sense of space and tranquility over the lovely, softly-lit dining room, long and narrow, decorated in billowing fabric.
The menu offers enjoyable and somewhat sophisticated Southern fare, including the likes of shrimp with superbly creamy grits and well seasoned "red gravy." During some weeknights and on weekends, live Jazz and Latin music plays. Call ahead for a reservation as the restaurant is sometimes booked for private parties. Buses and subway lines are not far, but driving is suggested, as valet parking is available.

Talay

Thai 🍴

A3

701 W. 135th St. (at Twelfth Ave.)

Subway: 125 St (Broadway)
Phone: 212-491-8300
Web: N/A
Prices: **$$$**

Mon – Wed dinner only
Thu – Sun lunch & dinner

Talay is the latest addition to the hip Harlem stretch along 12th Avenue, informally dubbed Viaduct Valley (or ViVa). Thai for "waterfront," this bustling, bi-level bistro-cum-lounge (formerly a 1920s freight house) ushers guests into its stylish space via an entry way flanked by two massive lion statues. Tasty Thai-Latin cuisine tops the bill of fare, co-created by Kuma Inn's King Phojanakong.

Vivid, distinct flavors define dishes such as crispy shrimp atop creamy plantains served with sweet-chili aïoli; grilled octopus with pickled bamboo shoots; and charred *bistek churrasco* served with three dipping sauces. Service is slow and getting there is a bit of a haul, but the food is well worth it. On weekends, a club scene takes over after hours.

Zoma 😳

Ethiopian 🍴

A5

2084 Frederick Douglass Blvd. (at 113th St.)

Subway: Cathedral Pkwy - 110 St (Central Park West)
Phone: 212-662-0620
Web: www.zomanyc.com
Prices: 😑

Mon – Fri dinner only
Sat – Sun lunch & dinner

Morningside Heights is enjoying yet another renaissance. Walk along Frederick Douglass Boulevard to see freshly updated storefronts and hip shops attracting young, vibrant newcomers by the thousands, alongside Columbia University's new housing and office expansions. Within this thriving area of great cultural diversity is a softly lit, open dining room adorned with indigenous fabrics and jewelry, where traditional Ethiopian cuisine flourishes. Here, the attentive staff present hot hand towels before a meal accompanied by *injera*—a soft, spongy, fermented bread—which serves as a utensil. Use this to delicately scoop deeply flavorful mouthfuls of refreshing tomato salad with sweet onions and hot peppers, or beef sirloin simmered in spices and clarified butter.

175

Lower East Side

Despite being one of New York's hippest neighborhoods, the Lower East Side has, for the most part, a refreshing lack of attitude and an astounding amount of local pride. "Come one, come all" has been its message to visitors since the 1880s, when it became the quintessential American melting pot. Though today's immigrants tend to be young artists, musicians and designers, artsy types aren't the only ones working on their craft on the Lower East Side. In recent years the neighborhood has become a breeding ground for new culinary talent, while history lives on in the district's many famous ethnic eateries.

THE GOVERNOR'S FARM

The area now known as the Lower East Side—clockwise from north, it is bounded by Houston Street, the East River, Pike Street, and the Bowery—was rural long after the southern tip of Manhattan was developed. Peter Stuyvesant, the last Dutch governor of Nieuw Amsterdam, bought much of the land in 1651 from the Native Americans. To facilitate transport between his farm, or *bouwerie*, and the urban market, he laid out a straight road now known as the **Bowery**.

GATEWAY TO AMERICA

The first mass migration to the Lower East Side occurred with the arrival of Irish immigrants fleeing The Great Hunger of 1845 to 1852. From the 1880s until World War I, millions of southern and eastern Europeans arrived via Ellis Island and settled in the Lower East Side, where they could meet other recently arrived immigrants. The neighborhood swiftly became the most densely populated in the country.

Eastern European Jews set down some of the strongest roots here, building synagogues and schools; publishing Yiddish newspapers; and opening Kosher delis. The Lower East Side was the original nosher's paradise, and for those in the know, it remains just that.

THE LOWER EAST SIDE TODAY

Today only 10 percent of Lower East Side residents are Jewish. The southern edge of the district is largely Chinese. Latinos still have a presence, but more prevalent—or at least visible—are the hordes of young hipsters who have transformed the once-gritty neighborhood into a free-spirited urban village.

Orchard Street between Canal and Houston streets is the district's spine; to the south, it's lined with bargain stores; farther north (around Broome Street), trendy boutiques begin. Stanton and Rivington Streets all the way east to Clinton Street are good for galleries, shops, and cafes. A carnival atmosphere prevails at night on and around Ludlow Street between Houston and Delancey, where restaurants, bars, and clubs stay full until the wee hours.

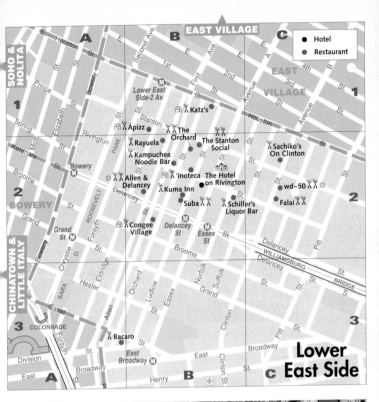

177

Allen & Delancey ✿

B2

115 Allen St. (at Delancey St.)

Subway:	Delancey St	Dinner daily
Phone:	212-253-5400	
Web:	www.allenanddelancey.net	
Prices:	$$$	

♿

Orianna Riley

New York's Lower East Side often does hip. Think young, sexy, and inviting, with sultry banquettes in back and intimate tables up front. Very rarely, however, does it also do warm, professional service (friendly being the very antithesis of cool), and food as elaborate and intricate as its stuffy uptown cousins. You'll find both at Allen & Delancey—the former, because owner Richard H. Friedberg has the brains to stay on-site and in-house to oversee operations; the latter, because Neil Ferguson is a topflight British chef who cut his teeth with fellow perfectionist, Gordon Ramsay. Reservations are tough, but no wonder: dishes change with the season, but might include a silky purée of caramelized bone marrow, shot with caviar and shallot; or perfectly golden chicken, studded with roasted maitake mushrooms, and cipollini onions, then sauced with crayfish velouté.

Appetizers

- Caramelized Bone Marrow, Caviar, Shallot Purée
- Sea Scallops, Celery Root Cream, Cipollini, Verjus
- Shavings of Hamachi, Pink Grapefruit Beads

Entrées

- Cod, Fennel, Lemon Confit, Oyster Veloute, Caviar
- Duck, Turnip Confit, Radishes, Foie Gras
- Lamb Persillade, Braised "Middle Neck", Potato Purée

Desserts

- Sweet-Cream French Toast, Oatmeal Ice Cream
- Chocolate-Peanut Butter Tart, Malted-Milk Sorbet, Whiskey, Vanilla Shake
- Passion Fruit Crème Brûlée, Coconut Sorbet

Ápizz

Italian ✗

B1

217 Eldridge St. (bet. Rivington & Stanton Sts.)

Subway: Lower East Side - 2 Av   Mon – Sat dinner only
Phone: 212-253-9199
Web: www.apizz.com
Prices: $$$

In a neighborhood trying to reconcile its past life (think housing projects and homeless shelters) with its glitzy new one (think Lauren Bush sightings and boutique hotels), Apizz is gloriously above the fray. Why? Because its simple, windowless Lower East Side facade hides the kind of cozy, impossibly quaint New York staple you wish there were more of—with warm, fuzzy lighting, good background music, and a young, sexy crowd. Okay, there is one diva—the fantastic brick-oven that dominates the room (their motto is "one room, one oven"), but it's earned its girth. Try the plump shrimp, roasted in a casuela, and served in a lemony bath of chorizo, toasted breadcrumbs and herbs; or a warm risotto, humming with mushrooms and freshly shaved parmesan.

Bacaro

Italian ✗

A3

136 Division St. (bet. Ludlow & Orchard Sts.)

Subway: East Broadway   Dinner daily
Phone: 212-941-5060
Web: www.bacaronyc.com
Prices: $$

 From Peasant owners Frank de Carlo and his wife Dulcinea Benson, Bacaro takes its name and inspiration from the pub-like wine bars popular throughout Venice. A warm and inviting glow sets Bacaro apart from its edgier surroundings, and features a sexy subterranean dining room. This setting, which once housed a gambling parlor, evokes an ancient cellar with candlelit nooks, weathered plaster walls, salvaged ceiling beams, and brick archways. The marble-topped bar is lit overhead by a blown glass chandelier, making it a lovely spot to enjoy a *crostini di giorno* or explore the all-Italian wine list. The menu highlights products of the Veneto region in items like marinated sardines, *baccala mantecato*, and lasagna Treviso with smoked mozzarella and radicchio.

Congee Village 😊

B2   Chinese ✗

100 Allen St. (at Delancey St.)

Subway: Delancey St   Lunch & dinner daily
Phone: 212-941-1818
Web: www.sunsungroup.com/congeevillage
Prices: 🍜

Porridge for dinner may not sound tempting, but with more than 25 varieties of *congee*, this attractive place is sure to win over even the most wary. This soothing specialty, popular throughout China, is served bubbling hot in an earthenware pot, ready to be seasoned with an assortment of tableside condiments. Besides the namesake signature, you can sample hard-to-find dishes like the sautéed short rib with black-pepper sauce on a sizzling hot plate, cold jellyfish, and rice baked with meat and vegetables in a bamboo vessel.

Located on the fringe of Chinatown, the multilevel space covered in bamboo and stone has a warm ambience. Large tables, a buzzing bar area and a host of private rooms fill the space with all the revelry of a town square.

Falai

C2   Italian ✗✗

68 Clinton St. (bet. Rivington & Stanton Sts.)

Subway: Lower East Side - 2 Av   Dinner daily
Phone: 212-253-1960
Web: www.falainyc.com
Prices: **$$**

With its concentration of good restaurants, Clinton Street is already a destination for foodies. Falai and its bakery just makes it more so. This sliver of a spot, with its hip lounge ambience, has an airy feel, even though the only window is at the front. During warm months, diners clamor for a table in the garden out back.

The Italian staff is welcoming and genuinely enthusiastic about the food—and for good reason. Trained as a pastry chef, Ioacopo Falai peppers his menu with sweet notes (cocoa, dates, raisins, apricots) that accent and enhance each dish. It may be a challenge to select between the many *dolci* on a full stomach, but it's worth saving room for the likes of *millefoglie* or an unexpected savory celery cake with milk gelato.

'inoteca

Italian ✗

98 Rivington St. (at Ludlow St.)

Subway: Delancey St
Phone: 212-614-0473
Web: www.inotecanyc.com
Prices: 💰💰

Lunch & dinner daily

Big Sister to 'ino in the West Village, 'inoteca caters to the chic, young Lower East Side set. This spot owes its popularity in part to co-owner Jason Denton, who also has a hand in Otto. True to its name (an *enoteca* is an Italian wine bar), the restaurant offers a superb selection of well-priced Italian wines from every region of Italy. Of these, 25 are available by the glass.

The menu emphasizes small plates and panini (perhaps stuffed with *bresaola*, fontina, and arugula, or roasted vegetables and fresh ricotta); pick up a copy of the 'inoteca's cookbook to learn how to perfect the art of this Italian sandwich. If wine and cheese is your thing, you can choose assortments of 3, 5, or 7 different types of Italian cheeses to sample with your vino.

Kampuchea Noodle Bar

Asian ✗

78 Rivington St. (at Allen St.)

Subway: Lower East Side - 2 Av
Phone: 212-529-3901
Web: www.kampucheanyc.com
Prices: **$$**

Tue – Thu dinner only
Fri – Sun lunch & dinner

It may not be priced like it came from a vendor's cart, but the cuisine at Kampuchea Noodle Bar nonetheless celebrates Cambodian street food. Divided among sandwiches (*num pang*), Cambodian savory crêpes, soups, and noodle dishes, the menu offers a comprehensive look at this satisfying fare. Best way to dine here? Order a little bit of everything. *Katiev*, or noodle soups, are the house specialty, and are brimming with everything from filet mignon to tofu to prawns.

The décor is part downtown New York, part kindergarten classroom, with its wooden counters complete with cubbyholes and hooks for storage, backless stools, and Mason jars filling in for water glasses. If you're looking to lunch, Kampuchea Noodle Bar serves it only on weekends.

Katz's

B1

205 E. Houston St. (at Ludlow St.)

Subway: Lower East Side - 2 Av
Phone: 212-254-2246
Web: www.katzdeli.com
Prices: 💰💰

Lunch & dinner daily

Established in 1888, Katz's is as much a New York institution as the Statue of Liberty. One of the few original Eastern European establishments remaining in the Lower East Side, Katz's attracts out-of-towners, residents and celebrities. In the never-ending debate over who serves the best pastrami in the city, Katz's often tops the list.

For an authentic experience, queue up in front of the salty countermen, collect your meal, and head to a table. What to order? Matzo ball soup and a pastrami sandwich—on rye, 'natch, and not toasted, please—with a side of fries.

Just be sure not to lose the ticket you get upon entering. It's your ticket out, and if you don't have it, they make such a fuss that you'll want to crawl under a table and hide.

Kuma Inn

B2

113 Ludlow St. (bet. Delancey & Rivington Sts.)

Subway: Delancey St
Phone: 212-353-8866
Web: www.kumainn.com
Prices: 💰💰

Tue – Sun dinner only

Grit meets glam in the Lower East Side as gentrification continues to take hold. At Kuma Inn, Chef King Phojanakong, a veteran of Daniel and Jean-Georges, brings a touch of culinary polish to the 'hood.' The second-floor dining room has a compact open kitchen and walls accented with bamboo and rice-paper sconces.

The décor is spare, allowing diners to focus on the food. Tapas-size portions are infused with the multicultural influences of Southeast Asia, reflecting the chef's own Thai-Filipino background. Order several items and share with some friends; just be sure to try the sautéed Chinese sausage with chili-lime sauce and the drunken shrimp.

Genteel service and a background soundtrack of the chef's favorite hits add to the ambience.

The Orchard

Contemporary ✗✗

B2

162 Orchard St. (bet. Rivington & Stanton Sts.)

Mon – Sat dinner only

Subway: Delancey St
Phone: 212-353-3570
Web: www.theorchardny.com
Prices: $$

Creative and funky, modern and cool, The Orchard sparkles as a star on the Lower East Side. This delightful place celebrates contemporary style with its light woods and warm beige walls covered by strips of mirrors. From the young waitstaff to the diverse crowd of diners, The Orchard gives off a hip, unpretentious vibe. Great food and a small room make reservations hard to come by.

The menu is Italian-inspired and upmarket, with an entire section devoted to crispy flatbreads (topped with steak tartare, royal trumpet mushrooms, or house-made hummus), a specialty here and great for groups—that is, if you can bring yourself to share. Entrées focus on inventive pastas like spaghettini with black tiger shrimp, crispy chorizo, and *panko oreganata*.

Rayuela

Latin American ✗

B2

165 Allen St. (bet. Rivington & Stanton Sts.)

Mon – Fri dinner only
Sat – Sun lunch & dinner

Subway: Lower East Side - 2 Av
Phone: 212-253-8840
Web: www.rayuelanyc.com
Prices: $$

This inspired "freestyle Latin" cuisine expresses an uninhibited journey through South America and beyond. Cuban-style pork; sugarcane-marinated duck with foie gras topped arepa; and paella infused with coconut milk, lemongrass, and ginger are stops along the way. A fine prelude to your meal is a selection from the lengthy ceviche list; each combines quality seafood and bracing flavors. The cocktail menu is comprised of quenching libations, like the passion-kumquat mojito or classic pisco sour. A slate-tiled bar, exposed brick walls, and iron grating filled with river rock outfit the lofty interior. These hard surfaces are softened by warm candlelight, gauzy fabric panels, hip crowd, and a majestic olive tree that stretches up through the mezzanine.

Sachiko's On Clinton

C2

Japanese ✗

25 Clinton St. (bet. Houston & Stanton Sts.)

Subway: Delancey St   Tue – Sun dinner only
Phone: 212-253-2900
Web: www.sachikosonclinton.com
Prices: $$

Named after owner, Sachiko Kanami, this comfortable spot draws a loyal clientele who clamor for the range of creative fare and seasonal specials. The attractive dining room has exposed brick accents, orange walls, and is supplemented by a charming garden. In addition to the rich, tender, and consistently fresh raw offerings neatly arranged at the intimate sushi counter, the kitchen team also displays skill in their cooked items like crab cream croquettes and foie gras topped sesame tofu. House specialty *kushiage* feature morsels of beef, chicken, or vegetables threaded on bamboo sticks, breaded in homemade *panko*, and deep-fried. The cocktail menu boasts a Japanese focus with sake making its way into cosmopolitans, margaritas, and mojitos.

Schiller's Liquor Bar

B2

European ✗

131 Rivington St. (at Norfolk St.)

Subway: Delancey St   Lunch & dinner daily
Phone: 212-260-4555
Web: www.schillersny.com
Prices: $$

A Keith McNally restaurant is a lot like the popular girl in high school. She's never the prettiest, smartest or funniest, but she has just the right combination to pop in a crowd. Schiller's Liquor Bar, like McNally's wildly successful Balthazar and Pastis, touts the same magical mix—though its components are breezy retro-bistro good looks, solid, if not wildly inventive, brassiere grub (don't miss the frites), and a prime location straddling a sunny corner of the Lower East Side. As to how best to describe the atmosphere that draws locals, day trippers and low-key celebrities alike, we direct you to the cheeky house wine list, categorized into *cheap*, *decent*, or *good*. A terrific cocktail list rounds out the drink list, including a spot-on Pimm's Cup.

The Stanton Social

B2

Fusion ✗✗

99 Stanton St. (bet. Ludlow & Orchard Sts.)

Subway: Lower East Side - 2 Av
Phone: 212-995-0099
Web: www.thestantonsocial.com
Prices: $$

Mon – Fri dinner only
Sat – Sun lunch & dinner

The Stanton Social has a finely tailored décor that pays homage to the haberdashers and seamstress shops that once dotted this trendy neighborhood. Vintage hand mirrors, woven leather straps, and wine shelves laid out in a herringbone pattern outfit the low-lit, dark-wood furnished space. Choosing from the generous list of ambitious multi-cultural small plates executed by Chef/owner Chris Santos is difficult—bring friends to ensure a wholehearted run of the menu. The signature sliders and French onion soup dumplings certainly deserve consideration. This entertaining fare is a perfect pairing with one (or two) of the bar's finely crafted cocktails or a selection from the well-chosen wine list. The second floor lounge offers the same menu.

Suba

B2

Spanish ✗✗

109 Ludlow St. (bet. Delancey & Rivington Sts.)

Subway: Delancey St
Phone: 212-982-5714
Web: www.subanyc.com
Prices: $$

Dinner daily

Hot, hot, hot. Spruced up in 2007, Suba's three sleek levels fill a former 1909 tenement from the ground-floor tapas lounge down the twisting steel staircase to the sexy Grotto; there, a polished-concrete dining island floats in an illuminated pool of water, and farther down still to the bright Skylight Room that does dual duty as a private dining space and a late-night weekend lounge.

The menu's been revamped too, offering a selection of small plates designed for sharing. Tempting creations like *gambas a la plancha* with chorizo and garbanzo purée reflect Chef Seamus Mullen's experience in some of Spain's top kitchens. You'll likely have trouble deciding between the wine selections on the Spanish-focused list and the creative sangrias.

wd~50 ✿

Contemporary 🍴🍴

C2

50 Clinton St. (bet. Rivington & Stanton Sts.)

Subway: Delancey St
Phone: 212-477-2900
Web: www.wd-50.com
Prices: $$$

 ♿

Wed – Fri lunch & dinner
Sat – Tue dinner only

It would have been easy for perennial it-boy chef, Wylie Dufresne, to rest on his laurels after locking up the Lower East Side fine dining scene. But no, the bold innovator who retooled New York's vision of molecular gastronomy with his strange and wonderful concoctions, is most definitely in. The menu at wd~50 changes often, and always walks the line—but there's rarely a miss. A smooth, pale-yellow popcorn soup gets a shot of color with a fan of succulent pink shrimp; a creamy passion fruit tart, studded with toasted meringue, puddled in nutty Argan oil.

The wine list is small, but nicely suited to the menu, and the décor is a clean mix of stone and wood, accented with splashes of bright color. Last year, lunch service began—add that to the mix of ultra-hip shops that have sprung up in the area, and you have a heck of a way to carve out an afternoon.

Appetizers

- Fried Quail, Banana Tartar, and Peppercress
- Smoked Eel, Salsify, Guava, and Puffed Yuzu
- Corned Duck, Rye Crisp, Purple Mustard, Horseradish Cream

Entrées

- Turbot, Barbecued Lentils, Cauliflower, Dried Apricots
- Lamb, Potato Noodles, Pretzel Consommé
- Pork Belly, Sunchoke, Ancho-Pineapple, Caper Emulsion

Desserts

- Toasted Coconut Cake, Carob, Smoked Cashew, Brown Butter Sorbet
- Cornbread Pudding, Lemon Grass, Prune
- Cherry-covered Chocolate, Molasses, Lime

Midtown East & Murray Hill

A bustling business district, the swatch of land east of Fifth Avenue contains some of the city's finest office buildings, from the Art Deco **Chrysler Building** to the modernist **Lever House**, as well as the spectacular Beaux-Arts **Grand Central Terminal**. All the way east, at the river, you'll find the headquarters of the United Nations. Tucked among these landmarks are historic hotels, posh shops lining Madison and Fifth avenues, and last—but far from least—a plethora of restaurants to suit every taste.

HUMBLE BEGINNINGS

The area bounded by Fifth Avenue and the East River, between East 30th and 60th streets, was not always the chic area it is today. In the early 19th century, steam-powered locomotives chugged down Park Avenue all the way to a depot on 23rd Street, bringing with them noise and dirt. Residents complained, and in 1854 an ordinance was passed banning trains south of 42nd Street. That helped pave the way for downtown development, but did nothing to improve the lot of those in Midtown East, whose tenements surrounded a sooty rail-yard that spread from 42nd to 56th Street.

UNDERGROUND RAILROAD

Enter railroad magnate "Commodore" Cornelius Vanderbilt (1794–1877), who opened the first Grand Central depot in 1871 on the present site of the Grand Central Terminal. Shortly thereafter, he began lowering the tracks feeding into it below street level, reducing some of the noise pollution. But smoke was still a big problem, and in 1889 the city demanded that the railroad electrify the trains or leave the city. To finance the electrification process, the Vanderbilts sunk the entire rail-yard fronting the depot below ground and sold the land above it to developers, who soon lined Madison and Park avenues with exclusive apartment buildings. The Grand Central Terminal you see today, which now houses a gourmet market and a sprawling dining concourse, was completed in 1913.

ONWARD AND UPWARD

After World War II, many of the apartment houses along Madison, Park, and Lexington avenues in Midtown were replaced by high-rise office towers. Today the area claims an eclectic mixture of old and new, including the residential enclave of opulent mansions, elegant brownstones, and converted 19th-century carriage houses known as **Murray Hill** *(between 30th and 40th Sts.)*. In quiet Murray Hill, foodies will discover a world of cuisines from sophisticated sushi to Indian curries to hearty steak.

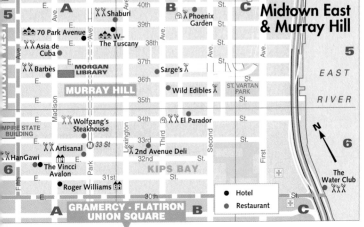

Midtown East & Murray Hill

5

EAST

RIVER

6

Murray Hill

Kips Bay

E. 40th St.
Shaburi
E. 39th St.
Phoenix Garden
70 Park Avenue
W- The Tuscany
E. 38th St.
Asia de Cuba
E. 37th St.
Barbès
MORGAN LIBRARY
Sarge's
E. 36th St.
Wild Edibles
ST. VARTAN PARK
E. 35th St.
Wolfgang's Steakhouse
E. 34th St.
El Parador
EMPIRE STATE BUILDING
33 St
33rd St.
Artisanal
2nd Avenue Deli
32nd St.
HanGawi
The Vincci Avalon
31st St.
Roger Williams
The Water Club
30th St.
Gramercy - Flatiron Union Square

● Hotel
● Restaurant

189

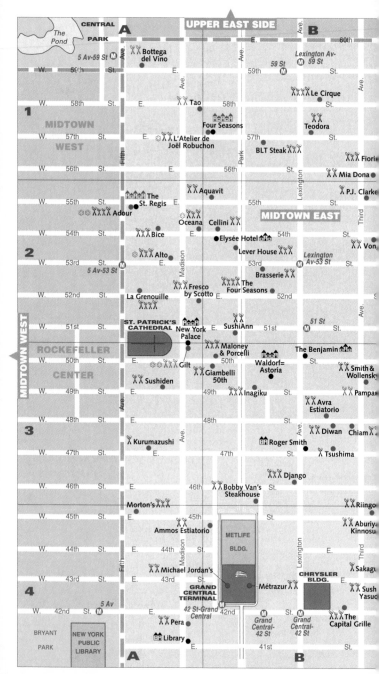

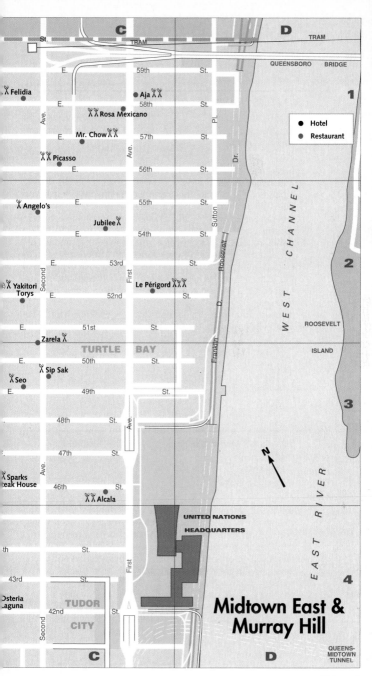

Midtown East &
Murray Hill

191

Aburiya Kinnosuke

B4

Japanese ✗✗

213 E. 45th St. (bet. Second & Third Aves.)

Subway: Grand Central - 42 St
Phone: 212-867-5454
Web: www.torysnyc.com
Prices: $$

Mon – Fri lunch & dinner
Sat – Sun dinner only

New York offers the world, and at Aburiya Kinnosuke, patrons are treated to an insider's view of Japan. From its mostly Japanese clientele to the extensive menu not often found here, this restaurant is the real thing.

Guests are invited to take part in the action here, where *shochu* cocktails involve hand-squeezed citrus, and grilled dishes require cooking over a small tabletop charcoal grill. *Yawarakani*, a pseudo-Japanese comfort food of ground-chicken mini-meatloaves cooked over open charcoal is one of the highlights and is served with a whisked egg for dunking. Ingredients are top-notch, and the chefs pay careful attention to detail.

Aburiya Kinnosuke requires advance booking, but once you're in, you won't be rushed through your meal by the

Aja

C1

Asian ✗✗

1068 First Ave. (at 58th St.)

Subway: 59 St
Phone: 212-888-8008
Web: www.ajaasiancuisine.com
Prices: $$$

Dinner daily

Inside Aja's windowless façade you'll discover a dark and temple-like décor constructed with stone walls, water elements, and a giant Buddha at the back of one of the small rooms. Loud contemporary music raises the volume of conversations, but this is of little concern to the mix of posh East Siders and young bankers with their dates who shun the sushi bar in favor of tables by the Buddha and side-by-side banquettes.

Strikingly fresh sushi, sashimi, and maki split menu space with the original and extensive Asian fusion menu. Flashy presentations have an Asian flair, with flaming rocks and colorful cocktails traveling to tables past admiring guests. You'll pay for the show, but high prices don't put a damper on the party.

Adour ✿✿

Contemporary XXXX

2 E. 55th St. (at Fifth Ave.)

Subway: 5 Av - 53 St   Dinner daily
Phone: 212-710-2277
Web: www.adour-stregis.com
Prices: $$$$

Tucked deep into the St. Regis New York—a bastion of old-school luxury if there ever was one—behind a gorgeous set of handsome wood doors, sits Alain Ducasse's Adour. Millions were dropped to create the over-the-top, lush interior design, and it shows—from the exquisite glass moldings to the plush seating to the sparkling glass wine cases—every detail is set to impress. Maybe too much so, for the wait staff occasionally reads a bit chilly.

Warm up with a sweetbread starter, pan-seared to perfection and served with one plump egg, poached *sous vide*, and flanked by toasted brioche. By the time you polish off a dessert of layered dark chocolate leaves, lined with orange-ginger sorbet and praline mousse, you're likely to have forgotten any service snags. It helps that the hosts, there to bid you good night with a smile, are as sweet as the chocolate leaves.

Appetizers	*Entrées*	*Desserts*
• Sweetbread "Meuniére", Egg Purse, Mushrooms, Toasted Brioche	• Duck Breast Filet "au Sautoir", Polenta, Shallots, Lemon	• Exotic Vacherin, Mango Marmalade, Passion Fruit Emulsion
• Cauliflower Velouté, Bagel, Comté Cheese	• Olive Oil-poached Cod, Prosciutto, Pepper-Onion "Piperade"	• Gala Apple Soufflé, Calvados Lady Finger
• Marinated Hamachi / Geoduck, Radish and Green Apple Mustard	• Glazed Pork Tournedos, Apple Ring and Budin Noir	• Raspberry Composition, Crème Brûle, Sablé, Yuzu Sorbet

Alcala

C3

Spanish ✖✖

342 E. 46th St. (bet. First & Second Aves.)

Subway: Grand Central - 42 St
Phone: 212-370-1866
Web: www.alcalarestaurant.com
Prices: $$

Mon – Fri lunch & dinner
Sat – Sun dinner only

A pan of rustic paella, a friend to share it with, and a seat in Alcala's covered garden on a clear summer day will capture the spirit of Spain's sun-drenched coast. Located just across from the United Nations, this neighborhood favorite serves Basque and other regional Spanish specialties to an international crowd in its cozy, brick-walled dining room.

At Alcala, the attentive staff caters to regulars as well as newbies with warm, old-school-style service. Begin with one of the authentic appetizers, then move on to hearty main dishes like roast baby pig or red piquillo peppers stuffed with codfish. Tempranillo, Garnacha, and Albariño number among the noteworthy Spanish varietals available to complement your meal.

Ammos Estiatorio

B4

Greek ✖✖

52 Vanderbilt Ave. (at 45th St.)

Subway: Grand Central - 42 St
Phone: 212-922-9999
Web: www.ammosnewyork.com
Prices: $$$

Mon – Fri lunch & dinner
Sat dinner only

This airy and attractive *estiatorio* occupies a winning spot, directly across from Grand Central Terminal, and adds Greek flair to an area overrun with Italian restaurants and steakhouses. Ammos bustles at lunch, when local business types drop in to grab a quick salad or linger over grilled fish, priced by the pound. Given its location, the restaurant quiets down noticeably at dinnertime. Modern takes on traditional Greek dishes fill the appealing menu, which includes an assortment of appetizers from house-made spreads to *saganaki*.

The modern Mediterranean décor supports the restaurant's name ("sand" in Greek) with natural light, sun-washed colors, blown-glass fishing buoys, and canvas umbrellas.

Alto ✿

11 E. 53rd St. (bet. Fifth & Madison Aves.)

Subway: 5 Av - 53 St
Phone: 212-308-1099
Web: www.altorestaurant.com
Prices: $$$$

Mon – Fri lunch & dinner
Sat dinner only

An authentic chunk of the Berlin Wall still marks the entrance, and its name continues to pay homage to Alto Adige, an Italian region that hugs the Austrian border. But four-year old Alto, having come under new ownership in 2008, has toned down its German influences in favor of more straightforward Italian fare; its trademark red chairs swapped out for a soothing brown and cream palette, where fresh-cut flowers dot the tables. Two things haven't changed—the impressive wine selection (though it doesn't quite compare to the thousands of display bottles that line the walls) and innovative cuisine that keeps getting better under Chef Michael White.

Super-fresh, seasonal ingredients find their way into homemade pastas, and entrees run the gamut from lamb to veal to fresh seafood—a wild striped bass, seared to perfection, is served over a clam and fennel pollen broth.

Appetizers	*Entrées*	*Desserts*
• Tuna, Bottarga, and Crema "Tonnata"	• Buffalo Milk Ricotta Tortelli, Mushrooms,Sugo	• Panna Cotta, Rhubarb Streusel Cake, Rhubarb Sorbet
• Truffle Mousse-stuffed Morels, Arugula, Parmigiano	• Rosemary-roasted Squab, Pistachio-crusted Foie Gras, Wild Flower Honey	• Budino: Carrot-Caramel Cake, Ginger-Spice Gelato, Candied Kumquats
• Seafood Salad of Shrimp, Scallops and Sea Beans	• Meat Ravioli, Parmigiano Fonduta	

Manhattan ▶ Midtown East & Murray Hill

Angelo's

C2

1043 Second Ave. (at 55th St.)

Subway: 51 St
Phone: 212-521-3600
Web: www.angelospizzany.com
Prices: 🥜🥜

Lunch & dinner daily

Angelo's is the kind of place you'd love to have as your neighborhood haunt. A cut above the rest in terms of service, presentation, and quality of the food, this family-friendly Midtown pizzeria draws a loyal coterie of locals.

No wonder. The thin-crust pies here are fantastic, topped with great ingredients and delivered to your table hot from the wood-burning oven. Fresh salads and pastas (think homemade spinach and cheese ravioli) equally accommodate small or large appetites in individual or family portions, and the price is definitely right. Not to mention the welcoming Eastern European servers, who win newcomers over with their upbeat attitude and spot-on timing.

There's even a second Angelo's on the West Side at *117 West 57th St.*

Aquavit

B2

65 E. 55th St. (bet. Madison & Park Aves.)

Subway: 5 Av - 53 St
Phone: 212-307-7311
Web: www.aquavit.org
Prices: $$$

Lunch & dinner daily

Everything about Aquavit is Scandinavian; its design, its cuisine, and its chef. Named for the Scandinavian spirit that figures prominently on its beverage menu, Aquavit occupies the ground floor of the Park Avenue Tower. There's a casual cafe and bar area up front; the more refined contemporary dining room, softened by beige tones and varnished woods, lies beyond.

Born in Ethiopia and raised in Sweden, Chef/owner Marcus Samuelsson excels at pairing unexpected textures and flavors, and fish dominates his à la carte menu. For dessert, go for the Arctic Circle—a luscious goat-cheese parfait filled with passionfruit curd and topped with tart blueberry sorbet. The restaurant even makes its own Aquavit, infused with everything from pineapple to pumpkin.

Artisanal

French 🍴🍴

A6

2 Park Ave. (enter on 32nd St. bet. Madison & Park Aves.)

Subway: 33 St   Lunch & dinner daily
Phone: 212-725-8585
Web: www.artisanalcheese.com
Prices: $$

Cheese is the focus of this Midtown brasserie, thanks to Chef/owner Terrance Brennan's passion for the stuff (Brennan also runs Picholine). From the house-blend fondue to the retail counter at the back of the restaurant where you can buy wonderful cheeses to take home, Artisanal plays up its strength.

There are other reasons to come here, though, starting with well-prepared French cuisine, such as bouillabaisse, *boudin blanc*, and hanger steak served—of course—with crispy frites. Then there's the prix-fixe lunch, a great bargain at $25 for three courses. And don't forget the thoughtfully chosen wine list; every selection is available by the bottle, the glass, or the taste. If you're not cheesed-out after your meal, try a cheese course instead of dessert.

Asia de Cuba

Fusion 🍴🍴

A5

237 Madison Ave. (bet. 37th & 38th Sts.)

Subway: Grand Central - 42 St   Mon – Fri lunch & dinner
Phone: 212-726-7755   Sat – Sun dinner only
Web: www.chinagrillmgt.com
Prices: $$$

A trendy venue in the Morgans Hotel in residential Murray Hill, Asia de Cuba still packs in a chic crowd, despite the fact that it's no longer new. Designer Philippe Starck fitted the striking bi-level interior with gauzy drapes lining the soaring walls, a 25-foot-high hologram of a flowing waterfall and a 50-foot-long, alabaster communal table running the length of the downstairs room.

Generously sized dishes marry elements of Asian and Latin cuisines in signatures such as *tunapica* (tuna tartare picadillo style), calamari salad, and *ropa vieja* of duck. Don't overlook sides like panko-crusted crispy plantains or Thai coconut sticky rice. Round up a few gorgeous friends who like to share, and order from the family-style menu.

Avra Estiatorio

B3

141 E. 48th St. (bet. Lexington & Third Aves.)

Subway: 51 St   Lunch & dinner daily
Phone: 212-759-8550
Web: www.avrany.com
Prices: $$$

Fresh fish nets the most attention here, and you can view a display of the day's catch on ice in the front dining room. Flown in fresh from Europe or purchased from New York's relocated Fulton Fish Market, fish and shellfish are brushed with olive oil and grilled whole over charcoal. Your choice will be priced per pound, so be forewarned if your eyes tend to be bigger than your wallet. Avra's spread *pikilia* (your choice of three) make an authentic and delicious way to start your meal.

This boisterous and always busy taverna-style eatery recalls the Mediterranean with its limestone floors, faux-stone walls, and arched doorways. In warm weather, you can sit inside or out, or compromise with a table near the doors that open onto the terrace.

Barbès

A5

21 E. 36th St. (bet. Fifth & Madison Aves.)

Subway: 33 St   Lunch & dinner daily
Phone: 212-684-0215
Web: www.barbesrestaurantnyc.com
Prices: $$

A sparkling diamond in an otherwise unpolished neighborhood rife with generic delis and overpriced Italian restaurants, Barbès glows with its friendly staff and traditional French-Moroccan fare. Brick walls and a beamed ceiling create a rustic mood in the cozy dining room, while the infectious Moroccan music lends an exotic note.

Here, the menu presents diners with a wide choice of items; dishes have a decidedly North African bent but with heavy Mediterranean influences (the names of the dishes—*moules à la Marocaine, crevettes aux pistou,* traditional *couscous Marocaine*—are all in French). The manager's presence ensures the warm quality of the service; he employs the requisite flourish when pouring mint tea into small Moroccan-style glasses.

Bice

A2

Italian XXX

7 E. 54th St. (bet. Fifth & Madison Aves.)

Subway: 5 Av - 53 St
Phone: 212-688-1999
Web: www.bicenewyork.com
Prices: $$$

Lunch & dinner daily

With over 40 restaurants worldwide, Bice has perfected its formula of preparing upscale northern Italian cuisine in settings appropriate to each location. What began in Milan has become a long success story in New York, with many years in its Midtown home. Here, they draw a well-dressed crowd to the fashionable dining room, as well as the more casual bar and cafe.

The menu is wide with extensive choices for each course. Preparations are fairly good and carefully prepared, though not necessarily creative. For this classic cuisine, there is a loyal following of diners who come carrying expense accounts to manage the prices.

The pace of these meals is relaxed yet efficient—a style long forgotten that is ideal for business or pleasure.

BLT Steak

B1

Steakhouse XXX

106 E. 57th St. (bet. Lexington & Park Aves.)

Subway: 59 St
Phone: 212-752-7470
Web: www.bltrestaurants.com
Prices: $$$$

Mon – Fri lunch & dinner
Sat dinner only

Why would a French chef name his restaurant after an American sandwich? He would, if he fancied his restaurant to be a contemporary bistro (B) and his name was Laurent Tourondel (LT). In fact, Bistro Laurent Tourondel is not a French bistro at all, but a Frenchman's vision of an American steakhouse. Sleek décor smacks of big-city sophistication, and the hip crowd with money to spend loves the noise and loud music.

On the menu, Japanese Kobe and American Wagyu beef complement the steakhouse classics, and many of the sides, like roasted hen-of-the-woods mushrooms or potato gratin, are served with a playful touch in cute cast-iron pans or copper pots. There are few bargains on the wine list, but it does offer a great selection by the glass.

Bobby Van's Steakhouse

Steakhouse ✗✗

B3

230 Park Ave. (at 46th St.)

Subway: Grand Central - 42 St
Phone: 212-867-5490
Web: www.bobbyvans.com
Prices: $$$$

Mon – Fri lunch & dinner
Sat dinner only

This scene is so powerful that it intoxicates. New steakhouse concepts may come and go, but a regular flock of brokers and bankers rule this stylish roost, where pricey wines and towering shellfish platters bear witness to the day's important dealings.

Service comes with flourish and perhaps a gruff edge, but with the obvious care required by Midtown movers and shakers. As the main attraction, meats are cooked exactly as ordered and carved tableside, with sides served family style.

After work, the bar gets boisterous as well-shaken martinis lift the mood. A separate menu of lighter fare is offered here, and addictive house-made potato chips adorn the bar.

Located in the landmark Helmsley Building, Bobby Van's has three other locations in Manhattan.

Bottega del Vino

Italian ✗✗

A1

7 E. 59th St. (bet. Fifth & Madison Aves.)

Subway: 5 Av - 59 St
Phone: 212-223-2724
Web: www.bottegadelvinonyc.com
Prices: $$$

Lunch & dinner daily

Manhattan outpost of the original in Verona, Italy, Bottega del Vino takes its wine seriously. The wine list features some spectacular Italian vintages—well worth a splurge. Painted on a beam along one wall, the sentiment *Dio mi guardi da chi non beve vino* ("may God protect me from those who do not drink wine") aptly sums up owner Severino Barzan's philosophy on the subject.

Delightful northern Italian dishes fill the menu with the likes of a perfectly executed *risotto all'Amarone*. With its low lighting and imported Italian furnishings, this restaurant begs you to bring a date—as long as the person who's paying has their platinum card in tow.

The front section is reserved for casual Bar Quadronno, offering a wide choice of panini and some of the best cappuccino in the city.

Brasserie

B2

Contemporary ✗✗

100 E. 53rd St. (bet. Lexington & Park Aves.)

Subway: Lexington Av - 53 St   Lunch & dinner daily
Phone: 212-751-4840
Web: www.rapatina.com/brasserie
Prices: $$$

Brasserie creates a 21st-century vision of its French counterpart with mod-retro design and interpreted standards. This dovetails nicely with its location in the basement of the 1958 Seagram Building, by Ludwig Mies van der Rohe. Cameras at the catwalk entry connect to a row of TV screens above the bar, so your arrival is on display to the dining room of people-watchers.

Aside from French classics reinvented à la mode, the menu pleases the largely corporate crowds with contemporary offerings like slow-smoked Berkshire pork loin or monkfish over cauliflower purée. Skip the mediocre pommes frites to save room for the decadent yet light and sugary chocolate beignets.

The Capital Grille

B4

Steakhouse ✗✗✗

155 E. 42nd St. (bet. Lexington & Third Aves.)

Subway: Grand Central - 42 St   Mon – Fri lunch & dinner
Phone: 212-953-2000   Sat – Sun dinner only
Web: www.thecapitalgrille.com
Prices: $$$$

Two blocks east of Grand Central Terminal, clubby Capital Grille occupies the ground floor of the complex that includes the famous Chrysler Building. The large space is opulent and elegant, a harmony of comfortable black and red leather chairs, banquettes, mahogany paneling, and gold-framed paintings.

Dry-aged steaks and juicy chops are hand-cut and perfectly grilled to your requested temperature. Given its location, this place stays busy, so book ahead. Also consider that the full menu is also available at the long bar. Professional staff ensures that any wait will be made comfortable.

Of course, a meal here sets guests back more than a few bucks, but the expense-account crowds are too busy brokering deals over lunch and dinner to mind.

Cellini

Italian 🍴🍴

B2

65 E. 54th St. (bet. Madison & Park Aves.)

Subway: Lexington Av - 53 St
Phone: 212-751-1555
Web: www.cellinirestaurant.com
Prices: $$$

Mon – Fri lunch & dinner
Sat – Sun dinner only

With its pleasant informality, lively atmosphere, fine selection of deliciously simple Italian classics, and efficient service, Cellini appeals to all. Even old school Italian-American standards, such as clams casino, are served with the care and culinary attention often reserved for fancier food. Good flavors and technique are demonstrated in pasta offerings, like spaghetti *frutti di mare*, tossed in olive oil, finished with white wine, tomato, and brimming with shrimp, clams, mussels, and scallops.

A concise, well-chosen wine list featuring Italian labels plus crowd-pleasers from around the world, and a polite waitstaff well-versed in the menu, justify Cellini's popularity. Best to reserve a table in advance, although walk-ins are accomodated.

Chiam

Chinese 🍴🍴

B3

160 E. 48th St. (bet. Lexington & Third Aves.)

Subway: 51 St
Phone: 212-371-2323
Web: N/A
Prices: $$

Sun – Fri Lunch & dinner
Sat dinner only

Don't confuse Chiam with the neighboring noodle joints. Chiam may not have the neighborhood authenticity of Chinatown, or the star appeal of Mr Chow, but it continues to win diners over with its serious Chinese cuisine and top-notch service. Think of this place, with its elegant dining room, quality wine list, and well-heeled clientele, as a choice for a special-occasion feast or for an expense-account business dinner.

Presenting Cantonese preparations with flair, the kitchen staff uses excellent products and a refined technique that yields consistently good and well-balanced fare. Dishes, such as the rich Grand Marnier prawns, are intended to be shared; order some steamed or sautéed vegetables to round out the mix.

Diwan

B3

148 E. 48th St. (bet. Lexington & Third Aves.)

Subway: 51 St
Phone: 212-593-5425
Web: www.diwanrestaurant.com
Prices: $$

Lunch & dinner daily

This is one of the few upscale Indian spots in the city with both a pleasant setting and refined cuisine. Set behind a wall of windows on a busy Midtown block, Diwan fashions an attractive lair of rich fabrics and low lighting. The professional and unobtrusive waitstaff enhance the low-key yet upscale ambience

A wide assortment of dishes takes the menu from classic to contemporary. Most everything is modernized; even traditional dishes are updated, honing in the flavors of vibrant spices and herbs. Tandoori items shine, the breads are terrific, and sharing is highly recommended. No need to fear spicy preparations; the kitchen will gladly temper heat to your liking.

Django

B3

480 Lexington Ave. (at 46th St.)

Subway: Grand Central - 42 St
Phone: 212-871-6600
Web: www.djangorestaurant.com
Prices: $$$

Mon – Fri lunch & dinner
Sat dinner only

In the bohemian spirit of jazz guitarist Django Reinhardt—whose improvisational riffs wowed 1930s Paris—this restaurant embraces the carefree soul of a gypsy. David Rockwell's design has withstood the test of time; indeed, many other establishments have attempted to imitate the creativity with which he outfitted the dining room, incorporating strands of beads and Moroccan-inspired fabrics and wallpapers.

For lunch, contemporary notes sing of modern salads, sandwiches (like a deconstructed lobster club), and light fare such as quality tuna tartare. Heavier international influences chime in at dinner. The downstairs lounge, popular with area post-work crowds, boasts its own food and drink menus. In warm weather, the outdoor seating gets standing ovations.

Manhattan ▶ Midtown East & Murray Hill

El Parador ☺

B6

Mexican ✗✗

325 E. 34th St. (bet. First & Second Aves.)

Subway: 33 St	Lunch & dinner daily
Phone: 212-679-6812	
Web: www.elparadorcafe.com	
Prices: $$	

Everything about El Parador is old-fashioned, but in the best possible way. Don't let the windowless façade or the location (near the entrance to the Midtown Tunnel) turn you away; inside, the upbeat Mexican ambience attracts a grown-up crowd who enjoy animated conversation and killer margaritas at the bar.

While the cuisine balances traditional fare with Americanized preparations, all the food bursts with flavor and good-quality ingredients. A line on the bottom of the menu sums up the restaurant's attitude, which is completely focused on the customer: "Please feel free to ask for any old favorite dish that you like." Even if it's not on the menu, they'll make it for you-and that includes special requests for fiery habañero salsa.

Felidia

C1

Italian ✗✗

243 E. 58th St. (bet. Second & Third Aves.)

Subway: Lexington Av - 59 St	Mon – Fri lunch & dinner
Phone: 212-758-1479	Sat – Sun dinner only
Web: www.lidiasitaly.com	
Prices: $$$	

For the past 25 years, Felidia has consistently attracted a loyal following of well-heeled regulars. TV personality and cookbook author Lidia Bastianich's flagship is housed in a cozy brownstone with a copper-topped bar and seating on two levels. Warm colors and polished wood are used throughout, with wine racks prominently showcasing the restaurant's extensive, mostly Italian list. Although Lidia is no stranger to the kitchen, Sicilian-born Chef Fortunato Nicotra mans the stoves, where he turns out tempting pastas like Istrian "wedding pillows" filled with cheeses, citrus, and raisins; or black and white fettucine with almond pesto; as well as regional fare like quail saltimbocca. Many dishes are elegantly finished in the dining room.

Fiorini

Italian ✗✗✗

B1

209 E. 56th St. (bet. Second & Third Aves.)

Subway: Lexington Av - 53 St
Phone: 212-308-0830
Web: www.fiorinirestaurant.com
Prices: $$$

Mon – Fri lunch & dinner
Sat dinner only

A little flower (*fiorini* in Italian) blooms on 56th Street in the form of Lello Arpaia's Italian eatery. In both the front room, featuring an elegant bar, and the intimate back room, honey-tone woods and pastel hues cast a warm, contemporary glow. Professional service adds to the upscale feel, where quality reigns in the straightforward, modern Italian cooking. It is a rare chef who chooses to focus on simple preparations and execute them with such excellence, rather than get distracted by overblown attempts at creativity. Thus, silky house-made *pappardelle* may partner with fresh crab meat, peas, and a perfectly balanced rosy tomato-cream sauce spiked with a whisper of vodka. A sharp espresso makes an outstanding end to the meal.

The Four Seasons

American ✗✗✗✗

B2

99 E. 52nd St. (bet. Lexington & Park Aves.)

Subway: 51 St
Phone: 212-754-9494
Web: www.fourseasonsrestaurant.com
Prices: $$$$

Mon – Fri lunch & dinner
Sat dinner only

There is nothing like a night in the pool room, known as the erstwhile country club of New York's elite. The décor—like the crowd—remains stunningly elegant. With monumental floral arrangements that change with the seasons, the entrance to this landmark building will take your breath away.
The food may be on par with a fancy wedding banquet and the service barely adequate for the undistinguished guest, but a quick glimpse at Henry Kissinger and cronies is worth the staggering price tag for one night among the powerful.
The Grill Room is the spot for lunch, where regulars have had their tables long-assigned on the legendary seating chart.
The bar is an impressive place for a cocktail and surely worth an early arrival to absorb the scene.

Fresco by Scotto

A2

Italian XXX

34 E. 52nd St. (bet. Madison & Park Aves.)

Subway: 5 Av - 53 St
Phone: 212-935-3434
Web: www.frescobyscotto.com
Prices: $$$

Mon – Fri lunch & dinner
Sat dinner only

Most folks know the personable Scotto family from their recipe demonstrations on the *Today Show*, so it is no wonder that their restaurant near Rockefeller Center is known to insiders as the "NBC Commissary." Despite a location that draws a crowd on expense accounts, Fresco By Scotto exudes a comfortable yet cosmopolitan aura. This casually elegant dining room offers unobtrusive service, and sound Italian-American cuisine. Lunch and dinner menus list rustic and robust appetizers as well as "Fresco Originals" like penne with chicken and veal Bolognese, a hearty bowl of steaming pasta in a chunky tomato-based meat sauce scented with aromatic root vegetables and finished with a touch of cream. In summer 2008, the Scottos opened Fresco On the Go at *40 E. 52nd St.*

Giambelli 50th

B3

Italian XX

46 E. 50th St. (bet. Madison & Park Aves.)

Subway: 5 Av - 53 St
Phone: 212-688-2760
Web: www.giambelli50th.com
Prices: $$$

Lunch & dinner daily

Family-run since 1960, Giambelli 50th offers the kind of old-world food and discreet service that seems to be vanishing from the New York dining scene. Three levels of dining include the clubby ground-floor main room that has hosted its fair share of power lunches. Upstairs, space for private parties includes the cozy wine room, displaying some exceptional vintages.

The restaurant's location, across from the New York Palace, has undoubtedly fostered the list of notable diners: mayors and minions, politicos, and pundits—even the Pope. From tripe Milanese to veal scallopine Marsala, expect consistently good traditional dishes. Be sure to peruse the hand-written wine list, as much a work of penmanship as it is a roster of international labels.

Gilt ✿✿

Contemporary XXX

455 Madison Ave. (bet. 50th & 51st Sts.)

Subway: 51 St
Phone: 212-891-8100
Web: www.giltnewyork.com
Prices: $$$$

Tue – Sat dinner only

Gilt/New York Palace Hotel

If one can manage to peel their eyes from the stunning interior of Gilt, housed in the New York Palace Hotel's historic Villard Mansion, they'll be pleasantly surprised to find food that rivals the surroundings. Chef Christopher Lee, who took the kitchen reigns three years ago, is known for his way with seafood. Wild Duxbury Mussels are fresh, plump, and bursting with flavor—resting on top, a crusty baguette smeared with creamy pistachio, ripe cherry tomatoes, and a heat-packing chipotle. A sweet, fork-soft Alaskan black cod is heavenly, topped with mandolin-thin slices of Asian pear and bathed in a smoky Miso broth. In between courses, take a second to sip on one of Gilt's California Cult wines and soak in that sexy interior—an ornate Italian renaissance showcase, replete with mile-high cathedral ceilings, glossy walnut paneling, and a marble fireplace in contrast with the 21st century décor.

Appetizers
- Yellowfin Tartare, Kimchi, and Scallion Pancakes
- Sea Scallop Ceviche with Sea Urchin
- Spotted Prawns with Smoked Ham & Potato Hash

Entrées
- Yellowfin "Wellington", Porcini, Foie Gras
- "Haus-Made" Bratwurst, Spätzle, Belgian Beer Cheese Sauce
- Lamb Shoulder Ragoût, Golden Raisin, Falafel

Desserts
- Chocolate "Solar System"
- Rhubarb Crumble, Honey Mousse, Berry Granité
- Meyer Lemon Panna Cotta, Pixie Mandarin Sponge Cake

HanGawi

A6

12 E. 32nd St. (bet. Fifth & Madison Aves.)

Subway: 33 St   Lunch & dinner daily
Phone: 212-213-0077
Web: www.hangawirestaurant.com
Prices: $$

Don't worry about wearing your best shoes to HanGawi; you'll have to take them off at the door before settling in at one of the restaurant's low tables. In the serene space, decorated with Korean artifacts and soothed by meditative music, it's easy to forget you're in Manhattan.

The menu is all vegetarian, in keeping with the restaurant's philosophy of healthy cooking to balance the yin and yang- or *um* and *yang* in Korean. You can quite literally eat like a king here; the emperor's roll and steamboat soup (on the prix-fixe menu) were once cooked in the royal kitchen. Of course, all good things must end, and eventually you'll have to rejoin the rat race outside. Still, it's nice to get away from the pulsing vibe of the city... now and Zen.

Inagiku

B3

111 E. 49th St. (bet. Lexington & Park Aves.)

Subway: 51 St   Mon – Fri lunch & dinner
Phone: 212-355-0440   Sat – Sun dinner only
Web: www.inagiku.com
Prices: $$$

Tucked into a corner of the Waldorf=Astoria, Inagiku may look a bit outdated these days, but the knowledgeable and charming service and top-quality Japanese cuisine more than make up for any fading décor.

The sizeable menu is divided between modern fusion dishes using Western ingredients and techniques, and traditional Japanese fare. Stick to the latter and you won't be disappointed. Sushi is expertly prepared and delicate tempura defines the art. Starters are perfectly done: the thin rice crêpes for the uni canapes are generously topped with vibrant uni; *uzaku*, a classic broiled eel salad, is accompanied by fresh cucumber and tossed in a light vinegar dressing. Everything comes elegantly presented with the appropriate garnishes and condiments.

Jubilee

C2

347 E. 54th St. (bet. First & Second Aves.)

Subway: Lexington Av - 53 St
Phone: 212-888-3569
Web: www.jubileeny.com
Prices: $$

Mon – Fri, Sun lunch & dinner
Sat dinner only

Your mother was right when she told you never to judge a book by its cover. From the outside, this little restaurant may not look like much, but inside lies a pleasant space with the welcoming feel of a family restaurant that you'd want to frequent regularly for the appealing Belgian cooking.

Prince Edward Island mussels are the signature dish; they're prepared five different ways, and served Belgian-style with frites, or with a green salad. Otherwise, the menu highlights such classics as roasted breast of chicken with pommes purées, duck leg confit, escargots, and a pavé of roasted salmon served with caramelized cauliflower. Desserts, including molten chocolate mousse cake, profiteroles, and crème brûlée are memorable.

Kurumazushi

J a p a n e s e ✗

A3

7 E. 47th St. (bet. Fifth & Madison Aves.)

Subway: 47-50 Sts - Rockefeller Ctr
Phone: 212-317-2802
Web: N/A
Prices: $$$$

Mon – Sat lunch & dinner

Midtown Manhattan is filled with big, ornate eateries where the food doesn't quite live up to the lavish surroundings—at Kurumazushi, you'll find the exact opposite. Simple lettering on the door of a nondescript office building is the only indicator of its presence; inside, guests enter a narrow foyer and head up a steep flight of stairs, or chance the tiny elevator to a second-floor sushi den, decorated in a traditional Japanese palette of red, white, and black. So why exactly is every midtowner-in-the-know happily rubbing elbows here come lunch hour? The exquisite sushi and sashimi omakase tasting menus, executed under head sushi master Toshihiro Uezu, no doubt—which some might argue have declined a bit over the last year, but is likely to still blow the socks off the uninitiated. Of course, so might the hefty bill that comes with your meal.

La Grenouille

French 𝗫𝗫𝗫𝗫

3 E. 52nd St. (bet. Fifth & Madison Aves.)

Subway: 5 Av - 53 St
Phone: 212-752-1495
Web: www.la-grenouille.com
Prices: $$$$

Tue – Fri lunch & dinner
Sat dinner only

Opened in 1962, La Grenouille has managed to remain the Masson family's bastion of traditional high-priced French cuisine in Midtown. Charles and Gisèle Masson founded the establishment; today Charles junior oversees the enterprise. A high coffered ceiling, silk wall coverings, and stunning arrangements of fresh flowers—a signature of the late Charles Masson the elder—create an Old World opulence in the lovely dining room, which is worthy of a special occasion for those who still prefer to be well-dressed for dinner.

Menu selections might include classically roasted chicken *grande-mère*, oxtails braised in Burgundy, and a divinely flaky warm apple tart. And don't overlook the signature dish: *les cuisses de grenouilles Provençale* (sautéed frogs' legs).

Le Cirque

Contemporary 𝗫𝗫𝗫𝗫

151 E. 58th St. (bet. Lexington & Third Aves.)

Subway: 59 St
Phone: 212-644-0202
Web: www.lecirque.com
Prices: $$$$

Mon – Fri lunch & dinner
Sat dinner only

Like many of its loyal ladies-who-lunch, the grand dame of New York restaurants, Le Cirque 2000, needed some time off to rest and revamp. After closing its doors in the New York Palace Hotel, the newest Le Cirque reopened in the stylish Bloomberg Building. This incarnation is a masterpiece of design. Huge curving windows add a modern feel, while the distinguished air of the past remains in the canopied ceiling and the burgundy carpets detailed with rich gold patterns.

Sirio Maccioni keeps a tight leash on his latest heir. It still draws one of the best power scenes in the city, with a mix of masters of the universe and socialites, who come here as much to be seen as they do for dishes such as Icelandic cod, Berkshire pork, and foie gras ravioli.

L'Atelier de Joël Robuchon ✿

Contemporary XX

B1

57 E. 57th St. (bet. Madison & Park Aves.)

Dinner daily

Subway: 5 Av - 59 St
Phone: 212-350-6658
Web: www.fourseasons.com/newyork
Prices: $$$$

♿

Housed in the upstairs lobby of the Four Seasons Hotel, the mood is sophisticated, but relaxed, at the midtown Manhattan outpost of L'Atelier de Joël Robuchon (there are eight locations worldwide). Expect nothing less than expert service and top-flight haute cuisine from the acclaimed Joël Robuchon. The menu is carefully executed under the watch of Chef Yosuke Suga, who spoils his mix of business clients and loyal regulars with the likes of perfectly smooth, seared scallops, fresh-off-the-boat from Maine, or a pan-sautéed *daurade*, bathed in an aromatic citrus broth, and touched with asian garlic bulbs. Those looking to soak in the extensive wine list and pick at small plates can head to the beautiful pearwood counter for a nice selection of warm and cold bites. Bonus entertainment—watching the open kitchen work their culinary magic from your cozy perch at the bar.

Appetizers
- La Langoustine: Crispy Langoustine Papillote with Basil Pesto
- Les Burgers: Beef and Foie Gras Burgers with Lightly Caramelized Bell Peppers

Entrées
- L'Amadai : Pan-sautéed Amadai served in a Lily Bulb Broth
- La Caille : Free-range Caramelized Quail Stuffed with Foie Gras, Potato Purée

Desserts
- Le Chocolat Sensation : Chocolate Cream, Bitter Chocolate Sorbet and Oreo Cookies
- Le Soufflé : Yuzu Soufflé Served with Raspberry Sorbet

211

Le Périgord

C2

French ✕✕✕

405 E. 52nd St. (off First Ave.)

Subway: 51 St
Phone: 212-755-6244
Web: www.leperigord.com
Prices: $$$

Mon – Fri lunch & dinner
Sat – Sun dinner only

The best things need not be the most contemporary, and Le Perigord bears witness to that fact. With a classic feel that dates back to the 1960s, this establishment cossets diners at tables with hand-painted Limoges china, crystal stemware, and fresh roses. A coffered ceiling and period chairs upholstered in willow-green fabric add further elegance as tuxedo-clad waiters proffer formal service to diplomats from the nearby United Nations. This is one of the few places in New York where one still dresses for dinner.

The time-honored French menu is comprised of traditional fare like veal kidneys with mustard sauce and *loup de mer* with wild mushrooms. For the pièce de résistance, desserts—including tasty seasonal fruit tarts—are wheeled to your table on a cart.

Lever House

B2

Contemporary ✕✕✕

390 Park Ave. (enter on E. 53rd St. bet. Madison & Park Aves.)

Subway: Lexington Av - 53 St
Phone: 212-888-2700
Web: www.leverhouse.com
Prices: $$$

Mon – Fri lunch & dinner
Sat dinner only

At Lever House, everyone feels important after walking through the well-lit tunnel leading to the stylish dining room. Since its opening, the restaurant has maintained a strong following, especially at midday when populated by well-dressed power brokers and fashionable ladies-who-lunch. Designer Mark Newson's retro-modern interior honors Park Avenue's first glass-clad tower, the landmark Lever House building built in 1952. A mid-century aesthetic prevails throughout with rounded corners, honey-toned wood and black leather furnishings. A honeycomb motif abounds, in the shape of visible wine storage, lighting fixtures, and carpet design. The fine food sent out by the kitchen features up-to-date, seasonally inspired fare, and a winning dessert selection.

Maloney & Porcelli

American ✕✕✕

B3

37 E. 50th St. (bet. Madison & Park Aves.)

Subway: 51 St
Phone: 212-750-2233
Web: www.maloneyandporcelli.com
Prices: $$$

Mon – Fri lunch & dinner
Sat – Sun dinner only

This upbeat spot exceeds expectations with its appealing, varied menu, and cheerful waitstaff—a far cry from your run-of-the-mill steakhouse.

One could order the giant, quality Porterhouse, cooked to order and carved tableside, but there are plenty of other enticing choices. Diners who pick a pizza appetizer and pasta main course have no need to envy a neighbor's filet. Sharing is recommended, as starters are entrée-size and sides served family style. Wine glasses and pepper mills are also enormous, supplementing the philosophy that more is more. Know that this is in keeping with the check; prices are anything but petit. Even so, the restaurant is appropriately jammed with an expense-account crowd and the bar remains a sought-after watering hole.

Métrazur

American ✕✕

B4

Grand Central Terminal

Subway: Grand Central - 42 St
Phone: 212-687-4600
Web: www.charliepalmer.com
Prices: $$$

Mon – Fri lunch & dinner
Sat dinner only

Grand Central Station usually evokes images of passengers dashing for trains. Yet, there is another side to this terminal, best seen from the serene perch at Métrazur (named for a bygone train that traveled the Côte d'Azur en route to Monaco). From its enviable east balcony setting, the restaurant transports diners from the hubbub below, while commanding spectacular views of the station's cavernous main concourse and celestial ceiling.

The food enhances this setting with a variety of contemporary American dishes incorporating premium seasonal ingredients, such as asparagus risotto with rabbit confit and pea leaves; or hand-cut tuna tartare, with wasabi cream, and ponzu. The bar is a primo spot for cocktails before catching a train.

Mia Dona

B1

Italian

206 E. 58th St. (bet. Second & Third Aves.)

Subway: 59 St
Phone: 212-750-8170
Web: www.miadona.com
Prices: $$

Lunch & dinner daily

Donatella Arpaia and Chef Michael Psilakis of Anthos opened this restaurant in February 2008. Designed to resemble a home, Mia Dona divides its long, narrow space into three separate areas. Patrons jostle for a place in the lounge, where dozens of black and white Fornasetti plates act as artwork on the whitewashed brick wall. Black-and-white floral wallpaper plays off the zebra-print carpet that links the two dining rooms.

Psilakis skillfully masks the complexity of his dishes, which are hearty and rustic. To start, *spiedini* feature perfectly grilled and skewered quail, sweetbreads, pork, merguez sausage, and lamb meatballs, while an entrée of ricotta gnudi explodes with flavor—accented by smoked speck, meaty mushrooms, and just the right amount of sage.

Michael Jordan's

B4

Steakhouse

Grand Central Terminal

Subway: Grand Central - 42 St
Phone: 212-655-2300
Web: www.theglaziergroup.com
Prices: $$$

Lunch & dinner daily

With Grand Central Terminal's painstakingly restored celestial mural overhead, Michael Jordan's offers dining under the stars anytime of day. Warm colors, wood panelling, and black-and-white photos of sleek locomotives brings glamorous Art Deco to the lofty mezzanine space.

At dinner, expect generous portions of well-prepared prime Angus beef, with warm and attentive, though occasionally flawed, service. Sides encompass traditional steakhouse carte, but be sure to save room for the macaroni and cheese, based on a recipe from the basketball star's grandmother. Lunch adds a reasonable pre-fixe menu and selection of lighter fare.

The elliptical mahogany bar is an agreeable setting for a happy-hour beverage, while the wine salon is well suited for a cocktail party.

Morton's

Steakhouse ✗✗✗

A4

551 Fifth Ave. (enter on 45th St. bet. Fifth & Madison Aves.)

Subway: 5 Av
Phone: 212-972-3315
Web: www.mortons.com
Prices: $$$

Mon – Fri lunch & dinner
Sat – Sun dinner only

Part of a Chicago-born chain that has mushroomed into a mega-chain with outposts all across the country, Morton's offers a similar experience no matter which location you visit. The Midtown Morton's—one of the older siblings—keeps with the clubby, masculine décor that characterizes so many steakhouses: mahogany paneling, low lighting, deep jewel tones, imposing chandeliers.

Your server will recite the menu while showing you samples of each main ingredient. A cart bearing baked potatoes, vegetables, and examples of all the cuts of beef offered is rolled to each table to help you make your selection.

The place has a split personality, depending on which day you go. During the week, the restaurant and bar both reek of power from the local corporate crowd. Tourists take over on weekends.

Mr Chow

Chinese ✗✗

C1

324 E. 57th St. (bet. First & Second Aves.)

Subway: 59 St
Phone: 212-751-9030
Web: www.mrchow.com
Prices: $$$$

Dinner daily

This Mr. Chow dates back to 1979 but still lures a high-profile crowd night after night. Actor, artist, restaurateur, and Renaissance man Michael Chow added interior design to his talents in creating this chic black and white dining room accented with a red fabric mobile overhead. The team of white jacketed servers makes closely placed diners feel posh and pampered. Regulars and cognoscenti know not to request the menu; have your waiter order for you (though you may want to include the fried seaweed) and don't be shy about dislikes. Find yourself distracted from your meal when the oft-performed noodle-making demonstration begins. It's impressive, as will be the check. Downtown residents will appreciate the TriBeCa location at *121 Hudson St.*

Oceana

A2

Seafood 𝕏𝕏𝕏

55 E. 54th St. (bet. Madison & Park Aves.)

Subway: 5 Av - 53 St
Phone: 212-759-5941
Web: www.oceanarestaurant.com
Prices: **$$$$**

Mon – Fri lunch & dinner
Sat dinner only

Paul Johnson Photography

At Oceana, the sophisticated seafood cuisine of Chef Ben Pollinger is expertly served amid elegance. Polished wood accents, dark blue carpeting, and nautical inspired murals, coupled with the polished staff, evokes the privileged feeling of dining aboard a private yacht. Sparkling freshness and vibrant flavors are evident in such creations as raw shrimp with *sopa ajo blanco* (an interesting play on white gazpacho made from *marcona* almonds and garlic) or steamed grouper with Asian vegetables and black bean purée. The dessert menu is a sweetly satisfying display of élan, featuring the likes of chocolate custard brownie with cinnamon-infused whipped cream. The wine list boasts over 1,100 labels, including an impressive selection of white Burgundy; the three-course tasting menu features exclusive pairings. The bar serves its own menu and makes a lovely after-work respite.

Appetizers

- Gnocchi, New Orleans Shrimp, Chanterelles and Pecorino
- Escolar Tartare, Pickled Papaya and Macadamias
- House-made Gravlax, Watercress, Radishes, Salmon Caviar

Entrées

- Sautéed Nova Scotia Lobster with Spring and Snow Peas, Orange-Lobster Reduction
- Taro-wrapped Pompano, Coconut-Cilantro Curry

Desserts

- Apricot-Almond Soufflé, Honey Ice Cream, Chocolate Dragee
- Frozen Banana Mousse, Sticky Lemon Rice, Black Pepper Meringue
- Tropical Fruit Soup with Crème Fraîche Sorbet

Osteria Laguna

Italian

C4

209 E. 42nd St. (bet. Second & Third Aves.)

Subway: Grand Central - 42 St
Phone: 212-557-0001
Web: www.osteria-laguna.com
Prices: $$

Mon – Fri lunch & dinner
Sat – Sun dinner only

Convenient to Grand Central Terminal and the United Nations, Osteria Laguna is tucked into the ground floor of a redbrick office building on a prime piece of Midtown real estate. Surprisingly charming for this stretch of 42nd Street, the dining space is separated into two rooms: a sunny, high-ceilinged front room with large windows and bare wood tables; and a back room where white-cloth-covered tables cluster.

A wide selection of homemade pasta and terrific, thin-crust, wood-oven-fired pizza star at lunch, when the room bustles with business diners. At dinner, additional entrées run from grilled branzino to veal saltimbocca, and a younger crowd composed of locals who work in the neighborhood holds sway, along with a cadre of tourists.

Pampano

Mexican

B3

209 E. 49th St. (bet. Second & Third Aves.)

Subway: 51 St
Phone: 212-751-4545
Web: www.modernmexican.com/pampano
Prices: $$$

Mon – Fri lunch & dinner
Sat – Sun dinner only

Expect upscale, elegant Mexican cuisine at Pampano—Maya's sophisticated young sibling. Both were sired by Richard Sandoval, who has created a mini Mexican-restaurant empire north of the border. Head upstairs for the airy, light-filled, white-washed dining room, where no matter the weather outside, the feeling inside evokes sun-bleached shores. When it's warm out, the open-air terrace is the place to be.

A selection of ceviche makes a great place to start, after some guacamole, of course. Seafood takes top billing on the menu, perhaps grilled shrimp over a goat cheese-stuffed Anaheim pepper. No meal here is complete without the tangy Pampano margarita, enhanced by hibiscus syrup and dried flowers. Finish with sips of a top-shelf tequila. During the week, for tasty lunch fare go to nearby cousin, Pampano Taqueria.

Pera

303 Madison Ave. (bet. 41st & 42nd Sts.)

Subway: Grand Central - 42 St
Phone: 212-878-6301
Web: www.peranyc.com
Prices: $$

Mon – Fri lunch & dinner
Sat dinner only

At lunch and dinner, Midtown business types like to loosen their ties and shake things up a bit at Pera. This self-proclaimed "Mediterranean brasserie," named for an elegant neighborhood in Istanbul, brings a new dimension to eating in staid Midtown.

Like the owners, the cuisine here is primarily Turkish: meze of homemade grape leaves, beef and bulgur tartare, or smoked eggplant dip served with crispy lavash; mains like the signature spiced ground lamb Adana cooked on an open-flame grill.

Wood, marble, and stone dominate the attractive interior, where an open kitchen and a hand-crafted communal table encourage a convivial spirit. Off the entrance, the zebrawood bar is a great place to grab a drink while you're waiting for friends to arrive.

Phoenix Garden

242 E. 40th St. (bet. Second & Third Aves.)

Subway: Grand Central - 42 St
Phone: 212-983-6666
Web: www.thephoenixgarden.com
Prices:

Lunch & dinner daily

You'll find this gem of a Chinese place tucked into the basement of a modest brick building in Murray Hill, where excellent Cantonese dishes keep locals coming back for more.

Since the menu cites some 200 different choices, it's worth requesting input from the friendly staff to assist in narrowing down your options. Whatever you decide on, don't miss the steamed shrimp and chive dumplings, pepper and salty shrimp, or any of the daily specials written on the board in the entryway (which may add the likes of Peking duck and steamed whole fish). The menu is meant for sharing, so bring as many friends as you can muster.

Prices can't be beat, especially considering that you can bring your own bottle (Phoenix Garden doesn't serve alcohol).

Picasso

Spanish ✗✗

C1

303 E. 56th St. (bet. First & Second Aves.)

Subway: 59 St
Phone: 212-759-8767
Web: www.restaurantpicasso.com
Prices: $$

Lunch & dinner daily

In a city where change is constant, it's comforting to find an unpretentious, widely appealing restaurant that has hardly changed through the years. This welcoming place with its warm and attentive staff is straight authentically Spanish, from the olives marinating in giant jars atop the bar to pitchers brimming with sangria.

Classically prepared Spanish favorites pepper the extensive menu, such as *mariscada* with its assortment of seafood and aromatic sauce. Everything satisfies, and nearly every preparation is deliciously abundant with garlic. All entrées come with a salad tossed in near-addictive dressing, and side dish—wise diners vary these to share.

The bar is an old-world spot for tapas, washed down with a glass of Rioja or amontillado.

P.J. Clarke's

Gastropub ✗

B2

915 Third Ave. (at 55th St.)

Subway: Lexington Av - 53 St
Phone: 212-317-1616
Web: www.pjclarkes.com
Prices: ⊖⊖

Lunch & dinner daily

Named for Patrick Joseph Clarke, who purchased the place in 1904, this saloon remains a slice of old New York, despite its change of ownership in 2002.

Pub fare still reigns at this former haunt of Frank Sinatra and Jackie O: big burgers, sandwiches, shepherd's pie, and a long list of beers on tap. The bar scene, usually packed four deep with one of the city's best happy-hour crowds, overshadows the food, but this doesn't faze the good-looking young professionals who come to meet and greet. If you have to wait for a table, the bar is the place to be.

The latest additions to the family include P.J. Clarke's on the Hudson *(Four World Financial Center at Vesey St.)*, and P.J. Clarke's at Lincoln Center *(W. 63rd St. at Columbus Ave.)*.

Riingo

205 E. 45th St. (bet. Second & Third Aves.)

Subway: Grand Central - 42 St
Phone: 212-867-4200
Web: www.riingo.com
Prices: $$

Lunch & dinner daily

Derived from the Japanese word for "apple" (as in the Big Apple), Riingo features celebrity chef Marcus Samuelsson's interpretation of Japanese and American cuisines. The stylish, contemporary restaurant, just off the lobby of the Alex Hotel, incorporates ebony wood, bamboo floor planks, and thoughtful touches such as custom-made ceramic sake sets. At the front of the restaurant, a small bar, lounge and a few sidewalk tables offer a pleasant setting for a post-work cocktail or fast business lunch.

In addition to the creative kitchen menu and extensive raw-bar selection, Riingo offers a full range of sushi and maki of impressive quality. Open for all-day dining, Riingo and its original menu rise a cut above your typical hotel restaurant.

Rosa Mexicano

1063 First Ave. (at 58th St.)

Subway: 59 St
Phone: 212-753-7407
Web: www.rosamexicano.com
Prices: $$

Dinner daily

A sure crowd pleaser, Rosa Mexicano promises good food and a good time, and it always delivers. While outposts have popped up in New York and other cities, the East Side original still wins raves on a nightly basis. The place is always packed (reservations essential) with a mix of young and old, families and singles.

With its terrific margaritas and extensive tequila list, the bar is the place to wait for a table or unwind after work. Guacamole made to order tableside, along with authentic entrées like *budin Azteca* (multi-layer tortilla pie), and *crepas de camarón* (corn crêpes filled with shrimp and napped with chile pasilla sauce) keep 'em coming back for more. Appealing desserts are worth saving room for—at least order one to share.

Sakagura

Japanese ✗

B4

211 E. 43rd St. (bet. Second & Third Aves.)

Subway: Grand Central - 42 St
Phone: 212-953-7253
Web: www.sakagura.com
Prices: $$$

Mon – Fri lunch & dinner
Sat – Sun dinner only

It's all about sake at Sakagura. Although the restaurant is located in the basement of a Midtown office building (enter the lobby and walk down the back stairs), this is as authentic a sake den as you'll find in the city. Here, you'll be transported to Tokyo with traditional Japanese décor, secluded booths, and tables filled with Japanese businessmen.

More than 200 kinds of sake are exquisitely presented in imported serving sets selected by the helpful staff. The menu plays a supporting role, designed to complement the sake list (no sushi is served, only sashimi, to best enjoy the sake). Other than that, the food doesn't skimp on variety, authenticity or quality. Share a few small plates as part of a lengthy ritual of nibbling and sake sipping.

Sarge's

Deli ✗

B5

548 Third Ave. (bet. 36th & 37th Sts.)

Subway: 33 St
Phone: 212-679-0442
Web: www.sargesdeli.com
Prices: 🍝

Lunch & dinner daily

Opened many moons ago by former NYPD sergeant Abe Katz, Sarge's is a classic New York deli that pulls in a steady stream of locals. Pastrami is king here, but you can't go wrong with any of the choices, which range from blintzes to matzoh ball soup. If you can squeeze in dessert after a deli Wellington (a diet-busting combo of corned beef, pastrami and potatoes baked in a puff-pastry shell), Sarge's serves a mean cheesecake.

Abe is no longer on hand to chat up the customers, but the chipper waitstaff makes everyone feel like a regular, and children are welcome. Still run by the Katz family, Sarge's is a Murray Hill must for a real New York deli experience.

For Long Island-bound commuters, Sarge's has a location in Syosset *(236 Jericho Tpk.)*.

2nd Avenue Deli

B6

D e l i ✕

162 E. 33rd St. (bet. Lexington & Third Aves.)

Subway: 33 St
Phone: 212-689-9000
Web: www.2ndavedeli.com
Prices: 💰💰

Lunch & dinner daily

Ignore the kvetching of those who complain that this deli is not the same now that it has moved to Midtown. Sure, the décor may be more deli-meets-Deco and there's a tad less attitude, but the food is every bit as good as it was on Second Avenue. Get over it already—this is still a true Jewish deli, and one of the best around by far.

What hasn't changed is the menu. It's still meat-only, no-dairy Kosher, with the same phenomenal pastrami, pillowy rye, tangy mustard, and fluffy matzoh balls in fantastic comforting broth. Go for the best of both worlds at lunch with the soup and half-sandwich combination.

In this location the deli also does takeout (popular with the Midtown lunch bunch) and delivery (popular with late-night partyers). Giant platters go equally well for a bris or a brunch.

Seo

C3

J a p a n e s e ✕

249 E. 49th St. (bet. Second & Third Aves.)

Subway: 51 St
Phone: 212-355-7722
Web: N/A
Prices: $$

Mon – Fri lunch & dinner
Sat – Sun dinner only

Seo is the lovely sort of neighborhood spot you'd like to be a regular at, so you could enjoy their authentic Japanese cuisine all the time. It's an understated place, located on a residential block near the United Nations, The Japan Society and the "Dag." In a neighborhood rich with Japanese eateries, Seo stands out for its excellent light dishes, such as miso-marinated cod, and sake-steamed clams and squid. They serve sushi and sashimi too, but don't let these dominate your meal or you'll miss out on the menu's variety.

Seo offers a good selection of sakes and beers to match the food. Sit at the sushi bar, or claim a table in the serene little dining room that overlooks a traditional Japanese garden behind the town house.

Shaburi

Japanese

A-B5

125 E. 39th St. (bet. Lexington & Park Aves.)

Subway: Grand Central - 42 St
Phone: 212-867-6999
Web: www.shaburi.com
Prices: $$$

Mon – Fri lunch & dinner
Sat – Sun dinner only

Shabu-shabu and *sukiyaki*, the family-style-do-it-yourself-Asian methods of cooking, are the specialty here at Shaburi. Outfitted with electric burners on each table and at each seat at the sushi bar, this well-kept, contemporary midtown spot is known for its fresh ingredients and pleasant service. Sushi is another popular pick, especially at lunchtime, where the mostly business crowd can be seen tucking into the prixe-fixe lunch special or bargain bento box. Not in the mood to cook, but still craving a cooked meal?

The menu offers a variety of alternatives from grilled Kobe beef marinated in sweet miso to *unagi haata*, barbequed eel layered with spinach and mushrooms.

Sip Sak

Turkish

C3

928 Second Ave. (bet. 49th & 50th Sts.)

Subway: 51 St
Phone: 212-583-1900
Web: www.sip-sak.com
Prices: $$

Lunch & dinner daily

Good, authentic Turkish cuisine still holds sway here at Sip Sak and peripatetic founding chef, Orhan Yegen, remains on board. He graces the upbeat dining room nightly with his charismatic persona and adds to the lively ambiance enjoyed by an international crowd of local residents.

The dining room has benefited from some decorative upgrades and now with colorful walls, dark wood tables, and abundant Turkish artifacts, it has a much warmer feel.

House specials like *manti* (aromatic beef dumplings in a yogurt garlic sauce) or stuffed cabbage arrive in abundant portions. Grilled octopus—a frequent daily special—is impeccably prepared, dressed simply in olive oil and herbs. A selection of Turkish wines and beers is offered, a fitting match to a meal here.

Smith & Wollensky

 B3

S t e a k h o u s e

797 Third Ave. (at 49th St.)

Subway: 51 St
Phone: 212-753-1530
Web: www.smithandwollensky.com
Prices: $$$$

Mon – Fri lunch & dinner
Sat – Sun dinner only

Part of a well-known chain with locations in 10 U.S. cities, Smith & Wollensky's 390-seat New York flagship opened in 1977—well before the current steakhouse craze—and still reigns as one of the city's most celebrated steakhouses. (Oddly, the restaurant's name is not related to its owners; founder Alan Stillman and his partner Ben Benson picked the two surnames randomly from the phone book).

USDA prime beef (dry-aged and hand-butchered on the premises) accounts for the constant crowds of agency types and other Midtowners who keep this place going strong. For night owls, adjoining Wollensky's Grill serves a less-expensive menu until two A.M. to nourish the raucus group of post-work partiers who hold sway at the wildly popular bar.

Sparks Steak House

 C3

S t e a k h o u s e

210 E. 46th St. (bet. Second & Third Aves.)

Subway: Grand Central - 42 St
Phone: 212-687-4855
Web: www.sparksnyc.com
Prices: $$$$

Mon – Fri lunch & dinner
Sat dinner only

With seating for nearly 700 people, Sparks is well equipped to handle crowds. Indeed, it has drawn hordes of expense-account types for years. The bi-level dining space feels even more gigantic on an evening when the place is jamming—which is most of the time. There's a raucous, masculine vibe, enhanced by large tables and the 19th-century landscapes of the Hudson River Valley that line the wainscoted walls.

Unlike many steakhouses, Sparks doesn't offer a Porterhouse, but thick cuts of phenomenal prime sirloin and lamb or veal chops will satisfy your meat cravings (for seafood lovers, lobsters weigh in from 3 to nearly 6 pounds). Waiting for a table here is de rigueur, but speedy bartenders will shake a frosty martini for you in the meantime.

SushiAnn

B2

38 E. 51st St. (bet. Madison & Park Aves.)

Subway: 51 St
Phone: 212-755-1780
Web: www.sushiann.com
Prices: $$

Mon – Fri lunch & dinner
Sat dinner only

This unpretentious haven with its L-shaped sushi bar and blond wood tables bustles at lunch with a business crowd and is peaceful at dinner serving a balance of tourists and regulars. The discreet staff welcomes both serious sushi aficionados and the California roll set with equal hospitality. SushiAnn should not be overlooked as it competes with the best sushi bars in the city.

A traditional Japanese experience can be had here from the top quality fish to the incredibly knowledgeable sushi chefs. Regulars develop a relationship with their favorite and enjoy a customized omakase from his repertoire.

A fine selection of cooked appetizers are worthy of consideration and the concise yet well-selected sake list offers plenty of *kanpai* for your yen.

Sushiden

A3

19 E. 49th St. (bet. Fifth & Madison Aves.)

Subway: 5 Av - 53 St
Phone: 212-758-2700
Web: www.sushiden.com
Prices: $$$

Mon – Fri lunch & dinner
Sun dinner only

Regardless of recent competition in the form of more modern and stylish spots, Sushiden remains popular for its traditional food and excellent service. The restaurant is an especially big hit with the business-lunch crowd that jams the place at midday—so be sure to make reservations.

While the menu offerings have been altered slightly to please the business diners, you can still find high-quality traditional sushi here (perhaps minus the spicy tuna and California rolls). Ask for the omakase, and the skillful sushi chefs will respond with a parade of items, each piece seasoned to enhance its flavor.

Branches cover the east and west sides of Manhattan; joining this east side location is another Sushiden at *123 West 49th St.*, near Sixth Avenue.

Manhattan ▶ Midtown East & Murray Hill

Sushi Yasuda

204 E. 43rd St. (bet. Second & Third Aves.)

Subway: Grand Central - 42 St
Phone: 212-972-1001
Web: www.sushiyasuda.com
Prices: $$$$

Mon – Fri lunch & dinner
Sat dinner only

Blond wood furnishings create a Scandinavian feel in this airy, contemporary dining room, which is cached away in an office building in the corridor between Grand Central Terminal and the United Nations. Seating at the counter is best if you want to order the omakase—just remember that counter reservations are limited to 90 minutes.

Everything on the menu is made from scratch and changes constantly, according to the market and the whim of Chef/partner Naomichi Yasuda. Turn your attention to the fantastic variety of sushi and sashimi, each item presented on a fresh Hawaiian *ti* leaf. Raw fish here is kept pristine, with no extraneous embellishments or garnishes to detract from the fresh flavors.

Tao

42 E. 58th St. (bet. Madison & Park Aves.)

Subway: 59 St
Phone: 212-888-2288
Web: www.taorestaurant.com
Prices: $$$

Mon – Fri lunch & dinner
Sat – Sun dinner only

Asia's tastiest dishes star at this former movie theater. It's hard to imagine catching a flick in this dramatic dining playground today, outfitted as it is with a Chinese scroll draped across the ceiling and a 16-foot-high statue of Buddha towering over a reflecting pool in the main dining room. The theater's former balconies now accommodate diners too— some 300 of them on three levels.

The menu spotlights a combination of Hong Kong Chinese, Japanese, and Thai dishes, including sushi and sashimi. Perfect for sharing, a host of small plates offers everything from dragon-tail spare ribs to lobster wontons. On weekend nights, Manhattan's young and restless turn out in droves to indulge in libations like the Zen-tini or Tao Love Potion #9.

Teodora

Italian ✗✗

B1

141 E. 57th St. (bet. Lexington & Third Aves.)

Subway: Lexington Av - 59 St
Phone: 212-826-7101
Web: N/A
Prices: $$

Lunch & dinner daily

Conveniently situated on a block of 57th Street that draws patrons from nearby residential and commercial districts, Teodora has the comfortable feel of a restaurant that's been around for ages. Two floors offer separate spirits, making it possible to enjoy the same cuisine in two distinctly different settings. Dark and lively, the downstairs room has a bit more charm, along with more noise and closely spaced tables. Upstairs is more quiet and conducive to privacy.

The mostly Italian waitstaff is well-versed in the menu, which emphasizes northern Italy in its fine array of traditional antipasti, house-made pastas, entrées, and side dishes. Simple means good here; there are no frills to steal attention from the food. Pricey reds, including labels not commonly found, dominate the wine list.

Tsushima

Japanese ✗

B3

141 E. 47th St. (bet. Lexington & Third Aves.)

Subway: Grand Central - 42 St
Phone: 212-207-1938
Web: N/A
Prices: $$

Mon – Fri lunch & dinner
Sat dinner only

There are few restaurant secrets left in New York, but Tsushima is one of them. Chances are, you haven't heard of it, but this place stands out among the competition in the thin slice of Midtown jammed with restaurants straight out of Tokyo. It's easy to walk right by Tsushima (it's located a few steps below street level), but once inside, you'll find a sultry décor that contrasts black wood with white leather seating.

Skilled chefs seamlessly juggle the standard table orders with the omakase offerings at the sushi bar, and the kitchen plays backup with an assortment of cooked courses. Though spicy tuna can be had, the chef's choice is the way to go, as Tsushima nets fantastic quality and interesting varieties of fish—all elegantly presented.

Vong

B2

Fusion

200 E. 54th St. (bet. Second & Third Aves.)

Subway: Lexington Av - 53 St
Phone: 212-486-9592
Web: www.jean-georges.com
Prices: **$$$**

Mon – Fri lunch & dinner
Sat – Sun dinner only

Designed by architects Philip Johnson and John Burgee, the 1986 Postmodern office tower dubbed "The Lipstick Building" is also home to Vong, where jewel-toned Thai silks, bowls of fragrant spices, and bamboo accents create an Oriental aura.

Tastes of Asia fuse with French technique in this cuisine, thanks to the years Alsatian-born Chef Jean-Georges Vongerichten spent cooking in Bangkok, Singapore, and Hong Kong. Although the kitchen stumbles at times, a codfish cooked *sous-vide* with an aromatic crust of cumin, herbs, and curry powder bears testament to the staff's potential.

Dessert, as in a deconstructed pineapple Napoleon—elemental as caramelized cubes of pineapple, ginger, coconut sorbet, and caramel-flavored tuiles—is worth remembering.

The Water Club

C6

Seafood

E. 30th St. (at the East River)

Subway: 33 St
Phone: 212-683-3333
Web: www.thewaterclub.com
Prices: **$$$**

Lunch & dinner daily

For years, birthdays, anniversaries and engagements have been celebrated at the Water Club, and, indeed, its setting is perfect for special occasions. Set on a barge in the East River, the dining room boasts floor-to-ceiling windows that overlook the river, and water views from every table. Marine signal flags hanging from the ceiling and a waitstaff dressed as a ship's crew complete the nautical theme.

The menu celebrates American dishes and spotlights seafood such as shrimp cocktail, grilled salmon, and Maine lobster. Meat dishes like Colorado rack of lamb and Long Island duck please landlubbers. Live piano music entertains nightly, and in summer, the Crow's Nest on the restaurant's upper deck offers informal outdoor dining and river breezes.

Wild Edibles

Seafood ✗

B5

535 Third Ave. (bet. 35th & 36th Sts.)

Lunch & dinner daily

Subway: 33 St
Phone: 212-213-8552
Web: www.wildedibles.com
Prices: $$

It's a fish market. It's a restaurant. It's an oyster bar. Wild Edibles is all those places rolled into one.

With four other markets in New York, including one in Grand Central Station, Wild Edibles prides itself on netting line-caught fish and organic produce from small farms. In the Third Avenue locale, a retail counter displays the day's catch, while a small bar and a few tables provide seating. A vast array of seafood fills the menu with an appealing mix of light fare and entrées—everything from oyster "flights," (with white wine or beer pairings) to fish cooked your way and accompanied with a choice of seasonings. Cheesecake is the only dessert option, and they don't serve coffee.

At lunch, it feels like you're eating in a fish store, but in the evening candlelight kicks in more atmosphere.

Wolfgang's Steakhouse

Steakhouse ✗✗

A6

4 Park Ave. (at 33rd St.)

Mon – Sat lunch & dinner
Sun dinner only

Subway: 33 St
Phone: 212-889-3369
Web: www.wolfgangssteakhouse.com
Prices: $$$$

&

After 40 years at the esteemed Peter Luger, former headwaiter Wolfgang Zwiener ditched retirement to strike out on his own across the river—a decision that has yielded mouth-watering results. Located in the former Vanderbilt Hotel dining room, the 1912 landmark space showcases a vaulted terra-cotta ceiling by famed architect Rafael Guastavino. The setting is handsome, but the steak's arrival refocuses all attention on the strapping portions of Porterhouse, hand-selected and dry-aged in house. Once the meat is basted with some of its sizzling juices, the feast will begin. Classic starters and sides like shrimp cocktail and creamed spinach are delightful distractions. Be sure to checkout the equally enjoyable TriBeCa location (409 Greenwich St.).

Yakitori Torys

C2

Japanese X

248 E. 52nd St. (bet. Second & Third Aves.)

Subway: 51 St
Phone: 212-813-1800
Web: www.torysnyc.com
Prices: **$$**

Dinner daily

Midtown has its fair share of Tokyo-style restaurants and Torys is no exception. Positioned on the second floor, this tranquil little yakitori house skewers up a remarkable variety of chicken parts and grills them expertly. From livers to tails, poultry rules the roost.

The kitchen's specialty is yakitori, but don't ignore the rest of their vast menu. The chicken soup here easily competes with grandma's version and do not miss their *gyoza*, a distant relative of the frozen versions found elsewhere.

The attentive staff will present your parade of courses and quenching libations at a relaxed pace; everything is cooked to order and there's surely no rush.

Zarela

C2-3

Mexican X

953 Second Ave. (bet. 50th & 51st Sts.)

Subway: 51 St
Phone: 212-644-6740
Web: www.zarela.com
Prices: **$$**

Mon – Fri lunch & dinner
Sat – Sun dinner only

Every day's a fiesta in this boisterous bistro, hung with bright paper garlands, ceremonial masks, puppets, and other Mexican artifacts— Zarela Martinez sees to that. The chef opened her restaurant here in 1987, and it's still going strong. Her secret recipe for fantastic, powerful margaritas is just one of the reasons.

A native of Mexico, Zarela courts a carnival ambience with lively music and food that's served family-style, in case you wish to share. In the evenings, the place teems with regulars and post-work revelers who often spill out onto the sidewalk while they wait to dig into flavorful regional Mexican like creamy *chilaquiles,* smoky *camarones enchipotlados,* or rich *cochinita pibíl,* whose enticing aromas fill the dining room.

Midtown West

When you think of Midtown West, Times Square probably comes to mind. True, brash **Times Square**, at Broadway and 42nd Street, demands your attention with its blazing marquees, but the neighborhood that runs from Fifth Avenue west to the Hudson River is so much more than that. Here you'll find **Bryant Park,** the gracious formal park behind the Beaux-Arts **New York Public Library**, and the site of New York's first World's Fair. This district is also home to the landmark 102-story Art Deco **Empire State Building**, as well as **Rockefeller Center,** headquarters of NBC studios and the city's famous ice-skating rink. For shoppers, **Macy's** anchors a frenetic commercial hub *(on Sixth Ave. at 34th St.)*, and **Diamond and Jewelry Way** *(W. 47th St., between Fifth & Sixth Aves.)* ranks as the world's largest district for diamonds and other precious stones.

If it's dining that interests you, look no farther. Midtown West holds a dense concentration of eateries,

Brigitta L. House / MICHELIN

from Restaurant Row (as West 46th Street between Broadway and Ninth Avenue is known) to the Time Warner Center on Columbus Circle—home to some of New York's most celebrated restaurants, not to mention a host of upscale shops.

FROM COUNTRY TO COSMOPOLITAN

In the colonial era, this slice of Midtown belonged to the city but was actually the country, as New York's population was concentrated well below Canal Street. By the mid-19th century, the area was covered with brownstone town houses—homes to upper-middle-class families who couldn't afford a mansion on Fifth Avenue. Upon the completion of the Sixth Avenue "El" (elevated railway) in 1878, a majority of these residents deemed the quarter too noisy and dirty, and with their Fifth Avenue neighbors, began moving uptown.

First known as Longacre Square, the trapezoidal plot formed by Broadway and Seventh Avenue between 42nd and 43rd streets was renamed in 1904 for the New York Times headquarters. On December 31 of that year, the new building on Times Square was christened with a brightly lit "time ball" lowered from atop the building precisely at midnight—a tradition that continues to this day. In 2007, the venerable newspaper moved into its new home, a stunning skyscraper designed by Renzo Piano, located a few blocks away.

The construction of **Rockefeller Center** between 1930 and 1940 permanently changed the character of the neighborhood. More than 225 buildings, mostly brownstones, were demolished to make room for the original 12 buildings of the complex, and the residential population was dispersed to other parts of the city. But with that loss came significant gain. The center was hailed as an architectural triumph. Rockefeller's insistence that early tenants be affiliated with the television and radio industries paid off well. Other media outlets soon gravitated to the district, boosting its worldwide visibility and local cachet.

In 1939, the opening of the **Museum of Modern Art** on West 53rd Street—a project championed by John D. Rockefeller's wife, Abby Aldrich Rockefeller—was equally prescient. The renowned MoMA now anchors one of the city's most vital museum districts.

THE DIVIDING LINE

Although Fifth Avenue officially separates the east and west sides of Manhattan, it is the Avenue of the Americas (still known as Sixth Avenue to locals, though it was officially renamed in 1945) that actually feels like the dividing line. In part, that's because its neighbors are so distinct. One block east, the department stores of **Fifth Avenue** ooze gentility. One block west, the fabled **Theater District** (spreading north from Times Square along Broadway) was inaugurated in 1895, when Oscar Hammerstein opened the Olympia theater complex at Broadway and 45th Street. In the subsequent three decades, some 85 theaters were built between Avenue of the Americas and Eighth Avenue. Today this area also teems with restaurants touting their pre- and post-theater menus, and service timed precisely to the 8:00 P.M. curtain.

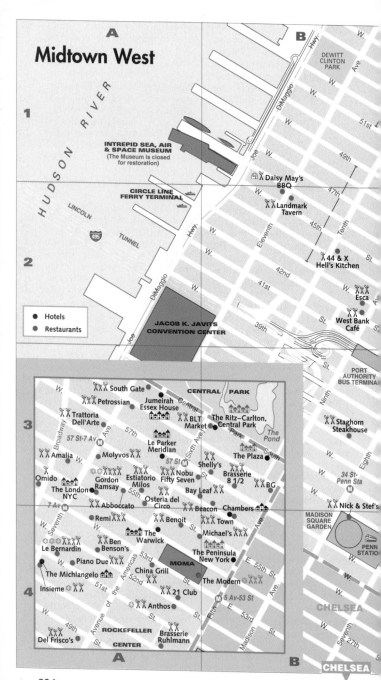

Midtown West

HUDSON RIVER

INTREPID SEA, AIR & SPACE MUSEUM
(The Museum is closed for restoration)

CIRCLE LINE FERRY TERMINAL

LINCOLN TUNNEL

JACOB K. JAVITS CONVENTION CENTER

- ● Hotels
- ● Restaurants

DEWITT CLINTON PARK

Daisy May's BBQ

Landmark Tavern

44 & X Hell's Kitchen

Esca

West Bank Café

PORT AUTHORITY BUS TERMINAL

CENTRAL PARK

South Gate

Petrossian

Jumeirah Essex House

BLT Market

The Ritz–Carlton, Central Park

Staghorn Steakhouse

Trattoria Dell'Arte

Le Parker Meridian

The Pond

Amalia

Molyvos

Shelly's

The Plaza

Omido

Gordon Ramsay

Estiatorio Milos

Nobu Fifty Seven

Brasserie 8 1/2

BG

The London NYC

Abboccato

Osteria del Circo

Bay Leaf

Nick & Stef's

Remi

Benoit

Beacon

Chambers

MADISON SQUARE GARDEN

Town

Michael's

PENN STATION

Ben Benson's

The Warwick

Le Bernardin

The Peninsula New York

Piano Due

China Grill

The Michelangelo

Insieme

21 Club

The Modern

CHELSEA

Anthos

Del Frisco's

ROCKEFELLER CENTER

Brasserie Ruhlmann

CHELSEA

234

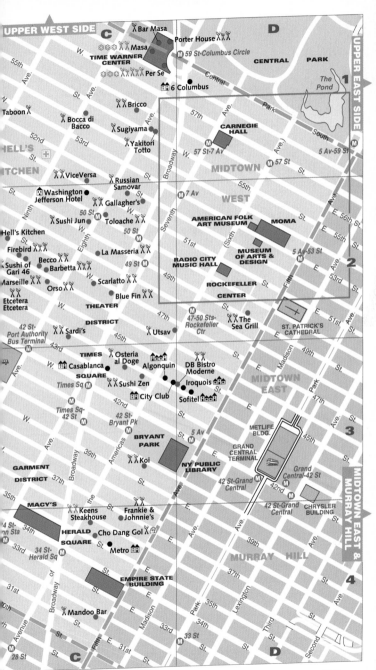

UPPER WEST SIDE

C

D

UPPER EAST SIDE

Bar Masa

Porter House

59 St-Columbus Circle

CENTRAL   PARK

W.

Masa

TIME WARNER
CENTER

Per Se

6 Columbus

The
Pond

Taboon

Bocca di
Bacco

Bricco

Sugiyama

57th

Ave.

CARNEGIE
HALL

Park

South

5 Av-59 St

1

55th

Ave.

N.

St.

52nd

53rd

Yakitori
Totto

W. 57 St-7 Av

57 St

HELL'S

ViceVersa

Russian
Samovar

Broadway

MIDTOWN

55th

Ave.

E. 56th

St.

KITCHEN

Ninth

St.

Washington
Jefferson Hotel

Gallagher's

WEST

7 Av

Seventh

AMERICAN FOLK
ART MUSEUM

(Sixth

MOMA

E. 55th

St.

St.

50 St

Sushi Jun

Toloache

50 St

51st

Eighth

MUSEUM
OF ARTS &
DESIGN

5 Av-53 St

53rd

Ave.

2

Hell's Kitchen

Firebird

Sushi of
Gari 46

Becco

Barbetta

La Masseria

RADIO CITY
MUSIC HALL

49th

49 St

Scarlatto

Fifth

Marseille

Orso

THEATER

Blue Fin

ROCKEFELLER
CENTER

51st

Ave.

Etcetera
Etcetera

W.

DISTRICT

47th

47-50 Sts-
Rockefeller
Ctr

The
Sea Grill

ST. PATRICK'S
CATHEDRAL

49th

St.

42 St-
Port Authority
Bus Terminal

Sardi's

45th

43rd

Utsav

Madison

E.

MIDTOWN
EAST

Park

47th

TIMES

W.

Casablanca

Osteria
al Doge

Algonquin

DB Bistro
Moderne

SQUARE

Times Sq

Sushi Zen

Iroquois

42nd

City Club

Sofitel

5 Av

METLIFE
BLDG.

45th

3

Times Sq-
42 St

42 St-
Bryant Pk

St.

GRAND
CENTRAL
TERMINAL

Grand
Central-42 St

W.

39th

BRYANT
PARK

5 Av

NY PUBLIC
LIBRARY

42 St-Grand
Central

42nd

St.

42 St-Grand
Central

CHRYSLER
BUILDING

St.

GARMENT

Broadway

Americas

Koi

Ave.

St.

DISTRICT

37th

MACY'S

the

St.

Keens
Steakhouse

Frankie &
Johnnie's

Lexington

MIDTOWN EAST &
MURRAY HILL

D

35th

34 St-
Penn Sta

HERALD

Cho Dang Gol

39th

34th

St.

34 St-
Herald Sq

SQUARE

Metro

33rd

MURRAY   HILL

37th

31st

EMPIRE STATE
BUILDING

35th

Park

Ave.

St.

Third

4

Broadway

St.

35th

34th

0th

Mandoo Bar

33rd

33 St

Ave.

St.

Second

28 St

St.

Fifth

E. 31st

St.

C

D

235

Abboccato

A3

Italian ✗✗

136 W. 55th St. (bet. Sixth & Seventh Aves.)

Subway: 57 St
Phone: 212-265-4000
Web: www.abboccato.com
Prices: $$$

Mon – Sat lunch & dinner
Sun dinner only

Brought to you by the Livanos family, whose stable includes Molyvos and Oceana, Abboccato bears the hallmarks of these experienced restaurateurs. Abboccato, located adjacent to the Blakely Hotel, combs the different regions of Italy for its cuisine and comes up with wines and tempting dishes such as ricotta *cavatelli* with house-made sausage, or grilled sirloin steak with white polenta, Gorgonzola, and anchovy oil. If you're dining with friends, the menu includes a section dedicated to *chiccetti*—small plates for sharing like *arancini* and *polpetti*.

Chic, modern styling lends an understated elegance to the 75-seat dining room, while the 20-seat terrazza opens onto the sidewalk, creating a sense of alfresco dining.

Amalia

A3

Mediterranean ✗✗

204 W. 55th St. (at Broadway)

Subway: 57 St - 7 Av
Phone: 212-245-1234
Web: www.amalia-nyc.com
Prices: $$$

Mon – Fri lunch & dinner
Sat dinner only

Cloaked in high design and backed by nightlife impresario Greg Brier, Amalia exudes hip. The dining room features exposed brick walls and distressed wood beams bedecked with ebony glass chandeliers and silk wallpaper. Located in a former carriage house next to the Dream hotel, Amalia's cuisine is as appealing as its setting is glossy. Warm and sunny Mediterranean flavors shine in creations like bacalao-stuffed piquillo peppers and lamb tagine with diced Asian pear and saffron broth. Tiramisu is given a whimsical twist as a sundae of mascarpone ice cream drizzled with espresso. There is also a subterranean lounge area where guests can start the party with a creative cocktail or shot of eau de vie in flavors like dried apricot and pomegranate.

Anthos ✿

Greek 🍴🍴

36 W. 52nd St. (bet. Fifth & Sixth Aves.)

Subway: 47-50 Sts - Rockefeller Ctr
Phone: 212-582-6900
Web: www.anthosnyc.com
Prices: $$$

Mon – Fri lunch & dinner
Sat dinner only

Anthos/Battman

A partnership of restaurateur/chef team Donatella Arpaia and Michael Psilakis, Anthos blooms with restrained elegance as touches of pale pink soften the chocolate-brown tones of the chairs and wood accents. The restaurant's name, which means "blossoming" in Greek, is echoed in the pastel cherry blossoms depicted in the artwork and in the back-lit bar mural.

Innovative and inspired Greek dishes are thoughtfully re-imagined with Chef Psilakis' bold yet balanced flavors. A raw meze selection to start would please the gods with tiny squares of uncooked fish—such as marlin artistically garnished with minced pear, delicate strands of saffron, and a touch of dried bay leaf; or luscious yellowtail under red beet gelée, with dried kalamata olives, and a layer of crispy bacon. Entrées of milk-fed chicken, or roasted lamb loin dusted in garlic and sage are equally Olympic in stature.

Appetizers
- Smoked Octopus, Fennel, Lemon Confit
- Grilled Prawn, Orzo, Smoked Chicken, Six-minute Egg
- Hilopita : Pork Belly, Artichoke-Lemon-Egg Emulsion

Entrées
- "Greek Risotto": Crab, Sea Urchin, Lobster, Caviar, Egg Yolk
- Grilled Loup de Mer, Medley of Winter Vegetables
- Spicy Shellfish Yiouvetsi Stew, Orzo, Saffron

Desserts
- Sesame Ice Cream, Metaxa-Caramel Halva
- Bougatza: Goat Milk Cheesecake, Pear and Goat Milk Caramel
- Baklava Trio, Almond Walnut Cake, Cinnamon Ice Cream

Barbetta

C2

Italian ✗✗✗

321 W. 46th St. (bet. Eighth & Ninth Aves.)

Subway: 50 St (Eighth Ave.)
Phone: 212-246-9171
Web: www.barbettarestaurant.com
Prices: $$$

Tue – Sat lunch & dinner

Steeped in history, from its landmark décor to a menu that features specialties dating back to 1906, Barbetta proves that old world glamour will always be fashionable. Still owned by its founding family, the dining room is bedecked with antiques, wood paneling, chandeliers, and potted trees. The Piedmont-influenced menu has offered risotto with wild porcini mushrooms, handmade *agnolotti*, and *zuppa inglese* since the turn of the twentieth century. The restaurant also boasts that it is the first in America to possess an espresso machine. Pair your meal with one of more than 1,700 different labels on the tremendous wine list. Scented by gardenia, oleander and jasmine, the secluded and covered garden is an oasis in the heart of the Theatre District.

Bar Masa

C1

Japanese ✗

10 Columbus Circle (in the Time Warner Center)

Subway: 59 St - Columbus Circle
Phone: 212-823-9800
Web: www.masanyc.com
Prices: $$$

Mon – Sat lunch & dinner

With its extensive menu and approachable prices, Bar Masa is a proper companion to Chef Masa Takayama's eponymous masterwork next door. Satisfy a yen for first-class fare without jeopardizing your retirement fund, and dig into the seasonal menu's structured listing of sushi offered à la carte, or a variety of grilled, braised, and fried dishes supplemented by rice and noodles. The décor of the slender room is earthy yet refined with pale walls tiled in Japanese limestone and dark wood furnishings. Gauzy fabric panels separate the popular bar area, which offers a well-chosen wine list embellished with several big ticket selections. More creative offerings may include the house Champagne cocktail made with muddled yuzu zest and rosewater.

Bay Leaf

Indian 🍴🍴

A-B3

49 W. 56th St. (bet. Fifth & Sixth Aves.)

Lunch & dinner daily

Subway: 57 St
Phone: 212-957-1818
Web: N/A
Prices: $$

In a sea of ethnic restaurants on a busy Midtown street, Bay Leaf stands out for its classic Indian cooking and enjoyable setting. This Indian eatery, on the ground floor of an office tower, is popular at lunch with the business crowd who come here for the well-priced buffet. It's also a sure bet for dinner, with a diverse assortment of à la carte items, including traditional curries and tandoori dishes. Expertly managed, the service is smooth from start to finish, and the staff helps guests navigate the many choices.

Bay Leaf shies away from the predictable décor with an elegant display of rich paneled woods, framed black-and-white photography and discreet Indian music. Service is also available on the terrace during warmer months.

Beacon

American 🍴🍴

B3

25 W. 56th St. (bet. Fifth & Sixth Aves.)

Mon – Fri & Sun lunch & dinner
Sat dinner only

Subway: 57 St
Phone: 212-332-0500
Web: www.beaconnyc.com
Prices: $$$

Open-fire cooking is the theme at Beacon's new Kitchen Counter, where co-owner/Chef Waldy Malouf uses top-quality ingredients to produce bold flavors. From comforting roasted chicken to sophisticated suckling pig, something here will appeal to most every appetite. For those who consider cooking a spectator sport, the open kitchen provides a mouthwatering view of the rotisserie, grill, and wood burning oven. This new dining counter places diners directly before the kitchen's warming blaze. Select from a trio of burgers at lunchtime, or graze through an assortment of small plates in the evening. Thursday nights offer a 12-course tasting menu, and generous portions are de riguer. The bar's innovative cocktail list draws a lively crowd.

Becco

C2

Italian ✕✕

355 W. 46th St. (bet. Eighth & Ninth Aves.)

Subway: 42 St - Port Authority Bus Terminal
Phone: 212-397-7597
Web: www.becconyc.com
Prices: $$

Lunch & dinner daily

Becco, which translates as "nibble", is owned by famed Italian food authority Lidia Bastianich and her son, Joseph. The Restaurant Row townhouse has long been a favorite pre-theatre dining choice, but the well-made hearty cooking served here makes Becco a destination in its own right. Exposed brick and terra-cotta tiles give the multi-room setting a warm vibe that is brightened by colorful Italian landscapes hung on the pale walls. Notice little images next to a number of menu items—these correspond to the specific cookbook in which Bastianich's recipe appears—inspiring diners to recreate the experience at home. Those looking for a great bargain should indulge in the *"sinfonia di pasta"* which features an unlimited amount of the chef's pasta selection.

Ben Benson's

A4

Steakhouse ✕✕

123 W. 52nd St. (bet. Sixth & Seventh Aves.)

Subway: 5 Av - 53 St
Phone: 212-581-8888
Web: www.benbensons.com
Prices: $$$

Mon – Fri lunch & dinner
Sat – Sun dinner only

If you grimace at the mere thought of fusion cooking, then this is the place for you. Since 1982, Ben Benson's has been serving prime cuts of USDA meats and other classic American fare to its contented macho clientele of power brokers and politicians (the names of the regulars are engraved on brass plaques set in the wainscoting). The huge menu includes the usual suspects (sirloin steaks, veal chops) but Southern fried chicken and crab cakes earn equal billing.

The high-ceilinged dining room is airier than many of the steakhouses in town, and this New York steakhouse remains stubbornly independent from chain ownership. For those who favor alfresco dining, the spacious sidewalk terrace provides a pleasant setting in nice weather.

Benoit

A4

French 🍴🍴

60 W. 55th St. (bet. Fifth & Sixth Aves.)

Subway: 57 St   Lunch & dinner daily
Phone: 646-943-7373
Web: www.benoitny.com
Prices: $$

With locations in Paris and Tokyo, New Yorkers now have the opportunity to experience the enchanting spirit of this wonderfully authentic bistro from Chef Alain Ducasse. A felicitous vibe pervades the meticulously designed room, exuding old world charm with oak-paneled walls, plush red furnishings, and a striking black and white bar. Like the Art-Nouveau lighting fixtures that formerly adorned this dining room as La Côte Basque, the menu respectfully honors the past. Treat yourself to classic delights such as the creamy, delectable duck foie gras, or rich *quenelles de brochet*, enhanced by a selection from the well-chosen, predominantly French wine list. Attention to detail adds a note of luxury one would expect from this world-famous chef.

BG

B3

American 🍴🍴

754 Fifth Ave. (at 58th St.)

Subway: 5 Av - 59 St   Lunch & dinner daily
Phone: 212-872-8977
Web: www.bergdorfgoodman.com
Prices: $$$

Since Bergdorf Goodman is the center of the universe for the pampered and privileged, it goes without saying that BG, the store's seventh-floor dining room, serves as a cafeteria to New York's champagne-sipping set. The word on the street is that Bergdorf's closed their old restaurant in favor of this sleek salon, decorated in haute Parisian style with hand-painted wallpaper and 18th-century-style chairs. Soft shades of blue, green and yellow lend a feminine mystique to the light-filled room. The menu reads like an upscale country club—deviled eggs, lobster salad, soufflé—and afternoon tea is served daily. For a less formal experience, try Bar III in the men's store across the street, where you can nosh on salads, sandwiches and soups while you sip a cocktail.

BLT Market

B3

American 🍴🍴

1430 Sixth Ave. (at 59th St.)

Subway: 5 Av - 59 St
Phone: 212-521-6125
Web: www.bltrestaurants.com
Prices: $$$

Lunch & dinner daily

The BLT empire continues to grow with the addition of Chef Laurent Tourondel's market-themed venture. The focus on seasonal, ingredient-driven cuisine is supported by menus that feature a monthly listing of peak produce and a blackboard of daily specials. Winter may bring spiced orange-glazed duck accompanied by collard greens and bacon. A few months later, this preparation may be updated to duck served two ways with spring onions and red currant jus.

The dining room, housed in the Ritz-Carlton Hotel, is an appealing union of city and country. Reclaimed wood furniture, antique farm tools, and black-and-white portraits of the restaurant's purveyors are complemented by velvet banquettes, colorful artwork, and large windows framing Central Park.

Blue Fin

C2

Seafood 🍴🍴

1567 Broadway (at 47th St.)

Subway: 49 St
Phone: 212-918-1400
Web: www.brguestrestaurants.com
Prices: $$$

Lunch & dinner daily

Hidden within the W Times Square Hotel, this member of the B.R. Guest restaurant group offers a hip retreat from this tourist-centric part of town. The downstairs dining space dazzles with its mirror-lined wall reflecting the wave motif sculpted in white plaster across the room. The second-floor balcony dangles a whimsical mobile depicting a school of fish.

Netting a steady stream of sea creatures, the menu features sushi and maki as well as raw bar items and caviar (all available at both lunch and dinner). Sustainable Scottish salmon, wild striped bass, and East Coast halibut vie for attention as entrées.

After work, the glass-walled bar on the corner of Broadway and 47th Street is usually packed with a happy-hour set who enjoy the Times Square view.

Bocca di Bacco

C1

Italian

828 Ninth Ave. (bet. 54th & 55th Sts.)

Subway: 50 St (Eighth Ave.)
Phone: 212-265-8828
Web: www.boccadibacconyc.com
Prices: $$

Dinner daily

This chicly rustic wine bar offers a deliciously varied menu, sure to please any mood. The space features heavy woodwork complemented by exposed brick walls, lined with shelves of wine and grappa bottles. Intimate seating is available, but groups or those interested in making new friends should opt for the communal tables, topped with slabs of white marble. Warm and welcoming, the front bar draws crowds of nearby residents and serves more than 40 wines by the glass from an all-Italian list. For a light snack, order a few of the *assagi*, like the chef's selection of cheeses served with fig jam and honey, or the meat-stuffed olives, fried crisp and delicious. More substantial offerings include excellent homemade pastas and simply prepared meat and fish.

Brasserie 8 1/2

B3

Contemporary

9 W. 57th St. (bet. Fifth & Sixth Aves.)

Subway: 57 St
Phone: 212-829-0812
Web: www.brasserie8andahalf.com
Prices: $$$

Sun – Fri lunch & dinner
Sat dinner only

Brasserie 8½'s individual style melds contemporary dash with a soupçon of decades past. You'll make a theatrical entrance down the brightly carpeted spiral staircase to reach the dining room. At the foot of the stairs, there's a circular lounge; a few more steps down, the brasserie is a big, bold, modern affair, with fabric-covered walls, leather booths, and a striking glass Léger mural walling off the kitchen.

Well-executed dishes are elegantly plated and take their inspiration from the Mediterranean (grilled octopus salad) to Asia (Japanese yellowtail with yuzu and pineapple-jalapeño sorbet). Service is attentive but speedy, ideal for those who need to get back to the office, or to go home to practice their grand entrances.

Brasserie Ruhlmann

French   ✕✕

A4

45 Rockefeller Plaza (bet. Fifth & Sixth Aves.)

Subway: 47-50 Sts - Rockefeller Ctr
Phone: 212-974-2020
Web: www.brasserieruhlmann.com
Prices: $$$

Mon – Sat lunch & dinner
Sun lunch only

Overlooking Rockefeller Center's Prometheus statue and garden arcade, this bustling brasserie's large sidewalk terrace is perfectly suited for alfresco dining. Owner Jean Denoyer (of La Goulue) named it as a tribute to French designer Emile-Jacques Ruhlmann.

The interior follows suit, incorporating faux ebony paneling, nickel-plated sconces, and a mosaic tile floor in swirls of burnt sienna, sky blue, pink, and white. Tables are furnished with burgundy velvet, high-backed chairs; alabaster lamps cast a flattering glow.

Executive Chef Laurent Tourondel, of the BLT empire, created this enjoyable menu of French classics. At dinner, changing *plats du jour* augment mains like N.Y. strip *au poivre*, mussels *marinière*, and braised rabbit *à la moutarde*.

Bricco

Italian   ✕✕

C1

304 W. 56th St. (bet. Eighth & Ninth Aves.)

Subway: 57 St - 7 Av
Phone: 212-245-7160
Web: www.bricconyc.com
Prices: $$

Mon – Fri lunch & dinner
Sat – Sun dinner only

Amore comes to mind when you see the rose-red walls and autographed lipstick kisses that cover the ceiling in this romantic Italian place. The dining space spreads over two floors, with the upstairs room being the sunnier and more tranquil of the two. If it's action you want, stick to the first floor, where chefs fire pizzas in the wood-burning oven and waiters scurry around, skillfully managing to keep the dishes coming without rushing diners. The two Italian owners play host and professional flirt to a bevy of regulars, many of them women.

The strength of Bricco's straightforward menu lies in its selection of flavorful homemade pastas, augmented by daily specials. Leaning toward Italy, the wine list devotes an entire page to Gaja Winery.

China Grill

A4

Asian 🍴🍴

60 W. 53rd St. (bet. Fifth & Sixth Aves.)

Subway: 5 Av – 53 St
Phone: 212-333-7788
Web: www.chinagrillmgt.com
Prices: $$$

Mon – Fri lunch & dinner
Sat – Sun dinner only

Opened more than 20 years ago, this first China Grill continues to be a perennial favorite and serves as the flagship of Jeffrey Chodorow's international restaurant organization. The sprawling interior designed by Jeffrey Beers is housed on the ground floor of the CBS building and features a multi-level dining room of 30-foot ceilings accented with white canopy light fixtures. The long bar area is a popular spot to unwind after a long day at the office; large tables enjoying ample portions of fun cuisine fill the soaring space with good-humored revelry. Served family style, the Asian-influenced menu shows strength in creativity with items like creamy miso-dressed salad topped with fried calamari, or risotto with edamame and grilled vegetables.

Cho Dang Gol

C4

Korean 🍴

55 W. 35th St. (bet. Fifth & Sixth Aves.)

Subway: 34 St - Herald Sq
Phone: 212-695-8222
Web: www.chodanggolny.com
Prices: 😊😊

Lunch & dinner daily

Named after a village in South Korea that's famed for its tofu, this unassuming eatery in Koreatown offers a break from the Korean barbecue served by the host of surrounding restaurants. Tofu, or soybean curd (*doo boo* in Korean) is the house specialty. Made fresh here each day, health-promoting tofu forms the basis of dishes from vegetable casseroles to pan-fried spicy octopus. Dishes are family-size and meant to be shared. An order of the *bulgogi* is easily big enough for several people, and appetizers can feed a hungry crowd. An abundance of plum wine, sake, and *soju* will liven up your meal in no time.

The friendly staff caters to a largely Korean clientele in a dining room decorated with wood beams and traditional Korean musical instruments.

Daisy May's BBQ 😊

Barbecue ✗

B2

623 Eleventh Ave. (at 46th St.)

Subway: 50 St (Eighth Ave.)
Phone: 212-977-1500
Web: www.daisymaysbbq.com
Prices: 🍴🍴

Lunch & dinner daily

Honey, grab your appetite and head straight for Daisy May's for some down-home finger-lickin'-good barbecue on Manhattan's wild West Side.

This sweet spot, complete with its barn-meets-school-cafeteria look, defies its location just northwest of the bright lights of Broadway. You'll find a motley bunch—everyone from bankers to bikers frequents this place for its fantastic food and friendly atmosphere.

Service-wise, you're on your own at Daisy's, where you place your order at the counter and are rewarded with a cardboard tray filled with chicken, ribs, pulled pork, or brisket with fixin's (Cajun dirty rice, baked beans, corn bread) alongside.

They don't serve alcohol, but the minty iced tea served in mason jars will quench your thirst.

DB Bistro Moderne

Contemporary ✗✗

D3

55 W. 44th St. (bet. Fifth & Sixth Aves.)

Subway: 5 Av
Phone: 212-391-2400
Web: www.danielnyc.com
Prices: $$$

Mon – Sat lunch & dinner
Sun dinner only

Stylish and exuberant, Daniel Boulud's contemporary take on the classic bistro features a lively front room dressed in red, accented with eye-popping floral photographs; or a more sedate yet equally attractive rear dining room. Thick linens, custom china, and a refined service team exhibit the chef's signature polish as does the contemporary French-inflected menu that satisfies the establishment's dapper patrons. Items such as lobster salad with pesto dressing and hanger steak with oxtail ragout reflect today's sensibilities; while crispy duck *confit* and *coq au vin* are tasty reminders of the hearty slow-cooked dishes of yore. Boulud's irreverent spin on the humble hamburger, here stuffed with foie gras and black truffles, has become a modern-day classic.

Del Frisco's

A4

Steakhouse 🍴🍴🍴

1221 Sixth Ave. (at 49th St.)

Subway: 47-50 Sts - Rockefeller Ctr
Phone: 212-575-5129
Web: www.delfriscos.com
Prices: $$$

Mon – Fri lunch & dinner
Sat – Sun dinner only

The McGraw-Hill Building's ground floor holds this sprawling steakhouse, a chain that originated in Dallas. Meat is the main attraction; portions range from a petit 6-ounce filet at lunch to a 48-ounce double Porterhouse for dinner to make any Texan proud.

Starters feature a house salad of iceberg and grated carrots studded with crumbles of blue cheese and garnished with strips of thick, crispy bacon. For dessert, the light creamy cheesecake has just the right texture.

Complementing its Midtown locale, Del Frisco's showcases a large L-shaped bar with comfortable leather stools and linen-covered tables set against window panels stretching to the second floor. The mezzanine dining area, accessible by a grand sweeping staircase, enjoys a quieter ambience.

Esca

B2

Seafood 🍴🍴🍴

402 W. 43rd St. (bet. Ninth & Tenth Aves.)

Subway: 42 St - Port Authority Bus Terminal
Phone: 212-564-7272
Web: www.esca-nyc.com
Prices: $$$

Mon – Sat lunch & dinner
Sun dinner only

Esca sparkles amid the perpetual motion in this clogged part of Midtown. A rustic retreat, the dining space is awash in creamy yellow under a burgundy ceiling. Wine bottles double as decoration, filling well-planned nooks, crannies, and shelves around the room.

Mario Batali and Joseph Bastianich joined Chef David Pasternack in founding this restaurant, where the day's *antipasti* tempt diners from the front room's farm-style table. *Primi* may include perfectly cooked, homemade black spaghetti with calamari, green chiles, and roasted garlic. As secondi, a daily fresh fish selection waits for you to take the bait—as the name of the restaurant translates. Inspired desserts may feature *torta al limone*, with layers of ethereal sponge cake and Meyer lemon curd.

Estiatorio Milos

Greek 🍴🍴🍴

A3

125 W. 55th St. (bet. Sixth & Seventh Aves.)

Subway: 57 St
Phone: 212-245-7400
Web: www.milos.ca
Prices: $$$

Mon – Fri lunch & dinner
Sat – Sun dinner only

It's not nice to fool Mother Nature, and at Milos, they don't try—they carefully source organic ingredients, so there's no need to do much to improve on them. The concept here is simple: you choose your fish from the fresh-from-the-sea array displayed at the counter, decide how much you want (it's sold by weight), and specify whether you want it to be charcoal-grilled or baked in sea salt. Soon, it will appear at your table, adorned with olive oil and lemon sauce. The Milos Special is the best starter, and deliriously sweet baklava makes the perfect ending.

The cacophonous dining room melds touches of industrial modern with Greek taverna in a bright setting. Prices can be high, but it's still cheaper than a trip to the Greek Islands.

Etcetera Etcetera

Italian 🍴🍴

C2

352 W. 44th St. (bet. Eighth & Ninth Aves.)

Subway: 42 St - Port Authority Bus Terminal
Phone: 212-399-4141
Web: www.etcrestaurant.com
Prices: $$

Tue & Thu – Sat dinner only
Wed & Sun lunch & dinner

Little sister to ViceVersa, Etcetera Etcetera shares the same combination of stylish surroundings and confident, affable service. Like its older sibling, the menu is Italian, but here they add Mediterranean accents. Ravioli filled with veal, raisin, and amaretti, and homemade potato gnocchi are melt-in-your-mouth good.

The Philippe Starck designed plastic chairs in pastel colors to complement the ebony woodwork and the gray ceramic-tile wall in the dining room; modern artwork and sculptures complete the picture. Located just two blocks from The Great White Way, Etcetera Etcetera makes a convenient and pleasant place for a pre- or post-theater meal, and the nightly three-course prix-fixe menu will make your wallet happy.

Firebird

C2

R u s s i a n XXX

365 W. 46th St. (bet. Eighth & Ninth Aves.)

Subway: 42 St - Port Authority Bus Terminal
Phone: 212-586-0244
Web: www.firebirdrestaurant.com
Prices: $$$

Tue – Sun lunch & dinner

Firebird celebrates "pre-Revolutionary" Russia in a decadent Theatre District brownstone replete with ornate Russian art, rare books, jewel-toned furnishings, and crystal lighting. This opulent atmosphere is further enriched by the well-orchestrated formal service team.

The menu lists classic Russian specialties such as borscht, chicken Kiev, and an extensive selection of caviar. The comfortable bar area is a lovely spot to sit back and peruse the encyclopedic vodka listing which represents more than 150 labels from such far-flung locales as China, New Zealand, and Scotland. Start your meal on a sweet note with the *tsartini*, made with honey-infused vodka, then end on one again, sipping strong black tea sweetened with preserved cherries.

44 & X Hell's Kitchen

B2

C o n t e m p o r a r y X

622 Tenth Ave. (at 44th St.)

Subway: 42 St - Port Authority Bus Terminal
Phone: 212-977-1170
Web: www.44andx.com
Prices: $$

Lunch & dinner daily

A corner location with lots of windows lends this restaurant a light and airy feel. When the weather cooperates, tables are set out on the sidewalk under the large, striped awning.

Inside, white and cream tones, molded plastic chairs, and leather banquettes create a cool, contemporary vibe. A quality mix of theatergoers and neighbors makes for a lively atmosphere. Advertising their motto, "a little bit of heaven in Hell's Kitchen," the gracious young staff sports T-shirts emblazoned with "Heaven" on the front and "in Hell" on the back.

American classics take on a 21st-century twist here; buttermilk fried chicken, for instance, comes with a chive waffle, and macaroni and cheese is given sophisticated oomph with Vermont cheddar.

Frankie & Johnnie's

Steakhouse ✕✕

C4

32 W. 37th St. (bet. Fifth & Sixth Aves.)

Subway: 34 St - Herald Sq
Phone: 212-947-8940
Web: www.frankieandjohnnies.com
Prices: $$$

Mon – Fri lunch & dinner
Sat dinner only

This location of the Frankie & Johnnie's steakhouse empire (the first was established in 1926 on West 45th Street) offers diners a little bit of history in the heart of the Garment District. The renovated town house was once the home of John Drew Barrymore. In fact, Barrymore's library, with its coffered ceiling and original fireplace, forms part of the masculine, wood-paneled dining room on the second floor.

Diners with booming baritone voices feel no need to tone down their bonhomie while chowing down on some serious cuts of prime dry-aged beef, but no one seems to mind the din. The all-male brigade of waiters is especially accommodating, and the restaurant even has a limousine service to shuttle guests anywhere in Midtown.

Gallagher's

Steakhouse ✕✕

C2

228 W. 52nd St. (bet. Broadway & Eighth Ave.)

Subway: 50 St (Broadway)
Phone: 212-245-5336
Web: www.gallaghersnysteakhouse.com
Prices: $$$

Lunch & dinner daily

Gallagher's, as they say, is truly "New York City to the bone." Established in 1927 next door to what is now the Neil Simon Theater, this culinary character satisfies carnivores with beef, beef, and more beef. That focus becomes clear as you enter to see rows of assorted cuts of beef hanging in the glass-enclosed meat locker, patiently aging. Inside the wood-paneled dining room, waiters wear gold-trimmed blazers, tables wear red-checked cloths, and walls are lined with photographs of Broadway stars, politicians and athletes of both the human and equine varieties.

While it doesn't come cheap, the beef shows a quality that really stands out. Surf and Turf, with its 10-ounce filet mignon and 8-ounce lobster tail and claws, always wins raves.

Gordon Ramsay at The London ❁ ❁

Contemporary 🍴🍴🍴🍴

A3

151 W. 54th St. (bet. Sixth & Seventh Aves.)

Subway: 57 St
Phone: 212-468-8888
Web: www.gordonramsay.com
Prices: $$$$

Sat – Wed dinner only
Thu – Fri lunch & dinner

©Tom Shelby

International celebrity Chef Gordon Ramsay offers New Yorkers a taste of his talents at his posh dining room located at the London NYC. Tucked off of the less formal space shared by London Bar and Maze, the elegant setting is done in a muted palette of pale celadon and soft grey with opulent appointments that yield an air of refinement indicative of the kitchen's creations. With seating for just 45 guests, attended by a perfectly polished and attractive service team, dining at Gordon Ramsay radiates luxury.

His cooking reflects a passion for the craft and an obsession to detail in offerings like honey and soy roasted quail with sautéed foie gras or a dessert soufflé flavored with pineapple, served with Thai curry ice cream. The chef's artful presentations are a concert of memorable tastes and textures from beginning to end.

Lunchtime offers very good value for the money.

Appetizers

- Cassoulet of Seafood with King Prawn Tortellini
- Foie Gras, Tapioca, Calvados Jelly, Candied Ginger
- Caramelized Calves' Sweetbreads, Pickled Vegetables

Entrées

- Venison Roasted in Cocoa Butter, Braised Cabbage, Bitter Chocolate
- Black Cod with Pigs' Tails and Caraquet Oysters
- Filet of Brandt Beef with Braised Kobe Short Rib

Desserts

- Pineapple Soufflé, Thai-Curry Ice Cream, Toasted Coconut
- Cinnamon Sablé, Lemongrass, Honeycomb
- White Chocolate Ganache, Rum Gelée, Basil Sorbet

Manhattan ▶ Midtown West

Hell's Kitchen

C2

679 Ninth Ave. (bet. 46th & 47th Sts.)

Subway: 50 St (Eighth Ave.)
Phone: 212-977-1588
Web: www.hellskitchen-nyc.com
Prices: $$

Tue – Fri lunch & dinner
Mon & Sat – Sun dinner only

As any New Yorker can tell you, this restaurant's name speaks to the 19th-century moniker for the surrounding neighborhood (between 34th and 59th streets, west of Eighth Avenue). At this hip Mexican eatery, the only thing devilish can be the wait you sometimes have to endure to get a table.

The "progressive Mexican" menu avoids the bland and predictable in favor of robust dishes executed with a true understanding of textures and flavors. Tamarind-marinated filet mignon chalupas and Herradura-cured wild salmon tostadas are light years away from the usual, while corn bread and black-bean purée provide a nice change from the ubiquitous chips and salsa.

A convivial atmosphere prevails in the narrow room, where tables line one side, and a bar lines the other.

Keens Steakhouse

C4

72 W. 36th St. (bet. Fifth & Sixth Aves.)

Subway: 34 St - Herald Sq
Phone: 212-947-3636
Web: www.keens.com
Prices: $$$

Mon – Fri lunch & dinner
Sat – Sun dinner only

This macho palace of steaks and single-malt Scotch has been around since 1885, the lone survivor of the erstwhile Herald Square Theater District. A palpable sense of history pervades the restaurant, which enforced a strict men-only rule until 1901. That's the year British actress Lillie Langtry challenged Keens' discriminatory policy in court, and won. Look up to see the restaurant's impressive collection of long-stemmed clay churchwarden pipes in racks lining the ceiling, another vestige of its men's-club days.

Hearty steaks and chops come in portions—and prices— hefty enough to satisfy the hungriest carnivores. A lighter pub menu of salads, burgers and sandwiches is also available at lunch and dinner.

Insieme ✿

Italian 🍴🍴

A4

777 Seventh Ave. (at 51st St.)

Subway: 50 St (Broadway)
Phone: 212-582-1310
Web: www.restaurantinsieme.com
Prices: $$$

Mon – Fri lunch & dinner
Sat dinner only

Chef and Sommelier co-owners Marco Canora and Paul Grieco offer their talent and skills at this refined uptown dining room, located in the Michelangelo Hotel (*see hotel listing*). The handsome décor is colored in pale earth tones, outfitted with sleek furnishings.

Insieme translates as "together," echoing the dual personality of this Italian menu where traditional items share equal billing with contemporary creations—the five course tasting menu represents each side. The chef's superior pastas include hearty *lasagna verde alla Bolognese* and au courant ramp fettucine with tomato and crabmeat. Entrées like the *zuppa di pesce* evoke the Old World while branzino with baby romaine, white anchovies, and a creamy lemon sauce takes familiar flavors in a new direction.

A passion for wine is evident in the carefully selected, informative, and enjoyable list.

Appetizers
- Asparagi con Uovo
- Hamachi "Affumicato"
- Beef Heart Risotto

Entrées
- Lasagna Verde alla Bolognese
- Zuppa di Pesce
- Branzino "Saltimbocca"

Desserts
- Crostata di Cioccolata
- Citrus Ascension
- Bomboloni

Koi

Fusion ✗✗

C3

40 W. 40th St. (bet. Fifth & Sixth Aves.)

Subway: 42 St - Bryant Pk
Phone: 212-921-3330
Web: www.koirestaurant.com
Prices: $$$

Mon – Fri lunch & dinner
Sat – Sun dinner only

♿

This New York offshoot of the über-trendy flagship in West Hollywood is aptly located in the Bryant Park Hotel, and it's always packed with the young, the restless, and the affluent. The first thing you'll notice is the enormous white lattice canopy that dominates the dining room; underneath it, many of the elements of feng shui have been incorporated into the eye-popping design (with the exception of the pulsating music all day).

The menu is equally à la mode: an extensive choice of sushi, sashimi, and rolls, as well as some original Pan-Asian fare. From the black-clad waitstaff and the chic plating to the A-list crowd, cool is the operative word at Koi. For a hipster's night out on the town, visit the equally trendy Cellar Bar.

La Masseria

Italian ✗✗

C2

235 W. 48th St. (bet. Broadway & Eighth Ave.)

Subway: 50 St (Eighth Ave.)
Phone: 212-582-2111
Web: www.lamasserianyc.com
Prices: $$

Lunch & dinner daily

♿
🍴
🎍
📱

A congenial midtown Italian modeled after the ancient farmhouses of Puglia, La Masseria's décor is portrayed to full effect with exposed wood beams, stucco walls, and generous touches of stone and brick. Despite its scope, the large space retains a hint of intimacy and has a warm, countrified feel that is an interesting contrast to the restaurant's home on the ground floor of a hi-rise apartment tower. The kitchen creates delightfully rustic fare in items like the creamy home-made stuffed fresh mozzarella—simplicity at its very best. Other offerings highlight a comforting, satisfying, Italian-American spirit, as in rigatoni bathed in rich, meaty "traditional Sunday grandmother's sauce."

Landmark Tavern

B2

Contemporary ✗✗

626 Eleventh Ave. (at 46th St.)

Subway: 50 St (Eighth Ave.)
Phone: 212-247-2562
Web: www.thelandmarktavern.org
Prices: $$

Lunch & dinner daily

Opened in 1868, the Landmark Tavern is one of the few original taverns remaining in New York. It's worth trekking to the far reaches of the West Side to experience this heritage restaurant, which still oozes with character.

A recent renovation spiffed up the place, but its aged patina and historical charm rest intact, along with the original speakeasy door and the bar carved from a single piece of mahogany. What has changed is the menu. Forget about corned beef and cabbage or bangers and mash; sophisticated cuisine tempts your taste buds with grilled Thai-marinated cuttlefish salad and lamb shank with cabernet mint *au jus*.

Mandoo Bar

C4

Korean ✗

2 W. 32nd St. (at Fifth Ave.)

Subway: 34 St - Herald Sq
Phone: 212-279-3075
Web: N/A
Prices:

Lunch & dinner daily

The next time you've exhausted yourself looking through the racks at Macy's, head over to Koreatown's Mandoo Bar to rest and refuel. As soon as you spot this tidy restaurant, you'll know its specialty—*mandoo* is the Korean word for "dumpling"—since the large window grants a view of uniformed women busily rolling out and filling circles of dough.

Eight different kinds of silky dumplings (steamed or fried and filled with pork, vegetables, seafood, or tofu) are the real reason to visit this pleasant, if somewhat Spartan, restaurant, but noodle and rice dishes are available too. For a tasty snack, try the Pajeon pancake, pan-fried and filled with squid, mussels, shrimp and vegetables.

The best part? It doesn't cost a lot of dough to eat here.

Le Bernardin ✿✿✿

Seafood 🍴🍴🍴🍴

155 W. 51st St. (bet. Sixth & Seventh Aves.)

Subway: 47-50 Sts - Rockefeller Ctr
Phone: 212-554-1515
Web: www.le-bernardin.com
Prices: $$$$
♿
🐾

Mon – Fri lunch & dinner
Sat dinner only

In a city where chefs change at the drop of a toque, it is remarkable that Le Bernardin has been under the same ownership since it opened in 1986, and that French-born Chef Eric Ripert has headed the kitchen since 1994. Such stability explains the effortless way in which this acclaimed restaurant operates.

A commendable list of 900 wines, spanning the decades from 1945 to the current year, provides an entrée to the prix-fixe menu (there's a chef's tasting too). A master in the treatment of fish, Ripert offers top-notch ingredients, organized under three categories: "almost raw," "barely touched," and "lightly cooked." Articulate preparations boast terrific flavor contrast, as in thin slices of fluke marinated in white soy and yuzu, then sprinkled with crispy puffed rice and briny flakes of seaweed.

At dinner the atmosphere is formal, and men are required to wear jackets.

Appetizers
- Smoked Salmon, Toasted Brioche, Caviar
- Seared Bluefin, Parmesan Crisp, Sun-dried Tomato
- Langoustine Curry with Heart of Palm Meunière and Chutney

Entrées
- Baked Lobster, White Asparagus, Sauce Gribiche
- Black Bass, Iberico Ham-Green Peppercorn Sauce
- Wild Salmon, Water Chestnuts, Pea Tendrils, Gingered Bok Choy

Desserts
- Amedei Chocolate Ganache, Sweet Potato Pearls
- Yogurt Panna Cotta, Red Grapefruit
- Gianduja Cream, Hazelnuts, Honey, Brown Butter Ice Cream

Marseille

C2

French ✗✗

630 Ninth Ave. (at 44th St.)

Subway: 42 St - Port Authority Bus Terminal	Lunch & dinner daily
Phone: 212-333-2323	
Web: www.marseillenyc.com	
Prices: $$	

Sunny yellow and sea-colored turquoise walls, large earthenware vessels, and patterned ceramic tile evoke la Côte d'Azur at this lively Hell's Kitchen brasserie. Wicker chairs and small tables are set up on the sidewalk; inside, large windows overlooking the restaurant's corner spot brighten the room.

The menu meanders through the Mediterranean, with lunch featuring a Niçoise salad, Tunisian chicken, and lamb couscous. Dinnertime offers more extensive entrées, from *goujons* of sole with arugula and endive salad to a short rib daube Provençale served alongside Roman gnocchi. In the center of the room, a mirrored column is stenciled with the selection of wines.

Marseille's location, two blocks west of Times Square, creates constant crowds.

Michael's

Contemporary ✗✗✗

A-B4

24 W. 55th St. (bet. Fifth & Sixth Aves.)

Subway: 57 St	Mon – Fri lunch & dinner
Phone: 212-767-0555	Sat dinner only
Web: www.michaelsnewyork.com	
Prices: $$$	

East Coast expense accounts meet West Coast cooking at this busy Midtown institution. California style infuses the interesting array of American dishes. Chef/owner Michael McCarty, who founded the original Michael's near the beach in Santa Monica in 1979, developed his market-driven menu way before using fresh seasonal fare was fashionable. Enjoy dishes like pan-roasted Atlantic cod and grilled Kurobuta pork chops at lunch or dinner.

In the airy dining room, light pours in from a wall of windows, illuminating the artwork on the peach-tone walls. Favored by media moguls, Michael's gets mobbed at lunchtime, and the waitstaff has to run at a big-city pace. The fact that everyone seems to be a regular here is proof enough that the brigade is up to the task.

Masa ✿✿✿

Japanese XX

C1

10 Columbus Circle (in the Time Warner Center)

Subway: 59 St - Columbus Circle
Phone: 212-823-9800
Web: www.masanyc.com
Prices: $$$$

Tue – Fri lunch & dinner
Mon & Sat dinner only

Welcome to the meal that will give your Mother a heart attack. Not because of its beautiful, soothing setting. Tucked into the 4th floor of the Time Warner Center, Masa is a temple of blond wood and stone. And not because of the service—which is the kind of unhurried, oh-so-on-it approach that lets you savor the moment, but never want for a thing. And certainly, undoubtedly, not for the unparalleled omakase—which, under the expert eye of celebrated Chef Masa Takayama, is a vivid, brilliant parade of otherworldly fish and extraordinary ingredients.

The menu changes nightly, but a fatty toro, minced with sea salt, might appear with a peak of glistening black caviar; or stacks of milky-white *fugu*, served over shiso blossoms, may come dusted with gold flakes. So what, pray tell, is the shocker? That would be the sobering tab at the end—an unprecedented $400 a head.

Appetizers
- Uni Risotto with Seasonal Truffles
- Toro Tartare with Caviar

Entrées
- From November through February Fugu Fish is on the menu prepared as a Sashimi Salad, as Fried Karaage, and as Sushi

Desserts
- From May through August, Hamo Fish is a seasonal item

The Modern

A4

9 W. 53rd St. (bet. Fifth & Sixth Aves.)

Subway:	5 Av - 53 St	Mon – Fri lunch & dinner
Phone:	212-333-1220	Sat dinner only
Web:	www.themodernnyc.com	
Prices:	**$$$**	

Sara Jaye Weiss

Housed in the Museum of Modern Art and operated by restaurant impresario Danny Meyer, the Modern caters to all tastes. The lively and energetic Bar Room is a popular choice for cocktails and a casual meal of small plates while the sophisticated and serene Dining Room, awash with daylight, serves up a commanding view of the Abby Aldrich Rockefeller Sculpture Garden.

The luxurious view is set off with designer tableware and a gracious service team that attends to all diners like VIPs. The sleekly outfitted setting is a fabulous canvas for the work of Alsatian-born Chef Gabriel Kreuther who puts his spin on contemporary cuisine. You'll relish his intriguing ingredients and combinations like Riesling poached foie gras with sweet peas, banana, and almond jus.

The voluminous wine list reflects the chef's heritage with an extensive selection of noteworthy Alsatian labels.

Appetizers

- Almond Panna Cotta with Yellowstone River Caviar
- Escargot, Potato Gâteau, Ginger-Parsley Jus
- Tartare of Yellowfin Tuna with Scallops

Entrées

- Duck Breast, Black Trumpet Marmalade
- Chorizo-crusted Cod, Harissa Oil
- Squab and Foie Gras, Caramelized Ginger Jus

Desserts

- Lemon Napoleon, Fromage Blanc Sorbet
- Pineapple Parfait, Coconut Tapioca
- Hazelnut Dacquoise with Milk Chocolate Chantilly

Molyvos

A3

Greek ✗✗

871 Seventh Ave. (bet. 55th & 56th Sts.)

Subway: 57 St - 7 Av   Lunch & dinner daily
Phone: 212-582-7500
Web: www.molyvos.com
Prices: $$

Part of the Livanos family restaurant empire, which boasts Oceana as its crown jewel, and named for the owner's birthplace on the island of Lesvos, Molyvos brings the home-style dishes of Greece to Midtown.
Chef/partner Jim Botsacos, whose signed cookbook is available for purchase, can claim his fair share of the restaurant's success. Dishes such as *paidakia skharas*, smoky grilled lamb chops served alongside the house potato *kefte* and a wood-grilled eggplant salad, are the reasons why.
A block south of Carnegie Hall, Molyvos is well situated for those attending a performance. Order the modestly priced pre- and post-theater menu (available Monday through Saturday before 7:00P.M. and after 9:30P.M., and all day Sunday) to get in and out in a jiffy.

Nick & Stef's

B4

Steakhouse ✗✗

9 Penn Plaza (bet. Seventh & Eighth Aves.)

Subway: 34 St - Penn Station   Mon – Fri lunch & dinner
Phone: 212-563-4444   Sat dinner only
Web: www.nickandstefs.com
Prices: $$$

Adjacent to Madison Square Garden and Penn Station, Nick & Stef's comes under the umbrella of Chef Joachim Splichal's Patina Restaurant Group, and is named for the chef's twin sons. The menu exhibits good variety for a steakhouse; a selection of seafood entrées, including grilled lobster, shrimp scampi, and jumbo lump crab cakes, balance the list of broiled steaks. The latter are served completely unadorned, so complement your meal with sides of hash browns, mac 'n cheese, or asparagus spears. Lunchtime highlights two burgers, appropriately named "The Nick" and "The Stef."
A suited clientele regularly fills this contemporary space, adorned with angled pine ceilings and warm tones.

Nobu Fifty Seven

A3

40 W. 57th St. (bet. Fifth & Sixth Aves.)

Subway: 57 St
Phone: 212-757-3000
Web: www.noburestaurants.com
Prices: $$$$

Mon – Fri lunch & dinner
Sat – Sun dinner only

Chef Nobu Matsuhisa has done it again, this time in Midtown. Nobu Fifty Seven's entrance may be sandwiched between two office buildings, but David Rockwell's sleek interior design, incorporates sake jugs hanging above the bar, exotic woods and rattan wall coverings. Low lighting creates a sultry mood—not an easy feat in a place as large and busy as this one.

The restaurant pulls in a stylish business crowd whose expense accounts can handle the hefty prices. Specialties include rock shrimp tempura (plump, batter-fried shrimp in a creamy and piquant chile sauce), and black cod with miso, a dish that made Nobu famous.

Creative à la carte offerings feature great variety, but you can always opt for the chef's omakase.

Omido

Japanese X

A3

1695 Broadway (bet. 53rd & 54th Sts.)

Subway: 50 St (Broadway)
Phone: 212-247-8110
Web: www.omidonyc.com
Prices: $$

Mon – Fri lunch & dinner
Sat – Sun dinner only

David Letterman has tickled your funnybone and now you're hungry. Sushi perhaps? Then head straight to Omido. Next to the Ed Sullivan theatre, this sleek cube of a space, encased in slats of dark wood, features a square counter lit overhead by translucent globes.

The selection of top notch sushi is skillfully prepared before your eyes; and in addition, the menu is bolstered by tempting cold and hot dishes, like a seaweed tasting with sesame ponzu, crisp and delicate tempura, or braised Kobe short ribs. At lunchtime, several bento box options are offered. Now for the punchline: the sake list is well chosen, desserts display talent, and the charming service team ensures satisfaction.

Orso

C2

322 W. 46th St. (bet. Eighth & Ninth Aves.)

Subway: 42 St - Port Authority Bus Terminal

Lunch & dinner daily

Phone: 212-489-7212
Web: www.orsorestaurant.com
Prices: $$

A respected member of the Restaurant Row dining fraternity, Orso nestles on the ground floor of a charming brownstone just steps away from the Theater District. As at its two other branches, in Los Angeles and London, the restaurant offers diners a wide choice of Italian fare, running the gamut from pizza and penne to swordfish and sausages.

Dressed in warm pastel shades, tables are set with patterned earthenware. Gracious servers accommodate those who come in for a quick meal before the theater, as well as patrons who are devoting the evening to dining. Star gazers take note: the later you come here, the more likely you are to see an actor from one of the neighboring theaters catching a post-performance bite to eat.

Osteria al Doge

Italian

C3

142 W. 44th St. (bet. Broadway & Sixth Ave.)

Subway: Times Sq - 42 St

Mon – Fri lunch & dinner

Phone: 212-944-3643

Sat – Sun dinner only

Web: www.osteria-doge.com
Prices: $$

Painted in sunny yellow, lit by wrought-iron chandeliers, and decorated with bright Italian ceramics, Osteria al Doge constantly plays to a packed house. The cuisine of Venice takes center stage here, with dishes such as *fegato alla Veneziana* (pan-roasted calves' liver in an onion and red-wine-vinegar sauce), and *brodetto alla Veneziano* (a mélange of seafood and shellfish braised in broth tinged with Pinot Grigio) paying homage to Italy's famous canal-laced city.

Set with linen placemats, fresh flowers, and glasses filled with crisp *grissini*, the long bar makes a comfortable perch for solo diners. Tables dress for dinner in the main room; service is attentive and friendly throughout.

Osteria del Circo

Italian ✗✗

A3

120 W. 55th St. (bet. Sixth & Seventh Aves.)

Subway: 57 St
Phone: 212-265-3636
Web: www.osteriadelcirco.com
Prices: $$$

Mon – Fri lunch & dinner
Sat – Sun dinner only

This Midtown osteria, run by the Maccioni family, explodes with exuberance, as its name would imply. Bright, billowing fabric overhead evokes the big top, a trapeze swings down above the bar, and colorful circus-themed artwork is displayed throughout the room.

Straightforward homemade pasta dishes may include *tagliatelle verdi alla Bolognese* or *pici alla Senese* with fava beans and pecorino cheese, while a hearty grilled ribeye steak or oven-roasted red snapper may be brought tableside for two. Attractively displayed on ice in the dining room, the day's catch bolsters the regular menu. The spotlight falls on Italian labels on the award-winning wine list. The service staff is professional and efficient, while maintaining the charm of this family operation.

Petrossian

French ✗✗✗

A3

182 W. 58th St. (at Seventh Ave.)

Subway: 57 St - 7 Av
Phone: 212-245-2214
Web: www.petrossian.com
Prices: $$$

Lunch & dinner daily

Linger on the sidewalk to marvel at the ornate Renaissance-style 1907 Alwyn Court Building that frames the entrance to Petrossian. Opened in 1984, this is the New York sister to Petrossian Paris, which has been delighting French diners since the 1920s. It was then that the two Petrossian brothers from Armenia made caviar the toast of Paris, and founded the company that now ranks as the premier importer of Russian caviar—the restaurant's specialty.

Located a block from Carnegie Hall, Petrossian showcases ingredients that are as rich as its surroundings, which are adorned with Lalique crystal sconces, etched Erté mirrors and Limoges china. The contemporary French menu, peppered with caviar and foie gras, is perfect for lunch, brunch, or dinner.

Per Se ❀❀❀

C1

Contemporary ⅩⅩⅩⅩⅩ

10 Columbus Circle (in the Time Warner Center)

Subway: 59 St - Columbus Circle
Phone: 212-823-9335
Web: www.perseny.com
Prices: $$$$

Mon – Thu dinner only
Fri – Sun lunch & dinner

Culinary genius in the house: check. Tiny, exquisite dishes fit for a museum: you got it. Odds of getting a reservation: about zero. In fact, the only inapt element to Chef Thomas Keller's critically-acclaimed Per Se might be the location—which happens to be, well, in a mall. A fancy mall, mind you—New York's Time Warner Center is positively jumping with celebrity chef eateries, but certainly not the bucolic Napa environs of his first restaurant, the French Laundry. But you're likely to forget that nagging detail the second you enter the serene, earthy haven that is Per Se.

The restaurant prides itself on precise, detailed service, so arrive early (and gentlemen, wear a jacket) to nurse a glass of wine at the bar and soak in dazzling views of Central Park.

Keller's signature opener—silky, caviar-topped oysters on a bed of tapioca pearls—begins what many contend is one of the finest meals in the country.

Appetizers

- Oysters and Pearls: Pearl Tapioca Sabayon, Island Creek Oysters, White Sturgeon Caviar
- Terrine of Foie Gras, Cauliflower Florettes, English Cucumber, Medjool Date Purée

Entrées

- Macaroni n' Cheese: Butter-poached Lobster, Parmesan Crisp, Mascarpone Orzo
- Calotte De Bœuf Grillée: Bone Marrow, Mushrooms, Asparagus

Desserts

- "Cashel Blue": Pickled Purple Top Turnips, "Purée de Pruneaux d'Agen"
- Chestnut Dacquoise, Whiskey-scented Chocolate Ganache, Vanilla "Icing" with Chestnut Ice Cream

Piano Due

Italian XXX

A4

151 W. 51st St. (bet. Sixth & Seventh Aves.)

Subway: 49 St
Phone: 212-399-9400
Web: www.pianoduenyc.net
Prices: $$$

Mon – Fri lunch & dinner
Sat dinner only

A Midtown office courtyard provides access to this restaurant, which encompasses two separate spaces. First, enter through Palio Bar, which showcases Florentine artist Sandro Chia's mural, depicting Sienna's famed Palio horse race, and envelops the large circular bar room in a riot of vibrant color.

An elevator transports diners to Piano Due on the second floor, where red velvet chairs accent the white walls, and natural light reflects off the vaulted ceiling. Glass objets d'art and colorful artwork add to the refined atmosphere.

At dinner the kitchen's ambition shows up in the likes of a peppercorn-crusted filet mignon; and *pappardelle alla cacciatora*, its sauce blending wild game with a hint of cream, Barolo wine, and bitter chocolate.

Porter House

Steakhouse XXX

C1

10 Columbus Circle (in the Time Warner Center)

Subway: 59 St - Columbus Circle
Phone: 212-823-9500
Web: www.porterhousenewyork.com
Prices: $$$

Lunch & dinner daily

Located in the Time Warner Center, Porter House shares the fourth floor with some impressive neighbors. Even so, Chef Michael Lomonaco's steakhouse sets a standard with top-quality ingredients and attentive service. A commanding view of Central Park is visible from most of the tables in the dining room, designed by Jeffrey Beers using chocolate brown leather, polished cherry, and cool stainless steel accents.

Although thick, juicy steaks and chops form the core of the menu, American seafood enjoys nearly equal billing. Desserts are wonderfully retro, recalling eras past with an ice-cream Sundae, baked Alaska, and classic New York cheesecake.

The extensive roster of wines focuses on the West Coast of the U.S., but remembers well-known European regions.

Remi

A4

Italian   XXX

145 W. 53rd St. (bet. Sixth & Seventh Aves.)

Subway: 7 Av
Phone: 212-581-4242
Web: www.remi-ny.com
Prices: $$

Lunch & dinner daily

Dreams of Venice come to mind when you enter this perennially busy Italian restaurant. Between the Venetian-glass chandelier, the mural of Venice that covers one wall, and the bright sunlight streaming in through the large front windows, there's much to suggest that lovely city. Indeed, *remi* means "oars" in Italian, a reference to the famous canals of Venice.

In keeping with this theme, the food derives much of its influence from the Veneto region. Dishes such as sautéed calf's liver, and ravioli stuffed with tuna are just two of Remi's signature dishes. Homemade pastas are particularly good, but be sure to leave room for *dolci* such as tiramisu and white-chocolate hazelnut semifreddo. Managers run the dining room with a watchful eye.

Russian Samovar

C2

Russian   X

256 W. 52nd St. (bet. Broadway & Eighth Ave.)

Subway: 50 St (Broadway)
Phone: 212-757-0168
Web: www.russiansamovar.com
Prices: $$

Dinner daily

It's no surprise that Russian Samovar borders the Theater District; this restaurant, with its flashy mix of Russian celebrities, bigwigs and hockey players, provides enough entertainment to rival Broadway. The crowd is raucous and the vodka is strong; guests can sample many varieties of the house-infused spirit available by the shot, the carafe or the bottle. Though the décor is one part Old World and one part Russian grandmother, this place shows diners a good time.

The staff can seem standoffish but are helpful even so. Authentic favorites, like crisp chicken Kiev, beef Stroganoff, hearty *pelmeni* (ground veal and beef dumplings in a light chicken broth), and the perfectly prepared blini, provide a taste of Moscow in the middle of Manhattan.

Sardi's

American ✗✗

C2

234 W. 44th St. (bet. Broadway & Eighth Ave.)

Subway:	Times Sq - 42 St
Phone:	212-221-8440
Web:	www.sardis.com
Prices:	$$$

Tue – Sun lunch & dinner

Grand dame of New York's theater-district restaurants, Sardi's has been serving patrons of the Great White Way since the 1920s. Stage-curtain red is the color scheme in the dining room, from the walls to the leather banquettes to the jackets worn by the mature brigade of waiters. And, of course, no self-respecting show-biz star can claim to have made it on Broadway until they see their caricature hanging among the framed portraits that paper Sardi's walls.

Exemplified by "Sardi's Traditions" like cannelloni au gratin, shrimp Sardi (sautéed in garlic sauce), and steak tartare, the American fare here provides ample sustenance to get you through a show. If you prefer to dine after the theater, Sardi's even offers a late supper seating.

Scarlatto

Italian ✗✗

C2

250 W. 47th St. (bet. Broadway & Eighth Ave.)

Subway:	50 St (Eighth Ave.)
Phone:	212-730-4535
Web:	www.scarlattonyc.com
Prices:	$$

Lunch & dinner daily

Conveniently located in the Theatre District, enjoyable cooking abounds at this neighborhood favorite. The likes of fork-tender *ossobuco d'agnello* with caramelized onions and stewed lentils tempt passersby, locals, and show-goers seeking fine Italian dining. The room is light and airy with pale stone accents, linen-covered tables, ivory leather seats, and exposed brick walls, featuring movie stills from the film *Roman Holiday*. Chef Roberto Passon's vast menu may feature antipasti specials like thin slices of grilled eggplant filled with finely diced prosciutto, arranged neatly beneath a layer of thick, well-seasoned tomato sauce. The generous pasta listing may include fresh fettucine with wild mushrooms and white truffle olive oil.

The Sea Grill

D2

Seafood ✕✕

19 W. 49 St. (bet. Fifth & Sixth Aves.)

Subway: 47-50 Sts - Rockefeller Ctr
Phone: 212-332-7610
Web: www.rapatina.com/seaGrill
Prices: $$$

Mon – Fri lunch & dinner
Sat dinner only

You'll descend in an elevator like a deep-sea diver down to this Rockefeller Center seafood emporium, where the blues and beiges of the stylish décor capture the colors of the sand and sea. You can enjoy the Sea Grill's magical setting overlooking Rock Center's skating rink (open October to April). Large windows peer out over the ice, where golden lights sparkle at night. In summer, the rink's space is filled with umbrella-shaded tables.

Offerings include everything from oysters and clams from the seafood bar to roasted whole fish and seafood prepared *a la plancha* (on a traditional cast-iron griddle). Whatever you choose, you'll savor a daily changing selection of fish and shellfish, fresh off the boat. Sides are sized for sharing.

Shelly's

B3

Italian ✕✕

41 W. 57th St. (bet. Fifth & Sixth Aves.)

Subway: 57 St
Phone: 212-245-2422
Web: www.shellysnewyork.com
Prices: $$

Lunch & dinner daily

There's something for everyone at this relaxed and casual crowd pleaser. Shelly's Italian menu runs the gamut from slow-braised lamb osso bucco, toothsome seafood risotto, and thin-crusted pizzas topped with San Marzano tomatoes, to a selection of *pesce* flown in daily. The raw bar displays sparkling offerings and is cleverly set up near the entrance to tempt arriving diners and passersby alike.

The brunch menu serves up the likes of chocolate chip French toast and includes an eye-opening cocktail. Shelly's convenient midtown location does not relegate its popularity solely to the work week. The slender, attractive room features burgundy banquettes and polished wood accents. The professional and friendly staff ensures a fulfilling experience.

South Gate

Contemporary 🍴🍴🍴

A3

154 Central Park South (bet. Sixth & Seventh Aves.)

Lunch & dinner daily

Subway: 57 St
Phone: 212-484-5120
Web: www.154southgate.com
Prices: $$$

Located in the newly refurbished art-deco jewel that is the Jumeirah Essex House, the hotel's new dining room is spectacular in its own right. A sexy vibe permeates the light and airy space, furnished with buff-colored swivel chairs, leather padded tables, and a wall clad in facetted panels of mirrored glass. The sleek bar area is accented with see-through columns displaying spirits and offers plenty of counter space for a comfortable solo meal or canoodling couple. Inspired by its posh Central Park location, the menu follows suit with an urbane take on seasonal cuisine in such dishes as flan of spring peas with morels and prosciutto, butter-poached lobster with kimchi, and cider-roasted apple crumble. Genuinely gracious service ensures a gratifying experience.

Staghorn Steakhouse

Steakhouse 🍴🍴

B3

315 W. 36th St. (bet. Eighth & Ninth Aves.)

Mon – Fri lunch & dinner
Sat dinner only

Subway: 34 St - Penn Station
Phone: 212-239-4390
Web: www.staghornsteakhouse.com
Prices: $$$

Shrimp cocktail, Caesar salad, baked clams, creamed spinach, onion rings and aged prime steak: there's a reason the oldies-but-goodies never go out of style. Staghorn Steakhouse is the place to go when visions of filet mignon and veal chops dance in your head.

Pay no attention to the Garment District location close to Penn Station and the Javits Center—although it's great for hungry conventioneers. Inside, the dining room eschews dark and clubby for a black and tan color scheme warmed by light wood floors and a handsome bar.

The staff is well dressed, professional and friendly. Be sure to ask your server about the daily specials, as well as wines available by the glass, since the menu only lists bottles and half-bottles.

Sugiyama

C1

Japanese ✕

251 W. 55th St. (bet. Broadway & Eighth Ave.)

Subway: 57 St - 7 Av
Phone: 212-956-0670
Web: www.sugiyama-nyc.com
Prices: $$$

Tue – Sat dinner only

When you walk into Sugiyama, the first thing you'll notice is the cloud of smoke rising from the red-hot stones on the tabletops, where beef or seafood are cooking. Welcome to the world of *kaiseki*, a traditional Japanese dining experience that ignites your taste buds with a parade of small dishes having an amazing richness and depth of flavor. If there's a time to splurge, this is it. Put yourself in chef Nao Sugiyama's hands and allow his talent to wow you.

Waiters explain the dishes and the concept; all you have to do is decide how many courses your appetite or wallet can accommodate. Reserve a space at the counter, where you can interact with the personable chefs and take in all the action. This is unquestionably the best seat in the house.

Sushi Jun

C2

Japanese ✕

302 W. 50th St. (at Eighth Ave.)

Subway: 50 St (Eighth Ave.)
Phone: 212-315-4800
Web: N/A
Prices: $$

Mon – Fri lunch & dinner
Sat – Sun dinner only

Sushi Jun proves the adage that good things come in small packages. This sliver of a restaurant, located on the ground floor of a Midtown tower, has just four tables and a small bar with seating for up to eight customers. What this place lacks in size it more than makes up for in substance, delivering some of the freshest and tastiest sushi around.

Chef Jun mans the sushi bar alongside two other sushi chefs who plate the rolls and sashimi on attractive pottery and sleek porcelain dishes. Fish is the focus, but sparkling clear clam soup, and vegetarian *namasu* illustrate the diversity of the dishes. You can order à la carte, or tuck into the sushi deluxe, which offers a market-based sampling that might include tuna, salmon, eel and fluke.

Sushi of Gari 46

Japanese ✗✗

C2

347 W. 46th St. (bet. Eighth & Ninth Aves.)

Subway: Times Sq - 42 St
Phone: 212-957-0046
Web: www.sushiofgari.com
Prices: **$$$**

Tue – Fri lunch & dinner
Sat dinner only

Chef Masatoshi "Gari" Sugio struts his stuff at the third in his mini-empire of sushi restaurants, this one on Restaurant Row in the Theater District. Here, he reels in fans of fantastically fresh and diverse sushi (think salmon with tomato; bluefin toro with tofu). The best seats in the house are at the sushi bar, where you can watch the chef perform his magic while you indulge in the day's *omakase*.

Count on consistency in piece after piece of splendid sushi, which hit their highest notes in the chef's 130 signature creations (there is no printed list; ask the chefs, if you're not familiar with Gari's cuisine).

A note for sake fans: the blended sakes available at Gari's other two restaurants are also available here.

Sushi Zen

Japanese ✗✗

C3

108 W. 44th St. (bet. Broadway & Sixth Ave.)

Subway: 42 St - Bryant Pk
Phone: 212-302-0707
Web: www.sushizen-ny.com
Prices: **$$$**

Mon – Fri lunch & dinner
Sat dinner only

Sushi Zen's soothing and peaceful interior is a pleasant contrast to its high-traffic, albeit convenient, Midtown locale. High ceilings, lots of natural light, and a sidewalk dining area made private by potted greenery and fabric panels are sure to create a sense of calm in this immaculate, well-run sushi-ya. Sit, take a breath, and let Chef/owner Toshio Suzuki stimulate your senses with his artfully prepared sushi and sashimi. Also discover a host of rolls; some traditional, like plum paste with shiso, and some original, like the Connecticut roll with eel and avocado. To best experience the chef's handiwork, order the omakase, which is based on the number of dishes you prefer. Accompany meals with a selection from the impressive sake collection.

Manhattan ▶ Midtown West

271

Taboon

C1   Middle Eastern 🍴

773 Tenth Ave. (at 52nd St.)

Subway: 50 St (Eighth Ave.)	Mon – Sat dinner only
Phone: 212-713-0271	Sun lunch & dinner
Web: N/A	
Prices: $$	

With its car dealerships and industrial spaces, Tenth Avenue in Midtown may lack the personality of many other New York neighborhoods, but it's worth visiting just for a meal at Taboon. This inviting Middle Eastern restaurant, named for its crackling wood-burning brick oven (*taboon* in Arabic), adds character to an otherwise barren street in Hell's Kitchen.

Taboon is that rare restaurant ideal for those dining alone or in groups. Meals begin with heavenly flatbreads, slathered with olive oil, sprinkled with rosemary and sea salt, and brought to the table still warm from the oven; fresh *tzatziki* serves as a sparkling accompaniment. Middle Eastern accents enliven delicious dishes, from a salad of red-wine-braised octopus to lamb osso buco.

Toloache

C2   Mexican 🍴🍴

251 W. 50th St. (bet. Broadway & Eighth Ave.)

Subway: 50 St (Broadway)	Lunch & dinner daily
Phone: 212-581-1818	
Web: www.toloachenyc.com	
Prices: $$	

♿

This festive Theatre-District newcomer, pronounced toh-lo-AH-tchay, features hacienda-inspired décor with dark wood, terra-cotta flooring, and hand-painted tile accents. Although the lively bar offers more than 100 tequilas, the talented kitchen commands your attention. Diners can choose a table in the two-story room, but a spot at the Ceviche Bar seats guests where morsels of fish are mixed with aromatics, guacamole is prepared in lava stone bowls, and bubbling hot quesadillas emerge from the brick oven. Grazing through the menu's handmade tacos and small plates is tempting, but save room for the likes of the highly enjoyable and flavorful chile relleno, stuffed with spinach and cheese, completed by dried fruit *picadillo*.

Town

Contemporary XXX

B4

15 W. 56th St. (bet. Fifth & Sixth Aves.)

Subway: 57 St
Phone: 212-582-4445
Web: www.townnyc.com
Prices: $$$

Sun – Fri lunch & dinner
Sat dinner only

At the Chambers Hotel *(see hotel listing)*, "a night on the town" translates as a meal at the property's stylish restaurant, located downstairs from the lobby bar. The understated yet hip décor, designed by David Rockwell in blond woods and cascades of beads, appeals to Gotham fashionistas and well-heeled tourists. Town opened in 2001 as the first independent venture of Chef Geoffrey Zakarian.

Modern and healthy cuisine depends on market availability, influencing menu selections that could include grilled sea bass served over artichoke leaves, or fresh asparagus salad. Many of the dishes are presented in a colorful neo-Californian style. Service is well-timed and courteous at this serious restaurant.

Trattoria Dell'Arte

Italian XX

A3

900 Seventh Ave. (bet. 56th & 57th Sts.)

Subway: 57 St - 7 Av
Phone: 212-245-9800
Web: www.trattoriadellarte.com
Prices: $$

Lunch & dinner daily

The nose knows. Take your cue from the much-larger-than-life nose sculpture that tops the entrance to Trattoria Dell'Arte. Designed as an idiosyncratic artist's studio, the interior exhibits unfinished paintings, sculptural body parts, and a gallery of works depicting Italian noses. The trattoria, bigger than it first appears, sits opposite Carnegie Hall, a location that assures the restaurant's constant buzz.

A long antipasto bar teems with assorted seafood, cured meats, and cheeses, while the menu offers a substantial selection of Italian favorites from *pappardelle* to *pesce*. Tasty pizza choices include *d'aragosta*, topped with a one-pound lobster, tomatoes, and mozzarella. Confident service adds to the contagiously exuberant air of the place.

273

21 Club

American 🍴🍴

21 W. 52nd St. (bet. Fifth & Sixth Aves.)

Subway: 5 Av - 53 St
Phone: 212-582-7200
Web: www.21club.com
Prices: $$$

Mon – Fri lunch & dinner
Sat dinner only

A dowager among New York City restaurants, the 21 Club started as a speakeasy during Prohibition. In the 1950s, the club debuted in its first film, *All About Eve*. Since then, the restaurant has starred in a multitude of movies, as well as playing host to a galaxy of stars, including Humphrey Bogart, Frank Sinatra, and Helen Hayes.

With its dim lighting and once-secret wine cellar (in a basement vault in the building next door), 21 Club still exudes a clandestine air. It's a place for power brokers, and the presence of a Bloomberg terminal in the lounge reminds guests that, in New York, money is big business. It's not a surprise that a jacket is required at this restaurant.

Cuisine sticks to the tried and true; 21 Classics, including the burger favored by Ari Onassis, provide the best traditional experience.

Utsav

Indian 🍴

1185 Sixth Ave. (entrance on 46th St.)

Subway: 47-50 Sts - Rockefeller Ctr
Phone: 212-575-2525
Web: www.utsavny.com
Prices: ⊜

Lunch & dinner daily

Don't let the plain bar area mislead you; climb the carpeted stairs to the upstairs dining room and you'll discover a posh formal setting, hovering above the 46th Street fray in an elevated bridge between two Manhattan office buildings. In this airy room, billowing fabric covers the ceiling, and leafy green plants soak up natural light from floor-to-ceiling windows.

Those in the know come for the bounteous lunch buffet (noon to 3pm daily), laden with a variety of meat (fish curry, tandoori chicken) and vegetable dishes (*daal bukhari*), plus salads, condiments, naan and dessert. Theatergoers can take advantage of the Broadway Special, a three-course pre-theater dinner (with a choice of appetizer, entrée and dessert) for less than $30.

ViceVersa

Italian ✗✗

C1

325 W. 51st St. (bet. Eighth & Ninth Aves.)

Subway: 50 St (Eighth Ave.)
Phone: 212-399-9291
Web: www.viceversarestaurant.com
Prices: $$

Mon – Fri lunch & dinner
Sat dinner only

Run by the experienced team of three Italian gents who cut their teeth at the venerable San Domenico on Central Park South (now closed), ViceVersa (pronounced VEE-chay versa) celebrates *la dolce vita*. The restaurant fashions an urbane ambience in its earth-tone dining space, highlighted by a zinc bar and softly lit wall alcoves displaying terra-cotta urns. Locals love the enclosed back terrace for summer dining.

Approachable fixed-price menus complement extensive à la carte offerings, all of which come to the table in artful array. Pastas are consistently good, and entrées (breadcrumb-and-caper-coated veal tenderloin; pistachio-crusted halibut) show a deft hand. Desserts, perhaps a bitter chocolate parfait with coconut truffle filling, prove irresistible.

West Bank Café

American ✗✗

B2

407 W. 42nd St. (bet. Ninth & Tenth Aves.)

Subway: 42 St - Port Authority Bus Terminal
Phone: 212-695-6909
Web: www.westbankcafe.com
Prices: $$

Lunch & dinner daily

Open for some 30 years, the West Bank Café is clearly doing something right. Located on the edge of the Theater District, this standby blends Italian influences with American know-how. Tasty selections might include refreshing tuna tartare, and homemade pappardelle topped with spicy sausage, tomato sauce and Greek yogurt.

From the framed windows and the pleasant jazz tunes piped in the background to the leather banquettes and soft lighting, the look is classic bistro. Though it attracts a larger and livelier crowd in the evenings, the West Bank Café makes an ideal choice for lunch as well. There's even a brunch menu featuring breakfast favorites ranging from eggs Benedict to brioche French toast, in addition to sandwiches and salads.

Yakitori Totto

Japanese ✗

C1

251 W. 55th St. (bet. Seventh & Eighth Aves.)

Subway: 59 St - Columbus Circle   Dinner daily
Phone: 212-245-4555
Web: N/A
Prices: $$$

Far from the offerings of New York City's ubiquitous hot-dog carts, yakitori is one of the most popular street foods of Japan. The term refers to a style of grilled meat, mainly chicken, that is marinated in a soy-based sauce and then cooked on a smoky charcoal grill. The result is tender, juicy and tasty morsels, many presented on skewers. Not for the faint of stomach, unconventional selections—chicken knees, bleeding chicken hearts on a stick, and chicken sashimi—are all specialties of the house.

Enjoy the sounds of Japanese pop and sultry jazz while you discover delectable treasures. Although the restaurant is well staffed, don't expect hovering service. Japanese culture dictates that servers stand back and wait to be summoned by patrons.

The ✿ award is the crème de la crème. This is awarded to restaurants which are really special for their cuisine.

MICHELIN ATLASES
Let your imagination take you away.

Get the most from your traveling with Michelin atlases
• Detailed road network coverage, updated annually
• Unique atlas format designed for the way you drive
• Route-planning made easy for business and leisure

www.michelintravel.com

SoHo & Nolita

The heart of Manhattan's downtown fashion scene, SoHo—short for South of Houston—is New York at its trendiest. Visitors flock to the district **(bound by West, Houston, Lafayette and Canal streets)** on weekends, when walking down the sidewalk is difficult given the proliferation of tables full of purses and jewelry, sunglasses and scarves, and "outsider" art. The restaurant scene here is as varied as SoHo itself and includes everything from pricey designer-decorated restaurants to tiny, decidedly un-trendy eateries.

Nolita (for North of Little Italy), Little Italy's über-fashionable sister, sits within that quarter's former limits; it stretches from Kenmare to Houston streets on Mulberry, Mott, and Elizabeth streets. The moniker Nolita came courtesy of real-estate developers, who in the 1990s wanted to distinguish it from the red-sauce joints of the old neighborhood. Today Nolita is chock-a-block with chic cafes that are ideal for people-watching.

THE CACHET OF COMMERCIALISM

Site of the first free black community in Manhattan, SoHo was settled in 1644 by former slaves of the Dutch West India Company, who were granted land for farms. In the early 19th century, Broadway was paved and a number of prominent citizens—including author James Fenimore Cooper—moved in, bringing cachet to the district. In the late 1850s, stores such as Tiffany & Co. and Lord & Taylor were joined on Broadway by grand hotels. Theaters, casinos, and brothels entertained visitors—and drove respectable middle-class families uptown. The exodus made room in the late 1800s for a slew of new warehouses and factories, many built with ornamented cast-iron façades that resembled carved stone. The area thrived as a commercial center until the 1890s, when fashionable businesses began relocating to Fifth Avenue.

ART BRINGS A NEW START

By the late 1950s the neighborhood was a slum known as "Hell's Hundred Acres," and city planners slated it for demolition to make room for an expressway until residents objected. Often in violation of building codes, painters and sculptors converted vacant warehouses into studios, galleries, and living quarters. An underground art scene took root and thrived until the early 1980s, when uptown galleries, boutiques, and affluent professionals began to push out the very artists who'd made the neighborhood so desirable.

Today few artists can afford to live or work in SoHo, and the migration of galleries northward to Chelsea continues. Locally owned boutiques have been largely supplanted by international couturiers, making SoHo a Mecca for moneyed fashionistas. Overflowing with traffic, pedestrians, and sidewalk vendors, **Broadway** is SoHo at its most commercial. Broadway's west end ranks as the neighborhood's premier corridor for fashion and art as well as dining.

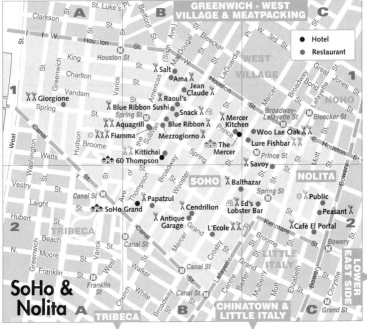

Ama

 B1

48 MacDougal St. (bet. Houston & Prince Sts.)

Subway: Spring St (Sixth Ave.)
Phone: 212-358-1707
Web: www.amanyc.com
Prices: $$

Mon – Thu dinner only
Fri – Sun lunch & dinner

Soft contrasts create a subtle and romantic atmosphere apropos to a restaurant which derives its name from the Italian word for love. A rustic yet sophisticated charm is enhanced with warm white walls, antique white wood floors, white paper covered tabletops, simple blond wood chairs and paneling, and amber track lights reflecting off a mirror lining one wall. Close set tables and two long banquettes along either wall further enhance the intimate feel in the narrow dining room. A ceiling fresco of pink blossoms and bushy green arrangements sitting atop the bar and in the cozy lounge area near the picture window adds welcome touches of the outdoors.

Fresh, Puglian influences reign on a menu offering house-made pasta dishes, antipasti, and secondi.

Antique Garage

 B2

41 Mercer St. (bet. Broome & Grand Sts.)

Subway: Canal St (Broadway)
Phone: 212-219-1019
Web: www.antiquegaragesoho.com
Prices:

Lunch & dinner daily

The name of this place tells you just what to expect: it's set in a former auto-repair garage converted to an antique store/restaurant. Filled with antique furniture, china and light fixtures—many of which are for sale—the cozy dining room feels more like a little country restaurant than a chic SoHo eatery. Seating is at tiny tables, or on low sofas, with coffee tables in between.

The food is the only thing notably Turkish here, and it's quite authentic and packed with flavor. Eggplant salad, grilled Turkish meatballs made with ground lamb and beef, and Mediterranean shrimp could be ordered as a meze selection to share or as progressive courses. Mint lemonade is freshly squeezed, and they brew an excellent cup of heady Turkish coffee.

Aquagrill

Seafood ✗✗

B1

210 Spring St. (at Sixth Ave.)

Subway: Spring St (Sixth Ave.)   Lunch & dinner daily
Phone: 212-274-0505
Web: www.aquagrill.com
Prices: $$

From the staggering selection of oysters at the raw bar to simple grilled fish, Jeremy and Jennifer Marshall's establishment aims to please all seafood lovers. The husband-and-wife team divides up the work here: Chef Jeremy watches over the kitchen while Jennifer oversees the dining room—decorated with lamps made of seashells.

The chef treats his fresh supplies with due deference, sometimes adding subtle Asian accents to enhance the preparations. Clever combinations, like falafel-crusted salmon are a hallmark of Aquagrill. Brunch is a real treat on weekends and lunch is always busy; but it's at dinner that the kitchen staff really struts their stuff. Service is smoothly choreographed, and an air of New York ambiance pervades

Balthazar

French ✗

B-C2

80 Spring St. (bet. Broadway & Crosby St.)

Subway: Spring St (Lafayette St.)   Lunch & dinner daily
Phone: 212-965-1414
Web: www.balthazarny.com
Prices: $$$

As one of the city's first French bistros, Balthazar reigns unrivaled for its authentic ambience, constantly animated by lively conversation. All the requisite late-19th-century Paris décor elements are here (red leatherette banquettes, mosaic tile floors), along with an eclectic crowd that runs from trendsetters to tourists. Part of Keith McNally's restaurant empire, Balthazar is still where the cool crowd hangs.

As for the menu, it's classic bistro; products are fresh, dishes are well prepared, and specials correspond to the day of the week. Baskets piled with fresh breads (baked at the restaurant's own bakery) and the shellfish towers are both as impressive to look at as they are to eat. Spilling out of a paper cone, the crispy frites are a must.

Blue Ribbon

B1

97 Sullivan St. (bet. Prince & Spring Sts.)

Subway: Spring St (Sixth Ave.)   Dinner daily
Phone: 212-274-0404
Web: www.blueribbonrestaurants.com
Prices: $$$

It's for good reason that the Blue Ribbon family is now liberally fanned across the city. Meet the catalyst for it all— Blue Ribbon Brasserie, a New York classic tucked into Soho's Sullivan Street. The restaurant's warm, engaging staff is a luxury in a neighborhood more inclined to make you feel plain than cherished—which is interesting, considering Blue Ribbon has its own celebrity following. Namely, the city's chef circuit, which regularly swings through the doors post-shift (the kitchen serves until 4:00A.M.) to indulge in fresh-off-the-boat shellfish and honestly-rendered comfort classics like grilled striped bass, flaky to the fork, and resting on a bright medley of summer vegetables; or a bright trio of fresh sorbet, served with a spoon and a smile.

Blue Ribbon Sushi

B1

119 Sullivan St. (bet. Prince & Spring Sts.)

Subway: Spring St (Sixth Ave.)   Lunch & dinner daily
Phone: 212-343-0404
Web: www.blueribbonrestaurants.com
Prices: $$

A few doors down from its sister, Blue Ribbon, the equally popular Blue Ribbon Sushi bears a sign so discreet you'd think they were trying to keep the place a secret. Inside the cozy, compact room, the chefs jostle for space to prepare their specialties behind the sushi counter.

Divided into sections by ocean (Atlantic and Pacific), the extensive menu of sushi is impressive and the fish supreme quality (especially the daily specials). Chef Toshi Ueki has serious technique and the caliber is impressive given the rest of the menu ranging from rock shrimp tempura to spicy tuna maki and all that faff. If you're going for dinner, be sure to get there early; the no-reservations policy means the restaurant fills up quickly.

Café El Portal

Mexican ✗

C2

174 Elizabeth St. (bet. Kenmare & Spring Sts.)

Subway: Spring St. (Lafayette St.)   Mon – Sat lunch & dinner
Phone: 212-226-4642
Web: N/A
Prices: ⊜⊜

There is something comforting about a place that doesn't try to compete with its fancy neighbors. In an area known for being a fashionista's Mecca, Cafe El Portal defies Nolita's hipper-than-thou vibe with its low-key design and casual ambience. Despite its less than impressive digs, this restaurant serves up some of the most authentic Mexican dishes in the city. Everything is made in-house at the tiny family-run place, from the fantastic tortillas to the piquant salsas.

The tiny bar boasts a tequila collection with more bottles than the restaurant has seats, and the cocktail menu goes well beyond your run-of-the-mill margarita. Reasonable prices and hearty portions are just a couple more reasons why locals love El Portal.

Cendrillon

Asian ✗

B2

45 Mercer St. (bet. Broome & Grand Sts.)

Subway: Canal St (Broadway)   Tue – Sun lunch & dinner
Phone: 212-343-9012
Web: www.cendrillon.com
Prices: $$

All too often, fusion cuisine merely reflects where the chef took his last vacation, but at this roomy SoHo restaurant, a real understanding of Asian culinary culture underscores the cooking. With Filipino cooking at its core, Cendrillon surprises with zesty and vivacious flavors, guaranteed to cheer the most sullen taste buds. Noodle dishes and Asian barbecue compete with tantalizing entrées, like grilled oxtail and salt-roasted duck. Although portion size is on the generous side, you'll definitely want to leave room for dessert. Check out the impressive selection of exotic Asian teas to round out your meal.

Like the fairy tale from which its name derives (*Cendrillon* is French for "Cinderella"), Cendrillon assures diners of a happy ending.

Ed's Lobster Bar

Seafood

C2

222 Lafayette St. (bet. Kenmare & Spring Sts.)

Subway: Spring St. (Lafayette St.)
Phone: 212-343-3236
Web: www.lobsterbarnyc.com
Prices: $$

Tue – Sun lunch & dinner

Finally East Siders have a simple seafood spot to call their own without having to trek to Mary's Fish Camp or Pearl Oyster Bar. It's not quite a shack, though it's certainly casual with its New England-style décor and inviting marble bar.
Ed McFarland (an alumna of Pearl) is throwing his hat in the "best lobster roll" ring, where his version deftly competes. Lobster meat piled on a bun slathered with butter, accompanied by perfect fries and Ed's pickles, brightens any stormy day. The kitchen is equally skilled with other sea creatures, and daily specials feature the freshest catch. Wines and beers harmonize with the saltwater menu. Though Ed's doesn't accept reservations, with a little more lobster to go around, the wait won't hurt so much.

Giorgione

Italian

A1

307 Spring St. (bet. Greenwich & Hudson Sts.)

Subway: Spring St (Sixth Ave.)
Phone: 212-352-2269
Web: N/A
Prices: $$

Mon – Fri & Sun lunch & dinner
Sat dinner only

All the buzz occurs inside rather than outside Giorgione, given its location on a quiet block in SoHo. Giorgio DeLuca (of Dean & DeLuca) owns this lively place, which you enter via the sleek bar. The narrow space continues, lined with chrome tables, white-leather seats and ice-blue walls that contribute to the cool vibe. Staff may be young and hip but don't give a whiff of attitude.
A cool, downtown crowd drops in for a select menu of terrific oven-fired pizzas, pastas, and fresh catch from the oyster bar. After dinner, you'll find it difficult to resist the sweet temptations of simple *dolci* with a perfectly brewed espresso .

Fiamma ❀

Italian 🍴🍴🍴

B1

206 Spring St. (bet. Sixth Ave. & Sullivan St.)

Subway: Spring St (Sixth Ave.)   Tue – Sat dinner only
Phone: 212-653-0100
Web: www.fiammarestaurant.com
Prices: $$$$

Courtesy of the Glass Restaurant Group

Stephen Hanson's sleek, carefully-appointed Fiamma, is on the gourmand's radar once again. The booster shot? A well-received debut by celebrated European chef, Fabio Trabocchi, who crossed the river to take over Fiamma's kitchen in late 2007. Trabocchi's specialty is turning Italian staples into symphonies of intricate flavors.

Dinner is served prix fixe style only (3 courses start at $85, and move upwards from there), and might include an impossibly thin cannelloni, plump with succulent lump crab meat; or a perfectly-seared trout floating in a lemony broth, pocked with chanterelles and fennel. For a final act, look for the creamy mascarpone panna cotta, laced with delicate honey gelato. Paired with a bitingly honest Sicilian red? *Finito.*

Appetizers	*Entrées*	*Desserts*
• "Il Crudo": Ahi Tuna, Pine Island Oysters, Fiore di Sale, Meyer Lemon	• Pasta Con Le Sarde: Bucatini, Aglio Olio, Calabrese Chiles, Sea Urchin, Sardine Gratin	• "La Panna Cotta": Mascarpone Panna Cotta, Corbezzolo-Honey Gelato, Date Purée
• "La Misticanza": Salad of Castelfranco Radicchio, Fried Organic Egg, La Quercia Prosciutto	• "La Porchetta": Roasted Bev Farm Ossabaw Pig, Violet Artichokes, Dill, Pancetta	• "Il Cioccolato": Amedei Chocolate, Nepitella Gelato, Basil Froth, Pistachio

285

Jean Claude

French 🍴

B1

137 Sullivan St. (bet. Houston & Prince Sts.)

Subway: Spring St (Sixth Ave.)   Dinner daily
Phone: 212-475-9232
Web: N/A
Prices: $$

Just add a plume of Gauloise smoke, and this little bistro could be on the Left Bank in Paris instead of planted in the heart of SoHo. Simply decorated with wine bottles and Gallic-themed posters, the dining room sports a lively, yet romantic, atmosphere—complete with French music playing in the background. Brown paper covers white linens on tables that snuggle so close together that if you like the looks of your neighbor, it wouldn't be difficult to start up a conversation about the tasty, classic French fare.

If you don't mind eating early, you won't need oodles of the green stuff to afford the inexpensive, three-course, fixed-price dinner menu (offered from 6:00 to 7:30 P.M., Monday through Thursday).

Kittichai

Thai 🍴🍴

B1

60 Thompson St. (bet. Broome & Spring Sts.)

Subway: Spring St (Sixth Ave.)   Lunch & dinner daily
Phone: 212-219-2000
Web: www.kittichairestaurant.com
Prices: $$$

Located in the fashionable Sixty Thompson Hotel *(see hotel listing)*, this sensual SoHo newcomer offers toned-down Thai cooking, thanks to chef Ian Chalermkittichai, who came to New York from the Four Seasons Hotel in Bangkok.

The food is as appealing as this exotic setting, where orchids float in bottles on lighted shelves, lush silk fabrics and Thai artifacts adorn the walls, and a reflecting pool forms the centerpiece of the dining room. Appetizers and entrées are modern and approachable, balancing European technique with New York accents and Thai inflections. Black-clad waiters can help you sort out which is which.

At times, the food seems more fusion than Thai, as the chopsticks on the table and the sashimi-style appetizers suggest.

L'Ecole 😊

B2

French ✕✕

462 Broadway (at Grand St.)

Subway: Canal St (Broadway)
Phone: 212-219-3300
Web: www.frenchculinary.com
Prices: $$

Mon – Fri lunch & dinner
Sat dinner only

If you want to be a guinea pig, this is the place to do it. The restaurant associated with The French Culinary Institute provides the opportunity for its students to show off what they've learned. They've certainly mastered the first rule of good cooking: use the best ingredients you can find and don't mess around too much with a good thing.

The kitchen earns top marks for its four- or five-course dinner menus, and the prix-fixe lunch menu is a great—and inexpensive—way to sample the flavorful regional French fare, which changes every six weeks. A conscientious student waitstaff caters to customers in a soothing yellow room decorated with photographs depicting the bustling world of a restaurant kitchen.

Lure Fishbar

C1

Seafood ✕✕

142 Mercer St. (bet. Houston & Prince Sts.)

Subway: Prince St
Phone: 212-431-7676
Web: www.lurefishbar.com
Prices: $$$

Lunch & dinner daily

If your credit card's not maxed out from visiting the Prada shop above this restaurant, Lure Fishbar makes a great place to drop anchor. It's decked out in a fantastic tiki-trendy style with angular porthole windows, semi-circular booths, teak paneling and tropical-print fabrics, reminiscent of a luxury ocean liner. The only thing missing from the maritime motif is the sound of waves crashing and the feel of sand between your toes.

Have a seat at the sushi bar and order a sushi-sashimi combo, or sit at the raw bar to share a shellfish plateau (in sizes small, medium and large). In the main dining room, you can net one of the fresh catches, which are as pleasing to the eye as they are to the palate. Just one visit and you'll be hooked.

Mercer Kitchen

B1

99 Prince St. (at Mercer St.)

Subway: Prince St
Phone: 212-966-5454
Web: www.jean-georges.com
Prices: $$

Lunch & dinner daily

When it opened in the basement of SoHo's Mercer Hotel *(see hotel listing)*, Mercer Kitchen took a position at the head of the culinary new wave. Today the restaurant, which owes its existence to wunderkind Jean-Georges Vongerichten, remains fiercely fashionable. This is the quintessential SoHo experience: a downtown crowd, chic décor, and a staff decked New York-style in black.

The menu appeals day and night with raw-bar selections, salads, sandwiches, and entrées that have roots in France but travel to faraway locales for inspiration. Raw tuna and wasabi dress up pizza; thinly shaved fennel forms a perfect salad; salmon swims with miso and bok choy . Take a seat at the bar for a glass of rose or a cool draft and you may even make a new friend.

Mezzogiorno

B1

195 Spring St. (at Sullivan St.)

Subway: Spring St (Sixth Ave.)
Phone: 212-334-2112
Web: www.mezzogiorno.com
Prices: $$

Lunch & dinner daily

A SoHo veteran established more than 12 years ago by Vittorio and Nicola Ansuini, Mezzogiorno (the name means "midday") re-creates the warm, vibrant atmosphere of the owners' native Florence. More than 100 Italian artists were asked to interpret the restaurant's logo, a smiling sun; their collection of collages, paintings and small objets d'art are displayed at one end of the room.

The Florentine theme continues in the menu that follows the seasons and reads straight from Italy. An extensive collection of pastas proves enticing, while meats are classically prepared. Pizzas are perfectly cooked in the woodburning oven and topped simply. Outside, the raised terrace provides a great vantage point for people-watching when the weather cooperates.

Papatzul

Mexican ✗

B2

55 Grand St. (bet. West Broadway & Wooster St.)

Subway: Canal St (Sixth Ave.)   Tue – Sat lunch & dinner
Phone: 212-274-8225
Web: www.papatzul.com
Prices: $$

Soho's sleeper hit. The Mexican restaurant, Papatzul, is a refreshing addition to the model-festooned neighborhood, with a vibe that's festive, but not so festive you can't linger over your conversation. Cool, but not so cool you get slapped with attitude. Laid-back service, genial prices, and old-school ambiance—need we go on? Head past the lively bar and you'll find a clump of closely-spaced tables with couples nursing pitchers of margaritas. Kick off your meal with a fresh shrimp, scallop and fish ceviche, dressed in a dense lime-tomato sauce and studded with avocado, jalapeno and cilantro. An entrée of rich, layered tortilla casserole with tender shredded chicken, is dressed in rich *pasilla chile* sauce, and then laced with a cool shot of crema.

Peasant

C2

Italian ✗

194 Elizabeth St. (bet. Prince & Spring Sts.)

Subway: Spring St (Lafayette St.)   Tue – Sun dinner only
Phone: 212-965-9511
Web: www.peasantnyc.com
Prices: $$

Chef Frank DeCarlo named his restaurant for his cooking style. Peasant emphasizes honest, Italian country fare, much of which is cooked in the wood-burning brick oven and served in terra-cotta pots.

Comforts are simple here, too, with church-pew seating, exposed brick walls and tabletop candles providing the main source of light. (Okay, the restaurant is dark, but who doesn't look good in dim, romantic candlelight? Besides, the menu is entirely in Italian, so you can always use the lack of light as an excuse to ask for a translation.) Rustic entrées include lamb with polenta, gnocchi with rabbit, marjoram, and fava beans, and steak Florentine. Pizza, with *pepperoncini* and *soppressata* or mortadella, among other toppings, is a sure-fire hit.

Public ✿

Fusion 🍴

C2

210 Elizabeth St. (bet. Prince & Spring Sts.)

Subway: Spring St (Lafayette St.)
Phone: 212-343-7011
Web: www.public-nyc.com
Prices: $$$

Mon – Fri dinner only
Sat – Sun lunch & dinner

Trendy Nolita location: check. Sexy, stylized nook-and-cranny seating: check. Irreverent, yet inexplicable theme (public buildings, in this case): check. New, buzz-worthy adjoining wine bar: check. So what doesn't Public have? The mediocre food and eye-rolling service that often beleaguers such places, for starters. Quite the opposite, in fact, with Chef Brad Farmerie spinning lovely fusion food (some call it *Australasian*), served by a professional staff in a super-slick setting. In between tea smoked salmon salads tossed with punchy vinaigrette, and heavenly sticky toffee puddings, you'd do well to wander through the labyrinth of rooms a bit.

Should you make your way next door, you'll find the Monday Room—a new wine bar (though there is no actual bar, just sexy leather banquettes) featuring a delightfully quirky selection of wines and an ambitious menu of small plates.

Appetizers	*Entrées*	*Desserts*
● Sweet Potato, Feta, Smoked Paprika Tortilla With Minted-Lemon Raita	● Snail-Oxtail Ravioli, Pickled Shiitake, Pea Shoots, Smoked Paprika Oil	● Sticky Toffee Pudding, Armagnac Ice Cream, Caramel Sauce
● Roasted Beet and Goat Cheese Arancini	● Mini Venison Burgers, Miso Bun with Tomato-Chili Jam	● Yuzu Cheesecake with Macadamia Nut Crust, and Basil Seeds
● Curried Lentil Spring Roll and Tamarind Chutney		● "Hokey Pokey" Ice Cream

Raoul's

B1

French ⚔

180 Prince St. (bet. Sullivan & Thompson Sts.)

Subway: Spring St (Sixth Ave.)
Phone: 212-966-3518
Web: www.raouls.com
Prices: $$$

Dinner daily

For any restaurant to survive for 30 years in this fickle business, they must be doing something right—and Raoul's does many things right. For starters, the kitchen turns out good classic French food, from skate with Manila clams to Colorado lamb with sweetbreads; the day's selection is presented on individual blackboards. You can't help but get caught up in the energetic atmosphere in the dimly lit main room, but if you're seeking a calmer spot for a quiet conversation, try the bright upstairs space or the tiny covered garden room.

This authentic bistro, its walls covered with arresting artwork, had its 15 minutes of fame in 2006 when it stood in for an upscale Beacon Hill eatery in Martin Scorcese's film, *The Departed*.

Salt

B1

American ⚔

58 MacDougal St. (bet. Houston & Prince Sts.)

Subway: Spring St (Sixth Ave.)
Phone: 212-674-4968
Web: www.saltnyc.com
Prices: $$

Mon – Sat lunch & dinner

The expression "neighborhood restaurant" is bandied about on a too casual basis nowadays, but Salt genuinely deserves the moniker. Diners are invited to sit at one of three communal tables in the middle of the simply furnished dining room. Here, you can rub elbows with other locals and catch up on some SoHo gossip. Or sit at a table near the large shop front windows.

Long Island duck breast, Alaskan King salmon, and New Zealand rack of lamb are some of the highlights from the brief menu that is a showcase in modern cuisine. Under the section "Protein + 2," select any two sides to accompany the main dish—a classic American mealtime formula. The menu makes fair use of fresh and flavorful combinations, incorporating seasonal and local meats and produce.

Savoy

American ✗

C2

70 Prince St. (at Crosby St.)

Subway: Prince St
Phone: 212-219-8570
Web: www.savoynyc.com
Prices: $$

Mon – Sat lunch & dinner

Like a fine wine, Savoy has only improved with age. Peter Hoffman and his wife, Susan Rosenfeld, opened with the intention of creating memorable meals from the best local ingredients. They still make good on their concept, which relies on their relationships with local growers. Elegant country cooking is expertly crafted from top-quality products here, taking care that the flavors of the main ingredients stand out. The same care applies to the wine list, which offers an intriguing selection by both the bottle and the glass.

The place occupies two floors of an 1830s town house, with a boisterous bar downstairs and a more peaceful dining area upstairs. If Savoy wasn't so successful, locals would gladly keep it as their own little secret.

Snack

Greek ✗

B1

105 Thompson St. (bet. Prince & Spring Sts.)

Subway: Spring St (Sixth Ave.)
Phone: 212-925-1040
Web: N/A
Prices: ⊜⊜

Lunch & dinner daily

Don't blink, or you might walk right past Snack. Seating just ten people at five lime-green tables, this sweet little Greek place offers a refreshing antidote to SoHo's über-trendy temples of gastronomy. Enveloped by photographs of Hellenic landmarks and shelves of Mediterranean grocery items, you'll feel transported to sunnier climes.

When you taste the fresh, authentic Greek cuisine, you'll half expect to feel sand between your toes. The friendly staff is more than willing to advise diners trying to choose from the delectable array of meze, sandwiches and savory pies (offerings are scrawled on a blackboard).

If you're craving souvlaki or stuffed grape leaves while in the West Village, visit the bigger Snack at 63 Bedford Street.

Woo Lae Oak

Korean 🍴🍴

148 Mercer St. (bet. Houston & Prince Sts.)

Subway: Prince St
Phone: 212-925-8200
Web: www.woolaeoaksoho.com
Prices: $$

Lunch & dinner daily

This Koreatown eatery solves New Yorkers' perpetual dilemma of whether to stay at home or dine out. Here, marble-top tables are outfitted with built-in grills to barbecue your own sea scallops and mahi mahi, or shiitake mushrooms and boneless Long Island duck breast. Less participatory options include traditional *bin dae duk* (mung bean pancakes) and *kal bi jim* (beef short ribs) prepared with authenticity and a flair for depth of flavor.

However, more than the cooking sets Woo Lae Oak apart from its more traditional neighbors. The fresh and attractive dining space, with a roomy, open floor plan still attracts a stylish downtown crowd.

A great value, the fixed-price *bann sang* individual lunch set includes some of the restaurant's most popular dishes.

For a pleasant stay in a charming hotel, look for the red 🏠...🏠🏠 symbols.

TriBeCa

An intriguing wedge of warehouses, loft residences, art galleries, and oh-so-chic restaurants, TriBeCa was named in the 1970s by a real-estate agent hoping to create a hip identity for the area. The acronym—which stands for Triangle Below Canal—stuck, and true to expectations, the area became trendy. TriBeCa hasn't been commercially influenced nearly to the extent that SoHo has, despite being home to dozens of celebrities, most notably actor Robert De Niro. For paparazzi-dodging starlets, that is precisely its appeal.

Technically, TriBeCa is not a triangle but a trapezoid. Its boundaries are *(clockwise from north)* Canal Street, Broadway, Murray Street, and the Hudson River. Greenwich and Hudson Streets are the main thoroughfares for dining and nightlife; art and interior-design stores are scattered throughout the neighborhood.

RESIDENTIAL, THEN AND NOW

Once used as farmland by Dutch settlers, the area now known as TriBeCa was included in a large tract granted to Trinity Church in 1705. In the ensuing century, wealthy families built elegant residences around Hudson Square (now the Hudson River Tunnel traffic rotary). A fruit and produce market opened in 1813 at the western edge of the neighborhood, but the quarter remained primarily residential until the mid-19th century. It was during this time that shipping and warehousing industries formerly located at the South Street Seaport moved to deepwater piers on the Hudson River. Five- and six-story "store and loft" buildings were erected around the district to accommodate the new trade. By 1939 Washington Market, as the area along Greenwich Street came to be known, and boasted a greater volume of business than all the other markets in the city combined.

In the 1960s, city planners approved urban-renewal projects that called for the demolition of many buildings along the waterfront. Luckily, enough of the old commercial warehouses remained to attract artists forced out of SoHo and others seeking cavernous industrial living space. Today, those same artists would be hard-pressed to afford such a space in TriBeCa; loft-apartment prices now start with the general term of no less than "seven figures."

TRENDY TRIBECA

Catering as they do to a local clientele of creative types, TriBeCa is a cool place to eat. You can either splurge on a meal here in expensive restaurants whose reputations precede them, or go for more modest fare. If it's a sunny day, snag an umbrella-shaded table outside—TriBeCa's wide sidewalks accommodate plenty of them.

Snag a ticket to a flick at the acclaimed **TriBeCa Film Festival**, an annual affair featuring over 250 films and 1000-plus screenings. Founded in 2002 to help restore lower Manhattan, this springtime event has become one of the leading film festivals in the world.

TriBeCa is also home to **Stuyvesant High School**, a prestigious institution specializing in mathematics and science, and one of the most prominent schools in the nation.

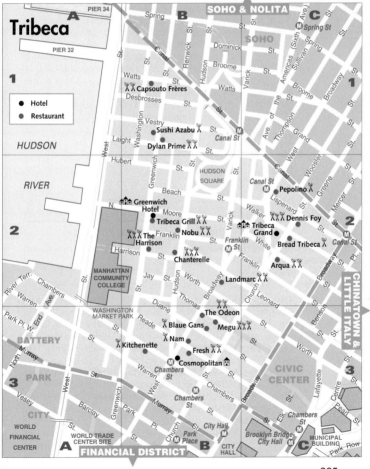

Tribeca

PIER 34
PIER 32

- ● Hotel
- ● Restaurant

HUDSON

RIVER

SOHO & NOLITA

SOHO

Spring St

Spring St

Canal St

Canal St

Capsouto Frères

Sushi Azabu

Dylan Prime

HUDSON SQUARE

Pepolino

Greenwich Hotel

Tribeca Grill

Nobu

Dennis Foy

Tribeca Grand

The Harrison

Bread Tribeca

Chanterelle

Arqua

MANHATTAN COMMUNITY COLLEGE

Landmarc

WASHINGTON MARKET PARK

The Odeon

Blaue Gans

Megu

Kitchenette

Nam

Fresh

Cosmopolitan

Chambers St

Chambers St

BATTERY PARK

CIVIC CENTER

PARK CITY

WORLD FINANCIAL CENTER

WORLD TRADE CENTER SITE

City Hall

Park Place

CITY HALL

Brooklyn Bridge City Hall

MUNICIPAL BUILDING

CHINATOWN & LITTLE ITALY

FINANCIAL DISTRICT

Arqua

C2   Italian 🍴🍴

281 Church St. (at White St.)

Subway: Franklin St   Lunch & dinner daily
Phone: 212-334-1888
Web: www.arquaristorante.com
Prices: **$$**

Recalling small hill villages in Italy's Veneto region, this corner trattoria celebrates northern Italy in its sunny-colored, light-filled space.

Thanks to Chef/owner Leonard Pulito, who named his restaurant after the Italian town where he and his family raised their own livestock and grew their own produce, the food at Arqua is executed with an eye for excellence. House-made *pappardelle* may be married to an earthy sauce made with duck and mushrooms, and sprinkled with parmesan to finish the dish; branzino is brushed with lemon and olive oil and grilled whole; thin scallops of veal have a natural affinity for wild mushrooms and Marsala.

Desserts from ricotta cheesecake to semifreddo do Italy proud, and gelati and sorbetti are made on-site.

Blaue Gans

B3   Austrian 🍴

139 Duane St. (bet. Church St. & West Broadway)

Subway: Chambers St (West Broadway)   Lunch & dinner daily
Phone: 212-571-8880
Web: www.wallse.com
Prices: **$$**

Taking over the space formerly occupied by Le Zinc, Chef Kurt Gutenbrunner (also of Wallsé) may have saved the zinc bar and the vintage art posters of the former tenant, but he has turned the menu upside-down with his Austro-German cooking.

Open for three meals as well as late-night noshing, the restaurant focuses on Austrian specialties, including an entire section devoted to sausages. The kitchen eschews the heavy hand often used in this style of cooking and instead offers light preparations of Austrian classics like Wiener Schnitzel, with each ingredient perfectly represented—down to the fresh-grated horseradish.

For dessert, the likes of cherry strudel, homemade ice cream coupes, and *Salzburger Nockerl* will leave you smacking your lips.

Bread Tribeca

Italian

C2

301 Church St. (at Walker St.)

Subway: Canal St (Sixth Ave.)
Phone: 212-334-8282
Web: www.breadtribeca.com
Prices: $$

Lunch & dinner daily

How downtown chow aficionados do lunch: crusty, overstuffed Italian sandwiches; a clean, cool, industrial layout; and a few famous actors chilling in the corner. With its long, wooden communal table and free WiFi—Bread Tribeca delivers the sort of bang-bang lunch that busy New Yorkers dream about, although the rustic Italian menu includes enough tempting pastas, pizzas, soups, and such, that it would be a shame not to linger longer and enjoy the chefs' myriad creations. Dip your spoon into a creamy, piping hot zucchini soup laced with a cool swirl of crème fraîche and a generous crush of black pepper. A luscious, creamy pumpkin cheesecake, served at room temperature and carrying hints of clove and cardamom, also delivers.

Capsouto Frères

French

B1

451 Washington St. (at Watts St.)

Subway: Canal St (Sixth Ave.)
Phone: 212-966-4900
Web: www.capsoutofreres.com
Prices: $$

Tue – Sun lunch & dinner
Mon dinner only

First, admire the stunning architectural details of the landmark 1891 building the restaurant has called home since 1980. Then, forget the slightly off-the-path location while you enjoy the view. Inside, howling steam pipes echo against carved wainscoting, dark wooden floors, and large jacquard-lined windows.

Enduring vision and commitment to providing great food and service are the hallmarks of this restaurant's sustained viability, and its place in New York culture. The honest and well-made menu may highlight a perfectly tender bœuf Bourguignon as well as sweet and savory soufflés—some of the best offered in the city. The restaurant serves as a friendly, intimate, and unpretentious foil to the hectic mega-restaurants in nearby TriBeCa and the Meatpacking District.

Chanterelle

B2

French

2 Harrison St. (at Hudson St.)

Subway: Franklin St
Phone: 212-966-6960
Web: www.chanterellenyc.com
Prices: $$$$

Mon – Wed & Sun dinner only
Thu – Sat lunch & dinner

The moment one approaches this corner location, with soft light emanating from the well-dressed large windows, it is clear that this is a truly special place.

Admire the potted greenery, elegant glass door, and vestibule upon entering this longstanding institution with a lofty reputation for quality. Inside, the host invites guests to a seating area where pieces by famous artists hang on the wall. Elegantly austere, the dining room is cool, open, and refined. Sensitive to the guests' every need, the efficient brigade of waitstaff are professional and attentive, to ensure a fine and enjoyable dining experience. This remains a popular spot for special occasions and celebrations. The innovative French menu is complemented by an impressive yet expensive wine list.

Dennis Foy

C2

Contemporary

313 Church St. (bet. Lispenard & Walker Sts.)

Subway: Canal St (Sixth Ave.)
Phone: 212-625-1007
Web: www.dennisfoynyc.com
Prices: $$$

Mon – Sat dinner only

Chefs are often compared to artists, but in the case of Dennis Foy, the analogy is unquestionable. Foy, both chef and owner, shows off his talents in the kitchen, where his cutting-edge cooking wins rave reviews, as well as in the dining room, where his paintings proudly hang.

The chef's adventurous spirit shines in his signature warm crab tian, a riff on crab cakes. Occasionally, he makes forays into molecular gastronomy, as in a "salt-cured terrine of foie gras, prunes, Eis and Snow."

Foy opened his eponymous TriBeCa restaurant in the space formerly occupied by Lo Scalco. The cathedral-like space, with its colorful arches, church-pew-like banquettes, and gold-leaf wallpaper, echoes the owner's creative soul.

Dylan Prime

B1

Contemporary ❌❌

62 Laight St. (at Greenwich St.)

Subway: Franklin St
Phone: 212-334-4783
Web: www.dylanprime.com
Prices: $$$

Mon – Fri lunch & dinner
Sat – Sun dinner only

Dylan Prime is kind of like the ideal man. With a menu that boasts a parade of masculine cuts like Porterhouse, filet mignon, or aged prime rib, it's undeniably a steakhouse. But unlike some of the more insecure shank shacks in town, this menu isn't afraid to show its softer side with delicate diver scallops, soft fried artichokes, and silky salmon tartare. Dylan Prime's split personality doesn't end there, either. The service is swift, but relaxed—and though the mood is dark, sultry, and romantic—thanks to low lighting, cozy banquettes, and flickering votives, there's plenty of leg room. The lunch set will find a nice deal in the $14 Dylan Prime Burger—a thick, juicy item on a warm, toasted brioche, stuffed with ruby-red tomatoes and homemade sauce.

Fresh

B3

Seafood ❌❌

105 Reade St. (bet. Church St. & West Broadway)

Subway: Chambers St (West Broadway)
Phone: 212-406-1900
Web: www.freshrestaurantnyc.com
Prices: $$

Mon – Fri lunch & dinner
Sat – Sun dinner only

Freshness is the mantra in this loft-like TriBeCa space. Marine colors, frosted-glass accents, and a wave motif overhead enhance the sea-themed dining space and entice a steady stream of loyal fish lovers.
A velvety piece of Atlantic cod, perfectly grilled with skin on to capture the natural juices, accurately represents the restaurant's unadulterated seafood preparations. Spare but delicious pairings, such as tender broccoli florets, simply dressed with fragrant olive oil and slivers of deep-fried garlic, complete the dishes.

The Harrison

B2

Contemporary XXX

355 Greenwich St. (at Harrison St.)

Subway: Franklin St
Phone: 212-274-9310
Web: www.theharrison.com
Prices: $$

Dinner daily

There's a fine line where downtown hip meets warm and inviting—and Chef/owner Jimmy Bradley walks it like a tightrope. He does it in Chelsea with his beloved Red Cat, as well as with The Harrison, which still manages, in its eighth year, to win over as many been-there-done-that locals as discriminating visitors. Maybe it's the beautifully prepared contemporary American cuisine—bold and seasonally inspired, but comfortingly familiar. A juicy, charred steak is packed with flavor and paired with sautéed Tuscan kale and sweet shallot confit, before getting kicked up with a spicy tomato sauce. Or maybe it's the slightly jazzy space itself, soaked in sexy amber lighting from the ribbon of red glass that runs along the windows.

Kitchenette

B3

American X

156 Chambers St. (bet. Greenwich St. & West Broadway)

Subway: Chambers St (West Broadway)
Phone: 212-267-6740
Web: N/A
Prices: ✑✑

Lunch & dinner daily

Kitchenette brings a taste of home to TriBeCa, where a Formica counter, swiveling barstools, and black-and-white floor tiles imbue this casual cafe with the nostalgic air of an old-fashioned luncheonette. The menu celebrates Americana, from freshly made cornbread to a tuna melt. Served on whimsical tables made from wooden doors, dishes such as moist, delicate turkey meatloaf with buttery mashed potatoes and silky-smooth gravy epitomize American comfort food. Kitchenette appeals to a wide array of diners, who love the retro feel and homey cuisine—since so many of them have children in tow, the next generation may appreciate this place just as much. Sibling Kitchenette Uptown (*1272 Amsterdam Ave.*) is a favorite with the Columbia University crowd.

Landmarc

French 🍴🍴

B2

179 West Broadway (bet. Leonard & Worth Sts.)

Subway: Franklin St   Lunch & dinner daily
Phone: 212-343-3883
Web: www.landmarc-restaurant.com
Prices: $$

Simple, modern bistro fare gets a kick in the pants at Landmarc, the 2004 brainchild of husband-and-wife team, Marc and Pamela Murphy. Blame the open grill, boldly placed just a few feet from the bustling bar, for transforming straightforward dishes like roasted chicken into expertly charred, juicy centerpieces. Plated alongside a mash of crushed russet potatoes and bright green *haricots verts*, the result is divine. The vibe at the TriBeCa space (there's another location uptown, in the Time Warner Center) is relaxed but trendy, with exposed brick walls, and a narrow second-floor balcony that opens up to the street in warm weather. Grape hounds will be happy to know that Landmarc's famed half-bottle list is still well-chosen, and gloriously within budget.

Megu

Japanese 🍴🍴🍴

B3

62 Thomas St. (bet. Church St. & West Broadway)

Subway: Chambers St (West Broadway)   Mon – Fri lunch & dinner
Phone: 212-964-7777   Sat – Sun dinner only
Web: www.megunyc.com
Prices: $$$

Sleek, gorgeous and sexy—Megu takes sweet advantage of TriBeCa's notoriously lofty digs. After a short descent down a row of stairs, visitors uncover a jaw-dropping décor, replete with a carved ice Buddha hovering over a pool strewn with rose petals. Above it, hangs a dramatic replica of a Japanese temple bell. Can the cuisine live up to this grand-scale design? Megu's kitchen thinks so—sourcing only the highest-quality ingredients, and turning out plates of bright, inventive Japanese delicacies, touched with influences farther afield.

Micro-greens wrapped in sheets of *yuba* are topped with a delicate mound of sashimi, and then drizzled with a sweet, spicy dressing. A midtown location provides an elegant Zen setting for the diplomat crowd (*845 UN Plaza*).

Nam

B3

Vietnamese

110 Reade St. (bet. Church St. & West Broadway)

Subway: Chambers St (West Broadway) Mon – Fri lunch & dinner
Phone: 212-267-1777 Sat – Sun dinner only
Web: www.namnyc.com
Prices: $$

Nam strives to please—and it does, bringing diners bounding back for the attentive service and alluring ambience. Slowly turning ceiling fans, backlit Vietnamese portraits, a wall lined with bamboo reeds, and natural light pouring in through the generously sized front windows all add to the appeal of this small, charming restaurant.

The food here may appear a bit scripted and the menu certainly contains no surprises, but there's something to be said for tried and true. Vietnamese standards such as *Ca Hap* made with perfectly steamed sea bass, bean-thread noodles, earthy yet sweet shiitake mushrooms, ginger, and scallions are rendered with good quality ingredients and a careful, if somewhat restrained, hand in the kitchen.

Nobu

B2

Japanese

105 Hudson St. (at Franklin St.)

Subway: Franklin St Mon – Fri lunch & dinner
Phone: 212-219-0500 Sat – Sun dinner only
Web: www.myriadrestaurantgroup.com
Prices: $$$$

In partnership with Drew Nieporent and actor Robert DeNiro, celebrity Chef Nobu Matsuhisa opened Nobu in 1994 to a large fanfare, and the restaurant continues to enjoy success today. Architect David Rockwell imagined the Japanese countryside in Nobu's dining room, replete with stylized birch trees and a wall of black river stones.

Nobu is best known for its seductive sushi and sashimi, but don't pass up Matsuhisa's appealing specialties like the miso-glazed black cod or monkfish pâté with caviar. Sharing dishes is the best way to "do" Nobu. Judging from the line-up outside, Nobu still packs 'em in nightly.

The chef's empire includes Nobu Next Door, offering similar food in a simpler setting, and Nobu Fifty-Seven in Midtown *(40 West 57th St.)*.

The Odeon

B3

American

145 West Broadway (at Thomas St.)

Subway: Chambers St (West Broadway)   Lunch & dinner daily
Phone: 212-233-0507
Web: www.theodeonrestaurant.com
Prices: $$

The story of The Odeon's longevity is a study in miracles. Opening in 1980, it has survived well past its own "15 minutes of fame," typical of the city's dining scene.

Perched from a bar stool, one can take in the Art Deco architectural details—from the dark hardwood bar and wall panels lining the dining room, to globe lights and lazy fans hanging from the ceiling. The warm tones and lighting set the tone of an otherwise lively room.

This lovely setting enhances the very enjoyable food. Items may include the Eden Brook trout, blending almond purée-butter, briny capers, and sweet tomato confit to create a depth of textural dimensions. The lunch special is a great deal for this neighborhood but, judging from the full dining room, it is no secret.

Pepolino

C2

Italian

281 West Broadway (bet. Canal & Lispenard Sts.)

Subway: Canal St (Sixth Ave.)   Lunch & dinner daily
Phone: 212-966-9983
Web: www.pepolino.com
Prices: $$

Named for a variety of wild thyme found in Tuscany, Pepolino and its original chef, Enzo Pezone, have been a TriBeCa fixture since 1999—this in itself is an accomplishment, considering this city's fickle restaurant scene.

Simple Tuscan specialties, neither stripped down nor re-imagined, bring enthusiastic visitors back for more. The menu may feature the fresh and light bread soup, *ribollita*, teeming with *cavolo nero*, root vegetables, tomatoes, beans, sprinkled with fragrant herbs. The heartier *fettucine al coniglio* is loaded with meaty morsels of tender stewed rabbit. Although the kitchen staff sometimes lacks focus, they nonetheless excel at creative fare such as the tomato-basil pâté that may be presented with bread at the beginning of the meal.

Sushi Azabu

B1

Japanese 🍴

428 Greenwich St. (at Laight St.)

Subway: Franklin St
Phone: 212-274-0428
Web: www.greenwichgrill.com
Prices: $$

Sun – Fri lunch & dinner
Sat dinner only

In the basement level of the Greenwich Grill, Sushi Azabu occupies a tiny cavelike space. A small counter welcomes patrons, who can find additional seating (for a total of 26 diners) in the scattering of rounded dark leather booths. Nature defines the décor: a floor fashioned out of river stones, a ceiling patterned with bamboo, walls covered in rice paper. Young and engaging, the sushi chefs entertain and chat with guests while preparing *nigiri* such as creamy amberjack, a briny giant clam, a sea scallop topped with grated green yuzu rind, and exceptionally fresh *uni* (sea urchin). Beverages include a list of sake, *shochu*, and beer.

Upstairs in the 1883 Romanesque Revival-style building, the Greenwich Grill serves contemporary cuisine with Pacific Coast sensibilities—as well as sushi.

Tribeca Grill

B2

Contemporary 🍴🍴

375 Greenwich St. (at Franklin St.)

Subway: Franklin St
Phone: 212-941-3900
Web: www.myriadrestaurantgroup.com
Prices: $$$

Mon – Fri lunch & dinner
Sat dinner only
Sun lunch only

This restaurant is rightfully a New York classic. Opened in 1990 by Drew Nieporent and Robert DeNiro, Tribeca Grill occupies the first two floors of a 1905 warehouse, which is also home to DeNiro's film company. Exposed pipes and brick walls preserve the building's industrial past and set the architectural standard for many modern TriBeCa eateries.

Beautiful people comprise a large part of the clientele, along with moneyed neighborhood residents. Ingredients are well-sourced in dishes such as a crispy, jumbo lump crab cake, served atop a bed of sautéed spinach, cauliflower florets, and a tomato confit studded with plump raisins and briny capers. For a savory dessert treat, pair a sampling of artisanal cheeses with a selection from the amazing wine collection.

Upper East Side

An enclave for the wealthy and fashionable, the Upper East Side represents a broad cross-section of New York neighborhoods and contains an impressive concentration of restaurants. In the area that stretches from Fifth Avenue to the East River, and from 60th Street to 96th Street, you'll find food to please every palate, from Austrian cuisine to vegetarian fare.

MUSEUM MILE

Rimming the east edge of Central Park, the Metropolitan Museum of Art, the Guggenheim Museum, the Jewish Museum, the Whitney Museum of American Art, the Frick Collection, the Neue Galerie, and the Cooper-Hewitt National Design Museum, are collectively known as **Museum Mile**. An impressive concentration of elegant shops, upscale restaurants, clubs, exclusive private schools and fabulous residences grace this area as well.

East of Lexington Avenue, where there's a significant population of single people, the atmosphere becomes more casual. Here, modern high-rise apartment buildings dominate, sharing space with a variety of pubs, sports bars and pizza joints.

FOREVER POSH

In the late 19th century, rich industrialists including Andrew Carnegie and Henry Clay Frick began building mansions on the large lots along Fifth Avenue, abutting Central Park. One of the first sections to be developed was around East 86th Street, where several prominent families of German descent, including the Schermerhorns, the Astors and the Rhinelanders, built country estates. Yorkville, as it was then known, soon moved east past Lexington Avenue and became a suburb of middle-class Germans, many of whom worked in nearby piano factories and breweries—although hardly a rathskeller survives today. In the 1950s, waves of immigrants from Hungary and Eastern Europe established their own communities, only to disappear as gentrification set in a couple of decades ago. Over the years, the posh East Side has been a magnet for celebrities— Greta Garbo, Andy Warhol, Richard Nixon and Woody Allen among them. Today, Fifth Avenue remains the neighborhood's most impressive thoroughfare, Madison Avenue is chock-a-block with chi-chi shops and art galleries; and Park Avenue is an elegant residential boulevard.

Brigitta L. House / MICHELIN

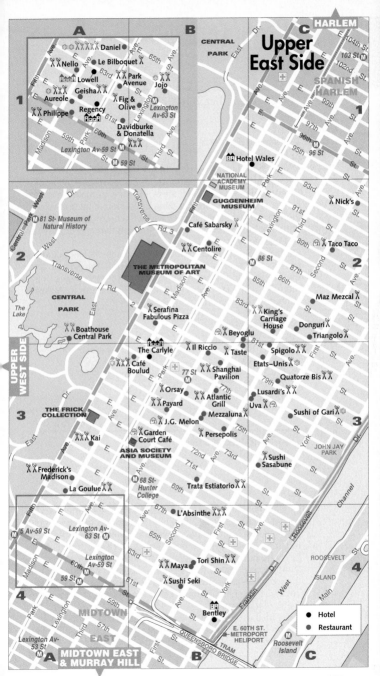

Upper East Side

HARLEM

SPANISH HARLEM

CENTRAL PARK

Daniel
Nello
Le Bilboquet
Lowell
Geisha
Park Avenue
Jojo
Aureole
Fig & Olive
Lexington Av-63 St
Philippe
Regency
Davidburke & Donatella
Lexington Av-59 St
59 St

Hotel Wales

Nick's

NATIONAL ACADEMY MUSEUM

GUGGENHEIM MUSEUM

Café Sabarsky

Taco Taco

Centolire

86 St

81 St-Museum of Natural History

Maz Mezcal

THE METROPOLITAN MUSEUM OF ART

Serafina Fabulous Pizza

King's Carriage House

Donguri

CENTRAL PARK

Beyoglu

Triangolo

The Lake

Boathouse Central Park

The Carlyle

Il Riccio

Taste

Spigolo

Etats–Unis

UPPER WEST SIDE

Café Boulud

77 St

Shanghai Pavilion

Quatorze Bis

Orsay

Atlantic Grill

Lusardi's

Uva

Sushi of Gari

Payard

THE FRICK COLLECTION

J.G. Melon

Mezzaluna

Kai

Garden Court Café

Persepolis

Sushi Sasabune

JOHN JAY PARK

ASIA SOCIETY AND MUSEUM

Frederick's Madison

68 St-Hunter College

Trata Estiatorio

La Goulue

5 Av-59 St

Lexington Av-63 St

L'Absinthe

ROOSEVELT

Lexington Av-59 St

ROOSEVELT ISLAND

59 St

Maya

Tori Shin

Sushi Seki

MIDTOWN EAST

Bentley

QUEENSBORO BRIDGE TRAM

E. 60TH ST. METROPORT HELIPORT

Lexington Av-53 St

MIDTOWN EAST & MURRAY HILL

Roosevelt Island

● Hotel
● Restaurant

Atlantic Grill

Seafood ❌❌

1341 Third Ave. (bet. 76th & 77th Sts.)

Subway: 77 St   Lunch & dinner daily
Phone: 212-988-9200
Web: www.brguestrestaurants.com
Prices: **$$**

Atlantic Grill is another drop in the bucket of the B.R. Guest Restaurant Group. The popular 200-seat restaurant hooks a very Upper East Side clientele (be sure to make advance reservations). One room is done in nautical blue and white; the other has a sunny aspect with cream-colored walls and potted palms. Sidewalk seating is in high demand during the warmer months.

Despite the restaurant's name, seafood selections, including raw-bar and sushi offerings, come from both the Atlantic and the Pacific. For dinner, go with one of the chef's entrées or try the fresh catch (anything from wild King salmon to Alaskan halibut), simply grilled.

Beyoglu

Turkish ❌

1431 Third Ave. (at 81st St.)

Subway: 77 St   Lunch & dinner daily
Phone: 212-650-0850
Web: N/A
Prices: **$$**

Small plates star at this meze house, where low prices and a casual, convivial atmosphere add to the appeal. The simple dining room with its bright walls and inlaid-tile tables sets the scene for sharing meze (the focus of the menu) from tangy homemade yogurt with cucumber and garlic to smooth stuffed grape leaves to a crunchy shepherd's salad. Most of the recipes—and some wine and beer offerings—come from Turkey, though Greek and Lebanese accents are found in many of the items.

If the idea of small plates doesn't float your boat, there's also a short list of daily specials, including meat kebabs and grilled fish. Your waiter will fill you in on the delightful desserts, such as baklava, and *kadayif* filled with almonds, pistachios, and honey.

Aureole ✿

Contemporary 🗙🗙🗙

A1

34 E. 61st St. (bet. Madison & Park Aves.)

Subway:	5 Av - 59 St	Mon – Fri lunch & dinner
Phone:	212-319-1660	Sat dinner only
Web:	www.aureolerestaurant.com	
Prices:	$$$$	

Taking up the first two floors of a 1920s brownstone, this beauty is stylishly bedecked with honey-toned woodwork, plush carpeting, and burgundy leather banquettes. Contemporary prints line the walls, while seasonal floral arrangements festoon the airy room. No doubt the flowers, an Aureole signature, will be part of the design when the restaurant moves to the new Bank of America building on Bryant Park in spring 2009.

Aureole belongs to Charlie Palmer's restaurant kingdom, with a second location in Las Vegas. At the helm in New York since early 2007, Chef Tony Aiazzi gives his creations a modern lift. The calamari and citrus salad is elevated as a deconstructed dish: a row of orange supremes; another of baby frisée; shaved fennel and sliced black olives in the center, surrounded by grilled calamari.

A well-chosen selection of 700 wines shows strength in European vintages.

Appetizers	*Entrées*	*Desserts*
• Rabbit in Three Preparations: Seared Loin, Rack Confit, Crisp Flank Schnitzel	• Coconut Curry-Poached Lobster with Napa Cabbage, Green Apple and Red Onion Sauté	• Red Berry Mille-Feuille, Lavender Crème Fraîche, Pistachio-Phyllo Crisps, Raspberry Sorbet
• Seared-Foie Gras, Caramelized Pears, Spiced Squash Waffle, Blackberries, Hazelnuts	• Caramelized Duck Breast with Candied Kumquats, Confit-layered Potatoes	• Hazelnut-Nougat Glace, Gingerbread Doughnut Holes, Grapefruit Sorbet

Boathouse Central Park

A2

American ✗✗

The Lake at Central Park (E. 72nd St. & Park Dr. North)

Subway: 68 St - Hunter College
Phone: 212-517-2233
Web: www.thecentralparkboathouse.com
Prices: **$$**

Lunch & dinner daily

You couldn't dream up a more romantic setting for a first date or a special occasion. Nestled on the shore of the lake in the middle of Central Park, the Boathouse features peaceful water views through its floor-to-ceiling windows. Built in the 1950s, Loeb Boathouse replaced the original two-story Victorian structure designed by architect Calvert Vaux in the 1870s.

Today the Boathouse is the only place in Manhattan for a lakeside meal. And the American fare (jumbo lump crab cakes, house-made pasta) makes it all the more worthwhile. On a sunny day, sit out on the deck and watch the boats float by. After lunch, why not hit the water with a gondola ride (advance notice required) or a rowboat rental?

Café Sabarsky

B2

Austrian ✗

1048 Fifth Ave. (at 86th St.)

Subway: 86 St (Lexington Ave.)
Phone: 212-288-0665
Web: www.wallse.com
Prices: **$$**

Wed – Mon lunch & dinner

Art alone is reason enough to visit the Neue Galerie, founded by cosmetics mogul Ronald Lauder to display his collection of early 20th-century Austrian and German art, as well as the collection of his friend, art dealer Serge Sabarsky. Besides fine art, you'll find a real gem in this 1914 Beaux Arts mansion, in the form of Café Sabarsky.

Old World charm oozes from the cafe, modeled on a late-19th-century Viennese *Kaffeehaus*. In the dining room, adorned with reproductions of Josef Hoffmann sconces, Otto Wagner fabrics and a Bösendorfer piano, chef Kurt Guntenbrunner (of Wallsé and Blaue Gans) offers fine Austrian cuisine. You'll find the likes of bratwurst and beef goulash here, but whatever you do, don't pass up the pastries!

Café Boulud ✿

B3

20 E. 76th St. (bet. Fifth & Madison Aves.)

Subway:	77 St	Tue – Sun lunch & dinner
Phone:	212-772-2600	Mon dinner only
Web:	www.danielnyc.com	
Prices:	$$$$	

Café Boulud/B. Wojcik

With Café Boulud, Chef Daniel Boulud pays homage to his family's convivial old farm cafe, located just outside of Lyon, in Saint-Pierre de Chandieu. The simply-appointed, intimate space, occupying the ground floor of the Surrey Hotel, doesn't pack much of a visual punch, but offers a nice reprieve from the Upper East Side's stuffier environs.

As to the food—well, there's nothing low-key about that. Earlier this year, incoming Chef Gavin Kayse gracefully took the reins on a menu that offers four themes: classic, seasonal, market, or exotic. A bone-in medallion of monkfish arrives impeccably bronzed, garnished with a creamy eggplant purée and lush, green emulsion of parsley. A tiny round of carrot cake, plump with sweetened cream cheese, is topped with frizzy shards of carrot; snuggled next to it, a decadent little globe of toasted-almond ice cream.

Appetizers
- Yellowfin Tuna Tartare "Niçoise"
- Vidalia Onion Velouté, Ramp Leaves, Crispy Onions
- Beef Tortellini, Broccoli Rabe, and Sauce Puttanesca

Entrées
- Seared Snapper, Soba, Shiitake and Dashi
- Chicken Breast, Mushroom Polenta, Cabbage
- Bacon-wrapped Veal, Glazed Sweetbreads, Carrot Purée, Jus

Desserts
- Raspberry- Pistachio Vacherin, Vanilla Chantilly
- Coffee Opera Cake with Chocolate Ice Cream
- Meyer Lemon Délice, Fromage Blanc Mousse, Blood Orange, Mimosa Sorbet

Centolire

Italian ✕✕

B2

1167 Madison Ave. (bet. 85th & 86th Sts.)

Subway: 86 St (Lexington Ave.)
Phone: 212-734-7711
Web: www.pinoluongo.com
Prices: $$$

Lunch & dinner daily

With 100 (*cento* in Italian) lire, you can go to America, or so an old Italian song goes. Accordingly, Tuscan-born restaurateur Pino Luongo opened Centolire to honor those Italians who, like himself, came to America to start a new life. Two dining spaces present different options: the more cozy and quiet downstairs room or the larger, more colorful upstairs area, accessed via a glass elevator.

At lunch, Centolire proposes a three-course menu of appealing Italian fare at a price you can't refuse. Dinner brings a range of entrées from *Stracotto di Manzo* to *Cacciucco alla Toscana* brimming with fresh fish and shellfish. Before you leave, check out the cookbooks written by Pino, which are displayed near the entrance.

Davidburke & Donatella

Contemporary ✕✕✕

A1

133 E. 61st St. (bet. Lexington & Park Aves.)

Subway: Lexington Av - 59 St
Phone: 212-813-2121
Web: www.dbdrestaurant.com
Prices: $$$

Lunch & dinner daily

Opened by David Burke and Donatella Arpaia, this restaurant reconfigures a traditional town house with geometric patterns, ebony parquet floors, and a palette that runs from chocolate brown to lipstick red. The place is constantly mobbed with a chi-chi cadre of diners.

Burke, who oversees the kitchen, describes his cooking style as "David Burke unplugged." You'll know what this means when you taste dishes such as day-boat scallops "Benedict," a take on the popular egg dish (in Burke's version, scallops replace the eggs, chorizo stands in for the ham, and a potato pancake masquerades as an English muffin). At lunch, the set menu is the best value.

The entire staff operates with noteworthy efficiency and grace.

Daniel ✿✿

French XXXXX

60 E. 65th St. (bet. Madison & Park Aves.)

Subway: 68 St – Hunter College
Phone: 212-288-0033
Web: www.danielnyc.com
Prices: $$$$

Mon – Sat dinner only

Let downtown have their hip—jackets are still very much required, thank you very much, for a trip to Daniel. And why shouldn't they be? This is renowned French chef Daniel Boulud's critical darling, after all; where his exquisite menu, carefully executed by his protégé, Chef Jean-François Bruel, meets a décor so grand it's blush-inducing. Walk the plush carpet of this cathedral-like space, which once housed the legendary Le Cirque, and soak in the silk drapes, carved ceilings, and massive floral displays. But then get down to business—what really sets critics' tongues wagging isn't the curtains, but Daniel's exquisitely rendered tasting menu, which might include an ethereally moist cod, fanned over morel mushrooms and wilted ramps; or a stacked lemon mousse and raspberry sorbet vacherin. The food is gloriously, unapologetically French; but the wine list ventures farther afield.

Appetizers

- Mosaic of Foie Gras and Black Angus Beef Cheek
- Trio of Sea Scallops: Ceviche, Tartare and Sashimi
- Fennel-Basil Ravioli with Littleneck Clam Emulsion

Entrées

- Braised Short Ribs and Seared Ribeye, Shallot Confit, Spinach Subric, Porcini
- Poached Halibut with Saffron-Mussel Velouté
- Squab, Foie Gras Pastilla, Avocado Chutney

Desserts

- Tasting of Mango with Roasted Sesame
- Brownie, Mascarpone Cream, Ethiopian Coffee Ice Cream
- Chocolate Biscuit, Roasted Cherries, Kierk Beer Sorbet

313

Donguri

C2

Japanese

309 E. 83rd St. (bet. First & Second Aves.)

Subway: 86 St (Lexington Ave.)
Phone: 212-737-5656
Web: www.dongurinyc.com
Prices: **$$$**

Tue – Sun dinner only

Owned by Ito En, a Japanese tea company (which also runs Kai), Donguri offers an extensive menu of authentic Japanese cuisine. With only 24 seats, this nondescript little place fills up quickly with a grown-up crowd who can afford the prices and appreciate the light, flavorful food.

Try one of the fixed menus, which might start with miso soup and a delightful plate of assorted appetizers, then progress through several more courses. Dinner may also be ordered à la carte—with a huge assortment of dishes to share—or go all out and order the chef's omakase. All products are ultra-fresh and specials change daily.

Fig & Olive

B1

Mediterranean

808 Lexington Ave. (bet. 62nd & 63rd Sts.)

Subway: Lexington Av - 63 St
Phone: 212-207-4555
Web: www.figandolive.com
Prices: **$$$**

Lunch & dinner daily

At this Mediterranean restaurant and olive oil shop (now with two additional locations), olive oil is treated with the same attention afforded fine wine. Each dish—from grilled lamb to mushroom carpaccio—is accented with a specific extra virgin oil. You'll find fragrant oils from France, Italy and Spain here, and the wine list echoes the same regions (with many selections by the glass).

Settle into the pleasant dining room on a time-out from strenuous shopping at nearby Bloomingdale's, and dig into tartines, carpaccio, crostini; or a charcuterie platter brimming with prosciutto, *jamón Iberico,* and *saucisson sec.* The bright food will revive you for further shopping adventures without an expanded waistline.

Etats-Unis ✿

C3

242 E. 81st St. (bet. Second & Third Aves.)

Dinner daily

Subway: 77 St
Phone: 212-517-8826
Web: www.etatsunisrestaurant.com
Prices: $$$

Truly a comfortable place to linger over a marvelous meal, Etats-Unis is a charming, family-run restaurant with a concise daily menu of internationally influenced dishes and baked-to-order desserts. Of course, the seasons inspire deeply flavorful offerings like house-made spaghetti tossed with sautéed tiger shrimp, day boat scallops, delicate lobster stock, basil, and a touch of cream. Freshly steamed, the warm date pudding is a house signature. This relative of sticky toffee pudding is served in a bed of caramelized rum sauce with a dollop of perfect *schlag*.

The little shoebox of a dining room was recently updated with new paint, light fixtures, and leather chairs, yielding an understated urban look that appeals to its patrons, attired in both suits and jeans. Directly across the street, cousin Bar Etats-Unis bustles with a lively crowd who enjoys its more casual menu.

Appetizers	*Entrées*	*Desserts*
• Gnocchi, Gorgonzola, Squash,Crispy Sage	• Sautée Cod, Mint-Cilantro Pesto, Tomatoes	• Date Pudding with Caramelized Rum Sauce and Freshly Whipped Cream
• Lettuce Salad, Caramelized Pear, Nuts Stilton Cheese	• Lobster Salad, Avocado, and Lemon Tarragon Dressing	• Baked-to-order Chocolate Soufflé For Two
• Seared Foie Gras, Roasted Grapes, Balsamic Reduction	• Braised Beef Short Ribs, Horseradish Potatoes	

Frederick's Madison

Contemporary ✗✗

A3

768 Madison Ave. (bet. 65th & 66th Sts.)

Subway: 68 St - Hunter College
Phone: 212-737-7300
Web: www.fredericksnyc.com
Prices: $$$

Lunch & dinner daily

Brothers Frederick and Laurent Lesort, known for Frederick's Bar & Lounge *(8 W. 58th St.)*, also preside over Frederick's Madison. The menu focuses on Mediterranean fare in the form of small plates, tartares, charcuterie and cheeses. Signature dishes include foie gras chaud-froid, which comes seared, and in a cold terrine served with kumquat jam; open ravioli of braised rabbit; and slow-baked cod with clam nage. In the dining room, blond woods, red velvet chairs, and Lalique light fixtures bespeak an elegance befitting the Upper East Side.

Spin-off Frederick's Downtown *(637 Hudson St.)* sits on a quiet Greenwich Village corner and offers a French bistro feel with plenty of outdoor seating.

Garden Court Café

Asian ✗

B3

725 Park Ave. (at 70th St.)

Subway: 68 St - Hunter College
Phone: 212-570-5202
Web: www.asiasociety.org
Prices: $$

Tue – Sun lunch only

Flooded by natural light in the glass-enclosed, plant-filled lobby of the Asia Society, this cafe is a far cry from your garden-variety museum restaurant. You may not hear much about it, but the Garden Court is worth seeking out, not only for its airy ambience but for the Asian dishes that expertly fuse elements of east and west.

Serving lunch Tuesday through Sunday, the Garden Court balances salads and sandwiches with seasonal entrées (Korean BBQ duck; steamed mahi mahi in a banana leaf). It's a quality show, right down to the careful presentation and good service—and the museum's entry fee is not required to access the cafe.

Don't miss the museum gift shop for cookbooks, teas, and wonderful gifts.

Geisha

Japanese ✗✗

A1

33 E. 61st St. (bet. Madison & Park Aves.)

Subway: Lexington Av - 59 St
Phone: 212-813-1112
Web: www.geisharestaurant.com
Prices: $$$

Mon – Fri lunch & dinner
Sat dinner only

Vittorio Assaf and Fabio Granato, the duo who brought Serafina to the Upper Eastside, strike again with Geisha—though this geisha den is more polished cool than bowing modesty. Decked out in origami and cherry blossom light fixtures, Geisha's vibrant two-floor space hums with the stylish, sophisticated crowd that pours in nightly—as often for the well-rounded cocktail list as for the food. The Asian-influenced menu, originally developed by Chef Eric Ripert of Le Bernardin, rounds the usual Japanese bases—sushi, sashimi and maki—but regulars may find themselves migrating to Geisha's sizable and creative salads. A rare duck breast with crackling skin gets a shot of texture from frisée lettuce, yellow raisins, and crunchy roasted pistachios.

Il Riccio

Italian ✗

B3

152 E. 79th St. (bet. Lexington & Third Aves.)

Subway: 77 St
Phone: 212-639-9111
Web: www.ilriccionyc.com
Prices: $$

Lunch & dinner daily

Located four blocks from the Metropolitan Museum of Art, Il Riccio makes a great lunch spot when you've had your fill of fine art. A shiny brass door beckons you into the restaurant, which sits on a busy street, surrounded by boutiques and eateries. Two different dining rooms here offer a comfortable respite from trekking through museum galleries.

Diners are cosseted at Il Riccio, where the chef takes great care in preparing Italian classics. Although the menu is not extensive, it does offer a nice range of dishes—the emphasis here is on pasta, from spaghetti with crab meat and tomato to gnocchi tossed in a bright pesto—along with a roster of daily specials. The short wine list celebrates Italian *vino*, including a page of pricey reserves.

J.G. Melon

B3

1291 Third Ave. (at 74th St.)

Subway: 77 St
Phone: 212-744-0585
Web: N/A
Prices: 😊😊

Lunch & dinner daily

Preppies still wanting a taste of the college life haunt J.G. Melon, where burgers and beers are the staples. The cheeseburger, cooked to order and served on a toasted English muffin, is arguably one of the best in the city, and the crispy, golden, cottage fries that accompany it perfectly round out the meal (literally, since the fries are round!). Cold nights bring customers begging for Melon's chili.

This place has been a New York institution for generations, and is always packed with neighborhood residents, including recent college graduates and young families with kids. Checkered tablecloths, wood floors and a long wooden bar give an amiable local pub feel, while the old-school staff makes everyone feel like a regular.

Kai

A3

822 Madison Ave. (bet. 68th & 69th Sts.)

Subway: 68 St - Hunter College
Phone: 212-988-7277
Web: www.itoen.com
Prices: $$$

Tue – Sat lunch & dinner

Secreted away above the Ito En tea shop, Kai occupies a hushed, Zen space. In front, diners are invited to tables looking over Madison Avenue, while the back counter affords a ringside view of the disciplined chefs at work.

The cuisine at Kai is unquestionably refined and though an a la carte menu offers quality choices, the talent lies in the tasting menus. The *kaiseki* menu (book in advance) displays brilliance and discipline as the chefs craft seasonal Japanese ingredients into meticulous preparations. As an alternative, the seasonal menu displays many of the same products with no less precision, served graciously by the thoughtful staff.

Seasonal sake pairings make a pleasant coupling and share distinctive sips at a nice price.

JoJo ✿

Contemporary ✗✗

B1

160 E. 64th St. (bet. Lexington & Third Aves.)

Subway: Lexington Av - 63 St
Phone: 212-223-5656
Web: www.jean-georges.com
Prices: $$$

Lunch & dinner daily

Jean-Georges Management

JoJo will always be special to its "father," superstar Chef Jean-Georges Vongerichten. After all, this restaurant was his first in New York City, launched in 1991. Christened with the nickname that Vongerichten knew as a boy, JoJo dovetails perfectly into this affluent neighborhood. The lovely town house contains a tiny bar area that cozies up to the front window. Beyond, the dining room creates a romantic lair filled with crystal chandeliers, rich tapestries, plush velvets, and fine silks.

Chef Ron Gallo possesses the confidence to coax the flavors out of great ingredients. He shows his talent to best advantage in the likes of a perfectly seasoned English pea soup, thick and aromatic, with just the right touch of herbs and cream. A seasonal chef's tasting augments the à la carte menu at dinner, while JoJo's daytime small-plates menu is popular with the ladies who lunch.

Appetizers
- Tuna Roll with Soy Bean Emulsion
- Goat Cheese, Potato Terrine, Mesclun, Arugula Juice
- Shrimp Dusted in Orange Power, Artichokes, Arugula

Entrées
- Codfish, Marinated Vegetables, Aromatic Sauce
- Sirloin Steak, Gingered Mushrooms, Soy Caramel
- Chicken, Olives, Coriander, Chick Pea Fries

Desserts
- Green Apple Pavlova, Thai Basil Seeds
- Warm Chocolate Cake with Vanilla Ice Cream
- Banana Brioche Pudding, Candied Pecans, Nutmeg Ice Cream

Kings' Carriage House

C2

American XX

251 E. 82nd St. (bet. Second & Third Aves.)

Subway: 86 St (Lexington Ave.)
Phone: 212-734-5490
Web: N/A
Prices: $$

Lunch & dinner daily

This restored carriage house is about as far from New York as you can get in New York. Run by Elizabeth King and her husband Paul Farell (who hails from Dublin), Kings' Carriage House resembles an Irish country manor, set about with Chinese porcelains, antique furnishings and hunting trophies on the walls. Its lovely ambience and personal service is perfect for charming a loved one or friend, or impressing out-of-town guests.

Simple and old-fashioned American dishes (as in a salad of grilled chicken breast and asparagus spears fanned over frisée; a dessert of ripe seasonal fruit) dominate the daily changing fixed-price menu. The lunch menu is especially inexpensive, but if you can't make it for a meal, do drop 'round for afternoon tea.

L'Absinthe

B4

French XXX

227 E. 67th St. (bet. Second & Third Aves.)

Subway: 68 St – Hunter College
Phone: 212-794-4950
Web: www.labsinthe.com
Prices: $$$

Lunch & dinner daily

Like a fine wine, L'Absinthe has improved with age. This upscale charmer has matured into a warm and amiable bistro with a soupçon of grace that raises it above similar restaurants. The remarkably accommodating staff caters to an understated, sophisticated clientele that one would expect to find in this quietly elegant setting.

The well-made menu highlights "brasserie classics," some offering modern touches, in addition to changing seasonal specials. A traditional steak tartare is quite good, served with mâche, and excellent frites. Separate menus are designed for holidays; this is truly a lovely spot for a celebration. For romance or dinner with the parents, it has the graciousness to impress—perhaps even more so after all these years.

La Goulue

A3

746 Madison Ave. (bet. 64th & 65th Sts.)

Subway: Lexington Av - 63 St
Phone: 212-988-8169
Web: www.lagoulurestaurant.com
Prices: $$$

Lunch & dinner daily

Named for the 19th-century Moulin Rouge dancer immortalized by Henri de Toulouse-Lautrec, La Goulue's zinc bar, antique mirrors, pressed-tin ceilings, and Art Nouveau fixtures fashion Belle Époque Paris. An upscale cast of serious diners have been seeking out this chic bistro since 1972.

Upper East Side attitude prevails at lunch, when moneyed patrons in designer clothes eye one another from tiny tables, tended by efficient, subdued waitstaff. A new chef has modernized some recipes, but classics remain excellent: foie gras is perfectly prepared, served with warm toasts, and the recommended glass of sauternes. Complete a meal with steak frites, topped off with the chocolate-drenched profiteroles . . . and a cardiologist on the side.

Le Bilboquet

A1

25 E. 63rd St. (bet. Madison & Park Aves.)

Subway: Lexington Av - 63 St
Phone: 212-751-3036
Web: N/A
Prices: $$

Lunch & dinner daily

There's no sign indicating Le Bilboquet's presence, but this swanky French restaurant is perpetually populated nightly with a sexy international crowd. Once inside, you'll observe that most of the patrons (many of them are French) seem to know each other, adding to the private-club ambience. This hotspot, with its tight quarters and loud music, is not the place for a quiet conversation, but if you're looking for a party, it's an ideal place to be.

The kitchen turns out French bistro cuisine and leaves the modern interpretations and fussy presentations to the competition. Steak tartare, roast chicken, *moules frites* and *salade Niçoise* are among the most-requested dishes. An insouciant attitude pervades the service, but the crowd never seems to care.

Lusardi's

C3

Italian ✗✗

1494 Second Ave. (bet. 77th & 78th Sts.)

Subway: 77 St
Phone: 212-249-2020
Web: www.lusardis.com
Prices: $$$

Mon – Fri lunch & dinner
Sat – Sun dinner only

After 25 years, Lusardi's still proves its commitment to running a great restaurant. Since Luigi and Mauro Lusardi first opened this neighborhood favorite in 1982, a loyal, well-heeled clientele have been indulging in delicious Italian cuisine. Fresh ingredients and careful preparation go into authentic fare such as their superb tortelli, delicate pasta enveloping spinach, mushrooms, and fontina cheese, blanketed in creamy truffle sauce. Even a humble salad shines here. Relish a quiet midday lunch or watch the room come alive in the evening hours, when packed with a coterie of devotees. Tiny, round, white-clothed tables lie in cozy rows down the elegant dining room; its classic, European décor continues to stand the test of time.

Maya

B4

Mexican ✗✗

1191 First Ave. (bet. 64th & 65th Sts.)

Subway: 68 St - Hunter College
Phone: 212-585-1818
Web: www.modernmexican.com
Prices: $$

Dinner daily

Maya practically defines casual elegance. Few restaurants are able to carry off being informal enough for a weeknight while being upscale enough for a weekend, but Maya expertly straddles that line. This spirited Mexican restaurant's pastel walls and vibrant artwork make it feel like an elegant private home, and its lively scene lures the right mix of a crowd.

Far from the burrito-laden menus of the competition, Richard Sandoval's menu reads like a love letter to Mexico. Time-honored culinary traditions are updated with a contemporary twist in many of the dishes, and a seemingly limitless margarita menu complements the elegant yet zesty creations from the devoted chef. Bursting with powerful flavors, meals here go well beyond fajita fare.

Maz Mezcal

Mexican ✗

C2

316 E. 86th St. (bet. First & Second Aves.)

Subway: 86 St (Lexington Ave.)
Phone: 212-472-1599
Web: www.mazmezcal.com
Prices: $$

Mon – Fri dinner only
Sat – Sun lunch & dinner

Simple Mexican food—and lots of it—leaves locals eager to return to Maz Mezcal, located on a busy block. Eduardo Silva now runs his family's East Side stalwart; after he took the reins several years ago, he renamed the place Maz Mezcal and then expanded it.

Flavorful Tex-Mex fare includes combination plates, as well as favorites such as enchiladas and fajitas. Dishes are tailored to mild palates in this family-friendly place, but if you prefer your food *picante*, the kitchen will be happy to spice things up. With more than 50 types of tequila, and its cousin, mezcal, available from the bar, you can count on a lively atmosphere almost every night. In warm weather, the party spills out to the backyard garden and the sidewalk seats.

Mezzaluna

Italian ✗

B3

1295 Third Ave. (bet. 74th & 75th Sts.)

Subway: 77 St
Phone: 212-535-9600
Web: www.mezzalunany.com
Prices: $$

Lunch & dinner daily

Mezzaluna is a restaurant that takes it name seriously. So much so, that they offered 20 meals to any artist (many of them Italian) who would agree to render his or her version of the restaurant's namesake crescent-shaped chopping knife. As you'll see, the 77 different versions that paper the walls each depict a unique take on this design and provide an eye-catching backdrop for well-prepared seasonal Italian dishes.

Founded by Aldo Bozzi, the restaurant has been around since 1984. Antiques imported from Italy and tables nesting close together add to the simple comfort and convivial atmosphere. From black linguine topped with fiery tomato sauce to brick-oven pizza, it's easy to see why the crowds line up here.

Nello

A1

Italian 🍴🍴

696 Madison Ave. (bet. 62nd & 63rd Sts.)

Subway: 5 Av - 59 St
Phone: 212-980-9099
Web: N/A
Prices: $$$$

Lunch & dinner daily

It's all about the Beautiful People at Nello. This place appeals to a moneyed, dress-to-impress clientele, who don't flinch at the restaurant's uptown prices. (Nello seems to keep pace with neighbors Givenchy, Christofle, Hermès and Lalique.) Inside, black-and-white photographs of an African safari adorn the walls, and little crystal vases of fresh flowers brighten the tabletops. Tables are tight, but with this chic crowd, it's all the more pleasing.

Nello is worth the splurge, not only for the delectable Italian cuisine and the charming waitstaff, but for the opportunity to see how the "other half" lives. Before you leave, pause inside the entrance to check out photographs of the rich and famous patrons who have dined here before you.

Nick's

C2

Pizza 🍴

1814 Second Ave. (at 94th St.)

Subway: 96 St (Lexington Ave.)
Phone: 212-987-5700
Web: www.nicksnyc.com
Prices: 💰💰

Lunch & dinner daily

New York has long been known for its pizzerias, and this one takes the cake—or, rather, the pie. The Manhattan satellite of the Forest Hills original, Nick's is everything you want a pizza place to be. The dining room is pleasant and cozy, the service is jovial and efficient, and you can watch the cooks hand-tossing the dough and firing your pizza in the wood-burning oven.

Pies turn out thin and crispy, spread with a good balance of tomato sauce, herbs and your choice of toppings. On the list of pasta (properly called "macaroni" in the traditional Italian-American lexicon) and meat entrées, half portions accommodate those with less hearty appetites—but with food this good at such reasonable prices, you'll want to rethink your diet.

Orsay

B3

1057 Lexington Ave. (at 75th St.)

Subway: 77 St
Phone: 212-517-6400
Web: www.orsayrestaurant.com
Prices: $$

Lunch & dinner daily

In true Parisian fashion, this smart brasserie at the corner of 75th Street overflows onto the sidewalk terrace through its large French doors. Inside, the Paris of the 1950s comes alive through the zinc bar, fan-patterned mosaic tile floor, mahogany paneling, and frosted-glass partitions.

The chef takes a few liberties with modern preparations, but the origins are French to the core. Lamb navarin, escargots, and steak tartare speak to the classic technique, while the likes of citrus-cured hamachi, or wild Duclair duckling with blood-orange glaze show contemporary flair.

Ideal for business or pleasure, Orsay's attractive bar provides a comfortable spot for guests dining alone to enjoy a glass of wine and a bountiful shellfish platter.

Park Avenue

A1

100 E. 63rd St. (at Park Ave.)

Subway: 59 St
Phone: 212-644-1900
Web: www.parkavenyc.com
Prices: $$$

Lunch & dinner daily

A dramatic improvement over its tired incarnation as the Park Avenue Café, this revamped space does something unique. Four times a year, the cafe closes for 48 hours and reopens with a completely different yet equally inspired mood, be it spring, summer, fall or winter. In a sort of architectural trompe l'œil, the design firm AvroKO—in concert with owner Michael Stillman—devised varied panels to fit the steel walls that frame the restaurant. Everything inside literally changes with the season.

The playful menu morphs cyclically too, with boosts from ingredients such as soft-shell crabs and rhubarb in spring, baby beets and vine-fresh tomatoes in summer. For dessert, the decadent and shareable "chocolate cube" is a chocoholic's dream.

Payard

B3

French 𝕏𝕏

1032 Lexington Ave. (bet. 73rd & 74th Sts.)

Subway: 77 St   Mon – Sat lunch & dinner
Phone: 212-717-5252
Web: www.payard.com
Prices: $$$

Famous for its handmade chocolates and mouth-watering French pastries, Payard is also a notable restaurant. Since you have to walk past the cases of tempting sweets to reach the dining room, there's always a danger that you'll decide to forget the main course altogether. If you do resist (until the end of the meal, that is), you'll be treated to modern French dishes such as sautéed East Coast halibut with classic ratatouille, roasted rack of lamb with Provençal vegetable bayaldi, and a tasty tart topped with rich duck confit, sweet parsnip purée and meaty lardons.

And don't even think of leaving without a sweet souvenir— perhaps a box of French *macarons*, some champagne truffles or a selection of *pâtés de fruits*—to tide you over until breakfast.

Persepolis

B3

Persian 𝕏

1407 Second Ave. (bet. 73rd & 74th Sts.)

Subway: 77 St   Mon – Sat lunch & dinner
Phone: 212-535-1100   Sun dinner only
Web: www.persepolisnyc.com
Prices: $$

This exotic Persian cuisine piques both interest and appetite, offering dishes fragrant with parsley, lemon, and saffron served with hospitality in an attractive setting. The large selection of salads and appetizers includes a trio of homemade yogurt seasoned with cucumber and dried mint, aged, dried shallots, and spinach with garlic. After a variety of starters, move on to flavorful meats such as marinated rack of lamb with eggplant purée, skewers of ground steak kebab, and saffron-marinated chicken. In lieu of the meat-focused entrées, there is also a mildly spiced vegetarian stew. Each entrée is accompanied by your choice of sour cherry-studded, almond-flecked, or dill-flavored rice. Takeout and delivery are popular options for locals.

Philippe

Chinese 🍴🍴

A1

33 E. 60th St. (bet. Madison & Park Aves.)

Subway: 5 Av - 59 St
Phone: 212-644-8885
Web: www.philippechow.com
Prices: $$$

Mon – Sat lunch & dinner
Sun dinner only

After more than 25 years at Mr. Chow in Midtown, Philippe Chow opened his own eponymous restaurant, on a very stylish block. The main room of this *tres chi-chi* spot, has a clean avant-garde look with leather banquettes lining the walls and vases of artfully arranged branches decorating niches between the dining room and bar.

His upscale Chinese cuisine ranges from striped bass Beijing to crispy duck. Entrées are sized—and priced—for two to three people (half-orders are available on some items). Noodles and dumplings merit a separate section on the menu; most every evening at 8:00 P.M., you can watch the chef craft traditional noodle dishes at a station in the middle of the dining room.

Quatorze Bis

French 🍴🍴

C3

323 E. 79th St. (bet. First & Second Aves.)

Subway: 77 St
Phone: 212-535-1414
Web: N/A
Prices: $$

Tue – Sun lunch & dinner
Mon dinner only

An Upper East Side favorite since 1989, Quatorze Bis now qualifies as a neighborhood institution. Dreams of Paris come to mind when drinking in this brasserie, with its marble-topped bar, French posters, and cozy banquettes; this décor is almost as delicious and authentic as the food.

French classics are executed with *savoir faire*, starting with the rustic *pâté de canard* served with cornichons, toast points, and a perfectly dressed salad. Other fine renditions of time-honored bistro favorites include juicy, tender steaks, drizzled with deglazed pan juices, accompanied by light crispy frites. Even the hottest day of summer is the perfect occasion to indulge in the comforting and delicious warm apple tart—happily, that's how it is always served.

Serafina Fabulous Pizza

Italian

B2

1022 Madison Ave. (bet. 78th & 79th Sts.)

Subway: 77 St   Lunch & dinner daily
Phone: 212-734-1425
Web: www.serafinarestaurant.com
Prices: $$

After browsing the tony boutiques of Madison Avenue, the Beautiful People head for Serafina Fabulous Pizza. People-watching is fantastic at this trendy Italian spot, best known for specialties cooked in its wood-burning oven. The second-floor dining room has a lively and energetic feel, while the third level boasts a retractable roof for alfresco dining in warmer months.

Snagging a seat at this popular spot may prove difficult in the evening, but great pizzas, fresh pastas, and grilled meats and fish make it well worth the wait. The gracious staff encourages those who wish to linger to sit back and enjoy a glass of the house sangria.

Six other Serafinas (all with the same menu) in Manhattan ensure that the party never ends.

Shanghai Pavilion

Chinese

B3

1378 Third Ave. (bet. 78th & 79th Sts.)

Subway: 77 St   Lunch & dinner daily
Phone: 212-585-3388
Web: N/A
Prices: ☜☜

While so many of the Upper East Side's restaurants seem to tailor their prices to an upscale clientele, Shanghai Pavilion is a real gem if you're looking for reasonably priced and sophisticated Chinese cuisine served in a pleasing, contemporary setting. Shanghai and Cantonese specialties cover all the bases, from pan-fried bean curd to steamed juicy buns filled with the likes of pork, with or without crabmeat. There's something for everyone on the generous menu, which also accommodates more westernized tastes.

If it's a traditional banquet you crave, call ahead to arrange it with the restaurant, then round up a group of friends for a multicourse feast. This isn't your average take-out joint—its food and décor rise well above the standard.

Spigolo

Italian XX

C3

1561 Second Ave. (at 81st St.)

Subway: 86 St (Lexington Ave.)
Phone: 212-744-1100
Web: N/A
Prices: $$

Dinner daily

Even at the beginning of the week, this sliver of a dining room is packed. The draw? Upper East Siders want to be among the lucky few (there are less than 20 tables) to relish the inspired Italian cooking at Spigolo.

Husband-and-wife team Scott and Heather Fratangelo met at the Union Square Café before opening this place. Food and wine are like religion here, and Scott pays serious attention to quality. Unusual yet rustic presentations, such as hake *acqua pazza* (served in a tomato-and-fish-based broth made with garlic and hot chile) are a sure bet, while more familiar dishes like light sheep's-milk-ricotta gnocchi with cream and pancetta are crowd pleasers. Heather plays the charming hostess when she's not whipping up delectable pastries.

Sushi Sasabune

Japanese X

C3

401 E. 73rd St. (at First Ave.)

Subway: 77 St
Phone: 212-249-8583
Web: N/A
Prices: $$$

Tue – Fri lunch & dinner
Sat dinner only

Nestled into the Upper East Side, the third outpost of the Sasabune family is paradise for the devoted followers who appreciate the premium quality fish with a palatable price tag. The style of rice preparation is unique here, with more assertive vinegar and warmer temperature.

Since Sasabune just serves sushi and sashimi omakase, it's not the place for newbies or picky eaters. In fact, the restaurant's motto clearly states "No Spicy Tuna. No California Roll. TRUST ME," so those hankering for tempura should steer clear.

However, the piscine parade—starting with yellowtail sashimi and finishing with the blue crab hand roll with its toasted nori juxtaposed with a creamy filling—is wholly gratifying and justifies the cult status of this modest spot.

Sushi of Gari ✲

Japanese 🍴

C3

402 E. 78th St. (bet. First & York Aves.)

Subway: 77 St
Phone: 212-517-5340
Web: www.sushiofgari.com
Prices: **$$$**

Tue – Sun dinner only

You're in excellent hands when you utter the magic two words, omakase please, at Sushi of Gari. This is no ordinary Upper East Side sushi den (though the simple, unassuming décor might suggest otherwise). This is the namesake restaurant of acclaimed sushi master, Masatoshi "Gari" Sugio—widely revered by sushiphiles across the city for his revolutionary ways with the fish.

A culinary walk with the master might include a silky sliver of red snapper, topped with tender young greens and a fried lotus chip, crunchy with sea salt; or a bright slip of salmon topped with a piping-hot roasted plum tomato, its outer layer gracefully charred into a sweet and smoky skin.

Be prepared to pay a bit for the show, for the omakase of genius doesn't come cheap. The good news is they don't stop serving until you crack, uttering those less-than-magical two words: "I'm full."

Sushi

- Bluefin Tuna with Creamy Tofu Sauce
- Salmon with Sautéed Tomato and Onion Sauce
- Miso-marinated Kanpachi with Daikon, Mint Paste and Garlic
- Torched Yari-Squid with Creamy Sea Urchin Sauce
- "Shabu Shabu" Snow Crab with Yuzu Sauce
- Herb-marinated Lobster with Mo-Jio
- Tempura Ice Cream with Strawberry Sauce
- Yuzu Panna Cotta

Sushi Seki

Japanese ✗

B4

1143 First Ave. (bet. 62nd & 63rd Sts.)

Subway: Lexington Av - 59 St
Phone: 212-371-0238
Web: N/A
Prices: $$$

Mon – Sat dinner only

A longtime neighborhood favorite, Seki is all about sushi, and the quality is just terrific. It can be a tough reservation to get, as the restaurant is both popular and small, but it's worth the advance booking to sample creations of the namesake chef, who once worked in the kitchen at Sushi of Gari.

In the modest dining nooks, the waitstaff keeps up a steady tempo, while at the cramped sushi bar, chefs craft fresh-from-the-boat products into tasty morsels. Regulars know to ask about the unique chef's sushi and daily specials that aren't written on the menu, but even the spicy-tuna set is well-fed here.

Late hours accommodate revelers who hanker for sushi after most places have closed. If you want first-rate sushi to go, Seki offers takeout.

Taco Taco 🍴

Mexican ✗

C2

1726 Second Ave. (bet. 89th & 90th Sts.)

Subway: 86 St (Lexington Ave.)
Phone: 212-289-8226
Web: N/A
Prices: 🪙

Lunch & dinner daily

If you're lucky enough to live within its delivery zone, chances are you've enjoyed a meal from Taco Taco, but this colorful Mexican restaurant isn't just for take-out.

Authentic Mexican and Tex-Mex dishes are some of the best in the city, and the prices here are as palatable as the food. Come hungry and tuck into everything from quesadillas served up Mexico City-style to huevos rancheros. Tacos are the house specialty; either the fried-fish taco or the "taco taco" (shredded pork in chipotle sauce) is sure to please.

You'll find many of the elements—tableside guacamole, a full bar offering tasty margaritas and many varieties of tequila—popular at pricier Mexican restaurants, but this neighborhood spot keeps it real. New sibling Móle (205 Allen St.) shares the same carte with the Upper East Side.

Taste

American ✗

B3

1411 Third Ave. (at 80th St.)

Subway: 77 St
Phone: 212-717-9798
Web: www.elizabar.com
Prices: $$

Lunch & dinner daily

Youngest son of the founders of Zabar's (New York's landmark West Side deli), Eli Zabar launched his second fresh-food market, Eli's, in 1998. Taste is adjacent to the market, a restaurant devised to pair small plates and changing entrées with Eli's favorite regional wines.

Drop in after work to sample affordable wines by the glass, and be sure to order something (like roasted eggplant and tomato tart or baby burgers on brioche) to nosh on. Dinner and brunch are full-service with appealing American cooking that's always full of flavor. At breakfast and lunch the setting is more relaxed and food is presented cafeteria-style. The menu always represents the tasty, home-style fare Eli's is known for—cooked better at his place than yours.

Tori Shin

Japanese ✗✗

B4

1193 First Ave. (bet. 64th & 65th Sts.)

Subway: 68 St
Phone: 212-988-8408
Web: N/A
Prices: $$$

Mon – Sat dinner only

From the outside this place doesn't look like much, but the sign reading "Authentic Japanese Food Culture" is your first indication that this team isn't fooling around. The sophisticated crowd of aficionados here reserves a seat at the counter, in order to catch the chefs in action.

You'll quickly find that this isn't your average yakitori and beer joint. The kitchen uses top-quality chicken and expertly seasons and grills every part of the bird from heart to skin. The chefs will adjust your menu upon request, but be open to necks or livers as they might turn out to be your favorites.

Note that before 10:00P.M. only fixed menus are offered. These include a dinner set and an *omakase*, and are truly the best way to sample the fare here.

Trata Estiatorio

B3

Greek ✗✗

1331 Second Ave. (bet. 70th & 71st Sts.)

Subway: 68 St - Hunter College   Lunch & dinner daily
Phone: 212-535-3800
Web: www.trata.com
Prices: $$$

Everything about this bright trattoria will remind you of the sea, from the crisp blue-and-white façade to the stone-washed white walls and the colorful mosaics of ocean life above the bar. The design lures a fashionable clientele who also frequent its sister in the Hamptons.

With the Greek Islands as a theme and fresh seafood displayed on ice by the open kitchen, what else would you expect but a daily changing list of fruits of the sea? Whole fish from around the globe are the house specialty; fresh catches like Alaskan Arctic char and African tiger shrimp are charcoal-grilled and priced per pound. Go for lunch if you want a bargain.

Don't overlook the wine list here; many Greek varietals are cited with descriptions of their characteristics.

Triangolo

C2

Italian ✗

345 E. 83rd St. (bet. First & Second Aves.)

Subway: 86 St (Lexington Ave.)   Dinner daily
Phone: 212-472-4488
Web: www.triangolorestaurant.com
Prices: $$

Although it's tucked away off the beaten track of upscale shops and world-class museums, Triangolo nonetheless keeps customers lining up outside. Why? Attentive service might be one reason. The warm décor in the simple dining room is another.

The greatest draw, though, is the generous menu of pastas, topped with hearty homemade sauces; *rotolo di pasta montanara* (rolled pasta filled with spinach, porcini and parmesan) is one of the signature dishes. Of course, you won't want to dive into the pastas without first sampling something from the long list of antipasti. And, by all means, save room for the tasty tiramisu.

Reasonable prices make one more reason why Triangolo might just be better than dining at your Italian grandmother's house.

Uva

Italian

1486 Second Ave. (bet. 77th & 78th Sts.)

Subway: 77 St
Phone: 212-472-4552
Web: www.uvawinebarnewyork.com
Prices: $$

Mon – Fri dinner only
Sat – Sun lunch & dinner

You'd never guess that this intimate little wine bar, with its mixed crowd, lively ambience, and impressive wine list (*uva* is Italian for "grape") was related to Lusardi's, an Italian stalwart in the Upper East. In Uva's rustic, dimly lit dining room, the friendly Italian staff wends their way around the tightly spaced tables, delivering plates and offering advice about the wine and food.

Surprisingly good cuisine, served in generous portions at reasonable prices, is a far cry from the generic Italian-American standards. Instead, Uva's menu encompasses a creative selection of house-made pastas, entrées, cheeses, and cured meats. There always seems to be a crush at the bar, where patrons can taste more than 30 wines by the glass.

Hotels and restaurants change every year, so change your Michelin Guide every year!

Upper West Side

Great cultural institutions and good food are what you can expect from the Upper West Side, along with tidy rows of restored brownstones and stunning apartment buildings bordering Central Park. Reaching from Central Park West to the Hudson River between 59th Street and 110th Street, the Upper West Side is home to the **Lincoln Center for the Performing Arts** and the **American Museum of Natural History.** This neighborhood is also where you'll run into some of the city's favorite food markets, such as Zabars *(80th St. & Broadway),* a family-run New York institution for more than 75 years.

FROM GOATS TO GLORY

Development has been relatively recent in this neighborhood. In the late 19th century, shantytowns, saloons and stray goats populated the area. This all changed in 1884 when Henry Hardenbergh built New York's first luxury apartment house—the celebrated **Dakota**—at 1 West 72nd Street. With its eclectic turrets, Gothic gables and ornate finials, the Dakota made a fitting setting for the 1968 film *Rosemary's Baby.* Over the years, the Dakota housed many celebrities, including Leonard Bernstein, Lauren Bacall and John Lennon.

After the Dakota came the ornate **Ansonia Hotel** *(2101-2119 Broadway)* in 1904, the first to have a drive-in courtyard, and the elegant **San Remo** *(145 Central Park West),* with its stunning Central Park views. These sumptuous digs appealed to many bankers, lawyers and other well-to-do professionals, who were followed in the 1930s by prosperous Jewish families relocating from the Lower East Side. These glorious private and public residences are made even more lavish with enclosed and beautifully landscaped gardens.

Gentrification of the older row houses in recent years has made the cross streets quite desirable, particularly among young professionals and college students. Today the Upper West Side's tree-lined residential blocks provide a quiet contrast to the bustle of Broadway, the area's commercial spine.

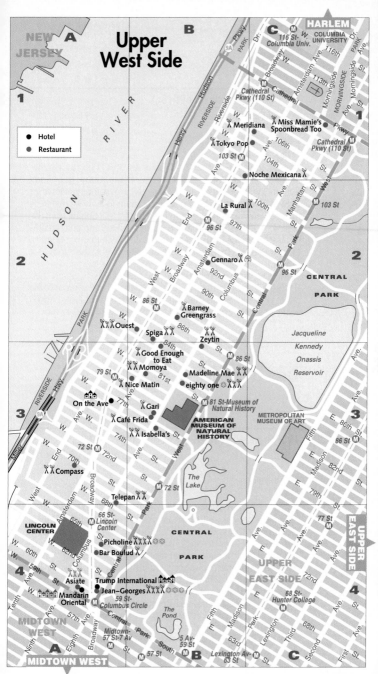

Upper West Side

NEW JERSEY

HARLEM

COLUMBIA UNIVERSITY

116 St–Columbia Univ.

Columbia Univ.

113th

Cathedral Pkwy (110 St)

Morningside

Cathedral Pkwy (110 St)

Legend:
- Hotel
- Restaurant

Meridiana

Miss Mamie's Spoonbread Too

Tokyo Pop

Noche Mexicana

103 St

La Rural

96 St

103 St

Gennaro

96 St

CENTRAL PARK

86 St

Barney Greengrass

Ouest

Spiga

Zeytin

Good Enough to Eat

Momoya

Madeline Mae

eighty one

Nice Matin

On the Ave

Gari

86 St

81 St–Museum of Natural History

AMERICAN MUSEUM OF NATURAL HISTORY

METROPOLITAN MUSEUM OF ART

86 St

Café Frida

Isabella's

72 St

Jacqueline Kennedy Onassis Reservoir

82nd

79th

Compass

Telepan

72 St

The Lake

77 St

UPPER EAST SIDE

LINCOLN CENTER

66 St–Lincoln Center

Picholine

Bar Boulud

CENTRAL PARK

72nd

68 St–Hunter College

Asiate

Trump International

Jean–Georges

Mandarin Oriental

59 St–Columbus Circle

The Pond

5 Av–59 St

63rd

MIDTOWN WEST

Midtown–57 St–7 Av

57 St

Lexington Av–63 St

MIDTOWN WEST

HUDSON RIVER

337

Asiate

80 Columbus Circle (at 60th St.)

Subway: 59 St - Columbus Circle
Phone: 212-805-8881
Web: www.mandarinoriental.com
Prices: $$$$

Lunch & dinner daily

Central Park forms the focal point for this 35th-floor aerie, located off the Mandarin Oriental hotel lobby (*see hotel listing*). Wrap-around windows showcase stunning views of New York City's first official Scenic Landmark, whose real trees trump even the sculpture of stylized branches hanging from the ceiling. A sophisticated palette of black, silver, and gold creates the backdrop for well-spaced tables and secluded banquettes, expertly served by uniformed team attentive to the room as a whole.

Artful preparations rely on quality ingredients to attain their flavorful, visually attractive results. An exotic yet approachable allure pervades meals that might start with a Kaffir-lime-infused seafood risotto and end with *kabocha* squash panna cotta.

Bar Boulud

1900 Broadway (bet. 63rd & 64th Sts.)

Subway: 66 St - Lincoln Center
Phone: 212-595-0303
Web: www.danielnyc.com
Prices: $$$

Lunch & dinner daily

The fourth and newest addition to Chef Daniel Boulud's New York brood isn't quite as fussy as older siblings Daniel, DB Bistro Moderne, and Café Boulud. Maybe it's because Bar Boulud likes to kick back a few now and then, as indicated by the wine barrel that marks the entrance. Inside the deep and narrow space, you'll find an ample grape list, divided into four whimsical categories: Discoveries, Classics, Legends, and Heartthrobs. The food doesn't stray too far from the classically-trained Boulud's wheelhouse, though—upscale French comfort food, with wine-friendly nibblers like charcuterie, pâtés, and terrines dominate the menu. Don't miss the luscious desserts, like a mocha tarte churned with creamy swirls of chocolate and coffee.

Barney Greengrass

B2

Deli ⑂

541 Amsterdam Ave. (at 86th St.)

Subway: 86 St (Broadway)
Phone: 212-724-4707
Web: www.barneygreengrass.com
Prices:

Tue – Sun lunch only

 Having just celebrated its 100th anniversary in June 2008, this Upper West Side institution looks forward to many more years of serving up the best smoked-fish platters around. New York's venerable "Sturgeon King" has truly earned its title.

In addition to serving breakfast, lunch, and supper until 5:00 P.M., they do double duty as a carry-out business and now take Internet orders. Whether you nosh in or take out, the deli sandwiches—piled high with pastrami, tongue, house-cured graviax or homemade egg salad, and served with a big crunchy pickle—are among the best in the city.

To eat here is to take a trip back in time. Service without ceremony but heavy NY attitude makes a trip to Barney Greengrass an authentic and essential experience.

Café Frida

B3

Mexican ⑂

368 Columbus Ave. (bet. 77th & 78th Sts.)

Subway: 81 St - Museum of Natural History
Phone: 212-712-2929
Web: www.cafefrida.com
Prices: $$

Lunch & dinner daily

The space formerly occupied by raucous Tequilla's on Columbus now houses a more serious Mexican restaurant. Red stucco walls and wrought-iron chandeliers retain the welcoming feel of a rustic cantina, but new owners have abandoned the run-of-the-mill burritos for cuisine rooted in regional Mexican traditions. Crowds of diners here appear to approve.

House-made sauces, moles, organic produce, and hand-made tortillas demonstrate attention to detail insuring complexity of flavors in dishes such as the lamb shank cooked in parchment, marinated in *guajilo* chile sauce, avocado leaf, and *hoja santa* (an aromatic herb). With their solid understanding of the cuisine, the kitchen staff freely and deftly adds heat to the dishes, presented by a friendly waitstaff.

Compass

Contemporary

208 W. 70th St. (bet. Amsterdam & West End Aves.)

Subway: 72 St (Broadway)
Phone: 212-875-8600
Web: www.compassrestaurant.com
Prices: $$

Mon – Sat dinner only
Sun lunch & dinner

Urbanista-sophisticates point themselves towards Compass for innovative American fare in polished, airy surroundings. Bright red accents enliven the fantastic back-lit bar, posh lounge with leather banquettes, and dining room in cooler tones; square slate-covered columns lend a sleek feel throughout.

Compared with its Upper West Side neighbors, this establishment displays culinary ambition, as in the juniper-crusted venison loin, served with braised shank ragout, herb gnocchi, Swiss chard, and *vincotto* jus. Starters like the tender and smoky grilled squid are refreshing, balanced, and well presented. Inventive cocktails and pairings from the well-chosen list of international wines further enhance meals, and help diners forgive the uneven service.

Gari

Japanese

370 Columbus Ave. (bet. 77th & 78th Sts.)

Subway: 81 St - Museum of Natural History
Phone: 212-362-4816
Web: N/A
Prices: $$$

Dinner daily

The Upper West Side outpost of Sushi of Gari (there are now three in Manhattan) fosters a hip aesthetic with its contemporary Asian décor and large glass windows facing the sidewalk.

While ingredients are top quality and everything is made to order, there is more focus on mass appeal here, with more guests appearing to choose à la carte rather than put themselves in the skillful hands of the sushi chefs, where the true beauty of Gari lies. A fine mix of sushi, including signatures by Chef Masatoshi "Gari" Sugio, and cooked dishes are all prepared with a modern touch. European influences are evident in items such as the foie gras and short ribs.

Offering a well-chosen list of sake and wine, plus professional service, Gari is packed nightly.

eighty one ✿

Contemporary 𝓧𝓧𝓧

B3

45 W. 81st St. (bet. Central Park West & Columbus Ave.)

Subway:	81 St - Museum of Natural History	Dinner daily
Phone:	212-873-8181	
Web:	www.excelsiorhotelny.com	
Prices:	$$$	

This newcomer's location on 81st Street accounts for the name. Across from the Hayden Planetarium, a handsome dining room with contemporary décor has landed. Crimson banquettes and a glass wall of wine create an appealing, lively space, perfect for friends, families, and celebrations.

Chef Ed Brown is the one to thank for the fresh flavors rarely found on the sedate Upper West Side. Luxury items—caviar from the Caspian Sea, truffles from France, pumpkin oil from Austria—punctuate a menu that shows off a modern twist. The kitchen creates seasonal dishes with a nice balance of texture, taste, and contrast. A poached egg with milk-fed Vermont veal sweetbreads served atop a toasted brioche in a pool of rich, meaty broth will give you the idea.

The bar and lounge at the entry is a sophisticated spot for a cocktail, appetizers, or wine from the smart selection.

Appetizers

- Baby Calamari a la Plancha, Pimento, Chorizo and Potato Sauce
- Poached Hen Egg, Green Asparagus, Parmesan
- Konpachi with Ginger Milk, White Soy

Entrées

- Halibut with Fennel, Meyer Lemon Salad, Roasted Fish Vinaigrette
- Roasted Chicken Breast with Fava, Lardo, Potato, and Peas
- Lamb Two Ways

Desserts

- Bourbon Banana Bread Pudding, Chocolate Gelato, Rum Raisins, Chocolate Butterscotch
- Greek Yogurt Cheesecake
- Cinnamon Sugared Peanut Fritters

Gennaro 😊

B2

Italian ✗

665 Amsterdam Ave. (bet. 92nd & 93rd Sts.)

Subway: 96 St (Broadway)   Dinner daily
Phone: 212-665-5348
Web: www.gennarorestaurant.com
Prices: 😊😊

New York may be renowned for its high-priced restaurants, but Gennaro is proof that terrific meals are available to everyone. A sampling of the value-driven wine selection, which leans heavily toward Italy, is displayed in the back of this lively room. The small, jovial space is crowded and often loud as attentive waiters carefully navigate between close, small tables. However, this remains a happy, chatty place, where guests are thrilled to see everything that comes their way.

The food is terrific—honest, well made, not terribly complicated, and absolutely satisfying. Pasta dishes are simply perfect; hear the "oohs" as diners are transported back to Italy.

Gennaro Picone's genuine trattoria deserves every single accolade it has received.

Good Enough to Eat

B3

American ✗

483 Amsterdam Ave. (bet. 83rd & 84th Sts.)

Subway: 79 St   Lunch & dinner daily
Phone: 212-496-0163
Web: www.goodenoughtoeat.com
Prices: $$

Serving breakfast, lunch, dinner, and takeout, Good Enough to Eat is an affordable neighborhood gem in an area quickly pricing such establishments out of reach. The décor is oddly endearing with its kitschy folk art and cows, cows, cows everywhere.

Chef/owner Carrie Levin has been serving the likes of old-fashioned grilled cheese sandwiches and organic roast chicken with mashed potatoes to repeat audiences since opening in 1981. Other creations may include a moist and buttery fish sandwich with tangy watercress and "funky" slaw. Join the masses in bringing the whole family; this children's menu has been taste-tested by young and picky palates.

Out front, the wide sidewalk accommodates outdoor seating, fittingly enclosed by a white picket fence.

Isabella's

Mediterranean ✗✗

B3

359 Columbus Ave. (at 77th St.)

Lunch & dinner daily

Subway: 79 St
Phone: 212-724-2100
Web: www.brguestrestaurants.com
Prices: $$

Lovely interiors, good service, and flavorful Italian food make Isabella's an enduring Upper West Side mainstay. Currently celebrating 20 years as an "Upper West Side Institution"— Isabella's boasts some of the better sidewalk real estate in the area. However, bi-level dining, adorned with greenery, and outdoor seating (weather permitting) does nothing to ameliorate long waits for tables, especially during weekend brunch.

Music keeps tempo with the bustling activity, while the charming and professional staff tends to diners relishing the likes of perfectly fried calamari with jalapeño accompanied by a duo of sauces, or capellini with tender scallops. For dessert, the warm brownie sundae is an explosion of pure American sweetness. For a small corkage fee, regulars may BYOB.

La Rural

Argentinian ✗

B2

768 Amsterdam Ave. (bet. 97th & 98th Sts.)

Dinner daily

Subway: 96 St (Broadway)
Phone: 212-749-2929
Web: N/A
Prices: $$

From the owners of Café Frida comes this Argentinian-inspired restaurant, tucked into the space that was home to Pampa. The environs may look gritty, but once you step inside the long, narrow room, the 'hood melts away in favor of a cozy den decorated with framed mirrors, wood-covered columns, and exposed brick walls. Out back, a charming patio adds outdoor seating, weather permitting.

Focused, not fussy, the cuisine dishes up good value as well as good flavor. Excellent-quality meats star at La Rural, named for the annual livestock show in Buenos Aires. *Parrillada* amounts to a carnivore's feast, sized for two. Theatrically served at table on a portable grill, the combination of different cuts of steak, short ribs, sweetbreads, and Argentinian sausages are all perfectly juicy and cooked to order.

Jean Georges

A4

Contemporary

1 Central Park West (bet. 60th & 61st Sts.)

Subway: 59 St – Columbus Circle
Phone: 212-299-3900
Web: www.jean-georges.com
Prices: **$$$$**

Lunch & dinner daily

Jean-Georges Vongerichten owns a galaxy of restaurants in New York City, but this one shines above the rest. On the ground floor of the Trump International Hotel, Jean-Georges wraps its space with huge window walls looking out on Columbus Circle. Adam Tihany sculpted the minimalist geometric motif, orchestrating the interior lighting to mimic natural light at different times of the day.

Extraordinary marriages of flavors and textures surprise in each course, and sublime ingredients are transformed by the hand of a master. Tender morsels of squab might be accompanied by Asian pear, candied tamarind, microgreens and orange jus; or red snapper crusted with crushed nuts, seeds and coriander. For quality and value, go for the prix-fixe lunch menu.

Adjacent to the dining room, casual Nougatine cafe serves breakfast, lunch, and dinner sans the formality or the hefty price tag.

Appetizers

- Bay Scallop, Winter Truffle Tartare and Croutons
- Foie Gras Brûlé with Sour Cherries, Candied Pistachios
- Sea Scallops, Cauliflower, Caper-Russian Emulsion

Entrées

- Roasted Sweetbreads, Licorice, Grilled Pear and Lemon
- Goat Cheese Royale, Roasted Beet Marmalade and Pistachios
- Gulf Shrimp and Smoked Bacon

Desserts

- Chocolate Poppy Seed Cake, Meyer Lemon Curd, Halva Powder
- Apple Confit, Pine Nut Sponge, Smoked Raisin, Tamarind Ice Cream
- Granny Smith & Fennel Sorbet, Candied Fennel

Madaleine Mae

Southern XX

B3

461 Columbus Ave. (at 82nd St.)

Lunch & dinner daily

Subway: 81 St - Museum of Natural History
Phone: 212-496-3000
Web: www.madaleinemae.com
Prices: $$

Looking for a change from the cadre of cookie-cutter concepts that have germinated recently on the Upper West Side? Make way for Madaleine Mae, a new restaurant that entices with its well-executed comfort food.

Jonathan Waxman, of Barbuto, has hit upon something unique here. Stop in for smoked ham and biscuits with gravy at breakfast, or classic sandwiches like a fried catfish po' boy at lunch. Dinner "standards" include an outstanding Lowcountry jambalaya, the bottom layer of rice browned to a perfect crisp in an iron skillet. Recalling the old days when southerners created folk remedies by distilling sugar cane, the mind-boggling assortment of house-made "rhum cures" at Madaleine Mae are still good for what ails you.

Meridiana

Italian X

C1

2756 Broadway (bet. 105th & 106th Sts.)

Dinner daily

Subway: 103 St (Broadway)
Phone: 212-222-4453
Web: N/A
Prices: $$

Welcoming and convivial, Meridiana is the kind of place just right for gathering with friends, chatting and getting to know people while tucking into a plate of delicious Italian food. Chef/owner Gianni "Johnny" Nicolosi and his wife, Pilar, have clearly come up with a formula for success. At the helm of this place since 1994, the couple still cossets diners in an inviting columned room painted with frescoes depicting a villa in Pompeii. Television screens are thankfully missing from the bar area.

Gifted hands in the kitchen make stalwarts such as *spaghetti con salsa di seppie al nero* new again, the al dente pasta caressed by a thick silky sauce tossed with diced calamari, fresh basil, tomato, and squid ink. Before you order, be sure to review the tempting list of nightly specials.

Miss Mamie's Spoonbread Too

C1

Southern ✗

366 W. 110th St./Cathedral Pkwy.
(bet. Columbus & Manhattan Aves.)

Subway: Cathedral Pkwy/110 St (Central Park West)
Phone: 212-865-6744
Web: www.spoonbreadinc.com
Prices: ⊜⊜

Lunch & dinner daily

This warm, welcoming atmosphere and service evokes an easygoing country setting—smack dab in the middle of the city. Homey, rustic touches, like kitchen implements hanging on the walls, mix well with retro red and yellow tile floors and Formica tables. The dining room floods with natural light, while pure, raw soul music plays in the background.

The menu is a celebration of Southern classics and does not veer much from this trajectory. However, this should not stop anyone from reviewing the daily boards for specials. Food this appealing, genuine, and satisfying can only be topped with perfectly sweet homemade ice tea and red velvet cake (a dark, moist, indulgent specimen of this classic dessert). Finish with the best coffee a dollar can buy.

Momoya

B3

Japanese ✗✗

427 Amsterdam Ave. (bet. 80th & 81st Sts.)

Subway: 79 St
Phone: 212-989-4466
Web: www.themomoya.com
Prices: $$$

Mon – Fri dinner only
Sat – Sun lunch & dinner

A welcomed newcomer to this (until recently) restaurant-starved stretch of the Upper West, Momoya's new uptown location appears more sophisticated than its Chelsea sibling, celebrated for its sleek setting and made-to-please sushi offerings. Curvaceous wood-textured walls disappear into the grey ceiling, leather booths, and slate floors. The marble sushi counter is complemented by sexy lighting, pulsating music, and a relaxed staff pacing service at a fine tempo.

Much care is taken with selection and preparation of ingredients—*toro* melts in your mouth, served alongside sweet sea urchin, spiked with a drop of soy. Desserts offer surprises that straddle East-meets-West cuisine with aplomb, as in the delicate *mille* crêpes with green tea and crème anglaise.

Nice Matin

Mediterranean

B3

201 W. 79th St. (at Amsterdam Ave.)

Lunch & dinner daily

Subway: 79 St
Phone: 212-873-6423
Web: www.nicematinnyc.com
Prices: $$

Named after the daily newspaper published in the major city on France's Côte d'Azur, Nice Matin transports diners to the sun-drenched Mediterranean coast.

Niçoise dishes here exhibit as many vibrant colors as appear in the room's luminous décor. Done up as a French cafe, the place asserts its unique personality by avoiding all the decorative clichés you find in many Gallic-style restaurants; lights dangle from the tops of high pillars that spread umbrella-like against the ceiling, and tables sport Formica tops.

The menu, like a tanned French lothario, wanders the wider Mediterranean region for its inspiration. Arctic char, roasted beets, fennel, and citrus sauce on Monday and old-fashioned roast duck on Saturday, bring fans in on specific days of the week.

Noche Mexicana

Mexican

B1

852 Amsterdam Ave. (bet. 101st & 102nd Sts.)

Lunch & dinner daily

Subway: 103 St (Broadway)
Phone: 212-662-6900
Web: www.noche-mexicana.com
Prices:

Tucked in between small restaurants and bodegas, Noche Mexicana is a great find. Bright and cheery, the restaurant's walls are papered with posters of artwork by Diego Rivera. The dining room is small, but authentic Mexican food is the real focus here, where an engaging staff with a warm spirit attends to guests. The *taco de lengua* may be messy, but the tender, tasty beef tongue dressed with cilantro, onions, and tomatoes, and wrapped in corn tortillas, is worth the laundry bill. You won't go wrong with the great tamales, *tingas,* or the *taco cesina* (filled with preserved beef). If you like your food *caliente,* make sure to request it spicy.

Grab a seat in the back of the restaurant, where you can watch those delicious tamales being made.

Ouest

B2

Contemporary XXX

2315 Broadway (bet. 83rd & 84th Sts.)

Subway: 86 St (Broadway)
Phone: 212-580-8700
Web: www.ouestny.com
Prices: $$$

Mon – Sat dinner only
Sun lunch & dinner

This polished restaurant from Chef Tom Valenti draws celebrities, media personalities, and neighborhood denizens alike. Past the perennially busy bar, you'll reach the large room at the back, which peers into the open kitchen. Bring some friends so you'll be more likely to snag one of the terrific circular booths covered in deep-red tufted leather. Low lighting turns Ouest into a romantic spot for dinner, while an Ouest Sour with yuzu and crispy poached eggs with house-smoked duck star at the lively Sunday brunch.

Behind the stoves, a veritable army of chefs riffs on American comfort food, resulting in dishes (such as crusted cod with mashed Yukon potatoes and pickled asparagus) that are high on originality and strong on presentation.

Spiga

B2

Italian XX

200 W. 84th St. (bet. Amsterdam Ave. & Broadway)

Subway: 86 St (Broadway)
Phone: 212-362-5506
Web: www.spiganyc.com
Prices: $$$

Dinner daily

Tucked away on an Upper West Side block, this delightful restaurant nestles tables into every available nook of its attractive dining room. Banquettes by the front windows, which overlook the street, are lined with colorful silk pillows. Sheaves of wheat in cylindrical vases add to the rustic tone set by exposed brick walls and rough-hewn wood paneling. Recently, Spiga's founding partner and chef—Salvatore Corea—sold the restaurant to his brother and moved on. The new chef has made few changes to the menu, which maintains a list of homemade pastas followed by *secondi* that are split between meat and fish dishes. Look for good offerings by the glass on the all-Italian wine list.

Service goes smoothly, and the new owner manages the small space with efficiency and grace.

Picholine ✿ ✿

A4

Mediterranean ✕✕✕✕

35 W. 64th St. (bet. Broadway & Central Park West)

Dinner daily

Subway:	66 St - Lincoln Center
Phone:	212-724-8585
Web:	www.picholinenyc.com
Prices:	$$$

It's best to think in terms of cat years when talking Manhattan restaurants. Case in point: on paper, Picholine will celebrate its sweet 16th this year, but this elegant Upper West Side steady is no kitten. With its jackets preferred policy and well-bred wine list, Terrance Brennan's sophisticated first-born has matured into graceful venerability over the last few years.

Besides, a classy facelift in 2006 (to a soothing lavender and cream motif) and a changing of the kitchen guards with the entrance of Chef Richard Farnabe, has breathed new life into Picholine.

With the focus squarely back on the food, look for crispy, roasted fillet of John Dory served with creamy leeks and cauliflower mousseline. For dessert, try the luscious rhubarb, surrounded by a chilled ginger soup and thumped with a dollop of fresh yogurt sorbet.

Appetizers

- Sea Urchin Panna Cotta, Chilled "Ocean" Consommé, Caviar
- "Bacon & Eggs", Polenta, Tuna Bacon, Truffle Toast
- Warm Maine Lobster, Green Papaya and Kaffir Lime-Lobster

Entrées

- Heirloom Chicken "Kiev", Liquid Foie Gras
- Sea Scallops, Cauliflower Silk and Blood Orange Grenobloise
- Red-legged Partridge, Tokyo Turnips, Foie Gras Sabayon

Desserts

- Caramel Apple Brioche, Salted Caramel Ice Cream
- Chocolate Soufflé, Peanut Butter Sorbet, Malt Foam
- Pear "Torchon" with Chocolate Soup

Telepan

American 🍴🍴

A3-4

72 W. 69th St. (bet. Central Park West & Columbus Ave.)

Subway: 66 St - Lincoln Center
Phone: 212-580-4300
Web: www.telepan-ny.com
Prices: $$$

Wed – Sun lunch & dinner
Mon – Tue dinner only

As one of the Upper West Side's favorite chefs, Bill Telepan continues to lure his loyal following to this sophisticated spot with seasonal dishes and a warm atmosphere.

Pecan-wood tables sit atop ash floors; bright, bold photographs grace green walls; and a glass-encased wine corridor bridges detached dining areas. The contemporary American menu's subtle Hungarian hints reveal the chef's roots (smoked trout on a potato-chive blini; sheep's milk ricotta blintzes); but fresh, high-quality ingredients from local greenmarkets are the real draw, not only providing produce but inspiration for changing menu items. The impressive wine list includes organic and biodynamic wines, further evidence of Telepan's commitment to agriculturally sound dining.

Tokyo Pop

Japanese 🍴

C1

2728 Broadway (bet. 104th & 105th Sts.)

Subway: 103 St (Broadway)
Phone: 212-932-1000
Web: N/A
Prices: $$

Lunch & dinner daily

The name says it all at Tokyo Pop, where a burst of bright colors creates a mood-lifting atmosphere. Diners who prefer to have a front-row seat to the action should head straight for the sushi bar, where the chef dazzles with his sharp skills. Sushi figures largely on the menu here, but the entrées are what really show off the chef's talent for combining textures and tastes. Unexpected items, such as the *agedashi* tofu and Sunrise Tapas roll, are standouts.

Although Columbia University reigns over the neighborhood, Tokyo Pop is far from a commissary for undergrads. This hip Japanese place can be a bit pricey, but its sushi and Asian-fusion fare is worth the price.

Zeytin

B3

Turkish ✗✗

519 Columbus Ave. (at 85th St.)

Subway: 86 St (Central Park West) Lunch & dinner daily
Phone: 212-579-1145
Web: www.zeytinny.com
Prices: $$

Step off the hubbub of Columbus Avenue into Zeytin and step into a sultry world of romantic, purple-hued walls, and low lighting. This seductive space is welcoming and intimate—perfect for a date.

Zeytin's traditional Turkish cuisine (the restaurant's name is Turkish for "olive") breathes new life into an area of the Upper West Side formerly dominated by run-of-the-mill restaurants. Ethnic-food lovers should head straight for this place, where intoxicating flavors and textures seduce diners. Eggplant-wrapped veal shank is unbelievably tender, while veal-, mushroom-, and cheese-stuffed pastries (*pachanga borek*) are delicate, yet receive high marks for flavor.

The best part? No passport is required for this culinary journey.

Couverts (✗... ✗✗✗✗✗) indicate the level of comfort found at a restaurant. The more ✗'s, the more upscale a restaurant will be.

351

John Peden / The New York Botanical Garden

The Bronx

The Bronx

The only borough attached to the mainland, the Bronx is marked by contrasts. Run-down apartment buildings and massive housing projects characterize the southern part of the borough. To the north, grand mansions and lush gardens fill prosperous sections such as Riverdale and Fieldston. Private foundations and grassroots citizen movements are successfully recreating the Bronx, and a vibrant community is slowly emerging.

MODERN MELTING POT

Named after Jonas Bronck, a Swede who settled here in 1639, the borough developed in the late 1800s. In 1904, the first subway line connecting the Bronx to the island of Manhattan opened, causing significant migration to this outlying borough. Grand Art Deco apartment buildings sprang up along the wide tree-lined thoroughfare called the **Grand Concourse**, attracting Jews from Eastern and Central Europe. Today, however, Hispanics make up more than half of the population, with African-Americans, Irish-Americans, West Indians, and others rounding out the cultural stew. A host of Italians settled in the Belmont area, though today they are mostly proprietors of local stores and shops; Albanian and Mexican immigrants now inhabit the neighborhood.

FROM BEACHES TO BASEBALL

Thanks to journalist John Mullaly, who led a movement in the late 1800s to buy inexpensive parcels of land and preserve them as parks, 25 percent of the Bronx today consists of parkland. This includes **Pelham Bay Park**, the largest in the city—with its sandy Orchard Beach. Beyond, tiny **City Island** is a gem of a beach community, complete with charming inns and seafood restaurants.

Located near the **Bronx Zoo** and **New York Botanical Gardens**, Belmont's main street, **Arthur Avenue**, lures diners from all over the tri-state area who come to eat authentic Italian fare, shop for fresh pasta, salami, and cheeses at their favorite food shops, and pick up fresh produce in the mid-avenue arcade.

Savvy shoppers flock to **The Arts and Antique District** of **Port Morris,** a collection of shops along Bruckner Boulevard, while a few blocks north on Alexander Avenue the charming **Mott Haven Historic District** *(between 137th-141st)* boasts beautiful Dutch- and Flemish-style homes.

Hunts Point, another notable South Bronx neighborhood, is known for its lively music and performing arts scene and is home to **The Bronx Academy of Arts and Dance**. Said to be the birthplace of hip-hop, rap, break-dancing, and salsa, this vivacious neighborhood has earned its borough the moniker "Boogie Down Bronx." Also worth visiting is **The Hunts Point Market**, the largest produce market in the country.

South of 161st Street, on the **Grand Concourse**, is the **Bronx Walk of Fame**, a series of lampposts sporting plaques with the names of famous Bronx natives such as General Colin Powell and Regis Philbin.

For breathtaking views in a bucolic setting, visit **Wave Hill**, a 28-acre expanse of public gardens overlooking the **Hudson River** and **Palisades**. As you weave your way through wild flowers and herb gardens, stroll up to the **Wave Hill House**, a historic country home built in 1843 and lived in by the likes of Theodore Roosevelt, Arturo Tuscanini, and Mark Twain.

Continue your tour of famed residences at **Poe Cottage** located at **Kingsbridge Road** and the **Grand Concourse.** Built in 1813, this little wooden cottage housed Edgar Allen Poe during the last years of his life, where he penned such great works as "Annabel Lee" and "The Bells." A federal and city funded restoration is planned for this aged abode, which will close during the winter of 2008 and reopen in 2010.

Sojourn to **Woodlawn Cemetery,** a 400-acre resting grounds for over 300,000 people including such esteemed individuals as Geraldine Fitzgerald, Herman Melville, Miles Davis, and many more. With its rolling lawns and beautiful memorials, this spectacular site is one of the largest burial grounds in New York City.

Summer 2008 saw the end of an era in the Bronx—it was the last season for venerable **Yankee Stadium**, built in 1923. The new stadium, which is scheduled to open in spring 2009 and retain the dimensions of the old field, will offer more amenities such as dining options and private luxury suites.

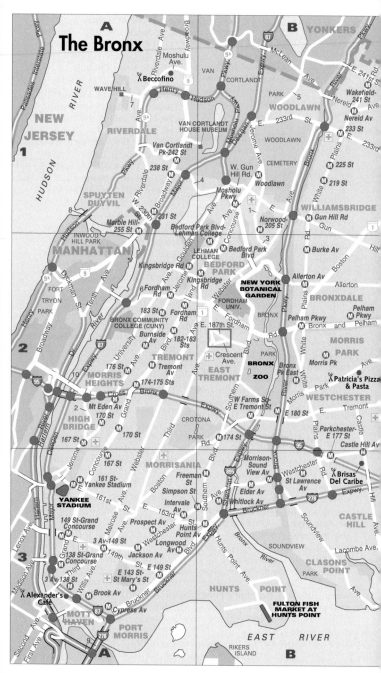

The Bronx

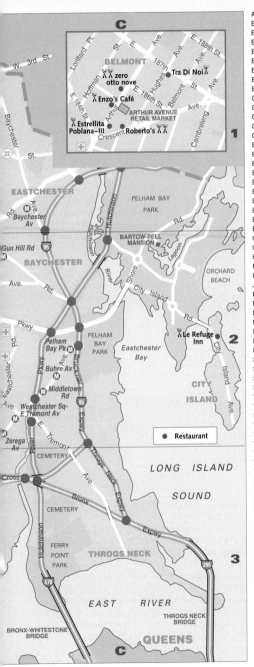

Alexander's Cafe

A3

129 Alexander Ave. (at Bruckner Blvd.)

Subway: 3 Av - 138 St   Lunch & dinner daily
Phone: 718-993-5281
Web: www.alexanderstogo.com
Prices: **$$**

Situated amidst an array of vintage shops, this affable eatery is the perfect end to an afternoon of ardent antiquing. Opened in July 2007, this cozy cafe sports a sleek and modern décor defined by dark wood tables, black leather chairs, soft lighting, and fresh flowers, which style an inviting atmosphere. In addition to a fixed menu, there's an affordable lunch buffet, and at least five daily specials; creative, quick-thinking cooks are dared to devise delicious eats from the owner's high-quality market picks of the day. Locals love the ever-changing selections, which could be grilled marlin steaks with buttery yellow squash and spinach, served with a savory avocado and pickle guacamole. Pair your meal with one of over a dozen unique beers offered.

Beccofino

A1

5704 Mosholu Ave. (at Fieldston Rd.)

Subway: 231 St (& bus BX9)   Dinner daily
Phone: 718-432-2604
Web: N/A
Prices: **$$**

Laughter abounds at unpretentious Beccofino, as locals sit and chat with family and friends—that is, until their plates arrive. At that point, conversation grinds to a halt as everyone digs into their dishes with gusto. Waitresses go the extra mile catering to diners' whims and smilingly field any questions about the menu. From starters such as stuffed eggplant, diners move on to gargantuan dishes of *spaghetti con scampi*, featuring an abundant amount of jumbo shrimp in well balanced, garlic-butter sauce, or plates overflowing with specialties such as the delicately flavored veal Sorrentino. This Riverdale charmer sends them all home satisfied.
Exposed brick walls, terra-cotta floors, soft lighting, and warm service enhance the pleasant rustic aura.

Brisas Del Caribe

Puerto-Rican 🍴

B3

1207 Castle Hill Ave. (bet. Ellis & Gleason Aves.)

Lunch & dinner daily

Subway: Castle Hill Av
Phone: 718-794-9710
Web: N/A
Prices:

This thriving neighborhood favorite delivers delicious Latin and Puerto Rican-influenced food for bargain prices. Bring a big appetite and a group of friends to tackle the abundant portions of *peril*, silky, and deeply flavored pork, slowly cooked, and served with yellow rice.

Welcoming and generous, the mostly bilingual staff attracts a regular clientele of families with children in tow, as well as food adventurers seeking new flavors. The restaurant is a popular local spot for a late night snack of Cuban roast pork sandwiches, accompanied by *morir sonando*, soursop, and wheat shakes.

A regular wait for a table (the restaurant does not take reservations) and steady take-out business are testament to this restaurant's quality and place in the community.

Enzo's Café

Italian 🍴

C1

2339 Arthur Ave. (bet. Crescent Ave. & 187th St.)

Tue – Sun lunch & dinner

Subway: Fordham Rd (Grand Concourse)
Phone: 718-733-4455
Web: N/A
Prices: $$

It's all in the family at Enzo's. This restaurant is run by Enzo DiRende, son of one of the founders of Dominick's, a veritable institution on storied Arthur Avenue—the Little Italy of the Bronx.

Enzo's is tucked between eateries that have been serving here for decades, but in this case, youth has the advantage. A stickler for hospitality, the manager fusses over the guests and every staff member has a smile.

Expect the familiar—linguini with red sauce and clams, whole fish Livornese and tiramisú—but the food is just like your *nonna* whipped up. The delicious crusty bread and desserts come fresh from bakeries in the neighborhood.

Enzo's has two locations in the Bronx: the newly refurbished and nice-looking original is located at *1998 Williamsbridge Rd*.

Estrellita Poblana III

C1

2328 Arthur Ave. (bet. Crescent Ave. & 186th St.)

Subway: Fordham Rd (Grand Concourse)
Phone: 718-220-7641
Web: N/A
Prices: 🍴

Lunch & dinner daily

New Yorkers may be surprised to find Mexican food in the Bronx's Little Italy, but this jewel box of a restaurant delivers the extraordinary. Powder-blue walls, wainscoting, hand-cut flowers, and helpful staff set the scene for quality, authentic Mexican fare.

Specials such as flavorful *budin* Azteca—a layered chicken tortilla pie with cheese—feature complex mole that is at once nutty, spicy, creamy, and thoroughly delicious. Tamales are only available on weekends, but there are numerous items—from empanadas to *camarones* Cancun—on the extensive menu. Fresh juices, *aquas frescas*, and *batidas* are sure to quench thirst and complement the wide range of mild to fiery fare. Of Estrellita's three Bronx locations, this is the most tranquil.

Le Refuge Inn

C2

586 City Island Ave. (bet. Bridge & Cross Sts.)

Subway: Pelham Bay Park (& bus BX29)
Phone: 718-885-2478
Web: www.lerefugeinn.com
Prices: $$

Tue – Sun lunch & dinner

City Island is a surprise haven of marinas, yacht clubs, and lovely Victorian homes anchored to the Bronx. One of the island's treasures is Le Refuge, an oasis of lovely ground-floor dining rooms inside a landmark home built c.1876 for wealthy oysterman Samuel Pell.

Overlooking the placid harbor, the inn is well-appointed with period antiques and crystal chandeliers. In warm weather, the veranda is set with small tables for sipping cocktails and relaxing before meals. From the kitchen come solid, well-composed standards like bouillabaisse or rack of lamb with bordelaise sauce, created by Chef/owner Pierre Saint-Denis. Service can be uneven, but it is easy to forgive this in light of a fine meal in one of the area's loveliest settings.

Patricia's Pizza & Pasta

Italian 🍴

1080 Morris Park Ave. (bet. Haight & Lurting Aves.)

Subway: Morris Park (& bus BX8)
Phone: 718-409-9069
Web: N/A
Prices: $$

Lunch & dinner daily

This casual eatery in the lively Italian-American section of the Bronx is open continuously from 11:00 A.M. until late in the evening, and perpetually full. It also does a healthy take-out business.

The devoted following truly loves the place as if home. Patricia's has the kind of menu where one can count on finding favorite comfort foods year after year, and where the same, warm Bronx waitresses-cum-sages tell it like it is. It's a familial experience in a setting that lacks pretense.

Generous portions of hearty Italian-American classics (linguini with white clam sauce or veal Sorrentino) are sure to satisfy. A selection of Bindi desserts are available along with a passable offering of house-style wines. A second location is in Throgs Neck (*3764 E. Tremont Ave.*).

Roberto's

Italian 🍴🍴

603 Crescent Ave. (at Hughes Ave.)

Subway: Fordham Rd (Grand Concourse)
Phone: 718-733-9503
Web: www.robertobronx.com
Prices: $$

Mon – Fri lunch & dinner
Sat dinner only

With the Italian food shops of Arthur Avenue nearby, it's no wonder that Roberto Paciullo's restaurant is the epicenter for Italian food in the Bronx. This is traditional Italian fare, simply the best you can find in this borough. House-made pastas share the menu with some familiar entrées and an extensive list of wines—the majority of them Italian. Check out the daily specials, but note that they're not advertised with prices (be sure to ask if you don't want to be surprised).

Amid the nondescript commercial buildings in this Bronx neighborhood, Roberto's stands out with its coral-colored façade and wrought-iron balcony. Inside, the rustic dining room mixes farmhouse tables with marvelous ceramic urns, some of them used as planters.

Tra Di Noi

C1

Italian

622 E. 187th St (bet. Belmont & Hughes Aves.)

Subway: Fordham Rd. (Grand Concourse)
Phone: 718-295-1784
Web: N/A
Prices: **$$**

Tue – Sun lunch & dinner

This spot isn't about haute cuisine, current twists, or bursts of innovation. It is famed for its good, classic, and popular Italian-American fare, served in a neighborhood surrounded by Italian markets. Here, generations of vendors sell *salumi* and baked goods; and with Mount Carmel Church and Borgatti's Ravioli only a few steps away, you will be flooded with nostalgia in this Bronx neighborhood with an Italian heart.

Families come to sample Chef/owner Marco Coletta's marvelous lasagna, linguini carbonara, or veal chop on the bone, with a side of artichokes and sweet-and-sour *caponatina*. And don't forget the homemade ricotta cheesecake.

The waitstaff speaks Italian, and the owner's wife will shower you with attention - transporting you virtually to the country itself.

zero otto nove

C1

Italian

2357 Arthur Ave. (at 186th St.)

Subway: Fordham Rd (Grand Concourse)
Phone: 718-220-1027
Web: www.roberto089.com
Prices: **$$**

Tue – Sun lunch & dinner

Arthur Avenue joyously welcomed Roberto Pacuillo's long-awaited second eatery, sibling to the wildly popular Roberto's, around the corner.

Zero otto nove (089) refers to the area code of Paciullo's beloved Salerno province; the trattoria celebrates the region's cuisine with robust pasta dishes baked in deliciously simple sauce, as well as a more sophisticated version of the rustic *baccalà e patate*, impeccably cooked, seasoned, and piping hot. Most items roast in the dancing flames of the magnificent wood-burning oven that anchors the space. Finish your meal with a short and utterly perfect espresso.

Styled as an historic Italian piazza, this space rises to a skylit mezzanine, set with more tables, all tended by extremely accommodating staff.

MICHELIN

Peter L. Wrenn / MICHELIN

Brooklyn

Brooklyn

New York's most populous borough, with more than 2.5 million residents, Brooklyn perches on the western tip of Long Island. Its landmass—second to Queens with 81.8 square miles—extends from the East River to Coney Island and from the Narrows to Jamaica Bay. Although almost half a million Brooklynites commute to Manhattan, the borough retains a distinctive, country-village atmosphere in its eclectic mix of neighborhoods.

BRIDGING THE GAPS

Founded by the Dutch in 1636, the area now called Brooklyn was first christened Breuckelen ("broken land" in Dutch) after a small town near Utrecht. By the time it became part of New York City in 1898, Brooklyn was flourishing as a center of industry and commerce. Its first direct link to Manhattan came in 1883 in the form of the **Brooklyn Bridge**. Then came the **Williamsburg Bridge** (1903), the **Manhattan Bridge** (1909), and the first subway in 1905. The 13,700-foot-long **Verrazano-Narrows Bridge**, completed in 1964, further facilitated travel between Brooklyn and Staten Island.

A TASTE OF THE NEIGHBORHOODS

A close look at Brooklyn reveals a patchwork of neighborhoods. **Prospect Park** is banked by several of them, including verdant **Park Slope**, a choice residential community. A notable attraction is the parks entrance, **Grand Army Plaza**, which houses the **Soldiers' and Sailors' Memorial Arch**, Brooklyn's version of the *Arc de Triomphe*.

Staid **Brooklyn Heights** reigns as a wealthy enclave of narrow, tree-lined streets bordered by historic brownstones. Don't miss a walk along the riverside **Esplanade**, which affords stunning views of Lower Manhattan.

Learn about the city's transportation history at the **New York Transit Museum** inside the now defunct Court Street subway station.

Traditionally an Italian, Hispanic, and Hasidic Jewish area, hipster **Williamsburg** now welcomes an influx of young artists. Brooklyn's **Bensonhurst** boasts a proliferation of pizzerias and pasta restaurants.

The area now known as **DUMBO** (Down Under the Manhattan Bridge Overpass) has transformed its 18th and 19th century warehouses and factories into luxury lofts, art galleries, theaters and restaurants. If you're in the area, don't pass up the classic photo op of the Manhattan Bridge, as seen from below.

In the northwestern section of the borough, the 36 blocks of **Boerum Hill** center on Smith Street, which is lined with boutiques and a wealth of good restaurants. Blue-collar **Red Hook** is now on the map as the docking site for the über-luxurious Queen Mary 2 cruise ship. Ikea recently moved into the neighborhood alongside a wealth of artists and industrial businesses. A resident artist coined the term "Residustrial" to describe this neighborhoods' eclectic character.

Attracting performers from all over the world, **BAM (Brooklyn Academy of Music)**, a **Green Point** cultural institution, is the place to go for cutting-edge theater, music, opera and dance. The art complex includes the **Howard Gilman Opera House**, the **Harvey Lichtenstein Theater**, and **BAM Rose Cinemas**. Philip Glass, Ingmar Berman, and Peter Brook are among artists who have showcased their work at this internationally esteemed establishment.

Coney Island's beloved **Astroland Amusement Park**, a three-acre expanse of carnival jubilance that defined the neighborhood's vibrant landscape, was sold to developers in 2007, marking the end of a 45-year era. You can still take a spin on the **Cyclone**, which was deemed a historical landmark in 1988, and whose property is owned by the City of New York. Among other things to see in Coney Island, stop by the **New York Aquarium**, the only one of its kind in New York; or usher in the summer season with the annual **Mermaid Parade**, a colorful march along the boardwalk, showcasing ocean-themed costumes and eclectic floats in honor of all things aquatic.

Less than a mile east of Coney Island, **Brighton Beach** is a thriving Russian enclave; head here for authentic blinis and borscht.

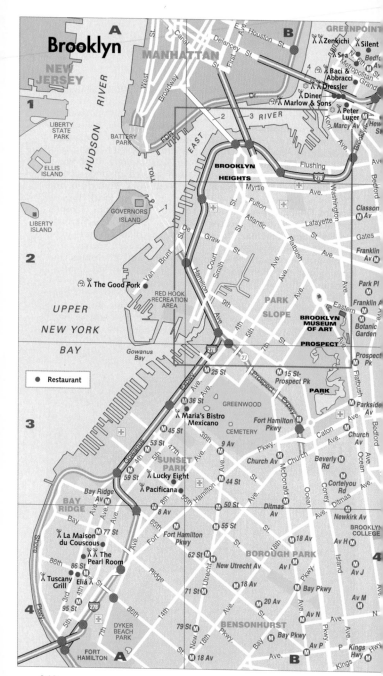

Brooklyn

A · B

GREENPOINT

MANHATTAN

Zenkichi · Silent
Sea
Baci & Abbracci
Dressler
Diner
Marlow & Sons
Peter Luger

NEW JERSEY

LIBERTY STATE PARK

ELLIS ISLAND

LIBERTY ISLAND

BROOKLYN HEIGHTS

Flushing

Classon Av
Gates
Franklin Av
Park Pl
Franklin Av
Botanic Garden

UPPER
NEW YORK
BAY

The Good Fork

RED HOOK RECREATION AREA

PARK SLOPE

BROOKLYN MUSEUM OF ART

PROSPECT

Prospect Pk

Gowanus Bay

25 St
36 St
Maria's Bistro Mexicano
45 St
53 St 47th
59 St
Lucky Eight
Pacificana

15 St-Prospect Pk

GREENWOOD CEMETERY

Fort Hamilton Pkwy

9 Av
Church Av
44 St
50 St
Ditmas Av

PARK

Parkside Av
Caton Av
Church Av
Beverly Rd
Cortelyou Rd
Ditmas Av
Newkirk Av

SUNSET PARK

BAY RIDGE
Bay Ridge Av
8 Av
77 St
La Maison du Couscous
The Pearl Room
Tuscany Grill
Elia
95 St

65th
Fort Hamilton Pkwy
62 St
New Utrecht Av
71 St
79 St
18 Av

BOROUGH PARK

Av H
Av I
Bay Pkwy
20 Av
18 Av
Av J
Av M
Av N
Bay Pkwy
Av P
Kings Hwy

BROOKLYN COLLEGE

BENSONHURST

DYKER BEACH PARK

FORT HAMILTON

● Restaurant

368

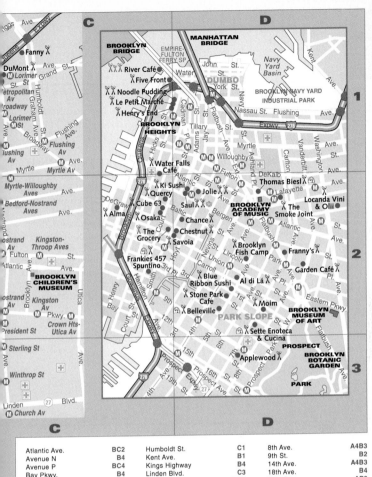

Al di Là

D2

Italian

248 Fifth Ave. (at Carroll St.)

Subway: Union St

Phone: 718-783-4565

Web: www.aldilatrattoria.com

Prices: $$

Wed – Mon dinner only

In a world of laminated menus, it's always a joy to find a daily changing bill of fare that actually bears the day's date. At this perennially busy Park Slope trattoria, husband-and-wife team Emiliano Coppa and Anna Klinger offer a balanced selection of seasonal Italian dishes that are both robust in flavor and generous in size. New Yorkers, not often known for their patience, wait quietly just to taste Klinger's risotto.

The high-ceilinged room boasts a faded chic, with its church-pew seats and eccentric touches, such as the coffee pots hanging from the walls. If you have questions about the menu, the knowledgeable staff can offer sound advice. Plan to get here early, though, since Al di Là's no-reservations policy means it fills up quickly.

Alma

C2

Mexican

187 Columbia St. (at Degraw St.)

Subway: Carroll St

Phone: 718-643-5400

Web: www.almarestaurant.com

Prices: $$

Mon – Fri dinner only
Sat – Sun lunch & dinner

With two private floors and roof-top belvedere offering views of lower Manhattan and the shipyards below, Alma thrives where others have failed. This local favorite also knows its clientele—appealing to hip, young ex-Manhattanites with children in tow, seeking live bluegrass, billiards, jukeboxes, and good food in a casual environment.

The contemporary Mexican fare comes in portions suitable to share, and often features subdued spices. A huge order of creamy, nutty guacamole is freshly mashed, yet lacks the oniony punch that might turn away pickier palates. The overstuffed poblano relleno is slightly smoky, perfectly charred, and served with a sweet potato *manzana* sauce spiked with chile. Steve's Authentic Key Lime pies are offered for dessert.

Applewood

Contemporary

D3

501 11th St. (bet. Seventh & Eighth Aves.)

Subway: 7 Av
Phone: 718-768-2044
Web: www.applewoodny.com
Prices: $$

Tue – Sat dinner only
Sun lunch only

Park Slope real-estate agents hoping to convince Manhattanites to make the big move across the river should bring them to Applewood. Set within a turn-of-the-century house, this place is a real neighborhood jewel, where everyone seems to know each other. David and Laura Shea run the restaurant with a passion that shines through in everything they do.

The pretty dining room boasts a fireplace to warm diners in winter, and a changing exhibit of works by local artists gives the place a homespun feel. In the kitchen, the best local organic produce, hormone-free meats and wild fish are transformed into excellent seasonal dishes, like vibrant pan-roasted Long Island hake and maple-brined Vermont pork, that are well balanced and full of flavor.

Baci & Abbracci 😊

Italian

B1

204 Grand St. (bet. Bedford & Driggs Sts.)

Subway: Bedford Av
Phone: 718-599-6599
Web: www.baciny.com
Prices: $$

Mon – Fri dinner only
Sat – Sun lunch & dinner

Dinner at this intimate, contemporary spot in the heart of the Williamsburg buzz will leave you giving kisses and hugs all around. The loveable menu welcomes with wide-open arms, offering enticing choices at each course. Final decisions are only further complicated by the daily specials created in the rustic, Italian style at which the kitchen excels.

Pizzas are the standout, with perfectly cooked thin crusts and an enticing assortment of toppings. The restaurant also serves a lovely brunch best enjoyed in the garden behind the restaurant, a supreme warm-weather setting.

Inside, the lighting is low and the ambience inviting, but if you live nearby and prefer to eat in, Baci & Abbracci will deliver its affectionate flavors right to your door.

Belleville

D2

330 5th St. (at Fifth Ave.)

Subway: 4 Av - 9 St
Phone: 718-832-9777
Web: www.bellevillebistro.com
Prices: ⊜⊜

Wed – Mon lunch & dinner

Belleville executes the informal French bistro concept perfectly in Park Slope, from décor to ambience to food. Decorated to appear old, Belleville looks comfortably worn, with mosaic floors, mirrored walls displaying the wine list, rows of wood-paneled banquettes, and tables nuzzled close together. In nice weather, windows open out on Brooklyn's busy Fifth Avenue and sidewalk seating.

The reasonably priced menu features well-prepared bistro fare from bourride to steak tartare to lusciously tender duck confit served beside a bundle of frisée and roasted baby potatoes. This is a welcoming neighborhood place for a lingering lunch, a romantic dinner or a weekend brunch. There's even a kids menu for little gourmands-in-training.

Blue Ribbon Sushi

D2

278 Fifth Ave. (bet. 1st St. & Garfield Pl.)

Subway: Union St
Phone: 718-840-0408
Web: www.blueribbonrestaurants.com
Prices: $$

Dinner daily

Brooklyn sushi lovers need not venture to Manhattan anymore with a Blue Ribbon Sushi located in Park Slope. This neighborhood favorite is the sister of the SoHo original *(119 Sullivan St.)* and is right next door to the casually elegant Blue Ribbon Brasserie.

This location provides equally delicate fare with original touches—but in larger surroundings and at a less frenetic pace (and with a no-reservations policy). Delight in the freshest sushi (which changes daily), or go beyond the status quo with the Blue Ribbon roll (half of a lobster topped with caviar). To help you narrow down your choices, sushi and sashimi are classified according to which ocean—the Atlantic or the Pacific—the fish comes from.

Brooklyn Fish Camp

Seafood ✗

D2

162 Fifth Ave. (bet. De Graw & Douglass Sts.)

Subway: Union St

Tue – Sun lunch & dinner

Phone: 718-783-3264

Web: www.brooklynfishcamp.com

Prices: $$

Since many Brooklynites work in Manhattan, the borough tends to be pretty sleepy during the day, and it can be hard to find a good place for lunch. Brooklyn Fish Camp has solved that problem for fish lovers in Park Slope.

Although the décor is inspired by the simple fish shacks of the rural South, the menu is a seriously focused celebration of the sea. An offshoot of the original Mary's Fish Camp in the West Village, this casual eatery sails away with top-notch seafood and enthusiastic service. The menu changes daily, based on the market, but owner Mary Redding's famous lobster rolls, fried-fish sandwiches, fresh grilled fish and selection of steamed or fried shellfish are always available. Order a side of spicy Old Bay fries to share.

Chance

Asian ✗

D2

223 Smith St. (bet. Baltic & Butler Sts.)

Subway: Bergen St

Lunch & dinner daily

Phone: 718-242-1515

Web: www.chancecuisine.com

Prices:

If you visit this Boerum Hill eatery, chances are you'll be enchanted. Brooklyn chef and restaurateur Ken Li runs the show at this modern Asian restaurant, which marries China and France for both its name and its inspiration.

Inside, the dining room says sleek with dark wood floors and walls, red chairs, and tables set with chopsticks on woven placemats. Large windows up front take in the street scene, while out back there is a small outdoor dining area.

The menu finds its heart in China, in a long list of dishes such as steamed pork dumplings, hot and sour soup, and Peking duck, but it ends up in France with foie gras and chocolate soufflé. Offering some 20 different choices, the Lunch Box special leaves nothing to chance.

Chestnut

D2

Contemporary ⟚

271 Smith St. (bet. De Graw & Sackett Sts.)

Subway: Carroll St
Phone: 718-243-0049
Web: www.chestnutonsmith.com
Prices: $$

Tue – Sat dinner only
Sun lunch & dinner

This Carroll Gardens eatery is the kind of place every neighborhood should have. Like its moniker, the philosophy here is comforting and seasonal. Chestnut's farm-reared chef spends time sourcing the best ingredients and then lets them shine in a menu reminding diners that the best supermarket is nature itself. The simple décor has just the right amount of personality, and the laid-back staff delivers genuinely warm service, starting your meal with fresh-baked bread and homemade pickles. Come on Tuesday or Wednesday nights to take advantage of the three-course, prix-fixe value menus. Or, order à la carte any night to dine on skillfully-prepared items that may include salt cod *brandade*, roasted chicken breast with sausage filling, or chocolate *budino*.

Cube 63

C2

Japanese ⟚

234 Court St. (at Baltic St.)

Subway: Bergen St
Phone: 718-243-2208
Web: www.cube63.com
Prices: $$

Lunch & dinner daily

Located in charming Cobble Hill, Cube 63 is the little sister of the original Lower East Side location, yet offers superior dining. The understated dining room pleasantly features dark-wood furnishings, pale blue walls, chic lighting, and sushi counter complemented by a back patio and two small lounge spaces. Cooked appetizers, noodles, and raw offerings are consistently well made and attractively presented. The large selection of sushi rolls feature firm, rich fish, and include curiosity-inducing house specials with names like the Tahiti roll (shrimp tempura, eel, cream cheese, avocado, and caviar) and the electric roll (tempura fried roll with salmon, whitefish, and crabmeat). Lunchtime offers reasonably priced specials with soup or salad.

Diner

American ✕

B1

85 Broadway (at Berry St.)

Lunch & dinner daily

Subway: Marcy Av
Phone: 718-486-3077
Web: www.dinernyc.com
Prices: $$

Williamsburg may be the current epicenter of hip and trendy, but this simple little corner spot is none of those things. Mark Firth and Andrew Tarlow painstakingly renovated the 1920s Kullman Diner, and though the result may be a little rough around the edges, its casual warmth brings regulars back time and time again.

Chef Caroline Fidanza provides them a skeleton menu of favorites including the excellent burger and the refreshing goat-cheese salad, both seen on more tables than not. Abundant daily specials are also offered, including both market-driven dishes and whimsical, fusion comfort food. Sure, the prices are reasonable and the service informal but this is no ordinary diner; they even publish a quarterly, aptly named, *Diner Journal*.

DuMont

American ✕

C1

432 Union Ave. (bet. Devoe St. & Metropolitan Ave.)

Lunch & dinner daily

Subway: Lorimer St - Metropolitan Av
Phone: 718-486-7717
Web: www.dumontrestaurant.com
Prices: $$

DuMont espouses its neighborhood's relaxed, edgy, and creative vibe. The multi-room space is warm and comfortably worn, furnished with dark-wood tables topped in brown paper, vintage tile floor, and cool leather seating handmade by the owner. There is also a lovely backyard with elevated seating called "the treehouse". Executive Chef Polo Dobkin draws crowds who clamor for the comforting and impressively prepared menu items. Favorites may include pan-roasted quail with cheddar polenta, NY strip steak with green peppercorn sauce, and of course, the DuMac and cheese (with *radiatore* pasta, a blend of cheeses, and studded with bits of bacon). Brunch keeps things rocking on weekends. For a quick burger and a beer, try DuMont Burger at *314 Bedford Ave.*

Dressler ⌘

149 Broadway (bet. Bedford & Driggs Aves.)

Subway: Marcy Av
Phone: 718-384-6343
Web: www.dresslernyc.com
Prices: $$

Mon – Fri dinner only
Sat – Sun lunch & dinner

Dressler/Jason Joseph

In Williamsburg, a neighborhood stuck in the hipster boom that defined it at the turn-of-the-millennium, a beacon of uptown elegance appears in Colin Devlin's Dressler. Not in the aesthetic of the place, mind you, which, like its local sister restaurants, DuMont and DuMont Burger, bleeds Brooklyn-cool—the cavernous space is a former printers shop redesigned into a glossy haunt, with mosaic tiles, polished mahogany and zinc-topped bar.

But in Chef Polo Dobkin's finely-tuned cuisine, which turns contemporary American fare on its pretty little head. Cool cubes of pickled watermelon find their way into a dish of pan-roasted quail and gooey cheese grits; and a perfectly-crisped roast chicken, studded with Crayola-bright veggies, gets hit with a sauce reduction impressive enough to raise a French eyebrow or two.

Appetizers

- Asparagus Vinaigrette, Herbed Olive Tapenade, and Parmesan
- Smoked Trout, Yukon Gold Galette
- Mushroom & Ricotta Raviolini, Parmesan Broth

Entrées

- Pan-roasted Cod, Roasted Tomato, Sea Beans
- Duck Confit Crépinette with Forestiere Potatoes
- Scottish Salmon, Sugar Snap Peas, Fava Beans, Tomato

Desserts

- Pineapple tart Tatin, Tequila Vanilla-reduction, Pineapple-Tequila Sorbet
- Bittersweet Chocolate Cream, English Toffee, Chocolate Shortbread and Salted-Caramel Ice Cream

Eliá

Greek ⅄

A4

8611 Third Ave. (bet. 86th & 87th Sts.)

Tue – Sun dinner only

Subway: 86 St
Phone: 718-748-9891
Web: www.eliarestaurant.org
Prices: $$

Long known to Bay Ridge residents, this little gem is no longer a secret. Now, regulars share their favorite Greek restaurant with diners from Manhattan. That said, everyone is treated like family at this affable and spotless taverna.

The chef sometimes steers the menu into uncharted waters with elaborate creations and mixed results. Hold steady with the simple, traditional dishes at which the kitchen excels, like classic *spanakopita* of spinach, leeks, and feta cheese layered in flakey, buttery phyllo dough, or baklava topped with nuts and a spiced citrus-infused syrup. Generous portions assure value for money. In the dining room, white-washed brick walls and marine blues evoke sun-washed stucco buildings and the color of the Aegean Sea.

Fanny

Mediterranean ⅄

C1

425 Graham Ave. (bet. Frost & Withers Sts.)

Lunch & dinner daily

Subway: Graham Av
Phone: 718-389-2060
Web: www.fannyfood.com
Prices: $$

Found near the Williamsburg chapter of the Sons of Italy and other vestiges of this once bustling Italian-American neighborhood, this warm and stylish French-Mediterranean restaurant is proudly serving delightful, delicious food.

The industrial-chic space is a sleek, monochromatic display of brushed cement, slate tiles, and metallic elements illuminated by clear, iridescent bulbs suspended from the tin ceiling over a wooden bar and tables.

Peek into the semi-open kitchen, as the crew thickly slices a lovely house-made pâté: moist, textured with creamy bits of liver, served with bread still warm from the bakery. Pan Bagna ("Big Wet") sandwiches slathered with excellent ingredients over yeasty brioche and an ethereal lavender blancmanger may round out the menu.

Five Front

C1

Contemporary 🍴

5 Front St. (bet. Dock & Old Fulton Sts.)

Subway: High St

Phone: 718-625-5559

Web: www.fivefrontrestaurant.com

Prices: $$

Wed – Mon lunch & dinner

Small and lovely, Five Front is located in an historic building in the desirable DUMBO neighborhood. On the walk from the High Street subway station, marvel at the magnificent Brooklyn and Manhattan Bridges that hover just overhead.

Bossa nova music, butcher paper on tables, and glimmering city lights make shadows dance on the walls, all creating a warm atmosphere. The snug dining space is divided into a front bar, a second small room with exposed brick, and a back room suited for groups. A bamboo garden is a delight in warmer weather.

Contemporary dishes are prepared using fresh ingredients and may include innovative takes on classics, such as bucatini served with pistachio-basil pesto. Service is attentive, professional, and warm.

Frankies 457 Spuntino 😊

C2

Italian 🍴

457 Court St. (bet. 4th Pl. & Luquer St.)

Subway: Carroll St

Phone: 718-403-0033

Web: www.frankiesspuntino.com

Prices: 💲

Lunch & dinner daily

Although *spuntino* loosely translates as "snack," Frankie's offers serious dining in a cozy setting. The initial food preparation takes place in the basement kitchen, while the rustic meals are assembled in the casual dining room, behind a counter stacked with charcuterie and crusty breads. This practice fills the room with mouth-watering aromas, as meatball parmigiana sandwiches and warm bowls of house-made pastas are plated and brought to the table.

Frankies attracts diners from young area newcomers to old-school Brooklynites, who know red sauce as "gravy." Weather permitting, the best spot to dine is the inviting back garden, illuminated by strings of tiny lights. Visit the Manhattan location on the Lower East Side *(17 Clinton St.)*.

Franny's

Italian

D2

295 Flatbush Ave. (bet. Prospect Pl. & St. Marks Ave.)

Subway: Bergen St
Phone: 718-230-0221
Web: www.frannysbrooklyn.com
Prices: $$

Mon – Fri dinner only
Sat – Sun lunch & dinner

Run by husband-and-wife team Franny Stephens and Andrew Feinberg, who share a passion for sustainable agriculture, Franny's is an inviting spot. A comfortable bar up front and a stack of highchairs for seating little ones imply all ages are welcome here.

The centerpiece of the open kitchen is the wood-burning brick oven from whose confines the individual-size pizzas emerge puffed and crispy. Affable servers will likely tempt you with at least one of the daily specials, but remember that the chef's selection of house-cured meats and small plates is also worth considering.

Decorated with greenery, strings of white lights, and a neatly arranged pile of wood to feed the pizza oven, the patio out back is the place to be on a warm evening.

Garden Café

Contemporary

D2

620 Vanderbilt Ave. (at Prospect Pl.)

Subway: 7 Av
Phone: 718-857-8863
Web: N/A
Prices: $$

Wed – Sat dinner only

This unassuming gem located a short distance from Prospect Park is lovingly run by John and Camille Policastro. He works the stove while she attends to diners in the intimate room: taking orders, serving food, and taking time to chat graciously with regulars. This neighborhood fixture attracts locals who want to spend an elegant evening out while staying close to home. Although there is no garden, the ambiance is completely fitting with latticework decorated walls, potted greenery, and cane chairs. The cooking is more traditional than daring but nonetheless impressive. An attention to detail makes the cuisine so enjoyable in items like crab and shrimp remoulade, arctic char with couscous, and an ice-cream topped brownie with bitter orange sauce.

The Good Fork

A2   C o n t e m p o r a r y   ✗

391 Van Brunt St. (bet. Coffey & Van Dyke Sts.)

Subway: Smith - 9th Sts (& bus B77)   Tue – Sun dinner only
Phone: 718-643-6636
Web: www.goodfork.com
Prices: $$

Red Hook, with its yet-to-be-gentrified warehouses and pot-holed streets, is not always easy to access (it's best to come by bus or car), but those who come to enjoy a cozy dinner at The Good Fork in this up-and-coming neighborhood will be deliciously rewarded.

Run by Ben Schneider (he built the restaurant) and his wife, Sohui Kim, this is the kind of adorable place where everything is as good as it looks. The eclectic menu zigzags from onion rings to *pappardelle* with wild boar, and if it seems scattered, that's the point. Showing the split personality between Chef Kim's classic training (seared duck, ravioli with butternut squash) and her proud Korean heritage (Korean-style steak and eggs over kimchee rice), the menu here truly has something for everyone.

The Grocery

C2   C o n t e m p o r a r y   ✗

288 Smith St. (bet. Sackett & Union Sts.)

Subway: Carroll St   Tue – Sat dinner only
Phone: 718-596-3335
Web: www.thegroceryrestaurant
Prices: $$

Opened in 1999, this Smith Street charmer helped put fine dining on the Brooklyn map. Today it continues to please a devoted following in a quaint space simply furnished with white paper-topped tables, whimsically accented with seasonal fruit. The verdant backyard is prized on warmer evenings, but beware that these precious tables are offered as first-come-first-serve. Chefs and co-owners Sharon Pachter and Charles Kiely run their operation with passion and a genuine regard for their guests satisfaction. The concise menu lists items that reflect the best of the season and local farmers' markets, such as roasted beets with goat cheese ravioli, stuffed whole boneless trout, and steamed spicy-sweet gingerbread pudding with roasted pineapple.

Henry's End

American ✗

C-D1

44 Henry St. (bet. Cranberry & Middagh Sts.)

Subway: High St
Phone: 718-834-1776
Web: www.henrysend.com
Prices: $$

Dinner daily

Brooklyn

For three decades, Henry's End has garnered respect from patrons who return again and again for casual and affordable American cuisine. The simple storefront features wood paneling, exposed brick, and amber lighting, lending a very old NY ambience well suited to this area of Brooklyn. Service is friendly and professional, with the chef popping out of the semi-open kitchen to greet and hug many of the arriving regulars. Families, couples on dates, and business types comprise the jovial crowd filling the narrow room. More ambitious menu selections may highlight game meats, such as the penne with aromatic, tender, and sweet rabbit sausage, bathed in robust and spicy tomato sauce. Good flavors and unique presentations combine in this solid comfort food.

Jolie

French ✗✗

D2

320 Atlantic Ave. (bet. Smith & Hoyt Sts.)

Subway: Bergen St
Phone: 718-488-0777
Web: www.jolierestaurant.com
Prices: $$

Lunch & dinner daily

Set on a rather nondescript stretch of Atlantic Avenue, Jolie beckons diners in Boerum Hill with its planters of greenery that decorate the sidewalk out front. Inside, a semi-circular marble-topped bar dominates the front of the restaurant, while the large dining room is in back. Walls do double duty as an art gallery; changing exhibits fill the space, lending an élan and sophistication to this *petit* bistro. As pleasant as the place is, the pièce de résistance is the walled garden area, *très jolie* indeed with its shade trees, flowering vines and market umbrellas.

Classic bistro fare fills the menu with such French favorites as roasted chicken breast stuffed with ricotta and fresh herbs; *escargots de Bourgogne;* and steak tartare *au Cognac.*

Ki Sushi

D2

Japanese

122 Smith St. (bet. Dean & Pacific Sts.)

Subway: Bergen St
Phone: 718-935-0575
Web: N/A
Prices: $$

Mon – Sat lunch & dinner
Sun dinner only

Ki Sushi proves that you don't need to go across the river to Manhattan to get great Japanese food. The highlight of this solid Japanese cuisine is its fantastic sushi—the omakase features seafood flown in from Tokyo's famous Tsukiji Market—but with items such as Chilean sea bass and grilled ribeye steak with truffle mashed potatoes, there's plenty to satisfy those who prefer their food cooked. House specialty sushi rolls include some eye-catching selections—Spicy Girl or Foxy Lady Roll, anyone?

The interior's Zen-chic design, complete with a water wall and potted orchids, may look the part of a hip hotspot, but the excellent service from welcoming servers shows that style doesn't trump substance.

La Maison du Couscous

A4

Moroccan

484 77th St. (bet. Fourth & Fifth Aves.)

Subway: 77 St
Phone: 718-921-2400
Web: www.lamaisonducouscous.com
Prices: $$

Wed – Mon lunch & dinner

Moroccan lanterns, bright pillows, shimmering burgundy accents, and a mosaic tile-backed fountain exotically festoon this tiny room, alive with a festive North African spirit. Fine flavors and textures combine in starters such as hummus and warm pita, spiced with cumin and paprika. Phyllo triangles filled with creamy goat cheese and black olive tapenade are deep fried, hot, and very satisfying. In addition to the more traditional lamb *tagines* or grilled kebabs, specials focus on French-Moroccan fusion cuisine. Desserts may include morsels of cinnamon-sugar dusted pastry filled with cheese and orange zest. Although the restaurant does not serve alcohol, the dedicated team running this neighborhood gem encourages diners to bring their own.

Le Petit Marché

French

46 Henry St. (bet. Cranberry & Middagh Sts.)

Subway: High St

Phone: 718-858-9605

Web: www.bkBistro.com

Prices: **$$**

Dinner daily

This quintessential bistro styles a cozy atmosphere of exposed brick walls, dark woods, lusty red and gold wallpaper, with paper-topped tables. More intimate than many of its neighbors, the "little market" fosters romance with candlelit tables nestling close together.

The husband-and-wife duo that own this spot manage the dining room with true hospitality, happy to assist with selections from the fairly-priced wine list. Gallic comfort food comes in combinations like pan-seared *magret* of duck set atop luscious chestnut purée, plated with plump cherries, or country pâté served atop mesclun salad with fig compote.

This charming *boîte* opened the day after Christmas in 2006, and from the looks of things, will be celebrating many holidays yet to come.

Locanda Vini & Olii

Italian

129 Gates Ave. (at Cambridge Pl.)

Subway: Clinton - Washington Avs

Phone: 718-622-9202

Web: www.locandany.com

Prices: **$$**

Tue – Sun dinner only

With its enchanting atmosphere, well-prepared rustic Italian cuisine, and personalized service, Locanda Vini & Olii merits a trip out to Brooklyn. François Louy, who owns the restaurant with his wife, Catherine, warmly greets guests to his Clinton Hill eatery. Housed in a century-old drugstore, the cozy dining room employs the former apothecary shelves and drawers to display cookbooks, wine bottles, and vintage kitchen equipment.

The cuisine, deeply rooted in Tuscan tradition, is often reinterpreted. Thus mildly sweet chestnut-flavored lasagna noodles might be layered with ground pork sausage, caramelized onions, and chickpeas; and grilled duck breast served simply with pan juices and a dollop of shallot marmalade.

If you're dining with a party of four or more, call ahead to request a tasting menu.

Lucky Eight

A3

5204 8th Ave. (bet. 52nd & 53rd Sts.)

Subway: 8 Av
Phone: 718-851-8862
Web: N/A
Prices: 💶

Lunch & dinner daily

With its plethora of dim sum spots, Chinese bakeries, and markets hawking everything from live bull frogs to fresh silky tofu, Sunset Park has emerged as Brooklyn's prominent Chinatown. From this, Lucky Eight's excellent food, good service, and pristine setting is an authentic and rewarding find.

Until late afternoon, pick from a list of some 40 items priced at 80 cents each. The laminated dinner menu is crammed with pages illustrating unique, regional Chinese fare. The (aptly named) signature dish, Pride of Lucky Eight, offers a sumptuous stir-fry of chives, celery, shiitake, and meaty abalone.

The highlight of the no-frills décor is the red-lacquer case at the back of the room, displaying shark fins and other artifacts.

Maria's Bistro Mexicano

B3

886 Fifth Ave. (bet. 37th & 38th Sts.)

Subway: 36 St
Phone: 718-438-1608
Web: N/A
Prices: $$

Lunch & dinner daily

Instantly amiable, with good food, excellent service, and no pretensions, dining at Maria's is akin to enjoying a meal with a dear friend. The bright-orange awning and open door invite customers from this industrial area of Sunset Park into Maria's cocoon-like space, where low lighting balances the vibrant wall colors.

At the back, a display of perfectly ripe, creamy avocados entices guests to begin with made-to-order guacamole. Menu items may include a chile relleno oozing with three cheeses, paired with a lusty chile sauce, at once creamy and smoky. Specials laud the kitchen's abilities; the lusciously flavored pork loin stuffed with zucchini blossoms and roasted poblanos, is presented as an alluring package on its colorful earthenware plate.

Marlow & Sons 😊

Gastropub ✗

B1

81 Broadway (bet. Berry St. & Wythe Ave.)

Subway: Marcy Av
Phone: 718-384-1441
Web: www.marlowandsons.com
Prices: $$

Lunch & dinner daily

By day, Marlow & Sons offers sandwiches and pastries in an urbane country store setting where shelves are chock full of provisions that include artisanal cheeses, gourmet pickles, and local honey. But at night, the back room becomes a jovial setting for dinner with its shabby-chic furnishings, sexy lighting, and lively crowd. The unassuming blackboard listing of specials may be difficult to read, but items like polenta soup, dressed with parmesan and olive oil, or a salted caramel tart topped with chocolate ganache makes the effort quite rewarding. Know that behind this simply stated menu is a sophisticated kitchen. To enhance the spirited atmosphere, there is a selection of boutique sparkling wines on the well-chosen list.

Moim

Korean ✗

D2

206 Garfield Pl. (at Seventh Ave.)

Subway: Grand Army Plaza
Phone: 718-499-8092
Web: www.moimrestaurant.com
Prices: $$

Tue – Fri dinner only
Sat – Sun lunch & dinner

Well known for its diverse dining choices, Park Slope now adds Korean as one more worldly option with the arrival of Moim, tucked away on a charming brownstone-lined street. The slender space mixes a chic palette of dark wood, cement grey, and green apple, with a small front bar where guests wait for tables while sipping lime and ginger sojutinis. Moim translates as "gathering," and the sizeable tables encourage sharing of the menu's polished yet inspired takes on Korean classics. *Pa jun* feature thick, smooth-textured pancakes copiously filled with tender scallion greens, squid, and shrimp; while hearty portions of meaty spare ribs in sweet-smoky sauce are creatively accompanied by caramelized chunks of iced sweet potatoes.

Noodle Pudding

Italian XX

C-D1

38 Henry St. (bet. Cranberry & Middagh Sts.)

Subway: High St   Tue – Sun dinner only
Phone: 718-625-3737
Web: N/A
Prices: $$

Named after a savory pudding baked with noodles and traditionally served on the Sabbath, Noodle Pudding embodies all the essential qualities that make up a beloved neighborhood restaurant.

For starters, there's no sign on the door; Brooklyn Heights' cognoscenti know where to come for good, honest Italian food. Servers are helpful and well-versed about the food and wine. An air of relaxation pervades the room, with its well-spaced bistro tables, terra-cotta floor, and soundtrack of American crooners.

Uniformly wonderful, top-quality meats, fish, and produce fill a menu that lists everything from inexpensive daily specials (rabbit marinated in red wine, then slowly braised and plated with polenta) to pasta, and roasted prime rib.

Osaka

Japanese

C2

272 Court St. (bet. De Graw & Kane Sts.)

Subway: Bergen St   Lunch & dinner daily
Phone: 718-643-0044
Web: www.osakany.com
Prices: $$

Osaka's plain brick façade blends in well with the village atmosphere of Cobble Hill. Inside the intimate, always-crowded dining room, black linens and bamboo accents play against pistachio-colored walls.

Named for Osaka-style sushi, featuring larger pieces of fish over smaller beds of rice, the restaurant offers an extensive selection of maki and chef's special rolls (there's even a "Viagra roll," with eel, avocado and sea urchin—the latter prized as an aphrodisiac) as well as raw seafood (sushi and sashimi are available as entrées or à la carte). Cooked courses include tempura, teriyaki, broiled black cod and grilled duck breast. If you're looking for a deal, try the combination boxes available for lunch and dinner.

Pacificana

Chinese ✗

A3

813 55th St. (at Eighth Ave.)

Subway: 8 Av
Phone: 718-871-2880
Web: N/A
Prices: $$

Lunch & dinner daily

The next time you're thinking dim sum, visit Sunset Park. This Brooklyn neighborhood, home to a fast-growing Asian population, is quickly becoming New York City's newest spot for Chinese food. Pacificana, with its crimson walls, vaulted ceilings, and semi-open kitchen framed by floor-to-ceiling fish tanks, is an elegant alternative to the bustle of Chinatown's Canal Street.

Sit back and relax while the smiling staff brings the parade of food to you. Carts overflow with a tempting array of typical dim sum fare—steamed dumplings, braised crab- and pork-filled tofu skin. There's also a full regular menu with house specialties like scallops with apples and macadamia nuts in a noodle nest, or lamb chops with black-peppercorn sauce.

The Pearl Room

Seafood ✗✗

A4

8201 Third Ave. (at 82nd St.)

Subway: 86 St
Phone: 718-833-6666
Web: www.thepearlroom.com
Prices: $$

Lunch & dinner daily

The wave-shaped awning is your first clue to the type of cuisine you'll enjoy at this Bay Ridge fish emporium. Fresh from seas around the globe comes a large array of well-prepared dishes, from seafood paella to jumbo Panama shrimp. And speaking of jumbo, the portions here are nothing to sneeze at. On weekends, the family-style brunch includes everything from homemade pastries and pancakes to steak and eggs.

Large windows add to the luminous feel of the room, with its shell-pink luster and aquatic-themed ceiling mural. This is a place that is as inviting in winter, with its open fireplace, as it is in the summer, when diners appreciate the spacious, covered terrace out back. Expect the service to be gracious and attentive any time of year.

Peter Luger ✤

B1

178 Broadway (at Driggs Ave.)

Subway: Marcy Av
Phone: 718-387-7400
Web: www.peterluger.com
Prices: $$$

Lunch & dinner daily

Peter Luger

A recent renovation has refreshed this venerable steakhouse, yet it is comforting to know that this is still all about steak. Originally opened in 1887, Peter Luger was sold upon the death of its namesake to Sol Forman in the 1940s, and is still owned by the Forman family. Today, Peter Luger continues to satisfy the cravings of carnivores by focusing on hand-selected USDA prime beef that is dry-aged in-house resulting in the meat's velvety texture and unmistakably rich flavor. Sharing is de rigueur; the menu offers sizzling platters of Porterhouse steak for 2, 3 or 4 people. The selection of side dishes is just as concise but equally delicious. The decadent creamed spinach and German fried potatoes are two delightful Luger traditions.

A dense slice of cheesecake or the "holy cow" hot fudge sundae will bring any meal to a suitably over-the-top close.

Appetizers
- Jumbo Shrimp Cocktail
- Sizzling Canadian Bacon
- Sliced Salad of Tomatoes and Onions with Peter Luger Sauce

Entrées
- Dry Aged, Family Selected, USDA Prime Porterhouse Steak for Two, Three or Four
- Double Thick Loin Lamb Chops
- Creamed Spinach for Two

Desserts
- Cheesecake Served with Homemade Schlag
- Pecan Pie
- Holy Cow Sundae

Quercy

French 🍴

C2

242 Court St. (bet. Baltic & Kane Sts.)

Mon – Fri dinner only
Sat – Sun lunch & dinner

Subway: Bergen St
Phone: 718-243-2151
Web: N/A
Prices: $$

Bistro décor in this attractive Cobble Hill eatery hearkens back to the 1950s with its blue and white linoleum floor, Formica bar, and red vinyl-covered banquettes. The food is classic bistro, too—think sautéed skate, steak au poivre, and for dessert, warm tarte Tatin topped with caramelized apples. Chef/owner Jean-François Fraysse named his establishment after his hometown in Southwest France; in true French fashion, the day's specials are written on a blackboard and presented to you along with a basket of country bread accompanied by butter and homemade strawberry jam.

Hip Brooklyn residents frequent Quercy for that intangible *je ne sais quoi*, or perhaps it's just for the good French comfort food served in an inviting atmosphere.

River Café

Contemporary 🍴🍴🍴

C1

1 Water St. (bet. Furman & Old Fulton Sts.)

Lunch & dinner daily

Subway: High St
Phone: 718-522-5200
Web: www.rivercafe.com
Prices: $$$$

Enchantment sets in the moment one steps onto cobbled Water Street and enters the restaurant's magnificent garden area. Inside, the elegant dining room is thoughtfully positioned to maximize a most unique view of the Brooklyn Bridge, towering above. This is all a far cry from the abandoned waterfront that visionary and pioneer Michael "Buzzy" O'Keefe revitalized when he opened the River Café back in 1977.

Yet this restaurant does not simply rest on its laurels and location; genuinely delicious and creative, contemporary cuisine is served by a staff focused on your comfort. The wine list offers a well-priced selection for this upscale destination. Water taxis from Fulton Street to the restaurant's adjacent landing simplify and enhance the trip from Manhattan.

Saul ⁕

D2

Contemporary 🍴🍴

140 Smith St. (bet. Bergen & Dean Sts.)

Subway: Bergen St
Phone: 718-935-9844
Web: www.saulrestaurant.com
Prices: $$$

Dinner daily

Saul/Ellen Wilson

A busy commercial street in Brooklyn's Boerum Hill is home to this 35-seat dining room, a magnet for the area's cosmopolitan mix of professionals and young families. Credit its popularity to Chef and co-owner Saul Bolton (who trained with Eric Ripert).

Guests are welcomed by the affable, well-informed staff into the humble interior, accented by exposed brick walls and a smattering of artwork.

Dishes here can be relished on multiple levels, from the outstanding ingredients and technique to the wonderfully combined flavors. Feast on top-notch, seasonal contemporary fare as in creamy asparagus soup studded with grilled spears and scented with sesame, or a delicate rabbit loin bound in crispy prosciutto. Bolton makes all the delectable desserts in-house, as in a blueberry almond tart served à la mode with lavender-honey ice cream, and the signature baked Alaska.

Appetizers

- Hamachi, Pickled Radish, Fava, and Ginger
- Pan-seared Red Mullet, Caponata, Candied Lemon
- Scallop Ceviche, Lime, Avocado, Kohlrabi, Cilantro

Entrées

- Sautéed Fluke, Asparagus, Yukon Gold Potatoes, Crispy Bacon
- Scallops, Granny Smith Apple & Radish Salad, Foie Gras Vinaigrette
- Roasted Breast and Leg Confit of Squab

Desserts

- Lemon Pound Cake, Jasmine-scented Raspberry Sorbet, Peaches
- Blueberry-Almond Tart, Lavender Honey Ice Cream
- Pistachio Parfait, Coconut Pudding

Savoia

 Italian

C-D2
277 Smith St. (bet. De Graw & Sackett Sts.)

Subway: Carroll St
Phone: 718-797-2727
Web: N/A
Prices: $$

Lunch & dinner daily

 Colorful earthenware plates, bare wooden tables and exposed brick enhance the rustic atmosphere of this Carroll Gardens charmer. At the pizza counter, a cook tearing leaves of fresh basil fills the room with a wonderful aroma, while the wood-burning pizza oven glows in the background.

No wonder that pizza is a hot item here. Toppings stray from the standard, with hot sopressata, fried eggplant and boiled egg among the many choices. There are plenty of other entrées, too—most of them focusing on Southern Italian traditions—from hearty fettucine *boscialo* (with a flavorful meat sauce kicked up with slivers of fried eggplant and nuggets of mozzarella) to a Sicilian-style beef cutlet. Personable and relaxed service adds to Savoia's casual vibe.

Sea

 Thai

B1
114 N. 6th St. (bet. Berry St. & Wythe Ave.)

Subway: Bedford Av
Phone: 718-384-8850
Web: www.searestaurant.com
Prices: $$

Lunch & dinner daily

 Resembling a trendy Manhattan lounge yet serving fresh, well-made Thai cuisine, Sea is an exotic bird among the small hipster bars of Williamsburg. The cavernous space pulsates with energy, and its popularity is enjoyed by a diverse clientele, from young families to larger after-work groups. The dining room, flanked by two bars, has an industrial-chic vibe with its concrete floor and cement walls complemented by a section of seating around a reflecting pool crowned by a life-size Buddha. Considering the festive environs, the staff is impressively gracious and attentive. The Thai-focused menu is reasonably priced and extensive in its offerings of dumplings, spring rolls, and salads along with curries and sautéed dishes available with a choice of protein.

391

Sette Enoteca & Cucina 😊

D2

Italian 🍴

207 Seventh Ave. (at 3rd St.)

Subway: 7 Av
Phone: 718-499-7767
Web: www.setteparkslope.com
Prices: **$$**

Lunch & dinner daily

Craving some Chianti and capellini? Then head straight for Sette Enoteca & Cucina, where the talented kitchen crew turns out consistently tasty Italian fare.

This Park Slope restaurant is popular with the neighbors—you'll find everyone from hip moms and their offspring to cool couples dining on pizza, pasta, and a host of entrées that includes crisp duck breast, wood-oven-roasted fish, and grilled hanger steak. The all-Italian wine list touts its *venti per venti*, 20 bottles for $20 each, and wines are also available by the quartino.

Don't expect exposed brick and candle-wax-covered Chianti bottles, though. Sette Enoteca & Cucina bucks the trend with its contemporary design (think blond wood tables and metallic-fabric-covered banquettes).

Silent H

B1

Vietnamese 🍴

79 Berry St. (at 9th St.)

Subway: Bedford Av
Phone: 718-218-7063
Web: www.silenthbrooklyn.com
Prices: 🍤🍤

Tue – Sun lunch & dinner

Chef/owner Vinh Nguyen struggled to find a Vietnamese restaurant to impress his visiting family, so he decided to open his own. Located on a quiet "Billyburg" corner, the pleasant room has a comfortable bar area and black-and-white photos of Vietnamese street scenes beneath ceiling fans with leaf-shaped blades. Nguyen's family cooking inspires the concise menu, offering home-style selections, like pork meatball ragu or caramelized black peppercorn fish, highlight the kitchen's use of fresh, high-quality ingredients to compose unique and flavorful dishes. A selection of "Viet-Tapas" may feature various rolls, shrimp toast, and beef carpaccio. Lunchtime offers the celebrated *banh mi*—crusty baguettes filled with meat and pickled vegetables.

The Smoke Joint

Barbecue

D2

87 S. Elliot Pl. (bet. Fulton St & Lafayette Ave.)

Subway: Lafayette Av
Phone: 718-797-1011
Web: www.thesmokejoint.com
Prices:

Lunch & dinner daily

You may leave smelling of hickory smoke, but the taste left in your mouth from this fantastic barbecue joint is worth the hungry stares you'll get from fellow subway riders. Settle down, grab a beer and dig into seriously smoky ribs coated with "jointrub"—a secret house recipe—and sandwiches, all served with a variety of sauces, including the lip-smacking-good "jointsmoke" and the spicy "hollapeno" varieties. Sides include the usual suspects, but the cayenne-spiked mac and cheese and the smoky, molasses-flavored barbecued beans are fantastic.

Despite its location near the esteemed Brooklyn Academy of Music, the setting is laid-back, and the staff is energetic, smiling, and just plain fun. Great prices leave an even better taste in your mouth.

Stone Park Cafe

Contemporary

D2

324 Fifth Ave. (at 3rd St.)

Subway: Union St
Phone: 718-369-0082
Web: www.stoneparkcafe.com
Prices: $$

Mon – Fri dinner only
Sat – Sun lunch & dinner

At this corner location, large windows peer onto Park Slope's vibrant Fifth Avenue thoroughfare and small park that is its namesake. Approaching five years in the area, Stone Park Cafe remains popular with neighborhood couples and families seeking seasonally inspired, creative fare. Offerings may range from smoked salmon cheesecake to lamb cassoulet. The $30 prix-fixe menu option is a very good value for such quality.

The light and airy interior is simply accented with exposed brick, light wood, and pale sage walls. A long bar near the entrance is a welcome spot for a pre-dinner cocktail. In the sunken dining room, tables are covered with white linens, brown paper, and clear glass votives. Weather permitting, al fresco sidewalk seating is available.

Thomas Beisl 🏚

D2

25 Lafayette Ave. (bet. Ashland Pl. & St. Felix St.)

Subway: Atlantic Ave - Pacific St
Phone: 718-222-5800
Web: N/A
Prices: $$

Tue – Sun lunch & dinner
Mon dinner only

Fort Greene is alive with the smell of strudel at Thomas Beisl. This Austrian *beisl*, or bistro, is run by Chef/owner Thomas Ferlesch, who manned the stove for 11 years as executive chef of the Upper West Side institution, Café des Artistes.
Located across from the Brooklyn Academy of Music, Thomas Beisl has the bistro look down with its white-paper-topped tables, terrazzo floor, and blackboard scrawled with the daily specials. Not to mention the engaging and attentive staff.
The menu reads like a love letter to Vienna with traditional Wiener Schnitzel, beef goulash, and homemade bratwurst rounding out the selections. Concertgoers drop in after the performance for Linzer torte, strudel, and *kaiserschmarren*, a souffléd pancake.

Tuscany Grill

A4

8620 Third Ave. (bet. 86th & 87th Sts.)

Subway: 86 St
Phone: 718-921-5633
Web: N/A
Prices: $$

Dinner daily

Bay Ridge's ever-changing demographic does not deter this charismatic, quintessential neighborhood restaurant from serving Italian-American favorites to a loyal cadre of locals, who come for dishes that burst with flavor as well as to share their latest adventures with the waitstaff.
The menu offers hefty portions of honest, good food, such as homey Hunter-style *farfalle* pasta baked in tomatoes, mushrooms, cheese, with sweet and hot sausage. Crostini of fresh, milky ricotta, roasted red bell pepper, and basil leaf over toast brushed with quality olive oil makes a wonderful prelude to any meal. Save room for decadent house-made desserts such as the pignoli tart—lemony and piney—in a crust that is truly worth every buttery calorie.

Water Falls Café

Middle Eastern

C1-2

144 Atlantic Ave. (bet. Clinton & Henry Sts.)

Lunch & dinner daily

Subway: Atlantic Av
Phone: 718-488-8886
Web: www.waterfallscafe.com
Prices:

Of the smattering of Middle Eastern restaurants on Brooklyn's Atlantic Avenue, Water Falls Cafe is the best of the bunch. It's not much on décor—simple white walls, basic black chairs, minimal artwork—but this family-run place dishes up terrific food at a great value.

Feisty and good-humored, the owner makes sure you are well taken care of, even if her mothering encourages you to eat every last bite—or at least take any leftovers home. The menu features typical Middle Eastern fare—hummus, shish kabob, kibbeh, and some of the best *fattoush* this side of the Arabian Sea.

There's an extensive list of freshly squeezed juices along with strong Arabic coffee and sweet mint tea. Alcohol is not served here, though you are welcome to bring your own.

Zenkichi

Japanese

B1

77 N. 6th St. (at Wythe Ave.)

Wed – Sun dinner only

Subway: Bedford Av
Phone: 718-388-8985
Web: www.zenkichi.com
Prices: **$$**

 This wood-clad Japanese *izakaya* is housed in a three-level space that feels wonderfully cozy and intimate. Dark furnishings, dim lighting, and a multitude of mirrors may make the setting difficult to maneuver, but the gracious staff safely escorts guests from the door to their own private dining nooks. Once settled and ready to order, summon a server with the tabletop call button. Zenkichi serves a selection of small plates designed for sharing and pairing with sake. The romantically inclined should choose the omakase for two which could include the likes of seared scallop and daikon salad, miso-marinated cod, and plum wine jelly for dessert. A return to the outside world will have you planning your next meal here—just be sure to call ahead for a reservation.

© Martha Cooper

Queens

Queens

Nearly as large as Manhattan, the Bronx, and Staten Island combined, the borough of Queens covers 120 square miles on the western end of Long Island. Thousands of immigrants arriving here each year makes Queens the most culturally diverse county in the U.S. They are drawn to the borough's relatively affordable housing, a family-driven quality of life, as well as the many tight-knit cultural communities formed by extended immigrant families.

THE QUEENLY BOROUGH

Queens' first permanent settlement was established by the Dutch at present-day Flushing in 1645. Clashes between Dutch and English settlers over freedom of worship marked its early years. When the English took over the colony of Nieuw Amsterdam in 1664, they named this county Queens, after Catherine of Braganza, wife of King Charles II of England. Until the mid-19th century, Queens remained a sparsely populated area of small villages and farms. As New York City grew, urbanization of Queens accelerated, attracting waves of German and Irish immigrants. In 1898, Queens was incorporated as a borough of New York City. The borough was first connected to Manhattan when the Queensboro Bridge opened in 1909; railway tunnels under the East River were completed the following year. With new transportation facilities making it easier for residents to commute to Manhattan, the population of Queens mushroomed in the 1920s. This era also cast Queens as a star of the silent-film industry, which operated some 20 studios in Astoria before relocating to sunny Hollywood, California—where the milder climate allowed filming outdoors year-round. By the 1970's, nearly 30 percent of Queens' residents were immigrants—that number has almost doubled today.

A CRAZY QUILT OF NEIGHBORHOODS

A seven mile span along The International Express (the New York subway 7 line) passes through the international smorgasbord that Queens offers. Restaurants in the neighborhoods along each stop reflect the borough's ever changing diversity.

On a stroll through **Astoria**, discover Greek grilled octopus and baklava; **Flushing** still reigns as Queens' most vibrant Asian neighborhood; **Jackson Heights'** global fare ranges from Indian tandoori dishes to Bolivian *arepas*; **Woodside** in some spots remains as an "Irishtown" but now includes Latin, Filipino, and Thai populations with restaurants and shops to match; in **Sunnyside** (one of the most diverse neighborhoods in the borough) you can eat your way through Korea, Columbia, Mexico, Romania, China, and Turkey.

These days, a cluster of factories in industrial **Long Island City** in western Queens are being renovated into artists' studios and living spaces. In Hunters Point—one subway stop from

Midtown—rapid gentrification is turning this working-class enclave into a desirable place to live, with rising housing costs to match. Vernon Boulevard, the main commercial thoroughfare, is now lined with diverse restaurants, bars, and shops.

ATTRACTIONS GALORE

For years, there wasn't much attracting tourists to Queens. Much has changed since with the openings of film studios such as **PS1 Contemporary Art Center**, the **Noguchi Museum**, and the **Museum of the Moving Image**. An old school and abandoned factories in Long Island City and Astoria were converted to house these new enterprises. Developed to accommodate New York's first World's Fair in 1939, the 1,275-acre **Flushing Meadows Corona Park** *(between 111th St. & Van Wyck Expwy.)* now contains the **Queens Museum of Art**, as well as a wealth of opportunities for sporting activities. The park also encompasses **Shea Stadium** (home to the New York Mets) as well as the **USTA National Tennis Center** (where the U.S. Open is held each summer). Of course, visitors traveling to New York by air all arrive via Queens, where both LaGuardia and Kennedy international airports are located.

© Martha Cooper

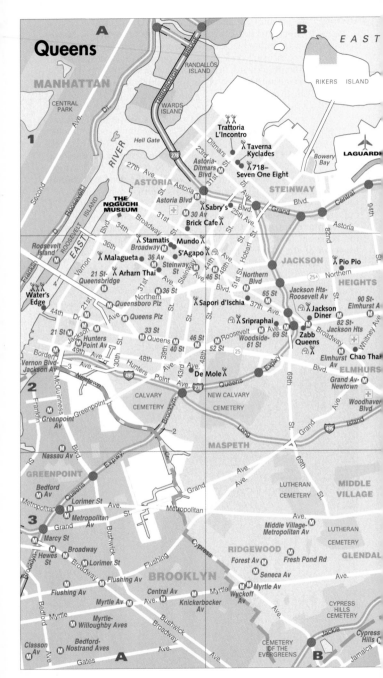

Queens

A **B**

EAST

MANHATTAN

CENTRAL PARK

RANDALL'S ISLAND

WARDS ISLAND

RIKERS ISLAND

Hell Gate

LAGUARDIA

Bowery Bay

Second Ave.

RIVER

27th Ave.

EAST RIVER

ROOSEVELT ISLAND

STEINWAY

ASTORIA

Astoria

23rd
Ditmars
Astoria-Ditmars Blvd.

Trattoria L'Incontro
Taverna Kyclades
718–Seven One Eight

Ditmars Blvd.

Astoria Blvd.

Astoria Blvd.
THE NOGUCHI MUSEUM
30 Av
Astoria Blvd
Sabry's
Brick Cafe

25th Ave.
Grand

Central

94th

Astoria

82nd

Broadway
31st
34th

Stamatis
Mundo
Malagueta
S'Agapo
36 Av
Steinway St.
Arharn Thai

JACKSON
Pio Pio

HEIGHTS

Vernon Blvd.
36th
Broadway
21 St-Queensbridge
Water's Edge

Northern Blvd.
46th
44th St.
48th

Northern Blvd
Sapori d'Ischia

65 St
Jackson Hts-Roosevelt Av
Jackson Diner

90 St-Elmhurst Av

82 St-Jackson Hts
Whitney Ave

Franklin

Roosevelt Island

44th Dr.
21 St
Jackson
Hunters Point Av
49th

Queensboro Plz
Queens Plz
33 St
Queens

46 St
Roosevelt Av.
Woodside-61 St

69 St
Broadway

Sripraphai
Zabb Queens
Elmhurst Av
Chao Thai

ELMHURST

Borden
Vernon Blvd-Jackson Av
48th
39th
40 St
43rd

De Mole

Queens Expwy
Long Island Expwy

Grand Av-Newtown

Woodhaven Blvd

McGuinness
Newtown
30th
Hunters Point Ave.
52nd

CALVARY CEMETERY
NEW CALVARY CEMETERY

MASPETH

69th St.

Grand

Greenpoint Av
Greenpoint

Nassau Av

GREENPOINT

Bedford Av
Lorimer St
Metropolitan
Metropolitan Av
Grand

Metropolitan
Grand

Metropolitan Av

Ave.

Ave.

LUTHERAN CEMETERY

MIDDLE VILLAGE

Marcy St
Broadway
Hewes St
Lorimer St
Flushing Av
Myrtle
Bushwick
Broadway

Flushing
Cypress

Middle Village-Metropolitan Av
LUTHERAN CEMETERY

RIDGEWOOD
Forest Av
Fresh Pond Rd

GLENDALE

BROOKLYN

Central Av
Myrtle Av
Myrtle-Willoughby Aves
Bedford-Nostrand Aves
Gates

Knickerbocker Av
Wyckoff Av
Myrtle Av
Seneca Av

CYPRESS HILLS CEMETERY

Classon Av

Bushwick
Broadway

CEMETERY OF THE EVERGREENS

Jackie
Cypress Hills
Jamaica

B

1

2

3

A

Arharn Thai

A2

32-05 36th Ave. (bet. 32nd & 33rd Sts.)

Subway: 36 Av
Phone: 718-728-5563
Web: N/A
Prices: ⊖⊖

Lunch & dinner daily

An easy train ride leaves you a block from this sleepy Thai place, surrounded by a lineup of restaurants that would suit the United Nations. Expect a room simply decorated with Thai handicrafts—many for sale—and service that is warm and eager to please.

The extensive menu offers a variety of chef's specialties and classics. *Mee Grob*, a contradictory composition of fried rice noodles, shrimp and tofu in a sticky tamarind sauce makes a bright starter, as does *Yum Koon Chieng*, a salad of Chinese sausage, cucumber, tomato and scallion tossed with lime juice and chile. Authentic spice levels may be toned down for Western palates, but large portions leave tasty leftovers to bring home. Traditional family-style dining is the best way to go here.

Brick Cafe

A1

30-95 33rd St. (at 31st Ave.)

Subway: Broadway
Phone: 718-267-2735
Web: www.brickcafe.com
Prices: $$

Mon – Fri dinner only
Sat – Sun lunch & dinner

Resembling a European country inn, with its lace curtains, chunky wood tables, tin ceiling and knick-knacks set around the room, the Brick Cafe wraps diners in a rustic, romantic atmosphere. This storefront eatery, set on a residential street in Astoria, is a good place to take a date.

In the candlelit room, you can share plates that take their cues from the southern regions of France and Italy. Salads range from Caprese to Niçoise, while entrées include everything from penne alla vodka to striped bass oreganata. For dessert, tiramisu and crêpes Suzette represent the cafe's Franco-Italian tendencies.

Locals favor the weekend brunch, which includes everything from omelets and French toast to octopus carpaccio and tuna tartare.

Chao Thai

Thai

85-03 Whitney Ave. (at Broadway)

Subway: Elmhurst Av
Phone: 718-424-4999
Web: N/A
Prices: 💰

Wed – Mon lunch & dinner

One of the best Thai restaurants in the five boroughs, Chao Thai makes up in taste what its décor lacks in style. It's a tiny spot of real estate in the heart of Elmhurst, sandwiched between Asian markets and restaurants of all types. Don't get distracted by piles of durian and jackfruit beckoning your wallet; save your *baht* for a coconut ice cream.

Skip the printed menu and ask staff to translate the long list of daily specials; this is where the kitchen's talent lies. These dishes are closer to Bangkok than New York and reflect the restaurant's commitment to feed a typically Thai clientele properly. Prices are low enough to order an extra dish or two. This popular place has limited seating, takes cash only, and is BYOB, so plan ahead.

De Mole

 Mexican

45-02 48th Ave. (at 45th St.)

Subway: 46 St
Phone: 718-392-2161
Web: N/A
Prices: 💰

Lunch & dinner daily

If you lived in Sunnyside, you'd likely be a regular at this charming Mexican bistro. Even if you don't, you might want to stop by the cozy brick-walled spot for its flavorful food and its surprising, European-influenced setting.

De Mole perfectly fuses real Mexican cuisine with a Balthazar-like touch on the details. The reasonably priced menu—supplemented by inviting daily specials—brings forth the best of Mexico, while fajitas, nachos and such are a nod to Mexican-American tastes. Even chips and salsa get bistro treatment as freshly fried tortillas are presented SoHo-style in a paper bag and served with an addictive smoky salsa.

The staff here could not be nicer and the restaurant has a family-fun feel.

Queens

Jackson Diner

37-47 74th St. (bet. Roosevelt & 37th Aves.)

Subway: Jackson Hts - Roosevelt Av   Lunch & dinner daily
Phone: 718-672-1232
Web: www.jacksondiner.com
Prices: 😎

You could call the décor in this Jackson Heights diner whimsical, or you could say it was gaudy, depending on your point of view. Either way, it's colorful and modern, from the 3-D leaves on the ceiling to the multi-hued chairs that are more functional than comfortable.

Don't come expecting burgers and milkshakes, though, since this diner is all about Indian cooking. If you like curries, masala dosa and tandoori dishes, Jackson Diner won't disappoint. The inexpensive lunch buffet offers a wide variety of Southern Indian dishes, including dessert, for one low price.

After lunch, spend some time exploring the immediate neighborhood, which teems with jewelry stores, sari shops and groceries, all peddling Indian wares.

KumGangSan

138-28 Northern Blvd. (bet. Bowne & Union Sts.)

Subway: Flushing - Main St   Lunch & dinner daily
Phone: 718-461-0909
Web: www.kumgangsan.net
Prices: $$

This establishment focuses on pleasure, with an attractively sprawling interior, lovely terrace with a burbling fountain, lush greenery, and a voluminous menu, as well as a sushi bar. Named for a range of mountains (translated as "Diamond Mountains") in North Korea, this local favorite perpetually buzzes with throngs of diners who partake in the well-made and satisfying fare. The large selection of steaming noodles, bubbling casseroles with chili-spiced broth, and barbecued meats are all made with authentic seasonings imported from Korea. To spark the taste buds, each table receives a generous selection of small dishes (*panchan*) at the start of the meal. Another location is in Midtown West (*49 West 32nd St.*), which is open 24/7 as well.

Malagueta

Brazilian

A2

25-35 36th Ave. (at 28th St.)

Subway: 36 Av
Phone: 718-937-4821
Web: N/A
Prices:

Mon – Fri dinner only
Sat – Sun lunch & dinner

Chef/owner Herbet Gomes and his wife, Alda Teixeire, have created an intimate and unassuming Brazilian bistro, offering a culinary homage to their culturally rich and brilliantly diverse homeland. Inside, olive green and deep red walls are judiciously covered with oil paintings, surrounding tables dressed with white linen, and fresh flowers.

Well-composed and authentic specialties like *peito de pato* (sautéed duck breast) or *moqueca de camarao* (shrimp stew with palm oil and coconut milk) tend towards the hot, salty, smoky, and sour ends of the flavor spectrum. Saturday diners should indulge in the hearty, flavorful, and rustic Brazilian clay-pot black bean stew, *feijoada compela*. Service is personable, well-informed, and dedicated to your enjoyment.

Mundo

International

A2

31-18 Broadway (at 32nd St.)

Subway: Broadway
Phone: 718-777-2829
Web: www.mundoastoria.com
Prices: **$$**

Mon – Sat dinner only
Sun lunch & dinner

Located just off of a busy Astoria thoroughfare, Mundo attracts crowds of hungry locals happy to have this little gem to call their own. The simple interior features a changing display of artwork and in warmer months, tables spill out onto the sidewalk giving the cozy space a quaint European atmosphere. The cuisine, much like the neighborhood, offers a diverse array of global representation. Appetizers like grilled halloumi cheese, empanadas, and edamame tastefully coexist with chicken Milanesa and beef-filled Ottoman dumplings.

Vegetarians will be pleased with the variety of meat-less items. Mundo's co-owners have put together an establishment that is sure to please—"Willie" Lucerofabbi warmly attends to the front-of-the-house while "John" Caner runs the kitchen.

Noodle House

38-12 Prince St. (bet. 38th & 39th Aves.)

Subway: Flushing - Main St   Lunch & dinner daily
Phone: 718-321-3838
Web: N/A
Prices: 🪙🪙

Also known as Nan Shian Dumpling House, it is easily found among a strip of restaurants reflecting the diversity of Flushing's burgeoning Asian population. Simply decorated, the comfortable dining room features rows of closely set tables and a mirrored wall that successfully gives the illusion of space. This enjoyable and interesting menu focuses on noodle-filled soups, toothsome stir-fried rice cakes, and the house specialty, steamed pork buns. These are made in-house and have a delicate, silky wrapper encasing a flavorful meatball of ground pork or crab and rich tasting broth. Eating these may take some practice, but take your cue from the slurping crowd: puncture the casing on your spoon to cool the dumplings and avoid burning your mouth.

Pio Pio

84-13 Northern Blvd. (at 84th St.)

Subway: 82 St - Jackson Hts   Lunch & dinner daily
Phone: 718-426-1010
Web: www.piopionyc.com
Prices: 🪙🪙

Spanish for "chirp chirp", this charming eatery serves up authentic Peruvian fare in a colorful, casual atmosphere; vibrant hues tint the walls while bright Peruvian paintings hang on exposed brick. True to its signature sound, Pio Pio calls attention to the chicken; exquisitely marinated, cooked rotisserie style, and served with a garlicky green sauce, this bird will have your taste buds tweeting in ecstasy. The sides are also something to sing about: try a generous plate of *tostones* (fried unripe plantains) or the zesty avocado salad. The combos—best shared—are a great value, offering a whole chicken plus two or more sides at a bargain price. On a sunny day, grab a table in the garden and cool off with a refreshing pitcher of sangria.

Sabry's

Seafood ✗

B1

24-25 Steinway St. (bet. Astoria Blvd. & 25th Ave.)

Subway: Astoria Blvd   Lunch & dinner daily
Phone: 718-721-9010
Web: N/A
Prices: $$

Located in an area of Astoria that's fast becoming known as Little Egypt, Sabry's serves seafood with Egyptian accents—starting with the large ice-filled case where the day's fresh catch is displayed. Prepared in the style of many Mediterranean eateries, fish from this case are grilled or baked whole, here with Middle Eastern flavorings like garlic, cumin, cardamom, and red pepper. Aromatic tagines, such as the shellfish version cooked in a heady tomato sauce, are another good option. Baba ghanoush is packed with flavor, and the freshly made pita bread makes a fantastic accompaniment.
If you must have a glass of wine, be aware that the restaurant doesn't serve alcohol, and you cannot BYOB. There are plenty of other options, though, like tasty mint tea.

S'Agapo

Greek ✗

A2

34-21 34th Ave. (at 35th St.)

Subway: Steinway St   Lunch & dinner daily
Phone: 718-626-0303
Web: N/A
Prices: $$

When in Astoria, go where the Greeks go, and in the case of S'Agapo ("I love you" in Greek), you'll quickly discover why this place is always crammed with Greeks, locals and Manhattanites sipping ouzo or a great bottle of wine.
Located on a quiet residential block bordering Astoria and Long Island City, S'Agapo is owned and managed by a charming couple from Crete. The taverna focuses on providing authentic food at palatable prices, with personal service.
Rustic preparations of perfectly grilled fish, lamb, and an extensive assortment of cold and hot appetizers mean that no diner goes away hungry. A number of Cretan specialties (house-made lamb sausage, Cretan cheese dumplings), as well as the quiet outdoor terrace, set S'Agapo apart.

Sapori d'Ischia

B2

55-15 37th Ave. (at 56th St.)

Subway: Northern Blvd
Phone: 718-446-1500
Web: N/A
Prices: $$

Tue – Sat lunch & dinner
Sun dinner only

Remember the movie *Big Night?* Like the Baltimore Italian restaurant that starred in that film, Sapori d'Ischia doesn't serve sides of spaghetti. In fact, their "house rules," posted at the bar, spell out a number of other things the restaurant doesn't do (for instance, they don't serve butter, grate cheese atop seafood or put lemon peel in espresso).

Set on an industrial-looking block in Woodside, Sapori d'Ischia started out as a wholesale Italian foods business. Over the years, owner Frank Galano (who runs the place with his son Antonio), added a market and then a small trattoria to the premises. Today, delectable pastas, low prices and a convivial atmosphere complete with live piano entertainment keep customers coming back for more.

Sentosa

C2

39-07 Prince St. (at 39th Ave.)

Subway: Flushing - Main St
Phone: 718-886-6331
Web: N/A
Prices:

Lunch & dinner daily

Sentosa, the Malay word for tranquillity, celebrates an agreeable intermingling of the mainly Chinese and Indian influences of Malaysia's multi-ethnic descendants. The restaurant features a contemporary setting with warm lighting, polished teak, and stone tiles. The flavorful menu offers fare such as *rendang*, a rich, flavorful stew made with tender cubes of beef simmered in coconut milk and chili paste; alongside a large selection of rice and noodle dishes, such as Mee Siam rice vermicelli, stir-fried with sweet chili sauce, cubes of fried tofu, bean sprouts, fresh shrimp, then topped with ground peanuts. Be sure to eat your vegetables; they are sautéed with alluring *belacan*, made from fermented, ground shrimp.

718 - Seven One Eight

French ✗

35-01 Ditmars Blvd. (at 35th St.)

Subway: Astoria - Ditmars Blvd
Phone: 718-204-5553
Web: www.718restaurant.com
Prices: $$

Lunch & dinner daily

What's in a name? In this case, 718 refers to the Queens' area code. No matter. This cozy French bistro provides a welcome addition to the Greek and Italian places that pervade the Astoria dining scene.

With its solid French base, the cuisine displays Spanish and American influences, all realized with fresh, seasonal products: shrimp meets mango in a salad, rack of lamb pairs with *piquillo* peppers, and thin-crust *tartes flambée* pay homage to that traditional Alsatian dish. Banana and chocolate bread pudding, and warm apple tart round out the scrumptious dessert menu.

Come Friday night and listen to music from the Casbah.

Spicy & Tasty

Chinese ✗

39-07 Prince St. (at 39th Ave.)

Subway: Flushing - Main St
Phone: 718-359-1601
Web: N/A
Prices:

Lunch & dinner daily

Teeming with a dizzying array of restaurants, bakeries and shops all catering to Flushing's booming Asian population, this Chinatown block draws a mix of New Yorkers in search of real Chinese food.

Spicy & Tasty fills that bill with fiery Szechuan cuisine that is remarkably consistent. Delicious dishes blend different degrees of heat, ranging from the mouth-numbing effect of Szechuan peppercorns to whole chilies marinated in sour vinegar that are merely warm by comparison. A few mild selections, which are no less tasty, will appeal to more prudent palates. Count on the kind staff for sound guidance regarding what to order.

The spacious dining room eschews Chinese lanterns and red walls in favor of light colors and wood sculptures.

Sripraphai

B2

64-13 39th Ave. (bet. 64th & 65th Sts.)

Subway: Woodside - 61 St
Phone: 718-899-9599
Web: N/A
Prices: 💰💰

Thu – Tue lunch & dinner

A meal at Sripraphai is an education in great and truly authentic Thai cuisine—its mostly Thai crowd is perhaps your first clue. This food goes well beyond expectation. The bright green papaya salad showcases beautiful and pliable threads of crunchy papaya tossed with lime, fiery chilis, and cilantro—a marvelous balance of flavors. Green curry redolent with coconut, pineapple chunks, and a whirlwind of subtle aromatics served over utterly scrumptious roast duck exemplifies this cuisine's melding contrasts of textures and divine flavors. Thai iced tea or grass jelly drinks are a sweet, cooling respite from the properly spiced plates.

Numerous servers work the contemporary, clean room; an expansive outdoor patio is perfect for al fresco dining.

Stamatis

A2

3114 Broadway (bet. 31st & 32nd Sts.)

Subway: Broadway
Phone: 718-204-8964
Web: N/A
Prices: $$

Lunch & dinner daily

Who says there's no longer any good Greek food to be found in Astoria? *Au contraire*, the neighborhood's Mediterranean heritage is alive and well at Stamatis. A block away from the subway, Stamatis delivers all the standards to an eager crowd, many of whom are Greek.

If you're hankering for spanikopita, hop on the train and head straight here. The restaurant's enormous menu runs all the bases, from meze to grilled whole fish, and each entrée comes with your choice of a classically Greek side item. Presentations are simple, but dishes are large on portion, flavor and quality.

After your meal, a complimentary dessert based on the daily selection of sweets (perhaps a cinnamon honey cake or a custard-filled pastry), will arrive at your table.

Taverna Kyclades

Greek ✗

B1

33-07 Ditmars Blvd. (bet. 33rd & 35th Sts.)

Lunch & dinner daily

Subway: Astoria - Ditmars Blvd
Phone: 718-545-8666
Web: www.tavernakyclades.com
Prices: ∞

This classic and beloved Greek taverna, helmed by a dedicated chef owner and staff, continues to serve fresh daily, grilled and fried fish (available for inspection in a showcase refrigerator in the semi-open kitchen), along with heaping portions of side dishes. A perfect spot to dine family style.

Years of non-stop service to a loyal and diverse clientele has not diminished the classic patina of the small, but warm and boisterous dining room. The setting here is no frills. Diners are seated on simple wood chairs elbow to elbow. Meals can also be enjoyed in the year-round and enclosed garden area. The surrounding space is crowded with back-to-back stores and restaurants. Service here is cool, helpful, and without attitude. *Opa!*

Trattoria l'Incontro

Italian ✗✗

B1

21-76 31st St. (at Ditmars Blvd.)

Tue – Sun lunch & dinner

Subway: Astoria - Ditmars Blvd
Phone: 718-721-3532
Web: www.trattorialincontro.com
Prices: $$

From the warm welcome you receive at Trattoria l'Incontro, you'll know immediately how important the customers are to Abruzzi native Tina Sacramone and her son, Rocco. Indeed, at this Astoria restaurant, the hospitality is as important as the food. The chef is frequently spotted in the dining area, greeting regulars and making sure everyone is happy with dishes such as Tina's homemade pastas. Risotto here is served in a crisp parmesan "bowl," a good example of how the chef improves on classic Italian fare.

In the dining room, beams punctuate the ceiling, and paintings of the Italian countryside fill the walls. The brick pizza oven, which is visible to diners, turns out a host of savory pies—and even a sweet one stuffed with chocolate.

Water's Edge

A2

4-01 44th Dr. (at the East River)

Subway: 23 St - Ely Av
Phone: 718-482-0033
Web: www.watersedgenyc.com
Prices: $$$

Mon – Fri lunch & dinner
Sat dinner only

Waterside dining with magnificent Manhattan views draws patrons to the Water's Edge. The entire back wall of the restaurant is made of windows, affording superb views of the East River and the skyscrapers of Midtown. Elegant table settings, Louis XV-style chairs, and live piano music fill the dining room, decked out with original artwork and Oriental rugs.

Menus change seasonally; expect skillfully prepared contemporary dishes like miso-glazed Chilean sea bass or lavender honey-glazed chicken.

If you're coming from Manhattan, make dinner reservations at Water's Edge, and take the complimentary boat shuttle to the restaurant from the 35th Street pier.

Zabb Queens

B2

71-28 Roosevelt Ave. (bet. 70th & 72nd Sts.)

Subway: 74 St - Broadway
Phone: 718-426-7992
Web: www.zabbqueens.com
Prices: $$

Dinner daily

Surrender to your adventurous palette and expect the unexpected at Zabb Queens, famed for its scrumptious Thai food. Showcasing the cuisine of the Issan region of Northeastern Thailand, this family-run restaurant aims to please with unique specialties such as crispy catfish *larb* with mango, cashews, chile, and lime juice; or delicious bowls of drunken noodles, evenly sautéed in sweet sauce with broccoli, beef, and tomatoes. Homemade coconut ice cream made rich with coconut meat and milk—is a delightful highlight that demonstrates the kitchen's dedication to quality. The staff is friendly and eager to assist in this well-maintained but unimpressive setting.

East Village sibling, Zabb City, also offers an exquisite Thai meal.

Peter L. Wrenn/MICHELIN

Staten Island

Staten Island

New York City's "forgotten borough," Staten Island is primarily a bedroom community, culturally and economically related more to New Jersey than New York. The island, 14 miles long and 8 miles wide, boasts more wide-open green space than anywhere else in the city.

To reach any of the restaurants here, you'll have to drive over the **Verrazano-Narrows Bridge,** or take the ferry. The borough's biggest attraction, the celebrated Staten Island Ferry carries more than 3-1/2 million tourists and commuters a year between Manhattan's South Ferry and St. George terminals, passing the Statue of Liberty each way. Stunning views of the Manhattan skyline and New York Harbor, especially at night, are priceless. So is the fare—the ride is free!

AN ISLAND REFUGE

Staten Island got its name in the early 1600s from Dutch merchants, who dubbed it Staaten Eyelandt (Dutch for "State's Island"). The first permanent settlement was established at Oude Dorp by Dutch and French Huguenot families in 1661. Over the next two centuries, the island thrived on farming and agriculture, ferrying goods to nearby Manhattan and New Jersey.

Staten Island's economy grew considerably in 1898, after its citizens voted to incorporate it as one of the five boroughs of Greater New York City. This move attracted hardworking immigrants—many of Italian and Irish descent—to its farms and factories, and hard-playing society folks to its resort hotels. The boom went bust after World War I, when many residents left to make their fortunes on the mainland. The borough blossomed once again when the **Verrazano-Narrows Bridge** opened in 1964, linking the island with Brooklyn and bringing an influx of Manhattanites seeking respite from the big-city buzz.

TODAY'S STATEN ISLAND

Though isolated, Staten Island is not without its attractions. Options for outdoor adventures are plentiful here, from beaches to parks to woodlands. Explore **The Greenbelt**, a 2,800-acre nature preserve, or take a stroll along **South Beach's** FDR boardwalk, a two and a half-mile stretch, said to be the fourth longest in the world. **Historic Richmond Town**, a 25-acre village *(441 Clarke St.)*, marks the site of one of the earliest settlements on the island. History comes alive here, thanks to costumed guides who demonstrate crafts like printmaking, tinsmithing, and weaving, regaling visitors with tales of 19th-century life in the former county seat. An unexpected treasure, the **Jacques Marchais Museum of Tibetan Art** houses rare objects from Tibet, Nepal, China, Mongolia, and India in an enchanted setting atop Lighthouse Hill.

© Martha Cooper

Staten Island

Restaurant

417

Aesop's Tables

B1

Contemporary ✕

1233 Bay St. (bet. Maryland & Scarboro Aves.)

Bus: 51 & 81
Phone: 718-720-2005
Web: N/A
Prices: $$

Tue – Sat dinner only
Sun lunch & dinner

As a nod to its namesake, charming, and amiable Aesop's Tables conjures a childhood fable. The room is filled with wicker chairs, French movie posters, chalkboards listing a fine selection of wines, and front windows filled with stuffed animals. Original tin ceilings, a small bar, and brick walls create a soothing atmosphere. Yet its greatest treasure may be the walled garden, weather permitting.

This unexpected Staten Island find is a local favorite, replete with long-celebrated entrées like meatloaf or ancho chile-crusted calamari. Lovely and perfect for a chilly evening, the harvest strudel wraps luscious chunks of apples, quince, and pears in a flakey, buttery crust. Locavores rejoice: ingredients, when available, are sourced from nearby farms.

Bayou Restaurant

B1

Cajun ✕

1072 Bay St. (bet. Chestnut & St. Marys Aves.)

Bus: 51 & 81
Phone: 718-273-4383
Web: www.bayoustatenisland.com
Prices: $$

Mon – Sat lunch & dinner
Sun dinner only

Hop the ferry from Manhattan to Bayou, where the good times roll and the down-home Creole cooking will make you yearn for The Big Easy. Despite its location in a nondescript neighborhood, if you close your eyes and step inside this faithfully recreated New Orleans bistro, you might think you're in the French Quarter. Exposed brick walls make a gallery for trumpets, banjos, Mardi Gras beads, and portraits of favorite son, Louie Armstrong.

Here, the party never ends, and the mood is infectious. The menu showcases what N'awlins does best, offering chicken and andouille gumbo, catfish po' boys with roasted-pecan gravy, seafood jambalaya, and crawfish étouffée. There's even grilled alligator, and for dessert, don't forget the fried cheesecake.

Beso

B1

11 Schuyler St. (bet. Richmond Terrace & Stuyvesant Pl.)

Lunch & dinner daily

Bus: N/A
Phone: 718-816-8162
Web: www.besonyc.com
Prices: $$

A free ride on the Staten Island Ferry from Manhattan will deliver you right across the street from this new addition to the island's dining lineup. Bring some friends to Beso ("kiss" in Spanish) to enjoy a fun night out without spending a fortune. Inside this lovely space, shawls double as window treatments, an antique Spanish sideboard forms part of the bar, and a white adobe fireplace is studded with colorful tiles. Locals love the grazing menu of vibrant tapas, which can include anything from *guajillo*-crusted tuna to *fundito* (broiled chorizo served in a green-chile and tomatillo sauce topped with melted Mahon cheese). And that's not all: entrées will pique your interest with the likes of a grilled ancho-crusted salmon fillet and a roasted duck breast glazed with honey and smoked chile.

Carol's Cafe

B1

1571 Richmond Rd. (at Four Corners Rd. & Seaview Ave.)

Wed – Sat dinner only

Bus: X15, 74, 76, 84, 86
Phone: 718-979-5600
Web: www.carolscafe.com
Prices: $$$

Well-known on Staten Island for the cooking school she operates above her restaurant, owner Carol Frazzetta presides over the kitchen here. Frazzetta graduated from Le Cordon Bleu and studied at the Culinary Institute of America before opening Carol's Cuisine (the cooking school) in 1972. It was only natural that she would follow suit with her own cafe.

Decorated with a feminine touch, evident in the pink-linen napkins, fresh flowers and hanging plants that decorate the interior, Carol's only serves dinner. The seasonal menu travels through the U.S. and Europe for inspiration, fixing on the chef's favorite dishes. With entrées like oven-roasted beef brisket and pancetta- and mushroom-stuffed veal chop, homework never tasted quite so good.

Fushimi

B1

2110 Richmond Rd. (bet. Colfax & Lincoln Aves.)

Bus:	51, 81	Mon – Sat lunch & dinner
Phone:	718-980-5300	Sun dinner only
Web:	www.fushimi-us.com	
Prices:	**$$$**	

Fushimi is one of the better Japanese restaurants on Staten Island. In a league of its own, the fare here is quite imaginative and inclines towards fusion. While the product may not be blue-ribbon, the presentation will certainly lure you—large white platters are elaborately decorated with fronds, tepees of bamboo, and the like. Despite its trite location, the expansive *mise en scéne* puts diners in a convivial mood, and is an ideal setting for the local crowd. The tiled foyer meanders into two areas: a bar packed with revelers sipping on drinks served in blue-tinged stemware, and a warm, whispery dining room/sushi bar filled with music and animated diners.

With its charming outdoor space (parking is available on premises), Fushimi is a magnet for visitors in the mood to lunch and lounge.

Nurnberger Bierhaus

B1

817 Castleton Ave. (at Davis Ave.)

Bus:	46, 96	Lunch & dinner daily
Phone:	718-816-7461	
Web:	www.nurnbergerbierhaus.com	
Prices:	**$$**	

Tradition reigns at this friendly Staten Island restaurant, complete with an Oktoberfest spirit and a waitstaff clad in German garb. Rustic German food is what the restaurant does best, and the meat-heavy menu focuses on generous portions of stick-to-your-ribs dishes like *Jägerschnitzel* and *Wurststellar mit allem drum & dran,* four types of sausage accompanied by sauerkraut and red cabbage. Desserts pile on more calories, in the form of German chocolate cake and *Apfelstrudel.*

Groups and families (a children's menu is available) are particularly drawn to the bierhaus, where they are welcomed with open arms and a full stein. The beer is reason alone to visit this place; several imported brews are available on draft, and even more by the bottle.

Panarea Ristorante

Italian 🍴🍴

A2

35 Page Ave. (bet. Boscombe Ave. & Richmond Valley Rd.)

Bus:	74	Lunch & dinner daily
Phone:	718-227-8582	
Web:	www.panarearistorante.com	
Prices:	**$$**	

♿

Don't be fooled by this restaurant's location in a strip mall; one step inside the etched-glass door, and you'll be won over by its casual elegance. Named for one of the more beautiful islands off the coast of Sicily, Panarea is owned by two Italian couples. From the wood-paneled bar topped with flower-filled Italian ceramic vases to the elegant dining room with its cozy fireplace to the lovely covered veranda, Panarea makes any occasion special.

The kitchen turns out well-prepared Italian classics, like tender grilled baby octopus and spaghetti *chitarra* with lobster sauce. All of the pastas are made from scratch, and the delectable desserts are homemade. Be sure to save room for one of the latter, washed down with a cup of the heady espresso.

Vida

American 🍴

B1

381 Van Duzer St. (bet. Beach & Wright Sts.)

Bus:	78	Tue – Sat lunch & dinner
Phone:	718-720-1501	
Web:	N/A	
Prices:	**$$**	

Festooned with braids of dried poblanos, this entryway opens to a luminous, immaculate room dressed in sunny shades of yellow, serving food that further brightens this Staten Island find. Vida indeed breathes new life into its dishes, many of which tip their hats to a Southwestern culinary heritage, like the hefty Mexican duo of corn tortillas filled with flavorful Chimayo chicken or juicy pulled pork.

Accompaniments are also perfectly cooked, such as the black beans that arrive heady with thyme and fired up with chili. Tempting as this menu is, innovative daily specials display care, creativity, and are not to be missed. Desserts, such as a dense, creamy pumpkin cheesecake perfumed with cinnamon and clove, showcase the best of each season.

Zest

B1

French ✗✗

977 Bay St. (bet. Lynhurst & Willow Sts.)

Bus:	51, 81
Phone:	718-390-8477
Web:	N/A
Prices:	**$$**

Tue – Sun dinner only

 ♿
 ☂

Inside this area's new and welcome French bistro, dark wood paneling, handsome wainscoting, and jazzy red portraits reinforce a "supper club meets the Mediterranean" aura. Lighting emits a romantic golden hue to warm the cozy dining room, where close tables are set with clean, crisp linens, and topped with a votive candle and fresh flowers. A semi-private room is a great option for larger parties. The restaurant also offers outdoor seating (weather permitting) and a top-floor lounge.

The French menu features familiar favorites such as hearty and aromatic cassoulet of white beans, tender lamb, and rich duck sausage, or a traditional tarte Tatin. Though prices may be pricey by neighborhood standards, the dishes are of surprisingly fine quality.

We try to be as accurate as possible when giving price ranges. But prices change daily so please confirm before booking.

Where to **stay**

Alphabetical list of Hotels

Where to stay

The Maritime

B3

363 W. 16th St. (at Ninth Ave.)

Subway: 14 St - 8 Av
Phone: 212-242-4300 or 800-466-9092
Fax: 212-242-1188
Web: www.themaritimehotel.com
Prices: $$$

121
Rooms

4
Suites

Polka-dotted with porthole windows, The Maritime Hotel is a 2003 reincarnation of the truly unique, 12-story white-tile edifice designed by Albert C. Ledner in 1966 to house the National Maritime Union. The location, amid Chelsea's art galleries and the Meatpacking District's hip nightlife, assures the property a clientele encompassing artists and fashionistas as well as business travelers.

A complimentary bottle of wine and a personalized note welcome guests to the cabin-like rooms, each echoing the nautical feel with its five-foot porthole window and palette of sea blues and greens. All include a CD player and a flat-screen LCD TV. Marble baths and 500-thread-count bed linens add the luxury of an ocean-liner state room. A warning to guests seeking peace and quiet: request a room on a higher floor rather than try and engineer the noise-reducing "window plugs" in the middle of the night.

Dining options include La Bottega, an Italian trattoria with a large outdoor terrace; and chic Matsuri (*see restaurant listing*) for Japanese cuisine. Between Cabanas rooftop bar and Hiro Ballroom, opportunities abound to drink in the Chelsea scene.

Manhattan ▶ Chelsea

The Bowery Hotel

335 Bowery (at 3rd St.)

Subway:	Astor Pl
Phone:	212-505-9100 or 866-726-9379
Fax:	212-505-9700
Web:	www.theboweryhotel.com
Prices:	$$$$

135
Rooms

7
Suites

The Bowery Hotel Source: Goode

This nondescript block of what was once known as Skid Row might seem an unlikely location for a trendy boutique hotel, but Eric Goode and Sean MacPherson (who brought you the Maritime in Chelsea) are betting that their new East Village property will draw hordes of hipsters and Europeans. Though the block can be dodgy late at night, it's within easy walking distance of New York's coolest 'hoods (East Village, SoHo, Nolita, Greenwich Village, Lower East Side).

From the outside, the hotel's new redbrick façade towers castle-like above neighboring structures. Giant black-paned windows give the building a pre-war charm. Step inside and you'll be engulfed in the dim, sultry lobby, where dark woods, fireplaces, velvet couches and mosaic mirrors create a distinctly Old World air.

Those huge, sound-proofed windows afford great city views, and paired with whitewashed brick walls, make the rooms seem larger. A mix of period and contemporary pieces add to the Art Deco-meets-21st-century design, while 500-thread-count bed linens, hi-def TV, and rainfall showerheads add luxury.

Look for the outdoor courtyard bar and restaurant Gemma to be popular with the in-crowd.

Manhattan ▶ East Village

Best Western Seaport Inn

33 Peck Slip (at Front St.)

Subway: Fulton St
Phone: 212-766-6600 or 800-937-8376
Fax: 212-766-6615
Web: www.seaportinn.com
Prices: $$

72
Rooms

Best Western Seaport Inn

This pleasant and welcoming Best Western hotel in Manhattan's Financial District is the perfect perch for history buffs seeking old New York. Cobblestone streets and Federal-style structures on the surrounding blocks transport visitors back in time to the 17th century, when the settlement known as Nieuw Amsterdam was taking shape. This hotel is just steps from the historic ships docked at South Street Seaport.

Tidy, well-kept rooms have recently been refreshed; all come equipped with an iron and ironing board, small refrigerator, safe, and complimentary wireless high-speed Internet access (available throughout the hotel). Rooms on the 6th and 7th floors offer private balconies overlooking the Brooklyn Bridge—a glittering sight after dark. These upgraded chambers also offer flat-screen TVs and whirlpool soaking tubs. Other perks include a complimentary continental breakfast each morning and fresh-baked cookies in the afternoon.

For shoppers, the mall at Pier 17 is a short walk away (where one can also catch a water taxi to Brooklyn). Also nearby are the skyscrapers of Wall Street and the greensward of Battery Park, which borders New York Harbor.

The Ritz-Carlton, Battery Park

A2

2 West St. (at Battery Pl.)

Subway: Bowling Green
Phone: 212-344-0800 or 800-241-3333
Fax: 212-344-3801
Web: www.ritzcarlton.com
Prices: $$$$

259 Rooms

39 Suites

If unique Art Deco furnishings, top-notch service, and stunning views of New York Harbor, the Statue of Liberty, and Ellis Island sound like your idea of a hotel, put on this Ritz. Occupying floors 3 to 14 of a 39-story glass and brick tower, the Ritz-Carlton, Battery Park lords it over a neighborhood that includes several museums as well as the greensward that defines the southwestern tip of Manhattan.

Guests nest here in spacious rooms and suites outfitted with Frette linens, featherbeds, and down duvets and pillows. Accommodations with harbor views have telescopes for checking out the dramatic waterscapes. All rooms provide a DVD Home Theater System, Bulgari bath amenities, plush terry robes and towels, wireless Internet access, complimentary evening shoeshine, and deep-soaking tubs.

Of course, the hotel offers 24-hour room service, but you can dine on prime Angus beef on-site at 2 West, or drink in the view along with a cocktail at the 14th-floor Rise bar.

If high-end shopping's your thing, you'll need to take a cab uptown. Otherwise, you can get in a good workout at the fitness center, then luxuriate all day at the top-of-the-line Prada spa.

Manhattan ▶ Financial District

Wall Street Inn

B3

9 S. William St. (bet. Beaver & Broad Sts.)

Subway: Wall St (William St.)
Phone: 212-747-1500 or 877-747-1500
Fax: 212-747-1900
Web: www.thewallstreetinn.com
Prices: $$

46 Rooms

Although it's not actually on the street that traces the wood-plank wall erected by Dutch colonists in 1653, this charming inn is nonetheless a good option for travelers with business on Wall Street. Tucked away off Williams Street, the Wall Street Inn fills two landmark buildings that date back to 1895 and 1920.

With in-room refrigerators, high-speed Internet access, a small basement exercise room, and complimentary continental breakfast, this low-key hotel offers good value for money. A small business center offers a full range of services. Early American period reproductions, floral prints, and marble baths fill the two classes (superior and deluxe) of tasteful rooms.

The back of the inn overlooks cobbled Stone Street, one of the narrow 17th century byways, which boasts some of the city's more renowned watering holes, namely Ulysses and Brouwers. While party-loving guests appreciate the ability to stumble back to the hotel, there is a downside. Despite the soundproofed windows, lower rooms on this side of the property are privy to the noise made by other revelers on a nightly basis.

The Carlton

88 Madison Ave. (at 29th St.)

Subway: 28 St (Park Ave. South)
Phone: 212-532-4100 or 800-601-8500
Fax: 212-889-8683
Web: www.carltonhotelny.com
Prices: $$$

293 Rooms

23 Suites

New and old dovetail seamlessly in this Beaux-Arts property, which premiered in 1904 as the Hotel Seville. In 2005 the hotel unveiled its $60-million renovation, led by architect David Rockwell. The project's showpiece is the grand three-story lobby. With its new entrance on Madison Avenue, this space synthesizes early-20th-century style with sleek seating and crystal chandeliers shrouded in cylindrical metal-mesh covers—a Rockwell signature. A sepia-toned portrait of the Hotel Seville, the lobby's focal point, glitters like a rainy scene through the three-story waterfall that envelops it.

All 316 rooms have a modern aspect and include geometric-print fabrics, 42-inch flat-screen TVs, and large work desks. Streamlined furnishings now complement such amenities as Frette linens, in-room wireless Internet access, plush robes, and Apple iHome sound systems.

Upstairs, a new steakhouse is slated to occupy the space recently vacated by Country restaurant. Off the lobby, casual-chic Café at Country serves breakfast, lunch and dinner, and its bar does a brisk happy-hour business.

Manhattan ▶ Gramercy & Flatiron

Gramercy Park Hotel

2 Lexington Ave. (at 21st St.)

Subway:	23 St (Park Ave. South)
Phone:	212-920-3300 or 866-784-1300
Fax:	212-673-5890
Web:	www.gramercyparkhotel.com
Prices:	$$$$

140 Rooms

44 Suites

Nikolas Koenig

The Gramercy Park has been hosting artists, writers and celebrities since 1925, but now its storied past is married to a fresh new look. With hip hotelier Ian Schrager and artist Julian Schnabel breathing new life into this property, the hotel is back and it's hot. Posh British-castle-meets-Gothic-Revival describes the dark lobby décor with its coffered ceiling, crystal chandeliers, and striking artwork by modern masters. Red velvet draperies and tapestry-print fabrics lend a masculine feel to the rooms. Thoughtful amenities range from a fully loaded iPod (upon request) to a key to Gramercy Park (impossible to access unless you live on the square overlooking the gated greensward).

Room service delivers a "best of" menu from famous area restaurants, just as bath products are chosen according to a "best of" list, with full-size versions available for purchase in the mini-bar.

Meanwhile, the celebutante scene at the Rose and Jade bars begs you to don your best Manolos, and the rooftop beckons the well-connected in warm weather. After a night of shameless partying, detox in the hotel's Aerospace gym, where views of the leafy park should soothe your throbbing head.

Inn at Irving Place

56 Irving Pl. (bet 17th & 18th Sts.)

Subway: 14 St - Union Sq
Phone: 212-533-4600 or 800-685-1447
Fax: 212-533-4611
Web: www.innatirving.com
Prices: $$$$

12
Rooms

Roy Wright

Infused with a 19th-century charm not often found in Manhattan hotels, this inn takes up two single-family brownstones built in 1834. To find it, look for the street number; the inn is unmarked. Walk inside and you'll be enveloped in a cozy parlor furnished with antique settees and armchairs covered in floral-patterned silk. If it's cold out, chances are the fireplace will be roaring.

A glass of champagne and a plate of cookies welcome you to your room. Decked out with hardwood floors and period furniture, each of the 12 guestrooms offers a work desk, a well-stocked minibar and a Sony CD/radio. Pedestal sinks, antique mirrors, and black and white tile decorate the large bathrooms.

In the morning, a continental breakfast including fresh-baked croissants and sliced fruit is served in the parlor or delivered to your room—whichever you prefer. For a civilized afternoon break, make reservations for the five-course high tea at Lady Mendl's tea salon. Cibar Lounge, also on-site, is a clubby place for a martini and light fare.

One caveat: If you're traveling with heavy luggage in tow, note that there's a steep flight of stairs at the inn's entrance.

Manhattan ▶ Gramercy, Flatiron & Union Square

W - Union Square

 B3

201 Park Ave. South (at 17th St.)

Subway: 14 St - Union Sq
Phone: 212-253-9119 or 877-782-0027
Fax: 212-253-9229
Web: www.whotels.com
Prices: $$$$

257 Rooms

13 Suites

Set on a prime corner of Union Square, this member of the W family is well located to zip uptown or downtown on the subway, indulge in world-class shopping, or walk to some of the best restaurants and bars in the city. Inside the landmark 1911 granite and limestone Guardian Life Building, David Rockwell redesigned interiors to maintain many historic details, such as the mosaic tile floors and original elevator fronts. Yet in quintessential W style, this hotel remains contemporary, with a two-story lobby and soundproofed guestrooms.

Even the least-expensive rooms are large by New York City standards, as are the well-equipped baths that feature Bliss spa products. Spacious closets, oversized work desks, robes, goose-down duvets and pillows, a 24-hour on-site fitness center, and a pet-friendly policy make guests equally comfortable for short or long stays. Prices are high, so book on weekends for the best deals.

The lobby's laid-back Living Room and the discreet, velvet-roped basement club, Underbar, accommodate those seeking seriously hip watering holes, while Olives (*see restaurant listing*) caters to diners craving fine Mediterranean fare.

Gansevoort

18 Ninth Ave. (at 13th St.)

Subway: 14 St - 8 Av
Phone: 212-206-6700 or 877-462-7386
Fax: 212-255-5858
Web: www.hotelgansevoort.com
Prices: $$$$

158 Rooms

20 Suites

Slick, sleek, swank: the upscale hotel in the Meatpacking District, the Gansevoort rises 14 stories above the burgeoning hip-dom of this once gritty area. Only the name, which belonged to the grandfather of Herman Melville, is historic. The lobby of this oh-so-cool property is outfitted in cherrywood paneling and Matisse-inspired carpet. Eelskin-covered columns and mohair panels add texture, and special attention has been paid to lighting effects throughout. Elegant rooms wear a dusky palette with touches of color, and huge windows overlook, from the high floors, the Hudson River and surrounding city. Bathrooms are large and luxurious.

The coup de grace is the hotel's rooftop, complete with its popular bar and 45-foot-long heated pool with underwater music.

Gansevoort's Hiro Salon and the GSpa and Lounge, both located in the basement, are still the rave. By day, you can pamper yourself with a multitude of treatments at the sultry spa; by night, the spa equipment is removed and the space morphs into a lounge. It's quite the neighborhood hotspot.

Manhattan ▶ Greenwich, West Village & Meatpacking District

The Hotel on Rivington

107 Rivington St. (bet. Essex & Ludlow Sts.)

Subway: Delancey St
Phone: 212-475-2600 or 800-915-1537
Fax: 212-475-5959
Web: www.hotelonrivington.com
Prices: $$$

89
Rooms

21
Suites

Grit and glamour collide on the Lower East Side, a neighborhood that has come into its own while retaining its diversity and refreshing lack of attitude. A great example of the area's newfound glamour, the Hotel on Rivington towers 21 stories above low-rise brick buildings. Floor-to-ceiling glass walls offer magnificent unobstructed views of Manhattan.

The remarkable result of a collaboration of cutting-edge architects, designers, decorators, and artists from around the world, this hotel combines sleek minimalist décor with ultramodern amenities, and, yes, comfort. If you notice anything else besides the view, you'll appreciate the Swedish sleep system that conforms to your every curve by sensing your body temperature and weight, as well as the Italian mosaic bathrooms decked out with heated floors, steam showers, and two-person Japanese-style soaking tubs. An on-site fitness facility, a DVD library of rare films, and a restaurant—Thor—serving market-fresh seasonal fare round out the amenities.

Largely populated by guests who work in the fashion, music, and media industries, the Rivington appeals to an artsy clientele who prefers not to stay in mainstream Manhattan.

The Benjamin

125 E. 50th St. (bet. Lexington & Third Aves.)

Subway: 51 St
Phone: 212-715-2500 or 866-233-4642
Fax: 212-715-2525
Web: www.thebenjamin.com
Prices: $$$$

112
Rooms

79
Suites

From its classic 1927 building (designed by Emery Roth and now beautifully restored) to its attentive service, The Benjamin serves up New York on a silver platter without a sterling-silver price tag.

This comfortable hotel hospitably accommodates business travelers, who appreciate practical details like kitchenettes, in-room business amenities, and 24-hour fitness center. It's the staff that makes the true difference here. Cheerful personnel go well beyond what passes for service at nearby business-oriented hotels, greeting guests by name and caring for them warmly. Dark wood furnishings and soft cream and taupe hues create a sophisticated haven from hurried Midtown, and rooms are amply appointed with lamps, hangers, Bose radios, and abundant towels in the small but elegant baths.

If stress has you tied in knots, visit The Benjamin's spa, where a comprehensive menu treats guests to a variety of ways to relax, rejuvenate, and revive. The Restaurant at The Benjamin and Emery Bar are convenient for a business meeting, and in addition to room service, with advance notice, the hotel will stock your fridge prior to your arrival with your favorite groceries and beverages.

Manhattan ▲ Midtown East & Murray Hill

Elysée

60 E. 54th St. (bet. Madison & Park Aves.)

Subway: 5 Av - 53 St
Phone: 212-753-1066 or 800-535-9733
Fax: 212-980-9278
Web: www.elyseehotel.com
Prices: $$$

89
Rooms

12
Suites

Elysée Hotel

Since the 1920s, the Elysée has earned a reputation as a discreetly private haven for writers, actors and musicians. Vladimir Horowitz once lived in the suite where his piano still stands; Tennessee Williams lived and died here (in the Sunset Suite); and Marlon Brando made this his New York home.

The period atmosphere lingers on in the Neoclassical-style furnishings, careful service, and agreeable rooms—some with terraces, kitchenettes, or solariums. Lovely bathrooms are clad in marble. Classic, yes, but modern conveniences like hotel-wide wireless Internet access, iPod docking stations, and two-line phones are available here, too.

Complimentary breakfast and evening wine and hors d'oeuvres are served in the second-floor Club Room. Since the hotel does not have an on-site fitness center, guests are offered complimentary use of the nearby NY Sports Club.

The Elysée may be best known—and loved—for its engaging Monkey Bar, where murals of frolicking monkeys, olive-shaped barstools, and piano music, along with a drink menu of classics, draw an attractive clientele.

Four Seasons New York

57 E. 57th St. (bet. Madison & Park Aves.)

Subway: 59 St
Phone: 212-758-5700 or 800-487-3769
Fax: 212-350-6302
Web: www.fourseasons.com
Prices: $$$$

305
Rooms

63
Suites

Noted architect I.M. Pei designed the monumentally elegant Four Seasons New York in 1993. Nothing is small about this property. The tallest hotel in the city, the limestone-clad tower soars 52 stories in a Postmodern style inspired by the 1920s. Inside the 57th Street entrance, you'll walk into a grand foyer decorated with temple-like pillars, marble floors and a 33-foot backlit onyx ceiling.

The hotel also boasts some of the city's largest rooms, which, at 600 square feet, are doubtless among the most luxurious as well. A recent refurbishment installed plasma-screen TVs in the opulent bathrooms, which also feature marble soaking tubs that fill in just 60 seconds. Top-drawer service includes a 24-hour concierge, perks for pets and children, and a fabulous newly redesigned spa offering a full spectrum of massages, facials, and body treatments. You'll find state-of-the-art exercise equipment, along with a whirlpool, steam room, and sauna in the fitness facility.

When you're ready to kick back with a martini, stop by The Bar, with its soaring ceilings and cozy curving banquettes. The intimate lounge called Ty serves afternoon tea as well as evening cocktails.

Manhattan ▲ Midtown East & Murray Hill

Library

 A4

299 Madison Ave. (at 41st St.)

Subway: Grand Central - 42 St
Phone: 212-983-4500 or 877-793-7323
Fax: 212-499-9099
Web: www.libraryhotel.com
Prices: $$$

60
Rooms

A welcoming inn well-located in Midtown, The Library keeps to a literary theme with its collection of 6,000 volumes (if that's not enough books for you, the New York Public and the Pierpont Morgan libraries are just minutes away). Each floor is numbered after a category in the Dewey Decimal System, and rooms contain books on a particular subject. Math maven? Request a room on the fifth floor. Literature your thing? Head to the 8th floor.

Rooms, though small, are comfortable, and manage to squeeze a basic desk, an all-inclusive entertainment center (containing bookshelves, drawers, a small closet, a mini bar, and a flat-screen TV) into the cramped quarters. Modern bathrooms come equipped with a hairdryer, magnifying mirror, and scale.

On the second floor, the Reading Room is where you'll find the complimentary continental breakfast laid out in the morning, snacks throughout the day, and the wine and cheese reception each evening. The comfy Writer's Den and the terrace Poetry Garden are perfect for—what else?—reading.

Don't let the address confuse you. The hotel's discreet entrance is actually set on 41st Street, just around the corner from Madison Avenue.

New York Palace

455 Madison Ave. (bet. 50th & 51st Sts.)

Subway: 51 St
Phone: 212-888-7000 or 800-697-2522
Fax: 212-303-6000
Web: www.newyorkpalace.com
Prices: $$$$

807
Rooms

86
Suites

The opulent Palace joins the historic 1882 Villard town houses with a contemporary 55-story tower built in 1980. The hotel's public spaces occupy the lavishly restored town homes built in the Italian Renaissance style, which you can enter through the lovely carriage courtyard on Madison Avenue. Fifth Avenue shopping, Rockefeller Center and Midtown cultural attractions all lie within easy walking distance.

Modern hotel rooms in the tower (floors 41 through 54), including 86 suites, are done in either traditional or modern style and provide all the amenities. The Palace houses a 7,000-square-foot spa and fitness club along with 22,000 square feet of excellent conference facilities. West-facing rooms have a stunning view of St. Patrick's Cathedral, just across Madison Avenue.

Gilt *(see restaurant listing)*, the Palace's acclaimed restaurant, offers cutting-edge cuisine and classic service in the space formerly occupied by Le Cirque 2000. Stop by the adjacent Gilt Bar and Lounge for a sophisticated cocktail in a striking contemporary setting.

Manhattan ▶ Midtown East & Murray Hill

Roger Smith

501 Lexington Ave. (at 47th St.)

Subway: 51 St
Phone: 212-755-1400 or 800-445-0277
Fax: 212-758-4061
Web: www.rogersmithhotel.com
Prices: $$

102
Rooms

28
Suites

Roger Smith

Art plays a big part in this comfortable hostelry, an easy walk from both Grand Central Terminal and the United Nations. The property's public spaces display permanent and rotating exhibits of original artwork—and the hotel even has its own exhibition space—The Roger Smith Lab Gallery, at the corner of 47th Street.

A mix of young and older guests favor this hotel for its good value given its level of comfort, helpful staff, and convenient location. Decorated in crisp New England country style, individually decorated rooms are made homey with live plants and shelves of books. You'll have everything you need here, from in-room mini-refrigerators and coffee-makers to complimentary wireless Internet access. Sunny junior suites claim coveted corner locations, and come with pull-out sofas for extra guests.

Other perks: there are iMacs in the lobby for accessing your email; the animated bar keeps late hours; and the small restaurant offers a limited menu for breakfast, lunch, and dinner. Decorated with wall murals and equipped with wireless Internet access, the hotel's Screening Room can accommodate business meetings as well as cocktail parties.

Roger Williams

131 Madison Ave. (at 31st St.)

Subway: 33 St
Phone: 212-448-7000 or 888-448-7788
Fax: 212-448-7007
Web: www.hotelrogerwilliams.com
Prices: $$$

191
Rooms

2
Suites

Hotel Roger Williams

Manhattan ▲ Midtown East & Murray Hill

Just blocks from the Empire State Building, this stylish boutique hotel makes a bright impression with its clean lines and pure colors. The "living room," as the lobby is called, is adorned with light wood paneling, soaring ceilings and 20-foot-high windows creating an airy, cosmopolitan feel. Comfy contemporary furniture scattered throughout the lobby provide classy spaces to meet and greet.

Though on the small side, rooms at "the Roger" all feature flat-screen plasma TVs, mini bars, Aveda bath products, and wireless high-speed Internet access. Splashes of tangerine, lime green, cobalt blue and red illuminate each room. The peppy colors aren't noisy and neither are the accommodations, thanks to well-insulated windows that help dampen the hustle and bustle of Midtown. Japanese-inspired double rooms add shoji screens and sliding-glass bathroom doors, while 15 garden terrace rooms enjoy private patios and stirring cityscapes. For security purposes, the elevator to the rooms cannot be accessed without a hotel key.

A help-yourself European style breakfast—ranging from fresh croissants to smoked salmon and prosciutto—is available in the mezzanine lounge each morning.

70 Park Avenue

70 Park Ave. (at 38th St.)

Subway: Grand Central - 42 St
Phone: 212-973-2400 or 877-707-2752
Fax: 212-973-2401
Web: www.70parkave.com
Prices: $$$

201
Rooms

4
Suites

This stylish member of the Kimpton Group fancies itself a Murray Hill pied-à-terre. Interior designer Jeffrey Bilhuber has outfitted the rooms to make guests feel at home: a contemporary vibe sets the tone with neutral hues of limestone gray, shimmery bronze, and light cocoa brown; connecting rooms are perfect for families. Come evening, guests gather around the limestone fireplace in the lobby to sip complimentary wine.

Steps from Grand Central Terminal, 70 Park is a stone's throw from the chic shopping on Madison and Fifth avenues. Animal lovers will appreciate that the hotel welcomes pets and Bryant Park is only a short walk away.

Rooms brim with electronic amenities, including a cordless phone with dataport, a CD/DVD player, and a 42-inch flat-screen TV. WiFi Internet access is available throughout the property. Creature comforts include terrycloth robes and slippers, L'Occitane bath amenities, and in-room spa treatments.

Don't want to miss your workout? Tune into the yoga channel on your TV, or hop on a treadmill at the nearby New York Sports Club where guests enjoy privileges. Off the lobby, SilverLeaf Tavern serves a limited menu of pub grub in addition to its full bar.

The St. Regis

2 E. 55th St. (at Fifth Ave.)

Subway: 5 Av - 53 St
Phone: 212-753-4500 or 800-759-7550
Fax: 212-787-3447
Web: www.stregis.com/newyork
Prices: $$$$

186 Rooms

70 Suites

The St. Regis Hotel

Stylish and elegant, and with service close to perfection, the St. Regis reigns among the city's finest hotels. Commissioned by John Jacob Astor in 1904, this Beaux-Arts confection at the corner of Fifth Avenue is located just blocks from Central Park, MoMA and other Midtown attractions. Its public spaces and lobby, from the painted ceilings to the marble staircase, are steeped in Gilded Age opulence.

Rooms fitted with elegant guestrooms are lined with silk wall coverings and custom-made furniture. Guests in the spacious suites (the smallest is 600 square feet; they range up to 3,400 square feet) are cosseted with extra luxuries, such as a bouquet of fresh roses delivered daily. Unparalleled service includes a butler you can call on 24 hours a day, an on-site florist, complimentary garment pressing when you arrive, and the exclusive Remède spa. Their signature massage calms jangled nerves with a mix of Shiatsu, Swedish, deep-tissue, and reflexology.

Be sure to stop in the King Cole Bar to peek at Maxfield Parrish's famous mural, and to sip a Bloody Mary, which was introduced here in the 1920s.

The Vincci Avalon

A6

16 E. 32nd St. (bet. Fifth & Madison Aves.)

Subway: 33 St
Phone: 212-299-7000 or 888-442-8256
Fax: 212-299-7001
Web: www.theavalonny.com
Prices: **$$**

80 Rooms

20 Suites

Right around the corner from the Empire State Building, this boutique property indulges business travelers with six meeting rooms and complimentary high-speed Internet access in each guestroom. Leisure travelers and theater lovers profit from The Avalon's setting, a short walk from Times Square and the bright lights of Broadway.

All appreciate large "Superior" rooms, each of which flaunt 27-inch flat-screen TVs, ample closet space, hairdryers, make-up mirrors, velour robes, and Irish cotton linens. Dark hardwood floors, earth tones (soft green, brown, and rust), and Italian marble baths accentuate the décor. At the top tier of room types, the 20 executive suites average 450 square feet and come with Jacuzzi tubs, Fax machines, sofa beds, and Bose Wave radios.

Just off the elegant lobby, which is set about with pillars and paneling, the Library/Club room is a den-like area with free access to WiFi and a personal computer. Guests also enjoy valet parking, thoughtful service, and discounted passes to the nearby Boom gym. The Avalon Bar & Grill serves a buffet breakfast each morning and American fare for lunch and dinner.

Manhattan ► Midtown East & Murray Hill

The Waldorf=Astoria

B3

301 Park Ave. (bet. 49th & 50th Sts.)

Subway: 51 St
Phone: 212-355-3000 or 800-925-3673
Fax: 212-872-7272
Web: www.waldorfastoria.com
Prices: $$$$

1235
Rooms

208
Suites

Nothing says New York high society like the Waldorf=Astoria. Built in 1931, the hotel blends exquisite Art Deco ornamentation and lavish Second Empire furnishings. The original Waldorf, built in 1893, was demolished along with its companion, the Astoria, to make room for the Empire State Building. The huge "new" hotel (including its boutique counterpart with a private entrance, the Waldorf Towers) occupies the entire block between Park and Lexington avenues at 49th Street. Its lobby features a striking inlaid-tile mosaic and Art Deco chandelier.

A $400-million renovation refreshed the grand dame; and deluxe fabrics as well as classic furniture dress the richly appointed and beautifully maintained rooms and suites, all outfitted with sumptuous marble baths.

Long a Midtown power scene, the mahogany-paneled Bull and Bear teems with brokers and finance types who come for the signature martinis, the dry-aged prime Angus beef, and the men's-club ambience. Also among the property's four restaurants, Peacock Alley (in the center of the main lobby) is worth seeking out for its elegant cuisine.

Manhattan ▶ Midtown East & Murray Hill

W - The Tuscany

120 E. 39th St. (bet. Lexington & Park Aves.)

Subway: Grand Central - 42 St
Phone: 212-686-1600 or 888-627-7189
Fax: 212-779-7822
Web: www.whotels.com
Prices: $$$

113
Rooms

7
Suites

Starwood Hotels & Resorts

Tucked away on tree-lined 39th Street, not far from Grand Central Station, The Tuscany (not to be confused with its sister spot, W New York - The Court, located on the same block and designed for business travelers) cultivates a sensual, relaxed atmosphere. It begins in the cozy lobby (or "living room" in W speak) done up in luxuriant purples, greens and browns. Velvets and satins, rich woods and supple leather add to the lush feeling of the space, which beckons as a comfortable spot for a drink or a private conversation.

Spacious rooms, highlighted by bold, deep colors and textures, feature original contemporary furnishings. Pillowtop mattresses, goose-down duvets, and spa robes make for a comfy stay. Bathrooms, however, are on the small side. In-room electronics include access to a CD/DVD library (high-speed Internet access is available for a fee). W's signature "Whatever, Whenever" service is available 24/7 by pressing "0" on your cordless, dual-line phone.

Athletic types will want to visit Sweat, the on-site fitness center. Before or after your workout, you can grab a quick bite at the Audrey Cafe.

Manhattan ▶ Midtown East & Murray Hill

Algonquin

59 W. 44th St. (bet. Fifth & Sixth Aves.)

Subway: 42 St - Bryant Pk
Phone: 212-840-6800
Fax: 212-944-1419
Web: www.algonquinhotel.com
Prices: $$$

150 Rooms

24 Suites

Algonquin Hotel

New York's oldest operating hotel was fully renovated in 2004 but remains true to its classically elegant roots and timeless aura. Best known for the the circle of literati, including Dorothy Parker and Robert Benchley, who lunched in the Round Table Room in the years after World War I, the Algonquin preserves the feel and look of a fine Edwardian club.

Rooms have been smartly upgraded to include all modern amenities (tastefully hidden); top-quality fabrics and fittings lend rich jewel tones to the accommodations. You may not want to arise from your pillow-top mattress, 350-thread-count linen sheets, down pillows, and the famous "Algonquin Bed." (Order one for home, if you like.) Each of the suites adds a fully stocked refrigerator.

For a taste of 1930s cafe society, step into the Oak Room, the legendary cabaret where famous audiences and performers (crooners Harry Connick Jr. and Diana Krall got their starts here) made merry. The mood lingers, and the shows still go on, with such talent as Andrea Marcovicci and Jack Jones. In the intimate Blue Bar, you'll find artwork by the late Al Hirschfeld, who was a regular.

Manhattan ▶ Midtown West

Casablanca

147 W. 43rd St. (bet. Broadway & Sixth Ave.)

Subway: 42 St - Bryant Pk
Phone: 212-869-1212 or 888-922-7225
Fax: 212-391-7585
Web: www.casablancahotel.com
Prices: $$

43
Rooms

5
Suites

Exotic tilework, warm wood paneling, and wrought-iron details greet guests at this European-style family-owned hotel. Convenient to Times Square and its many attractions, the Casablanca takes on the theme of the 1942 film starring Humphrey Bogart and Ingrid Bergman—without being kitschy. All the elements are here, from the pastel mural of the city of Casablanca that decorates the lobby stairway to the second-floor cafe called—you guessed it—Rick's.

With its tiled fireplace and bentwood chairs, Rick's Café is where you can wake up to a complimentary continental breakfast. In the afternoon, a selection of tea, coffee drinks, and cookies will tide you over until the wine-and-cheese reception at 5 P.M. Room service is provided by Tony's di Napoli restaurant, next door to the hotel.

The Moroccan ambience extends to the rooms, furnished with wooden headboards, damask linens, ceiling fans, and bathrobes. Guests enjoy free passes to the New York Sports Club, and a DVD library of films starring New York City.

No matter where you go when you leave this oasis, one thing's for sure: you'll always have the Casablanca.

Chambers

15 W. 56th St. (bet. Fifth & Sixth Aves.)

Subway: 57 St
Phone: 212-974-5656 or 866-204-5656
Fax: 212-974-5657
Web: www.chambershotel.com
Prices: $$$

72
Rooms

5
Suites

Behind its latticework door, the soaring lobby of this sophisticate sets the mood. It's all about art here: the hotel displays over 500 original pieces by young artists. Lobby furnishings and design details in various textures—warm wood floors, leather rugs, velvet sofas—complete the look of a swank town home. On the mezzanine, roving waiters provide refreshments all day, while books, art, and stylish seating create a comfortable atmosphere.

Explore the hotel's 14 floors, as each hallway houses a site-specific work of art. Guestrooms resemble urbane loft spaces with wide-plank hardwood floors and an eclectic but handsome blend of warm and cool materials—gray-washed oak furniture and details in blackened steel, chenille, leather, glass and artist's canvas. Ask and you'll receive; services include babysitters, a car and driver, in-room massage, and even a personal trainer on call.

For sophisticated contemporary fare, make dinner reservations at Town *(see restaurant listing)*; this restaurant also provides the hotel's room service.

Manhattan ▶ Midtown West

City Club

C3

55 W. 44th St. (bet. Fifth & Sixth Aves.)

Subway: 42 St - Bryant Pk
Phone: 212-921-5500
Fax: 212-944-5544
Web: www.cityclubhotel.com
Prices: $$$

62
Rooms

3
Suites

Originally conceived as an elite social club opened in 1904, The City Club now opens its doors to all. Located on 44th Street, the intimately scaled hotel is situated among a number of still active private clubs and has a sophisticated and exclusive ambiance with a petite lobby that feels more like the entryway of a private residence than a hotel. The rooms are attractively designed to maximize square footage with a handsome beige and brown color scheme dominating. Marble bathrooms are outfitted with bidets and Waterworks showers.

All guests enjoy complimentary high-speed Internet access as well as in-room DVD players, and electronic safe-deposit boxes. In the evening, turndown service includes a plate of freshly baked cookies. Truly spectacular are the hotel's three duplex suites, decked out with private terraces and circular stairways that lead up to the sleeping room from a well-appointed sitting room below. Room Service is provided by Daniel Boulud's DB Bistro Moderne (*see restaurant listing*) which connects to the lobby via a paneled wine bar.

Manhattan ▶ Midtown West

Iroquois

D3

49 W. 44th St. (bet. Fifth & Sixth Aves.)

Subway: 42 St - Bryant Pk
Phone: 212-840-3080 or 888-332-7220
Fax: 212-719-0006
Web: www.iroquoisny.com
Prices: $$$

105
Rooms

9
Suites

Well-known, well-kept and comfortable, the historic Iroquois evokes the mood of a private mansion. Modern European furnishings added during a recent renovation suit its 1923 vintage. A convenient library offers a computer with high-speed Internet access as well as a small selection of books.

Remodeled guestrooms are swathed in chocolate-brown, and offer luxuries like Frette linens, Simmons Beautyrest mattresses and goose-down pillows. Italian marble bathrooms sparkle in peach and cream. All rooms have both tub and shower, while the suites are equipped with Jacuzzi tubs. If you're sleeping in, press the button on your doorknob for privacy. Given the hotel's queenly grace, it's ironic to remember that bad boy James Dean lived in suite 803 from 1951 to 1953.

Amenities include a 24-hour exercise room featuring a Finnish sauna for the ultimate in relaxation (if you're planning to use the sauna, contact the front desk 30 minutes in advance). To savor the contemporary American cuisine at Triomphe restaurant, be sure to make a reservation; the intimate room is tiny and popular with theatergoers.

Manhattan ▶ Midtown West

Jumeirah Essex House

160 Central Park South (bet. Sixth & Seventh Aves.)

Subway:	57 St - 7 Av
Phone:	212-247-0300 or 888-645-5697
Fax:	212-315-1839
Web:	www.jumeirahessexhouse.com
Prices:	**$$$$**

448
Rooms

67
Suites

Jumeirah Essex House

This well-known Art Deco landmark opened in 1931 in its commanding site at the very foot of Central Park. Within easy walking distance of Carnegie Hall and the shops and restaurants of Fifth Avenue and the Time Warner Center, the Jumeirah Essex House welcomes guests in its impressive marble lobby.

A change in ownership passed this former Westin hostelry into the hands of the Dubai-based Jumeirah hospitality group. A major makeover has bestowed a new style on the hotel, whose lobby now sports an elegant Art Deco look, complete with sleek white leather arm chairs and two large photographs of Central Park, commissioned by the hotel from artist Atta Kim.

Warm, comfortable rooms have been refurbished with textured wall coverings and white damask linens. On one bedside table, a touch-screen-activated phone controls the room's lighting. The desk, with its halogen lamp, speedy Internet, and leather swivel chair, isn't a bad place to catch up on email.

Amenities include a fitness center, courtesy car service within a 10-block radius, and bicycles to ride through nearby Central Park.

Le Parker Meridien

118 W. 57th St. (bet. Sixth & Seventh Aves.)

Subway: 57 St
Phone: 212-245-5000 or 800-543-4300
Fax: 212-307-1776
Web: www.parkermeridien.com
Prices: $$$$

510 Rooms

221 Suites

To reach the lobby here, guests must pass through a columned, two-story-high hallway lined with marble, which sets the tone for the Parker Meridien experience. The hotel, just steps away from Carnegie Hall, Central Park, and the chic Fifth Avenue shops, divides its accommodations between the upper and lower tower—each has their own elevator bank.

Expect ergonomically designed rooms and suites to tout contemporary chic with platform beds, warm woods, 32-inch TVs, and CD/DVD players. There's a business center on-site, but if you prefer to work in your room, a large desk, high-speed Internet access, and a halogen reading lamp provide all the necessities.

In the morning, fuel up on tasty breakfast dishes at Norma's. Then get in a workout at Gravity—the 15,000-square-foot fitness facility—or take a dip in the enclosed and heated rooftop pool that overlooks Central Park. For dinner, choose between French bistro fare at Seppi's or a simple burger at the rough-and-ready burger joint.

Whimsical touches, like a "do not disturb" sign that reads "fuhgetaboudit," and vintage cartoons broadcast in the guest elevators, set this place apart from the standard Midtown business hotel.

Manhattan ▶ Midtown West

The London NYC

A3

151 W. 54th St. (bet. Sixth & Seventh Aves.)

Subway: 57 St
Phone: 212-307-5000 or 866-690-2029
Fax: 212-468-8747
Web: www.thelondonnyc.com
Prices: $$$$

549 Rooms

13 Suites

The London NYC is like a hop across the Pond without the guilt of those pesky carbon emissions. Formerly the Righa Royal Hotel, The London with its ivy-covered façade rises 54 stories above Midtown.

Guest suites epitomize modern sophistication with Italian linens, limed oak flooring, sectional sofas, and embossed-leather desks. Tones of soft gray, plum, sky-blue and crisp white dominate. Styled by Waterworks, bathrooms have the last word in luxury, with white marble mosaic-tile floors, double rain showerheads, and sumptuous towels and bathrobes.

Since service is a hallmark of The London, the expert concierge services of Quintessentially are on hand to assist you with any business or personal requests. Novel extras include complimentary cleaning of your workout wear, and an iPod docking station in each room.

The London is also known as the New York home of celebrity chef Gordon Ramsay. He may be infamous for his cantankerous spirit, but Gordon Ramsay at The London *(see restaurant listing)* impresses with its polished service and contemporary cuisine. For a casual alternative, try Maze for Ramsay's menu of small plates served in a sleek brasserie setting.

Manhattan ▶ Midtown West

Metro

C4

45 W. 35th St. (bet. Fifth & Sixth Aves.)

Subway:	34 St - Herald Sq
Phone:	212-947-2500 or 800-356-3870
Fax:	212-279-1310
Web:	www.hotelmetronyc.com
Prices:	$$

179
Rooms

3
Suites

Hotel Metro/Linda Davis

Though not hip or stylish, the Hotel Metro is nonetheless a good stay for the money. Located in the heart of the Garment District, near Penn Station (light sleepers take note that the hotel's location is not a quiet one), the building was constructed in 1901. An Art Deco-inspired lobby leads into a spacious breakfast room/lounge where tea and coffee are available during the day.

Guest rooms have been recently refurbished (the Metro opened its doors in 1995) and are equipped with mini-bars, and upgraded "plush-top" mattresses. Many of the marble bathrooms benefit from natural light, and the overall standard of housekeeping is good. The hotel now offers high-speed wireless Internet access, as well as a small business center. Rates include a complimentary continental breakfast served in the lounge area.

From the large rooftop bar (open from May through September), you'll have stunning views of the Empire State Building and the surrounding neighborhood, which includes Macy's, for all you hard-core shoppers.

Manhattan ▶ Midtown West

The Michelangelo

152 W. 51th St. (at Seventh Ave.)

Subway: 50 St (Broadway)
Phone: 212-765-1900 or 800-237-0990
Fax: 212-541-6604
Web: www.michelangelohotel.com
Prices: $$$

163
Rooms

15
Suites

Convenient to Times Square, the Theater District, Rockefeller Center and Midtown offices, The Michelangelo caters to both leisure and business travelers. A recent renovation has polished the two-story lobby, regal in its liberal use of marble, rich fabric panels, and crystal chandeliers.

Winding hallways have been freshened with new paint and carpeting; shelves of books add a homey touch. Attractively appointed with marble foyers, small sitting areas, down pillows and Bose radio/CD players, guest rooms are generous for Manhattan, with a standard king measuring about 325 square feet (upgrades get bigger from there). Marble bathrooms come equipped with hair dryers, make-up mirrors, deep soaking tubs, terrycloth robes, and even a small TV. Part of an Italian hotel chain, The Michelangelo interprets hospitality with *gusto di vivere italiano*. Turndown service, a complimentary continental breakfast, a small fitness center, and limo service to Wall Street on weekday mornings number among the amenities.

Chef/partner Marco Canora (also of Hearth) has added a touch of urbane flair to the hotel's erstwhile dining room with Insieme *(see restaurant listing)*.

The Peninsula New York

700 Fifth Ave. (at 55th St.)

Subway: 5 Av - 53 St
Phone: 212-956-2888 or 800-262-9467
Fax: 212-903-3949
Web: www.peninsula.com
Prices: $$$$

185
Rooms

54
Suites

This magnificent 1905 hotel serves beautifully as Peninsula's flagship U.S. property. When built as The Gotham, it was the city's tallest skyscraper, towering 23 stories, and today the property still sparkles.

Plush rooms exude a timeless elegance, and Art Nouveau accents complement their rich colors and appointments. Ample in size and well conceived for business travelers, each guest room provides a silent fax machine, wireless Internet access, and a bottled-water bar (with your choice of still or sparkling water). Service is a particularly strong suit at the Peninsula, and the smartly liveried staff effortlessly execute your every request.

You could spend hours in the 35,000-square-foot, three-story Peninsula Spa and Health Club, complete with its Jacuzzi, sauna, steam rooms, and luxurious indoor pool, but don't be late for afternoon tea or cocktails at the intimate Gotham Lounge. Ascend to the rooftop Salon de Ning before retiring to intimate Fives restaurant (on the second floor) for a romantic meal.

The Plaza

768 Fifth Ave. (at Central Park South)

Subway: 5 Av - 59 St
Phone: 212-759-3000 or 800-257-7544
Fax: 212-759-3001
Web: www.theplaza.com
Prices: $$$$

180 Rooms

102 Suites

The Plaza

This storied Beaux-Arts masterpiece is once again ushering the well-heeled and well-travelled through its gilded doors. Originally opened in 1907 and now managed by Fairmont Hotels & Resorts, this national historic landmark has been lavishly renovated to restore the past and embrace the future. The hotel's Fifth Avenue lobby has an ethereal feel with gleaming light-colored marble flooring, Baccarat chandeliers, and large picture windows framing the Pulitzer fountain in Grand Army Plaza.

Generously sized accommodations are elegantly appointed and equipped with a touch screen monitor that dims the lighting, adjusts temperature, and contacts guest services.

You won't want to leave the luxurious mosaic stone-tiled bathroom complete with 24 karat gold fixtures. The service is just as impressive as the surroundings. Each guest floor is staffed by a team of affable butlers, waiting to welcome you to your room upon arrival. Their service is made even more memorable when they ensure that you are attended to throughout your stay. The finishing touches are still being completed with a spa, retail arcade, and completely restored Oak Bar, due in the near future.

The Ritz-Carlton, Central Park

50 Central Park South (at Sixth Ave.)

Subway: 5 Av - 59 St
Phone: 212-308-9100 or 800-826-8129
Fax: 212-207-8831
Web: www.ritzcarlton.com
Prices: $$$$

213 Rooms

47 Suites

The Ritz-Carlton, New York, Central Park

Built in 1929 as the St. Moritz, the Ritz holds its place at the vanguard of luxury and graceful service among Manhattan's hotels. While the marble-floored reception lobby remains intimate, it opens into a grand two-story gathering space.

Sumptuous guestrooms are generously sized, beginning at 425 square feet and topping out at 1,900 square feet for the Central Park Suite. Steeped in Old World elegance, rooms dress up in rich fabrics, crisp, white 400-thread-count linens, and a plethora of fluffy pillows. Gleaming, oversized marble baths are stocked with large vanities, hairdryers, and Frédéric Fekkai products. Of course, all rooms have wireless Internet access, DVD players, and safes that can fit a laptop.

If stress has sapped your energy, a visit to the on-site La Prairie spa is in order. The massage menu tailors treatments to most every ailment of upscale urban life, including jet lag, shopping fatigue, and executive stress.

The addition of BLT Market brings a monthly changing menu of market-fresh breakfast, lunch, and dinner fare designed by Chef Laurent Tourondel. For afternoon tea or a well-shaken martini, stop by the clubby Star Lounge.

Manhattan ▶ Midtown West

6 Columbus Circle

D1

6 Columbus Circle (at 58th St.)

Subway: 59 St - Columbus Circle
Phone: 212-204-3000
Fax: 212-204-3030
Web: www.sixcolumbus.com
Prices: **$$**

88 Rooms

This new addition to the Thompson Hotels collection (which includes 60 Thompson in SoHo) sparkles with a hip vibe. You can't beat the location, across the street from the Time Warner Center and Central Park. Despite its ritzy setting, the urban retreat is casual in style and surprisingly reasonable in price.

Sixties-Mod describes the décor, which dresses the public spaces with teak paneling, molded chairs and leather sofas in a palette of earthy tones. The same spirit—and teak paneling—infuses the sleek rooms, where custom-made furniture and chrome accents abound. Walls are decorated with artwork by fashion photographer Guy Bourdin. Frette linens, soft lighting, iPod docking stations, and complimentary WiFi Internet access round out the amenities. Bath products are by Fresh.

Adjacent to the lobby, Blue Ribbon Sushi Bar and Grill adds a new concept by the well-known Blue Ribbon Restaurants group. Japanese fare here runs the gamut from hamachi to hanger steak. As for the young staff, they're friendly and helpful, catering to a clientele largely made up of savvy urban professionals and international visitors.

Manhattan ▶ Midtown West

Sofitel

45 W. 44th St. (bet. Fifth & Sixth Aves.)

Subway: 47-50 Sts - Rockefeller Ctr
Phone: 212-354-8844 or 877-565-9240
Fax: 212-354-2480
Web: www.sofitel-newyork.com
Prices: $$$$

346
Rooms

52
Suites

Located mid-block on 44th Street, this 30-story glass and limestone tower couldn't be more convenient to Fifth Avenue shopping, Times Square, and the Theater District. It's an easy walk from here to Grand Central Station too. Owned by the French hotel group— Accor—the Sofitel New York was designed by Brennan Beer Gorman and opened in 2000.

The Art Deco-style lobby is as welcoming as it is elegant, set about with blond wood paneling, green marble, and groups of sleek leather club chairs arranged on a colorful floral-patterned carpet. Off the lobby, Gaby Bar offers a stylish lounge in which to sip a cocktail, while its sister restaurant— also called Gaby—features flavorful French classics along with more contemporary fare for lunch and dinner.

Honey-colored velvet drapes, red chenille armchairs, sumptuous damask linens, and marble baths outfit the attractive and well-maintained guest rooms. The glass-topped blond wood desk paired with a cushioned leather chair caters to business travelers; Wi-Fi Internet access is available for a fee. A thoughtful touch for European guests, a voltage adaptor is included in each room.

Manhattan ▲ Midtown West

Warwick

65 W. 54th St. (at Sixth Ave.)

Subway: 57 St
Phone: 212-247-2700 or 800-203-3232
Fax: 212-247-2725
Web: www.warwickhotelny.com
Prices: $$$

359
Rooms

66
Suites

Newspaper magnate William Randolph Hearst built the Warwick in 1927 so that his lady friend, Marion Davies, could host their band of Hollywood and theatrical friends in style. Convenient to MoMA and the Theater District, the 33-story hotel underwent a facelift in 2001, and the smart guest rooms haven't lost their traditional feeling. Larger than many city hotel quarters, rooms here incorporate slick modern touches such as temperature controls that sense your presence. Go for broke and book the Suite of the Stars, where Cary Grant lived for 12 years; it boasts 1,200 square feet of space and its own wrap-around terrace.

For business travelers, high-speed Internet access is available throughout the hotel, and the business center in the lobby offers 24-hour fax and copying services. There's also an on-site fitness facility.

After working, or working out, treat yourself to a meal at Murals on 54, in full view of Dean Cornwall's wonderful murals depicting the history of Sir Walter Raleigh. Commissioned by Hearst in 1937 for the hotel's former Raleigh Room, these paintings have now been restored to their original luster.

Manhattan ► Midtown West

Washington Jefferson Hotel

C2

318 W. 51st St. (bet. Eighth & Ninth Aves.)

Subway: 50 St (Eighth Ave.)
Phone: 212-246-7550 or 888-567-7550
Fax: 212-246-7622
Web: www.wjhotel.com
Prices: $

135 Rooms

Washington Jefferson Hotel

Fresh, contemporary design at a decent price in Manhattan was once a pipe dream, but the Washington Jefferson Hotel delivers style without a high price tag. Located in the up-and-coming neighborhood of Hell's Kitchen, the hotel is close to the bright lights of the Theater District.

The lobby is warm and welcoming, and the staff ensures that all guests feel at home from the moment they step inside the doors. Rooms are somewhat Spartan, with platform beds dressed in crisp white linens, yet provide all the necessary amenities (TV with premium channels, radio/CD player). Clean lines extend to the bathrooms, outfitted with slate flooring and slate-tiled tubs. While standard rooms are on the small side, comfort is never sacrificed. Guests have 24-hour access to a small exercise room on-site, while serious athletes can take advantage of the reduced-price daily pass to Gold's Gym, available at the hotel's front desk.

Although there is no room service, you can enjoy lunch and dinner at the hotel's restaurant, Shimuzu. Sushi is a popular component here, but for those who prefer their fish cooked, the restaurant offers a delightful array of traditional Japanese dishes.

Manhattan ▶ Midtown West

The Mercer

B1

147 Mercer St. (at Prince St.)

Subway: Prince St
Phone: 212-966-6060
Fax: 212-965-3838
Web: www.mercerhotel.com
Prices: $$$$

67 Rooms

8 Suites

Even if your name isn't Leonardo DiCaprio, Cher, or Calvin Klein, you'll be equally welcome at The Mercer. Housed in a striking Romanesque Revival-style building erected in 1890, the hotel caters to the glitterati with discreet, personalized service, and intimate elegance. The modern lobby feels like your stylish friend's living room, complete with comfy seating, appealing coffee-table books, and an Apple computer for guests' use.

A Zen vibe pervades the guestrooms, fashioned by Parisian interior designer Christian Liaigre with high, loft-like ceilings, large windows that open, soothing neutral palettes, and Asian decorative touches. You'll find everything you need for business or leisure travel in your room, right down to scented candles and oversize FACE Stockholm bath products. Forgot something? The hotel's warm staff will gladly accommodate you with a laptop, a cell phone, or a fax machine in your room.

Sure, the hotel offers 24-hour room service, but in this case the food comes from Jean-Georges Vongerichten's Mercer Kitchen *(see restaurant listing)*, located in the basement. Don't fret if you get a room facing the street; soundproofing filters out the noise.

60 Thompson

60 Thompson St. (bet. Broome & Spring Sts.)

Subway: Spring St (Sixth Ave.)
Phone: 212-431-0400 or 877-431-0400
Fax: 212-431-0200
Web: www.60thompson.com
Prices: $$$$

85 Rooms

13 Suites

With its spare 1940s look inspired by French designer Jean-Michel Frank, 60 Thompson absolutely oozes SoHo style. The lobby, decorated in gray, brown, and moss-green tones, is accented by bouquets of fresh flowers, and natural light floods in from floor-to-ceiling windows.

Room sizes vary, but all sport a minimalist look, with crisp, white Frette linens standing out against a wall of dark, paneled leather. Amenities include flat-screen TVs in all the rooms, and high-speed wireless Internet access. (Business travelers take note that 60 Thompson has replaced the requisite in-room desk with a sitting area in its standard rooms.) Bathrooms are tiled with chocolate-colored marble and stocked with spa products by Fresh. For those who don't appreciate the smell of cigarette smoke in their room, the hotel devotes two entire floors to non-smoking chambers.

Check out the rooftop bar on the 12th floor, where you can sip a cocktail and drink in the great city views. In good weather, the rooftop scene is a hot one, whereas the lobby bar bustles year-round with a cool crowd. Downstairs, Kittichai restaurant *(see restaurant listing)* specializes in Thai cuisine.

Manhattan ▶ SoHo & Nolita

Soho Grand

B2

310 West Broadway (bet. Canal & Grand Sts.)

Subway: Canal St (Sixth Ave.)
Phone: 212-965-3000 or 800-965-3000
Fax: 212-965-3200
Web: www.sohogrand.com
Prices: $$$$

361
Rooms

2
Suites

Soho Grand Hotel

The architecture of this hip hotel recalls SoHo's industrial past, from the exposed-brick walls to the superb suspended steel staircase that connects the ground floor to the main lobby.

Two metal dog statues stand near the elevator, reminding guests of the Soho Grand's pet-friendly policy—what else would you expect from the same folks who own Hartz Mountain Industries? There's even a fish bowl in every room; if you grow attached to your new fishy friend, you're welcome to take him home with you.

And speaking of rooms, they're done in tones of gray and gold, with large picture windows overlooking the neighborhood. You'll relax in state-of-the-art style with Bose Wave CD/radios, in-room fax machines, and broadband Internet connections. Feel like splurging? Reserve one of the airy, two-bedroom penthouse loft suites. They boast their own wrap-around terraces for enjoying the awesome cityscape.

If you can't get a reservation at the Soho Grand, the hotel's nearby sister, the Tribeca Grand *(see hotel listing)*, may be able to accommodate you.

Cosmopolitan

95 West Broadway (at Chambers St.)

Subway: Chambers St (West Broadway)
Phone: 212-566-1900 or 888-895-9400
Fax: 212-566-6909
Web: www.cosmohotel.com
Prices: $

125
Rooms

Cosmopolitan

This privately owned seven-story hotel enjoys a valuable location in the heart of TriBeCa, while catering to more budget-conscious visitors to the city. Just a few steps away from Wall Street, SoHo, and Chinatown, the Cosmopolitan pulls in a steady clientele of business travelers and European tourists, who may appreciate the hotel's low prices, convenient setting, and cigarette-friendly policy.

The Cosmopolitan may lack the frills of some grander city hostelries, but guests can use the money saved on a room here to splurge on a show or dinner in a fine restaurant. Basic rooms are well-maintained, fairly spacious, and they all have private baths. Scant in-room amenities include a hair dryer, cable TV, a ceiling fan, and free wireless Internet access. Ask for a room on the back side of the hotel if worried about the street noise. Despite the fact that the entire hotel is smoking-friendly, the halls and the rooms seems absent of cigarettes traces.

The hotel does not offer room service, but the Cosmopolitan Café is right next door. This tiny eatery, with its rustic country style, makes a good spot for a light breakfast or to catch a quick sandwich at midday.

Manhattan ▲ TriBeCa

Greenwich Hotel

377 Greenwich St. (at N. Moore St.)

Subway: Franklin St
Phone: 212-941-8900
Fax: 212-941-8600
Web: www.thegreenwichhotel.com
Prices: $$$$

75
Rooms

13
Suites

♿

Spa

The Greenwich Hotel

Spanning the worlds of classic elegance and city chic, this TriBeCa newcomer was unceremoniously unveiled in spring 2008. Though the hoopla was kept to a minimum—despite the fact that Robert DeNiro and his son are partners—the Greenwich is a hotel to crow about. Attention to detail is evident here from the construction materials to the organic bath amenities, all reflecting au courant Italian sensibilities.

Among the 88 rooms, no two are alike. Carved pine doors open into refined chambers boasting Dux Siberian beds, custom-designed settees, and hardwood floors. Ten-foot-high ceilings create an airy feel. The same care is taken in the design of the bathrooms, with their brass hardware, Frette towels, and mosaic tiled showers. All the modern electronic amenities apply as well.

An on-site fitness center and a lantern-lit indoor swimming pool will take care of your exercise needs, while the Japanese-inspired Shibui spa spotlights relaxation with a shiatsu room and a room for traditional bathing rituals. Italian fare takes top billing at Ago, the new hotspot by Chef Agostino Sciandri.

Manhattan ▶ TriBeCa

Tribeca Grand

2 Sixth Ave. (at Church St.)

Subway: Canal St (Sixth Ave.)
Phone: 212-519-6600 or 877-519-6600
Fax: 212-519-6700
Web: www.tribecagrand.com
Prices: $$$

196
Rooms

7
Suites

Tribeca Grand Hotel

Swanky, hip, and Eurocentric, the Tribeca Grand fits its trendy neighborhood like a glove. Inside, the soaring open atrium lends the lobby an airy feel and a wall of lit votive candles stands in for a fireplace. Also in this space, the Church Lounge draws a crowd in the evening for light fare and libations. In warm weather, outdoor seating spills out onto Sixth Avenue.

Rooms in this sister to the Soho Grand are large, comfortable, and equally well-equipped for business and leisure travelers. The desk, accompanied by an ergonomic chair, is big enough to actually work on. WiFi Internet access and a fax/printer/copier are available in each room. The hotel says welcome with a long-stemmed rose on the bed and a dish of strawberries and chocolate, while a good night's sleep awaits you on the comfortable bed. Modern amenities include a flat-screen TV, a DVD player (the hotel owns a vast library of videos), and a Bose Wave radio. But if you prefer to read, the wing chair by the window is the perfect place to do so.

Lest you think this is an adults-only property, the hotel welcomes children of all ages as well as pets, with customized programs for both.

Manhattan ▶ TriBeCa

Bentley

B4

500 E. 62nd St. (at York Ave.)

Subway: Lexington Av - 59 St
Phone: 212-644-6000 or 888-664-6835
Fax: 212-207-4800
Web: www.nychotels.com
Prices: **$$**

161 Rooms

36 Suites

Bentley Hotel

Manhattan ► Upper East Side

It may be a little bit of a walk to the subway, Central Park, and the shops, but sitting right on the East River, with easy access to-and-from the airports, it's worth the extra blocks for the value and accessibility. The Bentley may not be new or trendy, but it makes a fashionable first impression. Floor-to-ceiling windows, geometric-patterned carpets, marble flooring, and contemporary furnishings fill the Art Deco lobby of this 21-story glass-and-steel office building, which was converted into a hotel in 1998.

By New York City standard, rooms are surprisingly spacious. A bit the worse for wear, furnishings and carpeting adhere to a neutral color scheme. Seating nooks by the windows take in views of the East River and the Queensboro Bridge. Families favor the extra space offered in the 36 suites, complete with pull-out sofas or futons. Given the location and moderate prices, this hotel is a good find.

The Bentley doesn't serve breakfast, but guests have complimentary access to a cappuccino bar 24 hours a day. If you don't feel up to dining out, the rooftop restaurant serves up panoramic city views with its limited menu. Valet parking, free daily newspapers, and concierge service count among other amenities provided.

The Carlyle

35 E. 76th St. (at Madison Ave.)

Subway: 77 St
Phone: 212-744-1600 or 800-227-5737
Fax: 212-717-4682
Web: www.thecarlyle.com
Prices: $$$$

123
Rooms

58
Suites

The Carlyle

Named for British historian Thomas Carlyle, this hotel epitomizes opulence with its fine artwork, Baccarat crystal light fixtures, and marble baths. Individually decorated Classic aka "standard" rooms are dressed in Louis XVI-style with original Audubon prints, 440-thread-count Italian linens, and elegant area rugs over wood floors. A select few of the Carlyle's roomy suites feature a baby-grand piano for the musically inclined.

Since it opened across from Central Park in 1930, The Carlyle has hosted every American president since Truman, along with a roster of foreign dignitaries from Prime Minister Nehru to Princess Diana—how's that for an A-list?

For entertainment, there's Café Carlyle, where Woody Allen regularly jams with the Eddie Davis New Orleans jazz band. Legendary Bemelmans Bar, renowned for its whimsical mural of characters from artist Ludwig Bemelmans' famous Madeline series of children's books, is a popular place for a cocktail.

With a contemporary menu almost as classy as the crowd it draws, the handsome Carlyle Restaurant proves a perfect complement to the hotel's sophistication. A new 4,000-square-foot spa called Sense is slated to open in the second half of 2008.

Manhattan ▶ Upper East Side

473

The Lowell

28 E. 63rd St. (bet. Madison & Park Aves.)

Subway: Lexington Av - 63 St
Phone: 212-838-1400 or 800-221-4444
Fax: 212-319-4230
Web: www.lowellhotel.com
Prices: $$$$

23
Rooms

47
Suites

A block from Central Park and close to Madison Avenue boutiques, The Lowell occupies a landmark 1928 building on a tree-lined Upper East Side street. The hotel's intimate size, discreet staff, and sumptuous ambience are the reasons most fans give for coming back time after time.

From the moment you step inside the silk-paneled lobby, you'll sense the European elegance that defines The Lowell. Guests here are cosseted in lavish suites, most of which have working fireplaces, private terraces (the Garden Suite has two terraces), and iPod docking stations. A recent renovation added new marble-clad baths—complete with mini TVs and Bulgari toiletries—king size, half-canopy beds, new designer fabrics, and upgraded kitchens to all accommodations.

The well-equipped fitness room adds thoughtful touches like magazines, cool towels, and fruit. If it's aerobics classes or an indoor pool you want, guests have complimentary access to the posh Equinox fitness club nearby.

Savor a hearty steak in the hotel's clubby Post House restaurant, or drop by the aristocratic Pembroke Room, all swagged in English chintz, for breakfast, afternoon tea, or weekend brunch.

The Regency

540 Park Ave. (at 61st St.)

Subway: Lexington Av - 63 St
Phone: 212-759-4100 or 800-233-2356
Fax: 212-826-5674
Web: www.loewshotels.com
Prices: $$$$

267
Rooms

86
Suites

This flagship of Loews hotel properties sits right on Park Avenue, just two blocks east of Central Park. Lush fabrics, Frette linens, CD players, TVs in the bathrooms, and double-paned windows are a few of the amenities you'll find in the contemporary-style rooms—the smallest of which is 225 square feet. Even Fido gets the royal treatment here with his own room-service menu and a dog-walking service.

Boasting a staff-to-guest ratio of 1 to 1, the hotel delights in serving its guests. Forget your reading glasses? Need a humidifier in your room? The Regency's staff is only too happy to oblige. Business travelers will appreciate rooms equipped with large writing desks, fax/printers, and high-speed Internet access. And if you need a haircut before that big meeting, there's even a beauty salon and barbershop on-site.

For that power breakfast, you need not go any farther than the hotel's 540 Park restaurant. For night owls, Feinstein's at The Regency (named for its owner, pop vocalist, and songwriter Michael Feinstein) offers big-name cabaret acts six nights a week.

Manhattan ▶ Upper East Side

Hotel Wales

C1

1295 Madison Ave. (bet. 92nd & 93rd Sts.)

Subway: 96 St (Lexington Ave.)
Phone: 212-876-6000 or 866-925-3746
Fax: 212-860-7000
Web: www.waleshotel.com
Prices: $$$

46 Rooms

42 Suites

Built in 1902, the Hotel Wales sits atop Carnegie Hill, on the same block with the mansion of steel magnate Andrew Carnegie. Close to Upper East Side museums (including the Metropolitan Museum of Art), the hotel exudes a countryside feel in its soothing lobby, complete with a fireplace, marble staircase, coffered ceiling, and mosaic floor.

All rooms profited from a recent renovation, which preserved the turn-of-the-century spirit with period furnishings, luxurious linens, down comforters, fresh flowers, and sepia-tone photographs of the neighborhood. The hotel's proximity to Central Park makes bringing your four-legged friend to this pet-friendly place all the more tempting.

Spend some time on the rooftop terrace, admiring the seasonal plantings and taking in the city views; or squeeze in a workout any time of day at the hotel's fitness studio. Continental breakfast is served each morning in the Pied Piper Room, decorated as a Victorian-era parlor. Delicious baked goods come compliments of Sarabeth's on-site restaurant and nearby Eli's gourmet market. Also on the property, Joanna's Italian bistro serves dinner and weekend brunch.

Manhattan ▶ Upper East Side

Mandarin Oriental

80 Columbus Circle (at 60th St.)

Subway: 59 St - Columbus Circle
Phone: 212-805-8800 or 866-801-8880
Fax: 212-805-8888
Web: www.mandarinoriental.com
Prices: $$$$

202
Rooms

46
Suites

Mandarin Oriental Hotel Group

Everything you could desire in New York City lies literally at the doorstep of the Mandarin Oriental. Occupying floors 35 to 54 in the north tower of the Time Warner Center, this hotel flaunts its enviable location overlooking Central Park. Also the site of such stellar restaurants as Per Se and Masa (*see restaurant listing for both*), hotel guests have direct access to the shops located inside the Time Warner Center at Columbus Circle. And don't pass up the contemporary Asian cuisine on-site at Asiate (*see restaurant listing*). Right next door (*60th & Broadway*), Jazz at Lincoln Center dedicates itself to this all-American art form with year-round jazz performances.

From the moment you enter to the moment you leave, the hotel's top-drawer service will make you feel like a VIP. Masculine yet delicate, modern yet timeless, guestrooms incorporate soigné touches such as cherry woods, silvery silks, and Fili D'oro linens. The view's the thing here; and the scenery is played up to full advantage with a wall of floor-to-ceiling windows in each room.

No visit to this unforgettable place is complete without a trip to the 36th-floor spa, which offers a customized "journey for the senses," booked in blocks of time rather than by treatment.

Manhattan ▶ Upper West Side

477

On the Ave

2178 Broadway (at 77th St.)

Subway:	79 St
Phone:	212-362-1100 or 800-497-6028
Fax:	212-787-9521
Web:	www.ontheave.com
Prices:	**$$**

242 Rooms

27 Suites

Michael Kleinberg Photography

Manhattan's Upper West Side teems with natural and man-made treasures, and this hotel is the perfect point from which to explore them. Whether seeking a run in Central Park or trek through the Museum of Natural History, guests are well-situated On The Ave. For shoppers and foodies, Time Warner Center offers an easy stroll to upscale boutiques and stellar restaurants.

Modern artwork surrounds the hotel's elegant lobby, where a pianist tickles the ivories on the baby grand piano each evening. Plush seating is strategically positioned throughout, fostering relaxation and conversation.

In the comfortable and beautifully-set rooms, flat-screen high-definition TVs, CD players, wireless Internet access, and black marble baths offer hip luxuriance, while Frette robes, down duvets, and Egyptian cotton linens will leave guests appropriately pampered. These flourishes help compensate for inconsistent guest services.

Rooms on the top three floors boast balconies that afford views of the Hudson River or Central Park. If your room lacks a view, take the elevator to the landscaped balcony on the 16th floor; this pleasant space offers Adirondack chairs for taking in the cityscape.

Trump International H

1 Central Park West (at Columbus Circle)

Subway: 59 St - Columbus Circle
Phone: 212-299-1000 or 888-448-7867
Fax: 212-299-1150
Web: www.trumpintl.com
Prices: $$$$

38
Rooms

129
Suites

An icon for its association with its flamboyant owner, this 52-story tower does Donald Trump proud. The location is ideal, with upscale shopping at the Time Warner Center and the attractions of Central Park right outside the door.

More than two-thirds of the accommodations—located on the 3rd through 17th floors—are spacious one- or- two-bedroom suites boasting custom-designed furniture and great city and park views. A blissful night's sleep awaits in lodgings that range from 460 square feet for a junior suite to 1,350 square feet for a two-bedroom unit. All have kitchens stocked with china and crystal; if you don't feel like cooking, you can arrange for a member of the staff from the stellar chef—Jean Georges' restaurant (see restaurant listing)—to prepare a gourmet meal in your room.

The 55-foot-long indoor pool is perfect for swimming laps, and the Techno-Gym equipment at the fitness center supplies a challenging workout (personal training and one-on-one yoga sessions are available).

Offering everything from complimentary business cards to free local phone calls, Trump's signature Attaché service caters to The Donald in everyone.

Manhattan ▶ Upper West Side

479

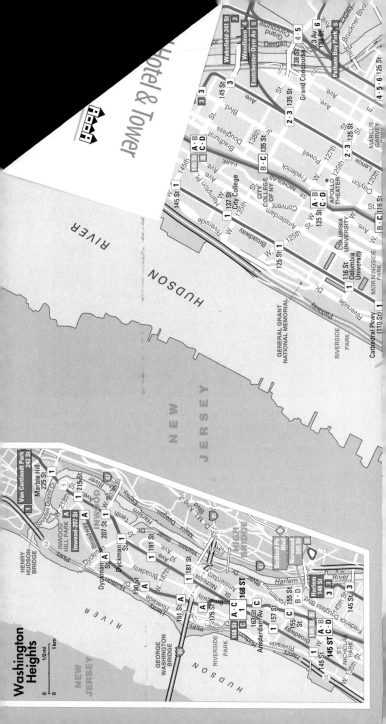